Long-Term Field Research in Social Anthropology

STUDIES IN ANTHROPOLOGY

Under the Consulting Editorship of E. A. Hammel,
UNIVERSITY OF CALIFORNIA, BERKELEY

Andrei Simić, THE PEASANT URBANITES: A Study of Rural-Urban Mobility in Serbia

John U. Ogbu, THE NEXT GENERATION: An Ethnography of Education in an Urban Neighborhood

Bennett Dyke and Jean Walters MacCluer (Eds.), COMPUTER SIMULATION IN HUMAN POPULATION STUDIES

Robbins Burling, THE PASSAGE OF POWER: Studies in Political Succession

Piotr Sztompka, SYSTEM AND FUNCTION: Toward a Theory of Society

William G. Lockwood, EUROPEAN MOSLEMS: Economy and Ethnicity in Western Bosnia

Günter Golde, CATHOLICS AND PROTESTANTS: Agricultural Modernization in Two German Villages

Peggy Reeves Sanday (Ed.), ANTHROPOLOGY AND THE PUBLIC INTEREST: Fieldwork and Theory

Carol A. Smith (Ed.), REGIONAL ANALYSIS, Volume I: Economic Systems, and Volume II: Social Systems

Raymond D. Fogelson and Richard N. Adams (Eds.), THE ANTHROPOLOGY OF POWER: Ethnographic Studies from Asia, Oceania, and the New World

Frank Henderson Stewart, FUNDAMENTALS OF AGE-GROUP SYSTEMS

Larissa Adler Lomnitz, NETWORKS AND MARGINALITY: Life in a Mexican Shantytown

Benjamin S. Orlove, ALPACAS, SHEEP, AND MEN: The Wool Export Economy and Regional Society in Southern Peru

Harriet Ngubane, BODY AND MIND IN ZULU MEDICINE: An Ethnography of Health and Disease in Nyuswa-Zulu Thought and Practice

Kenneth W. Wachter, Eugene A. Hammel, and Peter Laslett, STATISTICAL STUDIES OF HISTORICAL SOCIAL STRUCTURE

George M. Foster, Thayer Scudder, Elizabeth Colson, and Robert Van Kemper (Eds.). LONG-TERM FIELD RESEARCH IN SOCIAL ANTHROPOLOGY

Long-Term Field Research in Social Anthropology

Edited by

GEORGE M. FOSTER
Department of Anthropology
University of California
Berkeley, California

THAYER SCUDDER
Division of Humanities and Social Sciences
California Institute of Technology
Pasadena, California

ELIZABETH COLSON
Department of Anthropology
University of California
Berkeley, California

ROBERT V. KEMPER
Department of Anthropology
Southern Methodist University
Dallas, Texas

ACADEMIC PRESS   New York   San Francisco   London
A Subsidiary of Harcourt Brace Jovanovich, Publishers

NOV 05 1987

ACADEMIC PRESS, INC.
111 Fifth Avenue, New York, New York 10003

United Kingdom Edition published by
ACADEMIC PRESS, INC. (LONDON) LTD.
24/28 Oval Road, London NW1   7DX

Library of Congress Cataloging in Publication Data
Main entry under title:

Long—term field research in social anthropology.

    (Studies in anthropology)
    Proceedings of a symposium held in Burg
Wartenstein, Vienna, Austria, Aug. 20—Sept. 6, 1975.
    Includes bibliographies.
    1. Ethnology——Methodology——Congresses.
2. Longitudinal method——Congresses. I. Foster,
George McClelland, Date
GN345.L66   301.2'07'2   78—8828
ISBN 0—12—263350—4

PRINTED IN THE UNITED STATES OF AMERICA

To
LITA OSMUNDSEN
for her long-term interest in anthropology

Contents

INTRODUCTION

George M. Foster, Thayer Scudder, Elizabeth Colson, and Robert V. Kemper

8 FIELDWORK IN TZINTZUNTZAN: THE FIRST THIRTY YEARS
George M. Foster

Part III PROBLEM-ORIENTED STUDIES   **185**

9 FIELDWORK AMONG TZINTZUNTZAN MIGRANTS IN MEXICO CITY: RETROSPECT AND PROSPECT
Robert V. Kemper

10 MYSORE VILLAGES REVISITED
T. Scarlett Epstein

CONCLUSION: THE LONG-TERM STUDY IN PERSPECTIVE

George M. Foster, Thayer Scudder, Elizabeth Colson, and Robert V. Kemper

List of Contributors

Numbers in parentheses indicate the pages on which the authors' contributions begin.

Elizabeth Colson (1, 227, 323), Department of Anthropology, University of California, Berkeley, California

T. Scarlett Epstein (209), Institute of Development Studies, University of Sussex, Brighton, England

Hussein Fahim (255), Social Research Center, American University, Cairo, Egypt

George M. Foster (1, 165, 323), Department of Anthropology, University of California, Berkeley, California

June Helm (145), Department of Anthropology, University of Iowa, Iowa City, Iowa

Tamás Hofer (85), Ethnographic Museum, Budapest, Hungary

Robert V. Kemper (1, 189, 323), Department of Anthropology, Southern Methodist University, Dallas, Texas

Louise Lamphere (19), Department of Anthropology, University of New Mexico, Albuquerque, New Mexico

Richard B. Lee (303), Department of Anthropology, Toronto University, Toronto, Canada

William Mangin (65), Department of Anthropology, Syracuse University, Syracuse, New York

M. J. Meggitt (107), Department of Anthropology, Queens College, CUNY, Flushing, New York

Leopold Pospisil (127), Department of Anthropology, Yale University, New Haven, Connecticut

Alfonso Villa Rojas (45), Amores 1165-Dep. 5, Mexico 12, D. F., Mexico

Thayer Scudder (1, 227, 323), Division of Humanities and Social Sciences, California Institute of Technology, Pasadena, California

Evon Z. Vogt (279), Department of Anthropology, Harvard University, Cambridge, Massachusetts

Preface

This volume is rightfully dedicated to Lita Osmundsen, who not only encouraged us to plan a conference at Burg Wartenstein on the subject of the implications of long-term field research for the development of social anthropology, but also joined us in our discussions through the days of the conference, August 29–September 6, 1975. It was she who saw that our basic concern was with better standards of fieldwork. In retrospect, we see that in planning the conference we ought to have included some participants from other disciplines who have been involved in long-term studies—sociologists, psychologists, ethologists, and biologists face the same problems of maintaining continuity and comparability over time and of processing massive amounts of steadily accumulating data. But we assumed that initially we needed the common experience and disciplinary interests of anthropologists for a free, wideranging, no-holds-barred discussion. The conference was initially planned by Foster, Scudder, and Colson. Kemper, a contributor to the symposium who also served as recorder, was invited to join in the editing of the volume that would emerge from the conference. All participants rewrote their initial papers, some very extensively. The editors have to thank them for their patient acceptance of editorial suggestions. We also have to thank the staff of

Burg Wartenstein, that ideal setting for intellectual discussions, and the staff of the Wenner–Gren Foundation who most efficiently handled all the administrative details associated with the conference. We thank the Wenner–Gren Foundation for the grant that assisted in the editing process, the University of California for assistance in the preparation of the manuscript, Jason Curoe for editorial assistance, and Jane Taylorson and Toni Cord for typing much of the final copy. Grace Buzaljko assisted in the final editing.

Introduction

George M. Foster, Thayer Scudder, Elizabeth
Colson, Robert V. Kemper

THE SETTING

This volume is about a style of fieldwork in social anthropology. It came into being when a number of us, engaged in long-term research projects, began to realize that we were facing common problems arising from the peculiar nature of research that involves repeated visits to the same community or communities over a long period of time.

We were facing accumulating mountains of data and, since each piece of information might have value in a time sequence, we could not consider any information as having been dealt with when it had been once used in some publication. The classics of social anthropology, moreover, could not serve us as models for write-up or provide us with the means to describe and analyze the changing situations we encountered on each return: We needed more flexible models capable of incorporating time effectively. The anthropologist who spends a year or two in fieldwork can handle the material collected during that time period in a frame that purports to describe how people live and think. The anthropologist who makes one return visit to old haunts some years after a first study may find it easy enough to write about trends and see a trajectory of development.

1

Long-Term Field Research
in Social Anthropology

The anthropologist who makes repeated visits finds people behaving in response to particular concatenations of situations that may not repeat themselves: There is no easily discernible trajectory that can be described as a pattern of development, and if one cannot predict what situations people will face in the future, one cannot predict what they will be doing and what their expectations of each other will be on the next visit.

We were also interested in other facets of our experience, such as the effect of our own aging upon us as fieldworkers—how did changes in our status over time influence what we learned and how did aging affect what we regarded as important theoretical issues or how we viewed the problems faced by the people among whom we worked. There were also questions to be faced about the impact of repeated visits upon these people: What did we know about this? In a time when anthropologists were becoming steadily more aware of ethical problems associated with fieldwork and writing about living communities, we wondered if long-term research, with its massive accumulation of data on communities and individuals, might pose special problems.

It was these concerns that led to the planning of a conference on the implications of long-term field studies for social anthropology. We suspected that other anthropologists were facing the same questions, and might also have seen other issues that had escaped us. We hoped, by pooling experiences, to find answers for ourselves and for others who had already become engaged in long-term research or who might be beginning field studies that could develop into long-term research. The chapters in this volume emerged from that conference. (See Table I.1 on pp. 12–13, at the end of this chapter.)

THE GROWTH OF A FIELDWORK TRADITION

To appreciate why long-term study seems to be such a new development in anthropology, we need to look at the traditions of fieldwork from which it departs.

Anthropologists, as compared to other behavioral scientists, have been notably unconcerned with research design and data-gathering techniques. It is only a slight exaggeration to say that, until recently, we have felt that a well-trained ethnographer equipped with notebook and pencil could establish rapport with informants, ask questions, and return to home base with the data needed for description of the "culture" studied, and the formulation of hypotheses to explain what was seen and recorded. Other behavioral scientists wrote books and articles about research design, data-gathering techniques, samples, the canons of validity of data, and how to interview. They even described "participant observation." Most anthropologists felt, with unwarranted smugness we now recognize, that the "obvious"—doing what should come naturally to a well-trained researcher—hardly merited such formal attention.

Only in recent years have anthropologists begun to show serious concern with the history of research, with the origin and development of the assumptions that have underlain their fieldwork, with the relationship between techniques and end product. Fortunately, we now have a few good accounts of the research experiences of anthropologists, and of the fieldwork process itself (e.g., Freilich 1970; R. Wax 1971; Foster and Kemper 1974; etc.). From these accounts, and from retrospective analyses of anthropological research experiences, we now have a fairly clear picture of what we, as anthropologists, have done in the past, and where we are at the present.

Fieldwork in the Boasian Tradition

In the United States, cultural anthropology was once an historical discipline (in common with anthropology's other components, archaeology, physical anthropology, and linguistics). The transformation to a social science can be roughly dated as the period 1925–1940. When the goals of cultural anthropology (or ethnology) were clearly historical, a pattern of research developed which provided answers to many of the questions that were asked. The first task of the anthropologist, of course, was to "describe the culture" as completely as possible as well as, often, to measure a few heads and record a basic word list. The theoretical questions underlying this description were as follows: Where did this group originate? During a (usually presumed) period of migration, with what other groups did it have contact? What traits did it "borrow" from these other groups? What traits did it pass on to these groups? What traits did it invent? Culturally and linguistically, what are its generic relationships to other groups?

In the United States at least, this view of the task of anthropology can be described as the Boasian model, which prevailed for a half century or longer. Fundamental to the model was the assumption of a baseline, or aboriginal culture, an essentially static condition prevailing prior to major contact with Western civilization. The baseline culture could be described, in greater or lesser degree, by using a combination of the recollections of elderly informants and the techniques of historical reconstruction, using cultural, archaeological, linguistic, and occasionally physical data. The basic data-gathering technique consisted of finding elderly informants with good memories and questioning them about what they could remember. The time span over which the data were gathered was relatively unimportant, as long as one's informants lived and remained lucid. Five summer visits over 8 or 10 years or an equal amount of time in one solid block—methodologically it made no difference.

Lowie's research among the Crow Indians illustrates this assumption. He first visited the reservation in 1907, and then returned in 1910, spending at least a part of every summer through 1916 gathering data, returning for a short visit in 1931, and maintaining contact with the reservation after that date. Yet despite the time span—a full generation—between his first and last visits, he writes "The Crow experiences form a continuum in my consciousness. *Therefore I shall not give a separate account of each visit, but shall treat them all as constituting a single phenomenon* [Lowie 1959: 42; emphasis added]." Lowie's description of the Crow in his most comprehensive work is striking for the predominance of the past tense. Surely, notable changes in Crow life transpired between 1907 and 1931 (Lowie 1935); but neither these, nor the dynamic processes that produced them, seem to have been of much interest to Lowie. They had nothing to do with describing the baseline culture that he, and his contemporaries, considered to be *the* significant goal in anthropology.

Most American ethnographical research prior to the 1940s was carried out in relatively short visits, of a few weeks or months, sometimes repeated over a number of years. That there was a baseline when the ethnographer first appeared on the scene and began data collection and that this baseline could be critical to the study of how change takes place, apparently occurred to no one. As with Lowie, the date of recording any datum was not in itself of any importance.

Social Anthropology and the New Fieldwork

A revolution in field research took place when the significance of Malinowski's experiences in the Trobriand Islands began to be recognized. He had stayed in the Trobriands for a total of 24 months during the years of World War I and watched the Trobrianders as they went about their daily affairs and interacted with each other. He incorporated into his ethnographic account a description of what people did and the way they manipulated the rules they produced as cultural norms. Social anthropology, which emphasized a functional approach and the present, was the result. By and large, those anthropologists who adopted the new approach were uninterested in history. They were too busy recording what they saw and heard to spend much time on what had been. The new approach required more elaborate techniques for gathering information and the investment of sufficient time to be able to observe the changing routines associated with seasonal changes. Summer visits of a few weeks or several months could not produce descriptions that met the new standards. The ethnographer was expected to become immersed in the ongoing life of a new group of people and to learn their language. The new standard was first adopted in Britain, where the pattern of 2 to 3 years of fairly steady work on the same community came to be the accepted norm. In the United States, the system of graduate training and the pattern of funding for research usually reduced this period to a year or 18 months.

The wealth of data acquired during an extended field period exceeded by far that acquired in the earlier work, and this in turn called for new analytical methods. For the first time, the anthropologist could select data and choose among illustrative cases to make theoretical points. Earlier accounts, based on informant's descriptions and emphasizing historical reconstruction, had been fairly simple to compile and in the course of preparing a monograph almost all the collected data were used and appeared in print.

Continuities between the Two Styles

American anthropologists, who worked in the Boasian tradition, and the social anthropologists, who worked in the tradition of Malinowski, shared a major and critical assumption: A culture (or society) can be described once and for all! In the former case, that "once and for all," the baseline, is in the past; in the latter, it is the present. This is not an unimportant difference, but it seems secondary to the fundamental view of the anthropologist about a society, and the problems of anthropology. Both groups shared a static view of society.

Both groups knew that change occurs, but they viewed what had happened in a remarkably similar fashion: Relatively stable, slowly changing communities were jolted by massive contact with Western European civilization. One of two things then happened. For the Boasians, the jolt meant the essential destruction of the traditional way of life, the elimination of cultural forms that could be of any interest to the anthropologist. After all, they worked in North America, where vital native American cultures were undergoing the extreme pressure of the Indian reservation. For social anthropologists, who worked elsewhere in the world for the most part and among societies that were easily seen to be viable, ongoing communities, the jolt meant greater or lesser changes, the adoption of European traits, and particularly material culture. But the groups they studied had the vitality to withstand this shock, to reintegrate themselves around new elements and new conditions. They were believed to have achieved a new state of relative equilibrium. It was this reintegrated equilibrium that concerned the social anthropologist.

EARLY CONCERN WITH CHANGE

During the decade prior to World War II, anthropologists began to be concerned with contemporary changes. At the time of the Redfield–Linton–Herskovits Memorandum on Acculturation (1936), the new approach seemed highly original and promising. But by about 1960, major interest in acculturation had died out; the last formal gasp was perhaps the 1954 seminar sponsored by the Social Science Research Council.

In retrospect, what is striking about acculturation models developed by American anthropologists is that they were essentially static. They also concerned themselves with the fate of culture traits rather than with human beings. In this sense, the Boasian approach to culture as a collection of accidentally associated traits was adhered to, modestly modified to accommodate to the present. Acculturation studies therefore were essentially historical. They dealt with how contemporary cultures had come to be what they were. Acculturation models had little predictive value, and they were unconcerned with future changes. The same can be said of many of the studies of culture contact being carried out by British anthropologists at the same time.

THE BEGINNINGS OF LONG-TERM RESEARCH

In the same period that acculturation studies came to the fore, a new approach to field research slowly began to develop which ultimately may be as revolutionary as that associated with Malinowski. This is the long-term diachronic study which is the subject of the present volume.

Anthropologists who carry out long-term studies and who have worked among the same peoples for from 10 to 30 years are by no means concerned only with measuring change. They find that their depth of understanding increases in proportion to the length of time they spend in the community, but in this respect they are no different from Lowie and Boas, whose repeated visits to the Crow and the Kwakiutl led to the same result. The significant contrast with earlier work (for most anthropologists who have engaged in this kind of research) is the concern with the recording and measurement of change over the period of time the study continues.

For the first time in the history of anthropological field research, the date of recording data becomes itself a critical datum.

Realization of the revolutionary implications of long-term research in social anthropology has dawned slowly on anthropologists. Robert Redfield and Clyde Kluckhohn were probably the first to see the possibilities of the new approach. Kluckhohn's influence was the more decisive in the long run. His insight appears not to have come in a flash. His contact with the Ramah Navajo began in 1923, and further visits in subsequent years brought greater knowledge of the culture, and of the language. Influenced by Edward Sapir and John Dollard he decided, upon completing his doctorate in 1936, to begin a long-term study of the socialization of Navajo children. Believing the Navajo to be already well described, he assumed that an additional two summers of research would provide the background needed for his socialization studies. This proved not to be the case. Although he completed the draft of a Navajo monograph in 1938, he realized he had mastered neither the basic culture patterns nor the cultural dynamics of the group.

> Gradually there emerged the notion that the following of a small community and its culture through time was a needed experiment in anthropology. It seemed plausible that the lack of a time dimension was primarily responsible for the flat, one-dimensional quality which acute and sensitive scholars from other disciplines had noted in even the best of anthropological monographs [Kluckhohn 1949:v].

Kluckhohn's thinking was greatly influenced by Donald Scott, at the time director emeritus of the Peabody Museum of Harvard University. In correspondence, Scott stressed the significance of "continuous observation of the same persons in the same environment. . . . If biologists have found it profitable to spend their lives following the events in colonies of *paramecia,* it is likely that the science of man would be rewarded by intensive, longitudinal observations of a single community [Kluckhohn 1949:v]". Thus emerged "the fundamental idea of charting the fortunes of individuals and their culture through time," as well as the methodological strategies of multiple observations by different people, and multiple approaches by scholars from different disciplines (Kluckhohn 1949:v–vi). Some of the results of this new approach are discussed in Lamphere's article in this volume.

Kluckhohn's Navajo research has been widely recognized, and read, by American and foreign anthropologists. It is worth noting that three of the long-term projects described in this volume (Lake Powell, Chiapas, and Gwembe) have involved students of Kluckhohn's, and Pospisil acknowledges the influence of Kluckhohn on his own decision to engage in long-term research. Other anthropologists who today engage in continuing studies appear to have reinvented, or more or less accidentally fallen into the pattern of repeat studies, without conscious debt to the work of Kluckhohn. It was in the air, so to speak. Siegfried Nadel in lectures delivered in 1955 urged anthroplogists to undertake "continuous observations over really long periods [Nadel 1957:145–147]."

THE WENNER–GREN BURG WARTENSTEIN SYMPOSIUM

It was the recognition that something important was happening in anthropological research patterns, something about which very little was known, that led Foster, Scudder, and Colson to propose to the Wenner–Gren Foundation that a symposium be held at the Foundations' Burg Wartenstein conference center near Vienna, to explore the implications of long-term research in social anthropology. The organizers arbitrarily decided that for purposes of the symposium, "long-term" research would be defined as observations by one or more anthropologists of the same group over a period of 10 or more years. On the basis of this criterion, a list of possible participants was compiled—a list that numbered significantly more than the number of participants who could be conveniently accommodated at Burg Wartenstein. Using such criteria as kinds of societies studied, geographical location, nationality of the researcher, new kinds of research, and probable interest of readers in famous projects (e.g., Vicos, the Harvard Chiapas Project, and the Navajo), the list was trimmed to about 25 scholars who were approached as to availability. Only 15 whose essays appear in this volume were able to participate in the symposium. The symposium organizers believe that the range of experiences described is representative of anthropologists who have engaged in long-term research and that, collectively, the essays give a good picture of the present state of the art. As a result of the Burg Wartenstein conference, we have been made aware of the fact that many of our colleagues now see long-term research as both desirable and feasible. We believe that there are now at least 50 such studies in process.

Instructions to Participants

In the common anthropological tradition, the symposium organizers gave participants free range to describe what they thought were the most important aspects of their work. Within this flexible approach, we suggested that participants might group their data in four sequential sections:

A brief history of the research (identification of the research site, dates
of research, and participants involved)

Methodological questions (how is long-term research best planned,
research designs worked out, team members chosen, students
trained)

Research results (i.e., the major theoretical and factual findings to come
from the research)

Impact on the people studied

We believe this loosely structured approach has proven its utility; what
the essays may lack in direct comparability, they make up for in range of
ideas. Collectively they give few absolute answers, but they define the
parameters of the field and offer guidelines for future research.

Types of Long-Term Research

The major theoretical, methodological, and ethical problems with
which symposium participants wrestled, and the conclusions to which
they came, are summarized in the final chapter of this book. They are best
appreciated in the context of the individual case histories. But before
proceeding to these, it is necessary to stress that "long-term research" is
not a simple category, conforming to a model that almost all anthropologists follow, or ought to follow. In their initial instructions, the
conference organizers defined long-term research on the basis of a single
criterion: time span of the study. This definition is overly simplistic: It
suggests that the principal distinction between short- and long-term research is a simple dichotomy. Short-term research, according to this
definition, means investigations ranging in time from a few months to 2 or
3 years of more or less continuous data-gathering. During this period, field
research is the ethnologist's principal occupation. In contrast, long-term
research is a data-gathering process that stretches over a significantly
longer period, broken, for the ethnographer, by other duties, usually
teaching and associated university obligations. But within the long-range
model there is a great deal of variation: the total time span, the length of
the intervals separating distinct phases of the work, the number of investigators and their role–status relationships, and the goals of the research
itself—all these are important variables.

The major time span distinction is that between the "restudy" and the
"repeat" or "continuous" study. The former, best illustrated in this
collection by Epstein, consists of a major initial study followed after an
interval of some years by a (usually) much briefer visit. The primary
purpose of the "restudy" normally is to measure change, to see to what

extent earlier predictions have been borne out. Redfield's 6-week summer restudy of Chan Kom 15 years after he and Villa Rojas first worked there is a comparable example. That change is what concerned Redfield is apparent from his introduction: "Villa and I often talked of coming back to Chan Kom after the passage of years to see what had happened to the community. The villagers had committed themselves to progress and civilization so vigorously that one wanted to know what would come of it [Redfield 1950:x]."

Lewis's follow-up study of Tepoztlán (1951) is also a restudy, although rather different from those just mentioned in that he was more concerned with his own theoretical ideas and models than with changes per se. Yet, in subsequent publications, Lewis used Redfield's data as a basis for the measurement of change.

The "repeat" or "continuous" study pattern is illustrated by most of the contributions to this volume. Some have involved periodic visits after intervals of several years (e.g., Colson and Scudder, Lee and Fahim, Villa Rojas, Meggitt). Others are based on annual or near-annual visits over many years (e.g., The chapters by Foster, Hofer, Mangin, Pospisil, and Vogt). In contrast to the short restudy, with its primary emphasis on the measurement of change, anthropologists who engage in repeat or continuous studies are also likely to place equal emphasis on acquiring a deeper understanding of the culture itself. The author of one chapter in this volume—Vogt—goes so far as to say that his primary interest is in cultural continuities rather than change—in depth of understanding rather than the quantitative measures of progress.

In some ways overshadowing in importance the variation in time spans—but clearly related to the time-span dimension—is that in personnel and their relationships. At least four patterns are represented by conference participants:

1. The "loner," the independent researcher (Epstein, Helm, Meggitt, Pospisil, Kemper).
2. The "loner" and students (Foster, Fahim).
3. The "partnership" (Colson and Scudder, Hofer and Fél).
4. The "team" of colleagues, often including students (Lee, Mangin, Vogt and, in a somewhat different sense, all of the Navajo research described by Lamphere).

In various phases of their work, of course, individual anthropologists have worked under a variety of these conditions. Villa Rojas, for example, worked in partnership with Redfield, as a "loner" in Quintana Roo, and as a project director in Chiapas.

THE PRIMARY QUESTION: THE JUSTIFICATION FOR
LONG-TERM RESEARCH

The principal question that must be asked of long-term research is: Does it produce results not so easily obtained, if at all, from more traditional forms of anthropological research and are these results of such significance and importance as to justify the expenditure of money and professional time? That is, what is the balance of costs and benefits associated with long-term field research in social anthropology? Should young anthropologists routinely be encouraged to think in terms of repeat visits to their first research site? Should they take special pains to gather a set of minimum core data not necessarily central to their research problem, in case return visits should materialize? Or should planning be restricted to special situations that promise exceptional dividends in learning about changes and continuities in human societies and cultures? How many anthropologists should concentrate their research on the intensive study of a few groups and how many should conduct research for short periods among a wide range of populations and regions? There are no simple answers to these questions. We believe that the papers in this volume do, however, go a long way toward helping us to appreciate the parameters of long-term research, to understand how it compares with short-term fieldwork, and to realize what are some of its main costs and benefits. In the final chapter of this volume we summarize our thinking about these questions.

EXAMPLES OF LONG-TERM FIELD RESEARCH

The chapters included in this volume represent the work of anthropologists from the United States and several other countries. These anthropologists report on long-term projects conducted in foreign countries as well as in their native lands. All of the authors (save one) have observed the same population on two or more visits for at least 10 years. (Kemper has followed Tzintzuntzan emigrants to Mexico City for a shorter period, building on Foster's earlier records from the village and plans to continue to do so throughout his career.) As the information in Table I.1 shows, the chapters range widely over the world, treat a broad spectrum of societies, and have involved prodigious amounts of fieldwork by single ethnographers, partnerships, and large teams. Some of the chapters report on projects whose fame must stand the test of the next generation of anthropologists. One feature shared by all the projects is

TABLE I.1

Conference Participants, the Places of Research, and the Time Spans of Research

	Places of research discussed in conference	Time span of research	Total time in field (months)	Time span (years)
Colson	Gwembe Tonga (Zambia and Zimbabwe)	Oct 1956–Sept 1957; Jan 1960; Sept 1962–Aug 1963; July–Aug 1965; Sept 12–15 1968; June 1972–Jan 1973; June 1973–Sept 1973	36	17
Epstein	Two villages in Mysore State in S. India	Oct 1954–Sept 1956 and restudy July–Aug 1970	25½	11
Fahim	Nubian Village, Egypt	9 months in 1953–1964; 2 months in 1966; 2 months in 1969	21	16
Foster	Village in Mexico, Tzintzuntzan	1944–1946, 1958–1975	30	31+
Helm	Northwest Terr. Canada; Slave and Dogrib groups	1959–1960; 1962; 1967–1970; 1973 and 1974	32	15
Hofer	Átány Village, Hungary	1954–1975; project begun 1951 by colleague (Fél)	~15 [not including Fél]	24
Kemper	Mexico City, Mexico Tzintzuntzan Village	17 months in 1969–1970 and 2½ months in 1974	19¼	5
Lamphere	Navajo in U.S. Southwest, on reservation and off	Ramah 1936–1948 (Kluckhohn *et al.*), 1949–1954 (Vogt, Roberts *et al.*) & 1963–1964 (Lamphere, Reynolds; fieldschool); Sheep Springs 1965–1966; visits 1971, 1972, 1975 (Lamphere), Lake Powell 1974–1975 (Team)	21 herself; Kluckhohn ~ 36; other workers?	12 (Lamphere)
Lee	Botswana; !Kung, Africa	Aug 1963–Jan 1965; Aug 1967–May 1969; July–Aug 1973	38	10
Mangin	Vicos, Ancash, Peru	Project 1950–1954; Mangin: Sept 1951–1953, 1 month in 1957–1958–1959; 3 months in 1960; 1 month in 1961; various brief visits in 1962–1967; and 1975	32	24
Meggitt	Papua New Guinea; Mae Enga in Highland	1955–1957; 1960–1962; 1967, 1970, 1975	~30	20
Pospisil	Tyrol, Austria; Obernberg Village	Oct 1957–Sept 1963; 3 months summers 1964–1974; one month 1975	46	18
Scudder	Gwembe Tonga (Zambia and Zimbabwe)	Oct 1956–Sept 1957; Sept 1962–Aug 1963, Aug–Nov 1967; Apr–June 1970; Aug 1971; May–Nov 1972; June–Sept 1973	38	17
Villa Rojas	Chan Kom, Quintana Roo, Chiapas (Mexico)	1930–1933; 1935–1936; 1938; 1942–1944; 1955–1960; 1975	100	45
Vogt	Zinacantan and Chamula, Chiapas, Mexico	1957–1974. One or more annual visits of 2 weeks to 6 months	50	17

that they continue, either in yearly visits by a team of investigators or in a single anthropologist's plan to make another restudy a few years hence. It is this future orientation that sets these and other long-term research projects apart from one-shot studies. It is the commitment to open-ended, dynamic analysis of the changes and continuities of the human condition that marks long-term studies as a distinctively significant component of contemporary social anthropology.

BIBLIOGRAPHY

Foster, George M., and Robert V. Kemper (Eds.)
1974 *Anthropologists in cities.* Boston: Little Brown.
Freilich, Morris, ed.
1970 *Marginal natives: Anthropologists at work.* New York: Harper and Row.
Kluckhohn, Clyde
1949 Introduction: The Ramah project. In *Gregorio, the hand-trembler,* by Leighton, Alexander H. and Dorothea C. Leighton. *Papers of the Peabody Museum of Harvard University 40* (No. 1).
Lewis, Oscar
1951 *Life in a Mexican village: Tepoztlán restudied.* Urbana: Univ. of Illinois Press.
Lowie, Robert
1935 *The Crow Indians.* New York: Farrar and Rinehart.
1959 *Robert H. Lowie, ethnologist: A personal record.* Berkeley: Univ. of California Press.
Nadel, Siegfried
1957 *The theory of social structure.* London: Cohen & West.
Redfield, Robert
1950 *A village that chose progress: Chan Kom revisited.* Chicago: Univ. of Chicago Press.
Redfield, Robert, Ralph Linton, and Melville J. Herskovits
1936 A memorandum for the study of acculturation. *American Anthropologist 38:*149–152.
Wax, Rosalie
1971 *Doing fieldwork: Warnings and advice.* Chicago: Univ. of Chicago Press.

Part I

LONG-TERM RESEARCH IN HISTORICAL PERSPECTIVE

If time is the crucial dimension of long-term field research, then the history of specific projects should show how ethnographic procedures mirror changing fashions in anthropological theory. Whereas turn-of-the-century ethnologists were committed to salvaging information about native peoples facing "extinction" by the forces of European and American colonization, later fieldworkers focused on the acculturation of these populations in colonial empires and nation states. This shift from reconstructing the past to understanding the present transformed fieldwork styles. Brief summer field trips to many groups gave way to longer field seasons among the same group or in the same region.

By the 1950s, the significance of long-term studies was becoming clear to anthropologists interested in sociocultural change and economic development. The essays brought together in this section, all of which refer to studies begun before 1950, illustrate the interaction of method and theory during this important period in the growth of modern anthropology. The authors occasionally treat harshly their own shortcomings and those of their predecessors, but they also show that careful and patient research over several decades *may* lead

15

Long-Term Field Research
in Social Anthropology

to results unobtainable through conventional 12–18-month field trips.

In her critical review of anthropological research on the Navajo, Lamphere argues forcefully that fieldwork procedures are delimited by the theoretical framework of the investigators. The early focus on culture and personality studies by Kluckhohn and his students in the 1930s yielded, with the Ramah Project of the 1950s, to a greater concern with the interaction between culture, personality, and social structure defined according to Parsonian notions of functional integration. From the Ramah Project to the Lake Powell Research Project of the 1970s came an even larger shift in theoretical orientations. This multidisciplinary project operated within a theoretical framework, which emphasized regional ecology and policy-related issues. During these four decades, the Navajo have changed from being relatively isolated to being interwoven with social, economic, and political institutions of American society. Lamphere shows that the earlier studies neglected these external forces by treating the Navajo as if they lived in pristine isolation. As a result, data collected in the 1930s and 1940s often were too narrowly conceived to be valuable for scholars no longer interested in culture and personality issues. Lamphere also raises another difficult question regarding long-term studies: If we cannot know what theoretical issues and what kinds of ethnographic data will be important in 20, 50, or even 100 years, then, perhaps, we should shift our efforts to doing fieldwork *for* the population being studied rather than simply about it.

In contrast to Lamphere's review of earlier work among the Navajo, Villa Rojas offers a first-hand account of his fieldwork among the Maya covering some 45 years. He takes us from the ethnographically famous communities of Chan Kom and Tusik in Yucatan, where he worked in cooperation with Redfield during the 1930s, to Oxchuc in Chiapas, where he has worked intermittently since the 1940s. What began as a short-term involvement, leading to the Ph.D. degree, became a long-term commitment to fieldwork among the Maya. Like Kluckhohn, Villa Rojas became involved with a people with whom he had worked before his anthropological career began. More remarkable is Villa Rojas's continued fieldwork over such a long period. Although usually alone in the field, he was involved in two important team enterprises, first among the lowland Maya and later among the highland Maya. In recent years, Villa Rojas's position with the National Indian Institute has directly involved him with applied scientific research on the Maya and other indigenous populations in Mexico.

In retrospect, Villa Rojas echoes Lamphere by recognizing that he could have paid greater attention to external socioeconomic and political factors impinging on Indian groups. On the other hand, even though he now works in an agency devoted to applied anthropology and economic development, Villa Rojas still maintains a strong belief in the canons of science.

The case of the Quechua of highland Perú parallels that of the Navajo and the Maya. As reported by Mangin, the Vicos Project represented an attempt to blend scientific research and applied anthropology among this exploited population. Like Villa Rojas's work with Redfield, Mangin's participation in Holmberg's Cornell–Perú Project led to the Ph.D. degree. However, Mangin was involved in applied team research from the outset, whereas Villa Rojas came to this only in the later phase of his career. The Vicos Project represents a remarkable instance of anthropological fieldwork, yet Mangin believes that each return visit changes his view of the project. In this context, it is not surprising that no satisfactory overall evaluation of the Vicos experience has been written, although it is chastening to read Mangin's comment that "if we had had more money and greater local resources we might have done *more* damage." Mangin's own difficulty in assessing the Vicos Project certainly reflects his insistence on the importance of the personalities involved in the research. In contrast to Lamphere, who emphasizes theoretical issues and minimizes personalities, Mangin stresses that a project as complex as that in Vicos involves an interplay of personalities as important as that between theory and methodology. This is particularly true, he argues, because the separation of research from applied work at Vicos was never seriously attempted.

In contrast to the projects examined by Lamphere, Villa Rojas, and Mangin, the work of Hofer (and his senior colleague, Fél) among the peasants of Átány, Hungary, follows a quite different ethnographic tradition. It was the intent of Fél and Hofer to add to the body of national ethnographic literature, not to carry out research of theoretical significance or aimed at applied sociocultural change. As members of the culture being studied, Fél and Hofer had the advantage of being in or near the field situation on a continuing basis; not even Villa Rojas was a native Tzeltal speaker, and few of the Navajo or Vicos fieldworkers mastered the local languages. The result of their 20 years of research lies not just in their publications, but also in their collection of 3800 material artifacts and 10,000 photographs in the Budapest Museum of Ethnography. Átány became a living laboratory, readily at hand, in which new ideas about contemporary Hungarian life could be tested. Even so, it took a decade for the researchers to be on such intimate terms with the villagers that they could pass from the "front region" of the culture into the "back region," where the conflicts within the community could be properly understood. Because of this "deeper" and "thicker" knowledge of Átány, Hofer raises the possibility that long-term research in a single community may help to perfect the art of fieldwork itself and thereby make a significant contribution to the development of scientific methodology in anthropology.

It is interesting that Hofer and Villa Rojas take positive views of long-term field research, while Lamphere and Mangin are less sanguine about its value. Perhaps the early death of Kluckhohn and Holmberg, the guiding hands of the Navajo and Vicos projects, is the difference. Once these leaders were gone, the projects lost their corporate memory, the key to the ethnographic files. Later workers have had difficulty operating in this vacuum. The Navajo and Vicos projects represent, in a sense, a series of overlapping research efforts tied to a particular population while lacking the continuity and focus recognized as so important by Hofer and Villa Rojas. As we will see in the chapters in the rest of the volume, the social organization of long-term research projects, as Mangin points out so well for the Vicos case, may be as important in determining success or failure as are the methods and theories employed.

1

The Long-Term Study among the Navajo

Louise Lamphere

INTRODUCTION

Every anthropologist no doubt knows that the typical Navajo family is composed of a mother, a father, several children, and the visiting anthropologist. All of us who have conducted research on the Navajo Nation in New Mexico and Arizona have been constantly reminded through this anecdotal definition that these Native Americans are perhaps the most studied (and by implication the most overstudied) of all non-Western cultures. The Navajo, with a population of 130,000, are the largest Native American group in the United States, and their 18-million-acre reservation is about the size of New England. Anthropological research on the Navajo dates back into the late nineteenth century. The myriad of publications on the Navajo cover every facet of their lives.

This abundance of research on the Navajo gives us an opportunity to examine the special place of long-term research in comparison with shorter studies and to evaluate the contributions of long-term projects on the Navajo since the first one began 40 years ago. As anthropology has developed, the prevailing theories surrounding research on the Navajo have altered, as have the technique of data collection and codification. In

19

Long-Term Field Research
in Social Anthropology

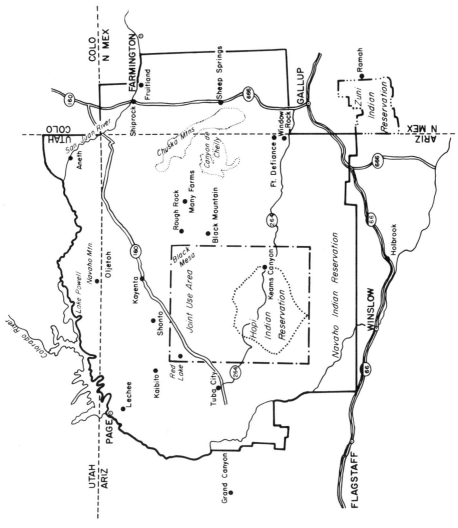

Figure 1.1. Navajo communities where long-term anthropological research has been conducted (see Table 1.1). Solid line indicates reservation boundary; dashed line indicates Navajo-Hopi Joint Use Area now being partitioned between the Navajo and Hopi Tribes; and

addition, the situation of the Navajo and other Native American groups has substantially changed. There is, I believe, a dialetical or interactive relationship between anthropological theory and method, on the one hand, and the economic, social, and cultural setting of the study population, on the other. The relationship that holds for one decade and determines the nature of research may not be relevant or useful 20 years later. Just as the data and results of a project begun in the 1930s might seem arcane and unhelpful given the needs of the present day Navajo population or the interests of contemporary researchers, so might ongoing or future research seem out-of-place and irrelevant 20 years from now.

Research on the Navajo has been extremely varied, both in terms of the topics chosen for investigation and the research design employed. Although much writing on the Navajo is intended to be about the Navajo Nation as a whole, most research has been carried out in the context of a particular community, a locale where researchers have lived and studied. Projects have been carried out by "lone" investigators, by teams of two, and by larger groups, either loosely or tightly organized. Long-term research has ranged from restudy of the same community by the same investigator, restudy by a different investigator (sometimes a student of the initial researcher), to continuous investigation by a number of investigators over a substantial period of time. In this chapter, I will focus on large-scale team research, beginning with the earliest and perhaps most famous, long-term Navajo research, the Ramah Project and the Comparative Study of Values in Five Cultures Project, both focused on the Ramah Navajo under the direction of Clyde Kluckhohn. Because of space limitations I will touch only lightly on long-term research as it developed in the period following the Ramah research (1957–1972). Instead, I will focus on a recent example of long-term Navajo research, the Lake Powell Research Project. A central concern of my discussion will be not only to compare the different organization of these projects, but to relate the theoretical framework of the investigators to the results of the research.

A final issue will be to examine the ethical aspects of each project especially in relation to the people studied. A number of Native American groups in the United States and Canada have begun to assert their legal rights and have attempted to alter their relationship to the economy and supralocal political institutions (such as the Bureau of Indian Affairs, county school boards and the Indian Health Service). In examining long-term research on the Navajo reservation, I hope to make the point that research problems and approaches are affected by the ethical stance of an investigator or team of researchers toward this growing self-consciousness of the Navajo.

THE RAMAH PROJECT

Kluckhohn conceived of the Ramah Project after he had completed his Ph.D. and had begun his appointment at Harvard University. He had already spent considerable time in the Ramah area, south of Gallup, New Mexico (during 1923 and in the summers of 1926–1929) and had written briefly about his experiences in his two chronicles of reservation travels, *To the Foot of the Rainbow* (1927) and *Beyond the Rainbow* (1933). The Ramah Navajo (population 400 in 1940) were pushed to the south of the town of Ramah when it was settled by Mormons in the 1880s and, at the time of Kluckhohn's initial study, lived in hogan clusters scattered over several townships. As an off-reservation Navajo population their claims to land have been tenuous. Mormon and Texas ranchers held some sections, interspersed with land allotted to Navajos during the early part of this century, bought by the Navajo tribe in the 1940s or still held by the Bureau of Land Management.

Kluckhohn's original plan had been to conduct a long-term study of the socialization of Navajo children using the Ramah community as an ethnographic backdrop. However, he was soon dissatisfied with the ethnographic phase of the project, feeling that his initial description showed that "we had not yet mastered the basic patterns, let alone the cultural dynamics [Kluckhohn 1949:v]." By 1939, Kluckhohn felt that a long-term study was necessary to overcome the "flat, one-dimensional quality" of most anthropological studies. He was impressed by the suggestion of Donald Scott, director emeritus of the Peabody Museum of Harvard University, that it would be useful to study a population over time, watching it change and grow.

The research gradually evolved into a multidisciplinary long-term project, since Kluckhohn felt that "multiple observations by different persons and multiple approaches by individuals who had received their training in various disciplines (Kluckhohn 1949:v,vi)" would enrich both ethnographic recording and the study of socialization. Alexander and Dorothea Leighton, both psychiatrists, were perhaps the most important contributors to the project during the 1939–1942 period; 15 graduate students in anthropology from Harvard and other institutions participated in summer fieldwork, and Kluckhohn lists several psychologists, physicians, and psychiatrists among his collaborators (Kluckhohn 1949:x). The loose integration of this team project seemed to complement its interdisciplinary character. Each fieldworker pursued topics of his or her interest or specialization or investigated a subject (e.g., the family as a "small-group culture" or Navajo ceremonialism) that seemed appropriate to the field situation (e.g., living with a family or attending the frequently held curing ceremonies).

By 1949, Kluckhohn felt that the aim of the project was a series of reports devoted to special topics (such as the history of the community, ceremonialism, social organization, and even basketry). Some studies would focus on theoretical topics, whereas others were to deal with the relationship of individuals to their culture; an overall report would integrate the various aspects of Ramah Navajo culture.

In other words, the goals of the project were broadly ethnographic and Kluckhohn was committed to a vision of ethnography that involved the accumulation of the minute details of everyday life, a commitment which was closely allied to his definition of culture. Culture for Kluckhohn consisted of "designs for living [Kluckhohn and Kelly 1945:97]" or "The set of habitual and traditional ways of thinking, feeling, and reacting that are characteristic of the ways a particular society meets its problems at a particular point in time [Kluckhohn and Leighton 1946:xviii]."

Following Benedict, Kluckhohn saw these structured ways of thinking and doing as "patterned." By *pattern* Kluckholn meant an overt, conscious aspect of culture, a discrete interrelated set of facts that produce structural regularities in the realm of ideas (ideal patterns) or consistencies in social relationships and action (behavioral patterns) (Kluckhohn 1941). In contrast, patterning at the covert level was characterized by the term *configuration,* a generalization from behavior that was largely unconscious or unverbalized by the participants in a culture.

The concepts of pattern and configuration helped Kluckhohn to deal with variation in Navajo life both in examining topics of general ethnographic interest (e.g., ceremonialism, social organization) and in studying socialization and personality. To ascertain overt patterns was to make sense out of the myriad details and to pull together conflicting statements about what should be done in a given situation and what individuals in fact do. This interaction between a definition of culture and Kluckhohn's commitment to detailed observation can be seen in his early work on Navajo religion (see bibliography in Kluckhohn 1962) and in his monograph on Navajo witchcraft (Kluckhohn 1944). In each publication, he dealt carefully with the number of informants consulted, the statements agreed on by most informants, and deviant statements. On some topics, his method was to gather "every (or virtually every) relevant datum" in the community being studied (Kluckhohn 1962:250). From this corpus of details on a particular topic Kluckhohn abstracted his patterns, often ethnographic generalizations (e.g., that ceremonial instruction is always paid for) or tabulations showing variation (e.g., the close biological relatives in the Ramah area from whom ceremonies were learned). Likewise, from detailed observations on a number of topics, Kluckhohn abstracted what he considered to be the important configurations or unconscious patterns of Navajo culture: "fear of malevolent intentions of other persons," "distrust of extremes," and "the spirit outlet" (e.g., a break in a pottery or weaving design) (Kluckhohn 1941:125). Unfortunately, a summary of patterns was often very abstract and disembodied from the data, so that it is often unclear how a particular pattern is related to information or tabulations presented elsewhere in the publication.

These same theoretical and methodological concerns—the collection of ethnographic details and the abstraction of patterns and configurations— also oriented Kluckhohn's study of socialization. Even Kluckhohn's definition of culture as abstracted patterns led him to be interested in the relationship between culture (as a set of elements described by the analyst) and the individual—the personality—who learns cultural patterns in the process of "culturalization." To understand this process and the resulting variation in personalities, the Ramah Project focused on the socialization of 48 children, a group selected by Kluckhohn and the Leightons to represent children from various age groups, economic backgrounds and family clusters (about one-third of the total number of children at Ramah). In making behavioral observations of children, the aim was to record everything seen and heard, checking observations against a list of important topics, so that relevant information would not be missed (Kluckhohn 1962:251).

In addition, Dorothea Leighton (and other fieldworkers) administered a number of psychological tests (intelligence tests; projective tests, including the Thematic Apperception Test and Rorschach; and a battery of psychological tests) to Ramah children, and these supplemented the observations recorded in field notes and kept in the growing Ramah Files. Most of the 48 children were followed over a period of several years and the results of the testing and case study material on individual children are reported in *Children of the People* (Leighton and Kluckhohn 1947) and several articles. Like the work on ceremonialism and witchcraft, the study of Navajo personality was designed to give a precise indication of the patterns of Navajo personality as well as an indication of the variation in individual personality configurations.

The loose organization of this team project probably facilitated the possibility of interdisciplinary work, a relatively new approach in the late 1930s, and allowed the collection of ethnographic material to progress along with the parallel culture and personality study. Both kinds of data were geared to producing detailed descriptions of Navajo culture and individual adaptations, rather than to isolating natural or cultural cycles or testing of hypotheses. From our vantage point today, it is easy to understand the limitations of the Ramah Project both in terms of data collection and theory. Most of the fieldwork took place during the summer months, although the Leightons' field research extended over most of the year. Most of the students conducted their studies in either one or two field seasons, worked through interpreters, and learned very little, if any, Navajo. The short exposure to Navajo culture and the lack of control of the language inhibited the kinds of topics that could have been studied and the ways in which data were collected and related to each other.

Information was kept on individuals and families in the community, and field notes were categorized under a set of topics devised by Kluckhohn (since the HRAF system had not yet been developed and adopted). These were kept in the Ramah Files at Harvard. Much of the material was collected in terms of the anthropologists' categories, not those of the Navajo. This is true of the Peabody Museum Papers on ethnobotany, land use, sex practices and reproduction, and the material on Navajo personality (which was interpreted in terms of the psychological categories worked out by professional psychiatrists and psychologists). It is less true of the material on ceremonialism by Kluckhohn and Wyman, where an elaborate system of translation of Navajo terms for ceremonies, parts of ceremonies, ritual paraphernalia, and plant medicine were worked out, and of the monograph on witchcraft in which Kluckhohn used Navajo categories to sort his data.

Researchers did pay attention to Navajo words and terminology (carefully noting down and translating names for plants, for example). However, the overall structure of what we now call a "domain" was not worked out. In some cases, today's reader cannot ascertain the significant Navajo categories and in others, where categories are presented, we cannot determine how they are ordered (e.g., in a taxonomy, paradigm, etc.). Even with the data on Navajo ceremonialism, I feel that the order is partly imposed by Kluckhohn and Wyman rather than being a reflection of an informant's ordering of events or terms. More useful than the Ramah Project writings on Navajo ceremonialism are the Navajo texts (often with interlinear translations) collected between 1929 and 1934 by Father Berard, since these provide raw material for understanding the content of Navajo ritual as well as the context of important symbols and concepts.

Since the 1940s the cultural neutrality of projective tests and the usefulness of interpreting modal personality structure or personality configurations have been questioned. Attention has turned away from "culture and personality" studies and focused on studies of symbolic interaction, cognitive development, or ethnopsychology (the study of personality and emotion in terms of native categories). Life history material has remained popular, but none of the Ramah life histories are as lengthy or as interesting as *Son of Old Man Hat* or *Sun Chief*. In other words, *most of the Ramah personality data do not fit into contemporary frameworks nor are they revelant to recent interests in social structure, economics, and political organization.*

Even the short description of Ramah social organization written by Kluckhohn and published posthumously (Kluckhohn 1966) is disappointing. As David Aberle (1973:90–93) has pointed out, Kluckhohn's tabulations were precise, but they tended to be enumerations on one variable, not associations of two or more variables. Connections between one pattern and another are not made, so that differences are not brought into conjunction with each other. Most importantly, interpretation is often substituted for explanation. From the Ramah monograph one gets no sense of how Navajo life fits together as a system and how personality, social structure, and culture are related. I feel that this is directly connected to the use of *culture* as a major organizing concept and the particular definition of culture which Kluckhohn used. By concentrating on *patterns* and *configurations,* and by abstracting these one by one from informant statements and behavioral observations, one gets little sense of the relationships among patterns. Where a relationship is presented, it is often imposed by the investigator and when a single pattern is explained, it is done through Western psychological theory or functionalism.

Finally, the focus on patterns meant that process was ignored. Kluckhohn had felt that he was working toward a more accurate description of the culture of a population in order to understand change, but, at least at this stage in the Ramah research, cultural cycles (such as that of domestic groups) were not studied nor were unidirectional changes analyzed (such as the importance of population growth for resource utilization, the increasing impact of neighboring groups, and the effect of institutions like schools on Navajo culture). In the period 1936–1948, I view Kluckhohn as still being under the profound influence of Boasian anthropology, committed to a view of culture as patterned elements without a clear framework for analyzing relationships among individuals, groups, and shared ideas except as abstract patterns.

Kluckhohn's theoretical framework and his commitment to precise ethnographic recording are also related to his position on the ethical responsibilities of the researcher. His views on the relationship between the anthropologist and the native community were expressed both in his publications and in "behind the scenes" activities on behalf of the Ramah Navajo and the Navajo Nation as a whole (Adair 1973). Kluckhohn accepted, implicitly, the relationship between a nation-state and an ethnic minority like the Navajo. He felt that one of the major questions of the time was understanding how minority peoples could be dealt with so that they would not be a perpetual problem and so that human values embedded in their lifeways would not be lost to the rest of humanity (Kluckhohn and Leighton 1946:xvi).

Kluckhohn viewed the situation of the Navajo in the late 1930s and early 1940s as "the nation's foremost Indian problem." He saw their situation as one of adjusting to (perhaps inevitable) "technological change," yet felt that this process could be less disruptive if "human needs" and cultural differences were taken into account. The problem was one of inadequate communication between administrators and Navajos, and Kluckhohn sought to make government and private programs more effective through social science research and publication which communicated the native culture to members of our own. "The central aim of this book," Kluckhohn and Leighton explain in discussing *The Navajo,* "is to supply the background needed by the administrator or teacher who is to deal effectively with the people in human terms [1946:xix]."

The anthropologist is therefore an "interpreter," a "broker," or "intermediary"—someone who translates native culture to those who have to "deal with" minority populations (teachers, health personnel, government agents, and other administrators). Even though the categories of the ethnography were those of current anthropological theory or derived from Western categories, the emphasis was on presenting Navajo culture in its own terms as "baseline," in order to record later changes and responses to contact with other cultures. In this conception of the anthropologist's role, there is little analysis of power relationships, of inequality, and poverty. Change is viewed as inevitable, the product of contact between two cultures (defined neutrally with regard to each other), and there is no analysis of the economic, political, educational, and religious institutions which impinge upon life within minority populations and determine relationships between traders and customers, teachers and students, doctors and patients, and government agents and clientele.

In a personal way, however, Kluckhohn did his best to make the wishes of Navajos known to the appropriate authorities. For example, he took an active role in helping the Ramah Navajo become part of the United Pueblo Agency (rather than under the jurisdiction of the more distant and unresponsive Window Rock Agency) and was an important witness for the Navajo Tribe in their Land Claims Case. Kluckhohn, in these and other activities, took the informal role of "broker," mediating between the Navajo and non-Navajos, much the same role he filled in the more formal context of published anthropological scholarship.

Kluckhohn saw no contradiction between purely anthropological and scientific problems and the potential usefulness of this material for those involved with policy decisions relating to Navajo life. He felt that his study of Navajo culture and personality patterns would lead to more humane decisions on the part of those who actually made policy with regard to health, education, and land use. His writings were not directed toward specific policy decisions, but in his personal actions he worked to bring about the decisions he felt Navajos wanted.

THE COMPARATIVE STUDY OF VALUES IN FIVE CULTURES

In 1948 the study of the Ramah Navajo became part of a new team project. In the years following World War II, Kluckhohn's participation in the formation of the Department of Social Relations at Harvard and his growing interest in the social theories of his colleague, Talcott Parsons, turned him to the study of values. Kluckhohn's predisposition for inter-disciplinary research was compatible with the philosophy of the department, and Parsonian structural-functionalism provided a more sophisti-cated formulation of the relationship between culture and personality. Parsons' analysis of the social system posited a series of analytic layers: the biological organism, the personality, the social system (with four functional sub-systems), and culture. Social interaction in Parsons' "ac-tion frame of reference" was oriented by "pattern variables" or, in later formulations by "value-orientations." Kluckhohn had disagreements with Parsons' framework (for example, in positing social structure as autonomous from culture), but the term value-orientation and sociological functionalism as an approach undoubtedly influenced his thinking about values (Edmonson 1973:176).

The Comparative Study of Values in Five Cultures Project was a 6-year project, funded for $100,000 by the Rockefeller Foundation and adminis-tered through the Laboratory of Social Relations under an Advisory Committee consisting of Kluckhohn, J. O. Brew, and Talcott Parsons. John M. Roberts and Evon Z. Vogt served as field directors, while during the 5 years between 1949 and 1953, more than 37 fieldworkers from a variety of social science disciplines conducted research on a number of projects.

The Values Project focused on an empirical study of values and their variation, using a comparison of five communities in the Ramah area: the

Mormons, the Texan Homesteaders, the Spanish Americans, the Zuni, and the Navajo. Kluckhohn felt that the Ramah area was an ideal setting for comparison since the five communities were small in size, were subject to the same historical process, and yet contrasted in important ways (Kluckhohn 1951a:ix).

The goal of the project was to explore why cultural variations and differences persisted among these communities, given the similar environment and technology available within the region. In other words, the project was to work towards a more complex understanding of one aspect of culture (values) rather than to study process and change as such. In this context, the Ramah Navajo became, not a sub-population within the larger Navajo culture (where generalizations could be made that applied to the Navajo as a whole) but one "society" to be compared with four others.

One of the immediate problems of the project was to define the concept of "values" and to provide a framework for studying them. In reaching an early definition, Kluckhohn utilized his previous writing on the concept of culture. He defined "values" in terms of "orientations toward experience which influence choice," a notion not too different from that of "pattern" or "configuration" (Edmonson 1973:168–169,174). Later, Kluckhohn's published definition included the notion of "the desirable" to distinguish values from culture in general. "A value is a conception, explicit or implicit, distinctive of an individual or characteristic of a group, of the desirable which influences the selection from available modes, means, and ends of action [1951b:395]."

During the course of the Values Project three schemes for the study of values emerged: Ethel Albert's classification (Vogt and Albert 1966) adopted the categories of Western philosophy; Florence Kluckhohn's sociological value-orientation scheme postulated variations in value-orientations along six universal dimensions (F. Kluckhohn and F. L. Strodbeck 1961); and Clyde Kluckhohn's own framework for comparison of value-emphases depended on binary oppositions derived from structural linguistics and distinctive feature analysis (Vogt and Albert 1966:12). Kluckhohn did not fully explicate his scheme until the mid-1950s after most of the fieldwork for the Values Project had been completed. It reflected his increasing disenchantment with functional explanations and the influence of structuralism on his thinking (see Lamphere and Vogt 1973:98–100). That no one scheme was adopted by all researchers reflected not only the difficulty of constructing a framework for studying a topic as abstract as values, but also the loose integration and interdisciplinary composition of the project.

Like the Ramah Project, the Values Project emphasized a permissive policy which allowed each fieldworker considerable freedom in choice of topic, methodology, and analysis. Not only were diverse definitions of "values" used, but some fieldworkers specialized in a single culture while others compared two or more of the five cultures. Some work focused on values, while other research concerned the relationship of values to an aspect of environment, personality, or culture (Vogt and Albert 1966:4). Taking all the projects together, it seems likely that each investigator acknowledged the relationship between his or her study and the general topic of "values," but focused on a topic of more immediate interest only peripherally related to values.

These studies of the Ramah Navajo did, however, build on the ethnographic and theoretical base already provided by Kluckhohn and his co-workers in the early 1940s. Some studies "filled in" data not previously collected, explicitly or implicitly using Kluckhohn's statements about Navajo cultural patterns and configurations in examining these "new" areas. Examples include the study of aesthetic and philosophical aspects of Navajo culture, including David McAllester's study of *Enemy Way Music,* George Mill's book on *Navajo Art and Culture* and John Ladd's monograph on Navajo ethics, *The Structure of a Moral Code* (all listed in the bibliography of Vogt and Albert 1966).

Of all these Ramah monographs, I have always been the most impressed by Ladd's book. Though based only on two months of fieldwork, it provides a "micro-level" analysis of Navajo "norms" and moral precepts which give an extremely accurate picture of what Navajos are like.

Two other studies, Vogt's *Navajo Veterans* (1951) and Rapoport's monograph on missionary activities (1954) expanded the use of psychological tests and life history data begun by Kluckhohn and the Leightons, and also dealt with change and acculturation. They illustrate both the type of culture and personality studies current in the early 1950s and the integration of anthropological, sociological, and psychological methods which was part of the Harvard Social Relations milieu. Both authors used Kluckhohn's list of implicit configurations as a "baseline" for determining Navajo values (Vogt 1951:35–38 and Rapoport 1954:51–54) and both designed their own psychological tests in addition to using more standard personality tests and collecting life histories. Furthermore, these studies entailed a research design more complex than anything attempted during the Ramah Project. Both investigators focused on subpopulations within the Ramah Navajo community and formulated specific hypotheses which could be tested with their data. Not only was hypothesis testing a more sophisticated approach than formulating questions, as Kluckhohn and his co-workers had done, but these hypotheses reflected, in each case, a model of the relationship between the individual personality, the social situation, and various aspects of culture (such as values). While the Ramah Project remained descriptive, these studies looked for relationships among variables and viewed aspects of Navajo life as forming some sort of "system."

Other aspects of the Ramah Project were carried on into the Values Project. Fieldworkers continued to contribute their field notes to the growing Ramah Files. New file drawers were set aside, some for each of the five cultures, and notes (dittoed in multiple copies) were filed on 5″×8″ sheets under as many HRAF system categories as applied to the material. Like Kluckhohn's previous categories, the new system was imposed from the outside rather than based on Navajo concepts. Even the schemes for describing values were derived from our own categories; this was perhaps necessary for cross-cultural comparison, but was not as faithful to Navajo distinctions as later approaches might have been.

An overall appraisal of the Values Project did not appear until 1966, several years after Kluckhohn's death. It contains comparisons among the five cultures on a series of topics rather than an overall synthesis of the study of values alone. By the time the book appeared, interest in values in anthropology had waned and other theoretical approaches and new methods had emerged.

The Values Project did not alter the anthropologists' relation to the native community, but did change their mission to the non-anthropological audience. Instead of emphasizing the practical and policy-oriented ways in which cultural interpretation could affect the actions of teachers, administrators and health personnel, the Values Project, partly because of its cross-cultural nature, aimed at a more abstract "scientific understanding" of values. The task was to understand "human behavior," the universal features of society and culture, rather than the workings of one culture or a particular community. This mirrors, I think, the turn away from "applied anthropology" or more action-oriented approaches in the late 1950s and 1960s in an attempt to build a more rigorous anthropology that could be more closely connected with cross-cultural generalizations and with the findings of other social sciences.

Just as the Ramah Project concentrated on the culture of the Navajo as more or less isolated from the social forces which impinged upon it, the Values Project was, in its original conception, a study of five isolated "cultures" or "societies" in isolation from the larger nation-state. It was perhaps naive to see each of these five communities as being five "societies" or "cultures." Important historical connections between the larger "cultures" and the Ramah area communities were ignored, and the power relationships among these populations and with outside forces were largely unexplored. All cultures were assumed to share the same technology, rather than having differential access to an economic system controlled outside the region, and the micro-environmental differences among their habitats were discounted. In discussing differences among the five "political systems," emphasis was on local decision-making patterns, while the implications of subordination to the wider society were not explicitly drawn.

RESEARCH ON RAMAH DURING THE 1960s AND 1970s

A third phase of research in the Ramah area has been mainly characterized by the presence of summer field schools in ethnography (in 1962, 1963, 1964, and 1972) and some individual short-term research (Blanchard 1971). As a participant in the 1963 field school supported by the National Science Foundation (Lamphere 1964) and as someone interested in the study of land use, domestic group organization, and authority patterns (Reynolds, Lamphere, and Cook 1967), I was in a position to understand the difficulties of the use of long-term research data by a "new generation" of anthropologists. I believe that problems in using previously collected material when no one with first-hand knowledge of that project is available, changes in research methodology, and changes in theoretical orientation which alter the usefulness of a given body of material are much more important in assessing the Ramah Project and the Values Project as examples of long-term research than are either their team composition or their loose organization.

As a well-studied community with already-established contacts and a substantial data file (located at the Laboratory of Anthropology in Santa Fe since their transfer from Harvard in 1963), Ramah should have been an ideal location for continued training and research in ethnography and social anthropology. However, Kluckhohn's death in 1960 severed the personal ties between anthropologists and the Ramah Navajo; many of Kluckhohn's students moved on to other research areas or began to work on other parts of the Navajo reservation. Links to individual families were lacking, as was someone with a thorough knowledge of the community who could have interpreted the masses of accumulated data. It was as if the "key" to the Ramah Files had died with Kluckhohn. Only hours of digging through "cut up" field notes revealed facts that might easily have come to light in a conversation with him.

Problems in using the files were related to the kinds of data collected and to the categories used in filing, which were in turn determined by the theoretical foci of the Ramah Project and the Values Project. Economic data were only to be found in "bits and pieces"; basic demographic, census, and land use data were incomplete. In general, it was difficult to gain an overall picture of the economic and social structure of the community, since Ramah research (intended as descriptive ethnography or studies of personality and values) had not focused on these types of data. For instance, in a recent search of the Ramah Files, I located the 1948 census but not a version updated through the 1950s. Particularly lacking was a classification of individuals into households and residence groups and the linking of these to a map indicating spatial location of kin groups and land use. Kluckhohn's genealogy of the Ramah Navajo (obtained from Richard Kluckhohn), the 1963 Tribal Census for Ramah, and the Allotment Files (then located in the Gallup Area BIA Office) were much more useful for constructing an analysis of residence patterns and land-use than anything I found in the Ramah Files.

LONG-TERM RESEARCH IN OTHER NAVAJO COMMUNITIES

While research in Ramah had focused on general ethnography, on Navajo personality, and later on values, fieldwork carried out by Malcolm Carr Collier at Navajo Mountain in 1938–1939 and by William Y. Adams 16 years later at Shonto indicated an interest in local social and economic organization, a trend which characterized much community research in the 1960s. Table 1.1 summarizes the research carried out in these and other communities (beginning with the Ramah research already discussed). Many projects began as individual, two-person, or team projects on a short-term basis and later were continued either by the same researcher or by another who had access to the original data. The two major projects involving more than two researchers were those sponsored by Cornell University at Fruitland and Many Farms. Both focused on culture change, the former on the ramifications of an irrigation project and the latter on the impact of a new health clinic, and both were very much in the main stream of 1950s "applied anthropology."

In many ways the research of the late 1950s and 1960s overcame the theoretical and methodological difficulties of the Ramah research. Fieldworkers did a much better job of collecting economic and social structural data on local communities. They went much further in understanding Navajo cultural categories. Better control of the language by several investigators made it possible to investigate problems (e.g., social structure, health, ceremonialism) according to Navajo taxonomy and conceptualization (see Witherspoon 1975). A "thicker," more complex

TABLE 1.1

Long-Term Navaho Research Projects[a]

Community	Investigators	Dates	Focus	Type of exposure	Organization
1. Ramah	Kluckhohn, Leightons et al.	1936–1948	Ethnography, culture, and personality	Initial Study; continuous (mostly summers)	New study; team: loosely organized
	Kluckhohn, Vogt, Roberts et al.	1949–1953	Values	Continuous	Team; loosely organized
	Field school students (Crocker, Jacobson, Cook, Hendel, Lamphere, Pandey Reynolds)	1962,1963, 1964	Social organization, ritual, mission activities	Summer; some restudy	Individual student projects
	Blanchard	1970–1971	Re-study of Nazarene Mission	One year restudy	Individual
	Blanchard and students	1972	PHS clinic, Ramah High school, Mormon Mission	Summer	Individual student projects
2. Navajo Mountain	Malcolm Carr Collier	1938–1939	Residence and local group structure	Initial study; one year	Individual
	Dorothea Leighton	1940	Culture and personality	Initial study; a few months	Individual with help of school teacher
	Mary Shepardson and Blodwen Hammond	1960–1962	Kinship and social structure	Restudy; three summers; access to Collier data.	New duo
3. Shonto	William Y. Adams	1955	Economic activities, social structure, and role of trader	Initial study	Individual
	Lorraine T. Ruffing	1971	Local economy and social organization, economic development	Restudy; access to Adams data.	New individual
	Scott Russell	1975–1976		Restudy	New individual

	Researcher	Year	Topic	Continuous	Team
4. Many Farms	Clifford Barnett, John Adair, Cara Richards and others from Cornell	1958–1961	Health and socioeconomic data	Continuous	Team
5. Fruitland	Cornell University Southwest Project (19 investigators, including Sasaki, Ross)	1948–1956	Culture change, economy and social organization	Continuous?	Initial study; team; loosely organized
6. Aneth	Harvey Moore (under direction of D. Aberle)	1953	Peyotism and socio-economic conditions	Initial study; summer	Individual
	Harvey Moore	1961	Culture change	Restudy of same sample	Same individual
	John D. Nielson	1966	Culture change	Restudy; without knowledge of Moore's data	New individual
7. Sheep Springs	Louise Lamphere and Terry Reynolds	1965–1966	Social organization and cooperation	Initial study; continuous for 15 months (Reynolds in summers)	Individual (duo in summers)
	Terry Reynolds	1971	Residence aggregation and dispersion	Continuous for several months (use of earlier data)	Individual (one of previous duo)
8. Red Lake/ White Mesa	Jerrold Levy	1960	Study of related camps (2 intermarried matrilineages)	Initial study	Individual
	Jerrold Levy and Stephen Kunitz	1967	Alcohol Study including some socioeconomic data	Restudy of same families	Same individual, plus new researcher and interpreter
	Lake Powell Research Project Fieldworker	1973	Socioeconomic survey plus fertility survey	Restudy of same families plus some new ones; (access to Levy's data)	Research assistant

TABLE 1.1 (*continued*)
Long-Term Navaho Research Projects[a]

Community	Investigators	Dates	Focus	Type of exposure	Organization
	E.B. Henderson	1974–1975	Genealogical study of King group adaptation	Restudy of same families (access to Levy's data)	Individual
9. South Tuba City	Jerrold Levy	1960	Socioeconomic Study	Study of 40 camps; detailed data on 13	Individual
	Jerrold Levy and Stephen Kunitz	1967	Alcohol study, including socio-economic data	Restudy of 13 camps (access to Levy data)	Same individual plus new researcher and interpreter
	Lake Powell Research Project Fieldworker	1973	Socioeconomic survey plus fertility survey	Restudy of 13 households plus new sample; access to Levy data	Research Assistant
10. Oljetoh Tsegi	Oswald Werner	1967–1972	Ethnomedical Dictionary	Summers	Individual with students
11. Rough Rock/Black Mountain	Gary Witherspoon	1966–1968	Social Organization & Kinship	Initial study Continuous for 2 yrs.	Individual

[a] Adapted mainly from Henderson and Levy 1975. Bibliography for each of these projects (except those of Werner, Witherspoon, Reynolds and more recent Lake Powell Research Project research) is available in the Henderson and Levy Bulletin.

understanding of Navajo culture and social relationships has come about not only from new methodological approaches and better collection of demographic, economic, and social structural data, but also from the sum total of a large number of short-term and long-term studies in different areas of the reservation.

In the meantime, the Navajo Nation has changed considerably. The Ramah community exemplifies some of these changes. Over the past 10 years the community has been more completely integrated into Navajo Tribal politics and programs. A new Chapter House has been constructed, an FM radio station started, and a community-controlled high school founded. The establishment of the school brought the Navajo into increased conflict with the local Mormon population; recently, a new multi-million dollar elementary and high school complex was built away from the Mormon town in the heart of the Navajo residential area. The new school and a recently finished "suburban" housing complex are the newest elements in the community's changed image.

These recent changes seem strangely unrelated and untouched by previous anthropological research. There has been some recent resentment against anthropologists; for example, the 1972 field school had difficulty placing students with families and gaining cooperation from some Navajos (Blanchard 1975:10). On the other hand, a student-published quarterly, *Tsá' ászi'* (The Yucca), illustrates how young Ramah Navajos are doing their own ethnography. The journal includes pictorial essays on cultural patterns (medicines, proverbs, traditional hair styles, and dress), and daily activities (how to shear sheep, butcher, weave a rug, prepare natural dyes, and make a silver bracelet). Drawings and poetry are also included. On the whole, the community has gained a more definite sense of itself, more control over its political affairs, and may come to question the validity of traditional anthropological research done by outsiders or its usefulness in terms of Ramah's own goals.

Throughout the Navajo reservation, the growth of County and Bureau of Indian Affairs (BIA) schools, Indian Health Service facilities, and new industries reflects the increasing impact of Anglo-dominated institutions. Government and tribal programs have increased, ranging from the poverty programs of the 1960s to legal services and community-controlled schools in the 1970s. The Tribal Government has faced complex disputes and negotiations regarding the Hopi–Navajo Joint Use Area, licensing of Anglo traders, industrial development, and natural resource utilization (including coal strip-mining and power plant construction). These developments indicate not only a new level of change for the Navajo Nation, but also the need for a new kind of anthropological research.

THE LAKE POWELL PROJECT, 1972-1977

The Lake Powell Research Project, "Collaborative Research on Assessment of Man's Activities in the Lake Powell Region," represents the involvement of anthropologists in interdisciplinary research with physical scientists and other social scientists. Through a large grant from the NSF RANN (Research Applied to National Needs) Program, geologists, biologists, geochemists, and other environmental scientists are studying the impact of the Glen Canyon Dam and Lake Powell on the surrounding environment as well as the development of coal burning power stations surrounding the lake. Anthropologists have been collaborating, not with psychologists, psychiatrists and sociologists, as in the Ramah Project, but with lawyers, political scientists, and medical personnel to study the impact of water and power development on human populations. The overall project is composed of many disciplinary and interdisciplinary subprojects, including three—anthropology, epidemiology, and law/political science—which deal with the Navajo in relation to Lake Powell. Each of these subprojects has centered on a narrow "problem" or set of topics; they employ a variety of techniques and team-research approaches. In addition, as data have been collected, new subprojects have evolved and additional staff have been added to conduct them.

The anthropology subproject, headed by Jerrold Levy (principal investigator) from the University of Arizona and Lynn Robbins (senior investigator) of the Huxley College of Environmental Studies, has focused on the economic impact of strip-mining and power plant construction on Navajo families in three communities: Page, its adjacent rural area (Lechee), and nearby Black Mesa. Several families in the adjacent Kaibeto–Red Lake area studied between 1960 and 1969 by Levy and Steven Kunitz are being used as a control group. These Lake Powell micro-studies are built on two kinds of previous research: (*a*) short-term, reservation-wide and community studies on such topics as social organization, homocide, suicide, and drinking patterns; (*b*) long-term contact with families in the Kaibeto–Red Lake area, supplemented by recent fieldwork on kin-group adaptations since the 1920s.

The micro-studies combined participant observation techniques with an extensive survey. A sample of 75–100 households in each community was queried regarding household and residence group structure, income and economic resources, industrial work experience, cooperative patterns, health, and political behavior. These data are being analyzed to document changes in the economy, social organization, and cooperative networks in the three communities. Other papers will deal with an analysis of Navajo voting patterns, an overall account of the impact of power production on Navajo development, and a study of Navajo participation in labor unions.

These anthropological micro-studies have involved a tighter program of team research than that conducted in Ramah, with the exception of Florence Kluckhohn's and Strodbeck's (1961) survey on value-orientations. This tight team organization was aimed at both the isolation of long-term trends and the testing of a series of specific hypotheses. The Lake Powell Research Project is well equipped to examine "process," especially long-range changes in the micro-economy and social organization of the Navajo and in the relationship of the Navajo Nation to the broader Anglo-American economy and political structure.

To complement these anthropological surveys, the law/political science subproject has taken a "case study" approach to understanding the history of Navajo water rights and how they have been affected by the legislation which permitted the construction of Lake Powell. In collaboration with the anthropology subproject it has investigated the history of the Navajo Generating Plant and the role of the Navajo Tribe in decisions to develop the coal resources on Black Mesa. This focus on the relationship between state government, Federal Agencies, private industrial interests, and the Navajo Tribe was missing in most previous ethnographic research.

The Lake Powell Research Project involves research with a policy orientation. Impact research of this kind views the Navajos as potential decision makers, not just as passive "reactors" to policies set by non-Indians. Clearly, the findings of the project have implications for Navajo decision making. For example, in deciding whether to sign contracts for a coal gasification plant on the Eastern reservation, it would be important for the Navajo Tribal Council to know what impact new jobs would have on Navajo families in the area. The Lake Powell data could help assess whether the Tribe should bargain for an increased number of more permanent jobs, or more importantly, if the income resulting from this kind of development will substantially improve the standard of living for the Navajo Nation.

In conducting policy-relevant research, especially when funded by sources outside the native community, there will certainly be non-native groups who might want to utilize the findings. For example, anthropologists who help to formulate environmental impact statements, especially those commissioned by private industry, may find that their reports are being used to "head off" adverse reactions to a power project which have formed at a local level or to convince Tribal leaders to sign necessary leases. Research which has the interests of supra-local institutions at heart may conflict with the sentiments of segments of a native population and, in turn, research which meets the needs of a native population or minority group may not be amenable to the goals of various state, federal, and private industrial groups.

CONCLUSIONS

Research on the Navajo has gone through three phases in the last 40 years. Long-term research has been important in all of them. In the first phase, represented by the Ramah Project, Kluckhohn and his students attempted to add to Navajo ethnography through research on specific topics which entailed careful attention to details and variation. The Ramah Project's aims—to follow a population over time—were extremely general by today's standards. Kluckhohn's theoretical interest in culture and in covert and overt patterning led him to generalized abstractions about Navajo culture phrased in anthropological categories, not those of the Navajo. His focus on culture rather than on social organization meant that data on economic, social, and political problems did not become integral to the analysis. The Ramah population was seen as a laboratory for understanding Navajo culture in general; the focus was on the community itself rather than on its place in the larger soeicty.

In the second phase, beginning with the Values Project in Ramah and continuing through some of the 1960s' community research, culture was still an important analytic concept, but more attention was paid to a theoretical framework which integrated various aspects of culture, personality, and social structure. The 1960–1962 re-study of Navajo Mountain, for example, provided excellent data on economic and social organization within a somewhat naive functionalist framework (Shepardson and Hammond 1970). Other researchers made progress in understanding Navajo social structure and culture in terms of Navajo categories (Witherspoon 1975; Lamphere 1977), but few were able to link changes in Navajo life to an analysis of American economic and political forces, except through a rather simplistic acculturation model (usually focused on the changing community rather than the forces for change).

Finally, the most recent phase of Navajo research, emphasizing regional and policy-oriented research and exemplified by the Lake Powell Research Project, has built on the previous long-term research projects (particularly on the Western reservation) to combine careful collection of local level socioeconomic data with analyses of the Navajo Nation's relationship to state, federal, and private industrial interests concerned with resource development. These current investigators have not been concerned with describing Navajo culture per se. Rather than treating local communities as isolates, they have explicitly studied the links between the Navajo and the ''outside'' world. The research has focused on policy-oriented problems; the results of particular studies may help Navajos in various tribal and government agencies as well as Navajos affected by local issues to make informed decisions about future development of their region.

The differences among these Navajo studies also reflect changes in anthropological theory over the past 40 years. From a focus on culture and personality to a more sophisticated model of society (Parsonian functionalism or British structural-functionalism), we have moved to a concern with hypothesis testing and the search for relationships among variables. At the same time, the Navajo themselves have changed from a relatively isolated population to one dominated by health, educational, and economic institutions derived from the larger society.

These institutions were present in the late 1930s and 1940s. Most anthropologists felt that change was desirable and would come with little disruption if the right government programs were implemented. This faith in the possibility of benevolent change overlooked the implications of this change for the future structure and economic base of the Navajo Nation. The Navajo Tribal Government, on the other hand, has become more powerful, commanding a large budget and making important economic decisions. Moreover, the Navajo have made some effort to control their own institutions (e.g. building their own community college and gaining contracts from the BIA to run several community-controlled schools). Anthropological research has had little impact on this emergence of the Navajo from a place of relative isolation to one of increased involvement in the U.S. political and economic structure.

If one takes the view, as I do, that research should in some way be related to the needs and interests of those being studied, then the cultural, values, and personality data collected during the years of research at Eamah are of little relevance to present-day Navajo. Furthermore, the framework and categories used in collecting the data make it less easily convertible into information which might meet present needs. The socioeconomic data collected in the 1960s are more relevant, but only if they can be related to long-term trends. The Lake Powell Research Project of the 1970s seems most likely to be immediately beneficial to the Navajo, but only part of its effort is anthropological.

In evaluating Navajo long-term research, it is easy to be pessimistic about the results of the research conducted so far and about the prospects for future long-term research among the Navajo. I would argue that it is *not* the organization of the research (i.e., whether conducted by an individual, pair, or team and whether loosely or tightly organized) that is crucial in producing long-term research that will stand the test of time. I have been more impressed with the role of theory in focusing research and in determining the kinds of data to be collected. However, anthropology has been characterized by major shifts in theoretical interest from one decade to the next, so that despite increasingly sophisticated theory and concomitant methodology, data collected in one decade may be of limited use to the next generation of anthropologists. As the Navajo case shows, we need to avoid this and consider what kinds of data will be most useful 10 to 20 years after a project has been started.

Navajo long-term research has not always realized the potential advantages of longitudinal study. Anthropologists are now beginning to have a complex and rich understanding of Navajo culture, but that seems to be as much a product of short-term research using new methodologies as of long-term research per se. In general, Navajo research has been largely unsuccessful in terms of understanding ''process'' and testing hypotheses over the long run, though some of the recent Lake Powell Research Project studies have focused on these issues.

Although the Navajo research does not meet ''ideal'' standards for long-term studies, two aspects of the Lake Powell Project indicate significant advances. First, unlike earlier studies which neglected the impact of non-Navajo institutions on local populations, the Lake Powell Project has done much to analyze local and supra-local structural relationships. This topic could certainly profit from additional long-term study. Second, I am encouraged by the increasing willingness to conduct policy-oriented research which might be relevant to the population studied. There may be an inevitable conflict between research that contributes to anthropological theory and that which contributes to policy recommendations of use to study populations. This is a difficult, but important question and one for which there will be no easy answer, but one which will effect the possibility and nature of long-term research in future years.

BIBLIOGRAPHY

Aberle, David F.
 1973 Clyde Kluckhohn's contributions to Navaho studies. In *Culture and life*, edited by Taylor, Walter W., Fischer, John L., and Vogt, Evon Z. Carbondale and Edwardsville: Southern Illinois Univ. Press. Pp. 83–93.
Adair, John
 1973 Clyde Kluckhohn and Indian administration. In *Culture and life,* edited by Taylor, Walter W., Fischer, John L., and Vogt, Evon Z. Carbondale and Edwardsville: Southern Illinois Univ. Press. Pp. 71–82.
Blanchard, Kendall
 1971 Religious change and economic behavior among the Ramah Navajo. Ph.D. disser-

tation, Department of Anthropology, Southern Methodist University, Dallas, Texas.

1977 The expanded responsibilities of long-term informant relationships. *Human Organization 36*(1):66–69.

Edmonson, Munro S.
1973 The anthropology of values. In *Culture and life,* edited by Taylor, Walter W., Fischer, John L., and Vogt, Evon Z. Carbondale and Edwardsville: Southern Illinois Univ. Press. Pp. 157–197.

Henderson, E. B., and Jerrold E. Levy
1975 Survey of Navajo community studies, 1936–1974. *Lake Powell Research Project Bulletin 6.* Los Angeles: Univ. of California.

Kluckhohn, Clyde
1927 *To the foot of the rainbow.* New York: Century.
1933 *Beyond the rainbow.* Boston: Christopher.
1941 Patterning as exemplified in Navaho culture. In *Language, culture, and personality,* edited by Leslie Spier. Menasha, Wisconsin: Sapir Memorial Publication Fund. Pp. 109–130.
1944 *Navaho witchcraft.* Boston: Beacon Press. Reprint.
1949 Introduction: The Ramah project. In *Gregorio, the hand-trembler,* by Leighton, Alexander H. and Dorothea Leighton. *Papers of the Peabody Museum of Archaeology and Ethnology 40* (No. 1): v–x.
1951a Foreword: A comparative study of values in five cultures. In *Navaho veterans,* edited by Vogt, Evon Z. *Papers of the Peabody Museum of Archaeology and Ethnology 41* (No. 1): vii–xii.
1951b Values and value-orientations in the theory of action. In *Towards a general theory of action,* edited by Parsons, Talcott and Shils, Edward. Cambridge, Massachusetts: Harvard Univ. Pres. Pp. 388–433.
1962 Studying the acquisition of culture. In *Culture and behavior: Collected essays of Clyde Kluckhohn,* edited by Kluckhohn, Richard. New York: Free Press of Glencoe. Pp. 244–254.
1966 The Ramah Navaho. *Bureau of American Ethnology, Bulletin 196, Anthropological Papers, No. 79.*

Kluckhohn, Clyde, and W. H. Kelly
1945 The concept of culture. In *The science of man in the world crisis,* edited by Linton, Ralph. New York: Columbia Univ. Press. Pp. 78–105.

Kluckhohn, Clyde, and Dorothea Leighton
1946 *The Navaho.* Cambridge, Massachusetts: Harvard Univ. Press.

Kluckhohn, Florence, and Fred L. Strodbeck
1961 *Variations in value orientations: A theory tested in five cultures.* Evanston, Illinois: Row, Peterson.

Lamphere, Louise
1964 Loose-structuring as exhibited in a case study of Navajo religious learning. *El Palacio 71*(1):37–44.
1977 *To Run after them: The social and cultural bases of cooperation in a Navajo community.* Tucson: Univ. of Arizona Press.

Lamphere, Louise, and Evon Z. Vogt
1973 Clyde Kluckhohn as ethnographer and student of Navajo ceremonialism. In *Culture and life,* edited by Taylor, Walter W., Fischer, John L., and Vogt, Evon Z. Carbondale and Edwardsville: Southern Illinois Univ. Press. Pp. 94–135.

Leighton, Dorothea, and Clyde Kluckhohn
1947 *Children of the people.* Cambridge, Massachusetts: Harvard Univ. Press.

Rapoport, Robert N.
  1954 Changing Navaho religious values: A study of Christian missions to the Rimrock Navajos. *Papers of the Peabody Museum of American Archaeology and Ethnology 41* (No. 2).
Reynolds, Terry, Louise Lamphere, and Cecil Cook
  1967 Time, resources, and authority in a Navajo community. *American Anthropologist* 69(2):188–199.
Shepardson, Mary, and Blodwen Hammond
  1970 *The Navajo mountain community: Social organization and kinship.* Berkeley and Los Angeles: Univ. of California Press.
Vogt, Evon Z.
  1951 Navaho veterans: A study of changing values. *Papers of the Peabody Museum of American Archaeology and Ethnology 41* (No. 1).
Vogt, Evon Z., and Ethel M. Albert (Eds.)
  1966 *People of Rimrock: A study of values in five cultures.* Cambridge, Massachusetts: Harvard Univ. Press.
Witherspoon, Gary
  1975 *Navajo kinship and marriage.* Chicago: Univ. of Chicago Press.

2

Fieldwork in the Mayan Region of Mexico

Alfonso Villa Rojas

INTRODUCTION

Writing at this time, I look back over nearly 50 years of professional research among Mayan groups in southern Mexico. In this chapter I present—by necessity in abbreviated form—some of my experiences during this period, emphasizing those that have implications for longitudinal, or long-term studies. As in all anthropological careers, a variety of chance influences and accidents impinged on formal planning to create the threads from which my experiences have been woven. So that the role of all these factors will be understood by the reader, it is necessary to begin with my earliest experiences. Among them were the task of breaking trail in the ethnographic investigation of difficult regions such as Quintana Roo and almost unknown areas in the highlands of Chiapas. The description of my first visits to these regions is given to illustrate the kinds of conditions that prevailed at that time, as well as to indicate the difficulties attendant on penetration of these regions.

The Indian groups that I first visited nearly 50 years ago were then characterized by hostility to outsiders and by a remarkable attachment to ancient traditions. Today they are becoming integrated into modern life

45

Long-Term Field Research
in Social Anthropology

and are strongly inclined toward innovation and city life. Some of their members have gone to college and one has even written a book on the culture of his own tribe. Among other factors, the spread of roads and transistor radios have given great impetus to this process of change. As will be seen, my long stays among these peoples and my great interest in their development has contributed significantly to my personal and professional development.

THE FIRST STEPS

The story began in 1927 when, for purely accidental reasons, I was obliged to abandon my studies at the university to become a school teacher in the village of Chan Kom, near Chichén Itzá, in Yucatán, where a distinguished group of North American archaeologists were discovering remarkable remains of the ancient Mayan civilization. Because of the location of Chan Kom, I was able to make friends with the members of this group, especially with its leader, Dr. Sylvanus G. Morley, who, with his agreeable, unaffected, and patient manner, created in me a growing interest in everything having to do with the practices and customs characterizing the people who left such remains. His generosity in permitting me to take books from his library to read at leisure in my retreat in Chan Kom permitted me to become familiar, little by little, with the most important authors on Mayan civilization and to acquire a fairly broad knowledge of the archaeology and ethnohistory of the entire Mayan region. Fortunately, by this time I could read both English and French without great difficulty. Pleased by the interest I showed, Morley later gave me the privilege of making an archaeological exploration of the famous *Sacbé,* or sacred route that crossed a good part of the Yucatán Peninsula (Villa Rojas 1934). With respect to my first contacts with Morley in Chichén Itzá, Redfield has left the following description:

> There Sylvanus G. Morley opened his generous nature to the young man, sharing with him his enthusiasm for the ancient Maya, and showing his interest in their descendants among whom Villa had come to live. When Villa rode back to Chan Kom, he brought with him books Morley had lent him about the ancient civilization, and these he read in the evening, lying in his hammock.
>
> It was these last events that brought about the choice of Chan Kom as one of four communities in which to study the ways of life in Yucatán: the task given me by Carnegie Institution of Washington. The village was chosen to represent village life in southeastern Yucatan: a life dependent upon markets and authorities of the city and yet shaped by a local, long-established, unwritten tradition. The relative progressiveness of Chan Kom was not a reason for its selection. The associations established with

the Americans at Chichén and the presence of a teacher who was soon to become an ethnological collaborator determined the choice [Redfield 1950:15–16].

My first meeting with Redfield occurred in Chichén Itzá, where he arrived in 1930, when I was barely 33 years old. At that time he was surveying Yucatán looking for appropriate sites at which to carry out research on his model of the folk–urban continuum. It was Morley who introduced me to Redfield and who suggested that I collaborate with him. Satisfactory arrangements were made, and I found myself associated with one of the most extraordinary men whom North American Anthropology has produced, both with respect to creative talent and character. His congenial and stimulating nature made it easy to get to know him, and he almost immediately gained my respect and cordial affection. As Redfield himself noted in the introduction to *Chan Kom: A Maya Village*, this first contact was really very brief, a matter of days, during which he instructed me on what I was to investigate.

As my first task, he asked me to keep a diary and to prepare reports on specific topics that he chose. From that time on, our correspondence was regular and extensive and of great benefit to me, since, in exchange for my reports, he sent long commentaries on methodological procedures. He suggested that, although my reports were extensive, they were deficient in significant details. For that reason I memorized a little verse of Kipling's which reads:

> *I keep six honest serving men*
> *(They taught me all I knew):*
> *Their names are WHAT and WHY and WHEN*
> *and HOW and WHERE and WHO.*

Even though this literary aid was very simple, it helped me a great deal, and my work improved.

The following year, our collaboration became closer because Redfield was able to stay in Chan Kom approximately 10 weeks, distributed in intermittent periods over a longer time span. During this period, I became aware of the meticulous way he recorded data and his insistence on the logical structure of the organization of these data.

Life in the field obviously agreed with Redfield; he seemed happy and carefree, and displayed an excellent sense of humor. His relations with his Mayan informants were somewhat paradoxical. On the one hand, he had a facility for making friends with people, on the other hand, he did not really establish close ties with his informants. At first I thought this was because his physical type was so different from theirs: he was tall, white-skinned, angular, and semibald. Later I came to realize it was due to his limited knowledge of Mayan, and to a way he had of asking complex questions that informants found difficult to answer. In any event, his three principal informants (D. Eus, D. Fano, and D. Nas), who spoke Spanish fairly well and were among the most important people of Chan Kom, communicated well with him and developed a genuine affection for him. Naturally, his interests included all of the community, and he endeavored to have contact with the largest possible number of informants, utilizing the aid of those who knew Spanish.

Despite his linguistic handicap, he possessed a special sense for capturing the point of view of the Indians and for evaluating their personality. He liked nothing better than to be present, simply as an observer, at all kinds of gatherings and social occasions in which the people of Chan Kom behaved spontaneously. Later, alone in our hut, he would comment about everything he had seen and comprehended at those gatherings.

His interviews with the few informants who knew Spanish were well planned, although they were carried out in a deceptively casual manner, as a simple chat which gradually led to the topic he wished to define, enlarge upon, or come to know better. His interview style was not a matter of simple questions and answers; rather, he allowed his informants great freedom of expression. Except for numerical data, typical phrases, or specific names, he took few notes in front of his informants. Later, alone, he recorded the most important points and, in the evening, wrote very detailed notes.

He was enormously inquisitive, anxious to pursue to the smallest detail those topics that interested him. From time to time he complained that our observational capacities had fairly important limitations. For example, he once noticed a bottle tied to the trunk of a papaya tree. When he learned that this was a custom, the object of which was to increase the number of papayas produced, he knew the bottle must have been there for some time and that we had not previously noticed it, despite having passed it on numerous occasions. This clear deficiency in our data gathering led to a good discussion about the necessity of cultivating the spirit of observation—always looking for elements significant to the theme being investigated. He was able to go without sleep all night, so as to observe some special ceremony being carried out by a shaman; later he would interview individually all of the principal participants in the ceremony. In this way, he obtained a comprehensive and integrated understanding of everything he had seen.

Customarily he would dedicate the entire day to his work; he did not read novels while in the field, nor did he feel upset, nervous, or apathetic, as often happened to Malinowski, according to his "Diary." In the evenings, when he was in a mood for talking, he gave me the opportunity fully to enjoy his wisdom. He had two favorite topics: scientific method and literary criticism. It was easy to see that he was very familiar with the literature of his day; among the authors I remember from his chats are Henri Barbusse, Thomas Mann, Erich Maria Remarque, Thornton Wilder, and Sinclair Lewis, all of whom were in vogue at that time.

In contrast to his severe and sometimes cold bearing, he had a gentle and sensitive spirit and a strong feeling for his family. I realized this in that same year of 1931 on a trip we made to the distant and almost unpopulated territory of Quintana Roo, searching for the most hostile and backward Indians of the entire Yucatán Peninsula. Deep in the jungle we stopped at a mule drivers' camp. Upon finding out that some of them were going to Peto, where there was a post office, Redfield immediately forgot his fatigue and wrote a long letter to his wife. This act impressed me since it revealed his affectionate sensitivity. Days later, on the way back, at a bend in the trail we found an Indian carrying a fawn. Redfield immediately bought it as a surprise gift for his daughter Lisa, then a little girl, who was living with her mother in Mérida. Suffering a thousand discomforts, he took it with him to the train station in Peto, where he could obtain a bottle and milk to feed it properly. Throughout the ordeal, he took care of the fawn as if it were a human child. Such were my first contacts and impressions of this exceptional teacher who, by his example and his word, was able to awaken in me a genuine interest in social research.

EXPERIENCES AMONG THE MODOC INDIANS

As might be expected, by that time I was competent in the analysis of concrete situations in which social relations could be traced clearly and precisely by using participant observation and all the other techniques of control appropriate to that type of study. For that reason, the fieldwork experience that I undertook in 1934 as part of my anthropological training at the University of Chicago (which I had begun in 1933) was not very stimulating to me. The experience took place among the Modoc Indians located in the small settlement of Sprague River, Oregon. Six students from different universities participated in it, under the direction of Dr. Leslie Spier. Of my fellow students, I only remember Philleo Nash and a woman with the last name of Alpenfels. We camped on the outskirts of the town and had contact with the natives only at certain times when we interviewed two or three professional informants who charged $1 per hour of "work." My informant was named Peter and he lived in a pretty bungalow in which he had a special room for receiving anthropologists.

He possessed, in addition, an automobile used by his daughters to go to the nearby city of Klamath Falls to shop and have their hair fixed. After 2 weeks trying to record Peter's memories of the practices and customs of his parents and grandparents and how they resembled and differed from those of their neighbors, the Klamath Indians, I became very frustrated. I realized that while I was cooped up in that room recording things of the past, with all of their uncertainties and oblivious to time, remarkable things were happening outside which could have shed much light on the nature of the accelerated change which these people were experiencing with the arrival of the products and effects of the dehumanizing mechanization of modern life.

To save my sanity, I abandoned the group and traveled on my own through the Indian zones of southwestern United States. Nevertheless, for a long time I felt remorse for having left such a nice and congenial group in such abrupt fashion. The recording of historic antecedents is, of course, important when it leads to a better understanding of the present, but it should be carried out with greater rigor than that which I observed on that occasion among the Modoc. The form in which I myself have used such antecedents has been presented in some of my writings (e.g., Villa Rojas 1945, 1947, 1963, 1964).

ETHNOGRAPHIC EXPLORATIONS AMONG
THE MAYA OF QUINTANA ROO

In writing about this phase of my ethnographic work among the Maya of the Yucatán Peninsula, I shall have to be extremely brief. I mention it only because of its intimate connection with the studies I conducted in Chan Kom with Redfield. At that time, the Maya of Quintana Roo represented the least acculturated point on Redfield's folk–urban continuum: The region occupies the eastern zone of the peninsula, which was practically unpopulated in the central area.

The Indian groups, isolated there under the tall forests of *chicozapotes* (sapodilla trees), were descendants of the great armies which, in the previous century, supported the bloody "caste war" against the whites, which left a total of 300,000 dead. After being defeated and with the passing of the years, the Indians withdrew to that central region which, since then, had been considered "forbidden ground" for non-Indians.

It was my job to put an end to that isolation by serving as intermediary between the government and the last rebel groups. My uninterrupted stay of almost a year among them represents the most difficult and fascinating experience of my entire career and illustrates the great caution and tact that an ethnographer must exercise in order to return safely from incursions among hostile and distrustful people. The harvest of information I was able to obtain has been presented in my book, *The Maya of East-Central Quintana Roo* (Villa Rojas 1945). I will try to summarize the essential elements of that experience.

As mentioned earlier, in 1931 I made a preliminary trip into Quintana Roo with Redfield, visiting only two peripheral points. The following year, I made a 4-week trip that allowed me to visit almost all the villages established there, which I found to be organized in tribal groups controlled by a military theocratic government. Each group had, as a center, a sanctuary where a "speaking cross," functioning as an oracle, was worshipped; that is, the organization was similar to that of the Maya in the pre-Hispanic era. On this occasion, I had the good fortune to discover the group that was most closely tied to its old customs and was also the most reluctant to start dealings with the outside world. Having lost our way, we came to a village of a little more than 100 inhabitants whose appearance exactly duplicated that described by the first chroniclers. Its settlers, nude from the waist up, showed the most astounding surprise upon seeing two strange men arrive on horseback. They immediately forced us to dismount, with insults and threats of aggression if we could not satisfactorily explain the motive of our trip. They simply would not believe that we had lost our way. When, after an hour, the main leaders arrived, I asked to speak with them alone in one of their small chapels. Since I spoke their language fairly well and knew something of their idiosyncrasies, the dialogue developed in terms of mutual understanding. I explained that my mission was to buy chicle, which seemed reasonable to them. In this way we overcame the first stumbling block and were able to leave safely 2 hours later. The place, I learned, was called Tusik and, from that moment, I decided it was the appropriate place for an intensive, long-term study. The problem was to win the confidence of the Indians so that they would let me live among them.

To achieve this goal, when months later I returned to the same town I came as a traveling salesman, bringing with me three mules loaded with products in greatest demand, such as salt, soap, *manta* (cotton cloth), machetes, axes, and glass beads and jewelry for women. Since I sold everything at incredibly low prices, the people's attitude toward me gradually changed from hostility to tolerance, and they allowed me to stay among them about 5 weeks. I used this time to visit other villages and even their "sacred center." During this time they did not forget about chicle, their principal export resource. So, with the help of Morley I arranged with North American firms established in Mérida to purchase chicle from them. The Indians were also helped by having offered to them at cost the large copper cauldrons used in boiling down chicle.

With this evidence of friendship, the Indians no longer doubted my good intentions and—at long last—they gave permission for me to move in with them. They made available to me a hut in the village of Tusik and opened the doors of their sanctuary and all the other places to me. My stay in the area, accompanied by my wife, lasted from September 1935 to July 1936.

As might be expected, we very soon became participant observers of the life of the community, participating in all their activities, both profane and sacred and also in their worries and joys. As with the Indians, the state of the *milpa* (cornfield) so intimately tied to the vagaries of the weather, formed an important part of my worries, as did rumors of the passage of federal soldiers through the area and the ups and downs of the price of chicle. I had to add a porch to our hut so that our neighbors would have a proper place for their chats and gossip. I gained the confidence of the scribe of the tribe (the only one who knew how to read and write in the Mayan language), who controlled the "sacred papers" of their ancestors, to the point of permitting me access to his archives; these papers included old Catholic almanacs, prayers, and diverse reports on topics of history and folklore. The scribe also kept, as something special, a heretofore unknown version of the books of Chilam Balam, post-Hispanic codices that contain a great deal of what previously was inscribed in hieroglyphics. This particular version is now known among specialists as the "Chilam Balam of Tusik." Regrettably, the original was stolen years after my departure by newspapermen who visited the region.

In view of my total immersion in the world of these Indians, it is easy to understand that the daily recording of my notes was always behind schedule: The experiences of the day greatly exceeded what could be written at night. Only when the town became empty because of the demands of work in the *milpas* or the pastime of hunting was I able to relax a bit and catch up on my notes. At such times, I could also reflect on the content of the material, plan further inquiries, or formulate hypotheses. Since the porch to my hut had become a sort of communication center to which people desirous of information came from all over the region, it was easy for me to gather data on any topic in a spontaneous and uninhibited way.

There were, of course, distrustful individuals who continued to have doubts about the real purpose of my stay with them, even though I periodically supplied them with merchandise at cost and took care of them without charge when they suffered illness or accident. The fear of losing their autonomy and of being turned over to the government was very deep-rooted among these Indians, even including my most devoted informants. Almost continually there were ominous rumors about possible surprise attacks by federal soldiers. Then, one day, the moment arrived when I had to tell the Indians that the Mexican government was about to open a road across their territory, which could cause serious consequences if they did not take proper steps to have the lands that belonged to them legally recognized in the form of *ejidos*. The impact of this startling news on the leaders of the tribe who had gathered in my hut was one of incredulity, and at first they showed disbelief. How was it possible that I, who had always been on their side, could now propose to them that they come to terms with their natural enemy, the Mexican government? Could it be that I was a spy of that government who had penetrated their ranks to "sell them" later? Some said, in an angry tone, that they were the ones who could grant lands to that government and not the reverse; others blamed me for my supposed false loyalty; and still others asked for more information. The whole time I remained calm, willing to give them all the explanations they requested. I emphasized that I had always been unarmed, even though they all boasted of their good shotguns and machetes. Finally I proposed that they discuss the matter among themselves and that my wife and I would wait outside for their decision. After an hour they called to tell me that they would accept my proposal with three conditions:

1. They had to be guaranteed exclusive use of the tribal lands.
2. Their customs had to be respected and they could not be forced to change their ways.
3. A group of Indians led by "Lieutenant" Evaristo Sulub who, 2 years before, had done away with a detachment of soldiers who had tried to capture them, had to be allowed to return to their home town.

All this seemed reasonable to me, and I promised to take the necessary steps to achieve it.

To finish this story, after several months of dealings with General Rafael Melgar, governor of that federal territory (now the state of Quintana Roo), he agreed to all requests and turned over to the Indians the maps and titles of the lands which, by tradition, they considered their property. The ceremony took place in the sacred capital itself in May 1937, long after I had completed my studies. In addition to General Melgar and his retinue, the famous Mayan scholar Alfredo Barrera Vázquez, whom I invited, and I were present. At the moment of presentation of the legal documents, a small incident occurred which might have had grave consequences: Upon checking the maps we found that the "holy town" or capital of the tribe did not appear on them. This alarmed the Indians greatly, since they thought this oversight had been intentional. Fortunately, the surveyors who had made the maps were present and the governor instructed them immediately to extend the boundaries to include the disputed area, so that everyone was happy. The event ended with a banquet served by the Indians, immediately after which the general and his retinue left, since they did not feel entirely safe. Thus the last redoubt of rebellion resulting from that uprising known as the "caste war," which began in 1847, came to an end. (For more information on this war, see Villa Rojas 1945:34–35.)

I continued to visit the region sporadically, moved by the desire to see the Indians' progress in the process of integration into national life. At present, although the "holy town" and its "guards" continue to exist, the people are more inclined toward progress than toward tradition. In fact, some members of the new generation already have obtained academic degrees at the National University of Mexico in Mexico City. One, a grandson of an old informant, is now the representative of his district in the Quintana Roo House of Representatives. It has been a dramatic change.

ETHNOGRAPHIC RESEARCH AMONG
THE TZELTAL INDIANS OF CHIAPAS

In accordance with Redfield's plan of long-term studies in the Mayan region, I was commissioned to undertake investigations among the Tzeltal group located in the central part of the State of Chiapas, Mexico. This group numbered 45,737 members, of whom 32,359 spoke no Spanish; this figure gives some idea of the cultural conservatism and geographical isolation of these people. They lived scattered in small *municipios* ("municipalities") of 3000 to 5000 inhabitants, each of which—although the term usually is not used in Mexico—could be considered a sort of "tribe," for each group had its own dialect, form of local government, dress, and other unique cultural characteristics. A few Ladino (i.e., Mestizo) families, largely dedicated to commerce, resided in the *cabeceras,* the administrative centers of these *municipios,* but most of the Indians lived in smaller settlements some distance away, in forested areas, coming to the *cabecera* principally for major religious activities and to make purchases. Hostility between the two groups had led to armed conflicts in 1914, 1917, 1930, and 1935.

Since this region was practically unknown ethnographically, I decided first to make an exploratory trip to gain a general idea of its principal cultural configurations, thus to be able to select the most traditional group for intensive study. The topography of the region is extremely broken; with altitudes fluctuating between 2200 and 10,000 feet above sea level, the climate varies from hot and humid in the lowlands to very cold and foggy in the highlands. Accompanied only by an interpreter, I made this trip on horseback in February and March of 1938. In all I visited 15 *municipios,* 7 of which were in the cold, foggy zone, inhabited by Indians of great reserve, seemingly always wrapped in wool ponchos. The other 8 in the hot zone, were inhabited by less withdrawn people who dressed in light cotton clothing. In only three places in the highlands—Cancuc, Oxchuc, and Tenejapa—did I find Ladinos remaining, because of fear of a new uprising among the Indians. In Cancuc, the only Ladinos I encountered were hog buyers who still remembered the bloody events of 1935, when armed Indians drove out the few members of this ethnic group that owned stores. The stores themselves were burned to erase all traces of their former owners.

By contrast, in the lowlands, from Ocosingo northward, travel conditions were more favorable; the terrain was less rough, and the Indians dealt with Ladinos more easily. The latter condition may stem from the fact that beginning in the middle of the nineteenth century, coffee plantations had been established in this region, and through these the Indians had had more contact with people and things from the outside world.

The trip through the highlands was extraordinarily fascinating for me, both because of the beauty of the countryside which unfolded in a topography of summits, gorges, and pine forests, and because of the strange customs I was discovering daily: clans and lineages as in the time of the ancient Maya; the persistence of the *calpul* social organization of Nahua origin; of transforming witch *naguals,* and many other cultural aspects clearly pre-Hispanic in origin. In Oxchuc, where I arrived at the time of carnival, I witnessed the "Dance of the Flags" which I was never again to see. There, despite their suspicions, the Indians allowed me to examine the sacred book they call *Cajualtik* (i.e., "Our Lord"), which they kept in a small palm frond chapel in the middle of the forest, far from any Ladinos (Redfield and Villa Rojas 1939:107–119). I must emphasize that at no time did I resent the inconveniences and difficulties of the trip, since everything was new and exciting for me.

Intensive Studies among the Tzeltals

As a result of that exploratory trip, I selected the highlands for study and, in particular, the municipality of Oxchuc which, as just pointed out, was one of the most conservative of all groups. I conducted this investigation during two periods totaling 19 months of residence among the Indians: May 1942 to April 1943, and December 1943 to June 1944. At that time the municipality had a population of 3034: 1596 men and 1438 women. It was necessary to prepare carefully for entry into any of the hamlets of the municipality. As a first step I dedicated 3 weeks to gathering all possible data from the archives and government offices in Ciudad de Las Casas, the commercial and administrative center of the highland area. At that time its population was approximately 20,000, and it had hotel services, banks, telegraph and mail services, health facilities, and the like. There I was able to gather abundant information about the communities of Oxchuc, Tenejapa, and Cancuc which formed the most conservative centers in the entire area. Talks with plantation owners, rural school teachers, officials, and traveling salesmen who, in one way or another had had dealings with those Indians, led me to choose a settlement called Dzajalchen ("Red Cave") as my place of residence; this place was strategically located a short distance from the spot where the boundaries of these three groups meet. In addition, the place had a minuscule school attended by children from eight settlements, which indicated that the Indians had lost something of their isolation, reserve, and suspicion of outsiders.

I spent my first days in Dzajalchen in the shack which served as the school, taking advantage of the friendship I had been able to establish in Ciudad de Las Casas with the teacher. Later, the teacher and his students (none over 14 years of age) helped me to build a small wattle-and-daub palm-thatched hut in which to live. Once I had accomplished this, I began to make brief excursions in the environs over the rough and uneven paths of that remote corner of the Sierra; at times the teacher himself accompanied me, explaining the character and peculiarities of the most important individuals of that small world. With regard to the Indians, their manner was reticent and distrustful, one of displeasure when we dared to look about inside their huts. This attitude was more noticeable when I went out alone; then, the huts closed up and the Indians (especially the women) hid themselves or ran into the underbrush. Through the school teacher I found out that it was believed I didn't have a wife, an unnatural and suspicious thing in an adult. To remedy this situation my wife, who was living in Mexico City, came to live with me. Her presence helped greatly and distrust began to decrease to the point that we were able to exchange visits with some of the families. I must add, nevertheless, that there were a few exceptional cases of individuals friendly towards me from the first days of my arrival. There were two in particular who were interested in having news from the outside world and also in learning to read and write. Both became excellent informants and, with the passage of time, became "cultural promoters" (teachers) of the National Indian Institute.

As to why I stayed in Dzajalchen, the Indians were satisfied with the explanation that I wanted to live with them to learn their customs and later teach them to my people. The proof of this for them was in the interest that my wife and I placed on everything they did and said. Since we were also eager to do something to benefit the community, I decided to set up a simple first aid center with a few basic medicines, such as vermifuges, aspirin, argyrol for the eyes, different analgesics, antiseptics for sores and wounds, and antidiarrheal medicines. The results were extremely gratifying and soon my hut was visited by Indians from many places, including Tenejapa and Cancuc. This simple medical treatment seemed so effective that some came to request cures for alcoholism. Moreover, they perceived its effectiveness to extend to their own magical system; they assured me that it was also good to combat *naguals* and witches' curses. The most common explanation given on this point was that the many medicines with a disagreeable odor or taste caused the *naguals* and other evil spirits to leave the body of the victim. The *naguals* do not like the Ladino odor, some of the patients would say.

Months later, when the people had become accustomed to my presence and had recognized my power over *naguals,* it was possible for me to build a bigger, more solid and comfortable house, in the style of the Ladinos of the area; that is, with a shingle roof, walls, and a wood floor. Nearby I built a spacious open porch of palms, with a railing on the sides and low benches, to be used as a social center. It promptly became popular with the Indians. There were always people there talking, listening to our record player, arranging personal matters with the "Principals" (elders of the community) or simply waiting to be treated for some illness. In this way our house and our activities became just another institution within the cultural system of the group. This technique of working gave me the opportunity to be in constant communication with the neighborhood and to have timely knowledge of activities, gossip, and daily incidents. Thus I could know ahead of time where a wedding was to take place, or a funeral, a party or whatever other event which should be recorded. At times I would go to the river to bathe, or wander through the hamlets with no other purpose than passing the time of day or observing my friends in their habitual tasks. My observations and data were recorded at length in diary form and in special notebooks dealing with special topics. I could use my field notebook freely in front of the Indians without causing any objections. In general, with the exception of a few exceedingly shy or distrustful individuals, people were always willing to give the information I requested. There were, of course, some topics which caused reticence, about which the Indians showed a certain degree of anxiety while speaking. Among these were genealogies, wealth, religion, witchcraft, and sex. Ultimately I came to understand that this anxiety was due to the fear of *naguals* who, it was thought, were everywhere trying to listen to people's sins.

Because of the strict separation of the sexes in daily life, my informants were mostly men; only three or four middle-aged and a few elderly women became friendly and communicative with us. Usually they talked with my wife or with our cook (who came from Tenejapa), to pour out their troubles or problems. Although I am fluent in Mayan as spoken in Yucatán, Tzeltal is a very different branch of this family. I only learned to use the phrases necessary to be able to participate in simple conversations. I could understand a good deal, but I couldn't speak to any great extent. Consequently I always used an interpreter in complicated matters and in all those instances where it was essential to capture every nuance of meaning. Therefore, some of the Indians who had worked on coffee plantations and hence could express themselves fairly well in Spanish were helpful to me.

My Relationships with the Tzeltals in Subsequent Years

Even though Redfield's initial plan to make a comparative study of different regions in the Mayan area had to be suspended when the Carnegie Institution terminated its Meso-American program, my relationships with the Tzeltals were renewed from time to time during later years: At times it was as a consultant on studies being carried out in Oxchuc from 1953 to 1968 (see Siverts 1969 and Harman 1974), and at other times as an applied anthropologist paid by the Mexican Government. Actually, I didn't renew direct contact with these Indians until I returned to the region in 1955 to do applied research.

During the following five years I remained in the region as Director of the local "coordinating center" of the National Indian Institute which was charged with promoting the socioeconomic development of the highland Tzeltal and Tzotzil communities. Although my office was in Ciudad de Las Casas I spent a good deal of time traveling through these communities, especially those where I had lived years before. I found the changes which had occurred during the intervening decade to be remarkable, especially the progress of schools and the new world view which was developing among the Indians: Their basic attitude toward life was less oriented toward tradition and more so to the resources of modern technology. Consequently the influence of the old people and of the *naguals* had decreased considerably. The two boys who had become attached to me in 1942 when I began my work there were now "cultural promoters" (rural teachers) and active proponents of social change (see Harman 1974:155), and Dzajalchen now had stores, a good school, medical services, and two basketball teams!

On the other hand the combination of serious land erosion and a rapid increase in population had created serious economic and social problems. As a government representative I was in the fortunate position of being able partially to alleviate the impact of these conditions by helping people obtain new lands in thinly populated areas of Chiapas.

In this applied phase of my work I was most impressed by the degree of anomie characterizing many of the Indians. Although they had by no means completely broken with their traditions and former way of life, I attributed this anomie to the process of accelerating change they were experiencing. These conditions continue: The old people are frustrated because they no longer have their former influence, while the young people, although attracted by modern technology, still do not understand the system of ideas associated with it. The situation seems very different from that reported by Margaret Mead in Manus.

Before leaving this descriptive section I want to ask, and attempt to answer, a few questions about the work I did. I continue to believe, of course, that participant observation, when it really means intimate coexistence with the local people, is essential to the best fieldwork. Only in this way can the elusive small details, the *imponderabilia,* of daily life, be known. Our close contact with local people has always led to excellent rapport, the only basis on which really reliable information can be obtained. In retrospect, there are certain themes I wish I had known enough to pursue more thoroughly: ethnohistory, for example. As a case in point, I gave little attention to the meaning of caves in the lives of the Tzeltal, simply because I was ignorant of the importance they had had in the cult of the ancestors, whose funeral urns were kept in them. Among the Maya of Yucatán, too, I underestimated the importance of lineages, and failed to gather data on kinship, *nagualism,* pagan ceremonies, and other topics that I might have investigated.

Perhaps I should also have placed greater emphasis on the socioeconomic and political forces within the larger society, which play important roles in the exploitation of the Indians. Although I came to understand the cultural system of Oxchuc municipality and its similarities to and differences from surrounding municipalities fairly well, my knowledge of the power structure of the Ladino city of Las Casas was very superficial. Yet it is this power structure which, to a large extent, explains why the Indians remain attached to their ancestral conditions, and still constitute a despised caste within the larger society.

Considering the simplicity of field research in an earlier period, my financial support for the Tzeltal work was adequate. In these times of Jeeps, tape recorders, motion picture cameras, and even computers, the cost of a similar study would be much greater. It was time, rather than money, that I lacked; I would have liked more time to gather data, to digest these data, to organize my materials, and to write up my findings.

RESULTS OF MY WORK

Of the several dozen articles and two or three books I have published on my research, I will dedicate a few lines to those which appear to have been most significant. *The Maya of East-Central Quintana Roo* is, of course, one of the most important, since it deals not only with ethnography, but also with archaeology and history (Villa Rojas 1945). Even though 30 years have passed since its publication, no similar study has been made in that region; on the other hand, parts of it have frequently been plagiarized. The same can be said about "Notes on the Ethnography of the Tzeltal Indians of Oxchuc," whose 800 microfilm pages have served as the basis of many publications of younger scholars (Villa Rojas 1946). The intimate "interior view" of an Indian life style revealed in that "diary" could only be the product of a long residence among them, as well as a genuine participation in the problems of the community.

My Chiapas papers deal with a variety of themes; collectively they are important in demonstrating the remarkable persistence of ancient Mayan social institutions and belief systems through four centuries of European conquest and domination. "Kinship and Nagualism in a Tzeltal Community," which was well received by Mayan scholars, resulted from a lecture I gave at Northwestern University, invited by Sol Tax (Villa Rojas 1947). At the time I was at the University of Chicago; thus I had time to reflect on the implications of and the interrelationships among the diverse aspects of the culture under study. The topic interested me because my data revealed a previously unknown, completely Indian means of social control which undoubtedly had survived through many centuries. On that occasion I also offered for the first time evidence of the existence of clans and lineages among the Tzeltal, as well as a tendency toward cross-cousin marriage. Years earlier Fred Eggan had noted how rare this type of marriage was in native North America and how few the references were to its existence in Central and South America (Eggan 1934). Hence, the solid documentation of this marriage system in contemporary southern Mexico contributed significantly to our understanding of New World kinship systems, and particularly that of the pre-Hispanic Maya.

Later, in an article published in Spanish (in English, "Nagualism as a Means of Social Control Among the Mayan Groups of Chiapas, Mexico"), I amplified my earlier study (Villa Rojas 1963). Using more recent information gathered by Calixta Guiteras, Evon Vogt, Marianna Slocum, and others I was able to confirm the observations presented in 1946. Coupled with historical sources, which were very useful to me, the contemporary ethnographic data enabled me to prove that the *nagualism* practices I had found in Oxchuc were the same as those of the ancient Maya. The persistence of purely Indian forms among the Tzeltal was again made clear in a subsequent paper also published in Spanish (in English, "Barrios and Calpules in Tzeltal and Tzotzil Communities in Contemporary Mexico"); the *calpul* form of social organization of today clearly has its roots in purely Indian institutions (Villa Rojas 1964).

The paper, whose title in English would be "Concepts of Time and Space among Contemporary Mayan Groups," was somewhat different in nature, although not entirely disassociated from social organization (Villa Rojas 1968). My purpose again was to show the persistence over a thousand years of a number of basic concepts which still regulate the lives of the Mayan Indians of Chiapas.

MUTUAL IMPACTS

Throughout these pages I have given incidental information on the consequences of my presence on the people whom I have studied. I think in all cases the consequences have been favorable. Chan Kom, for instance, became—in the opinion of its neighbors—"the best town of the region." In Quintana Roo I helped the Indians obtain lands as well as political peace, and in Oxchuc in addition to obtaining land for them I awakened in the people an interest in change. In the places I have worked the attitude of the people toward me has continued to be one of great cordiality and appreciation. On occasion I have written to literate members of the community asking for further information on some topic and they, in turn, from time to time, have written asking for some favor, which I have always tried to fulfill if at all possible. On the few occasions I have lent money it has always been returned. Unlike the situation occasionally described in other places—the Navajo come to mind—no informants have become dependent on me. In general, the people with whom I have worked have behaved with remarkable dignity. They have, however, shown little curiosity about my scientific work, and in none of the places I have worked have they read my books. In Chan Kom, however, Redfield's voluminous English work is kept as a "sacred book," shown only to distinguished visitors.

Prolonged contact with the same people over decades has also had an impact on me; it has served as a point of reference better to appreciate the changes that have taken place within myself. To return to a community, be it Chan Kom or Oxchuc, and find that the boys who were my informants are now old men surrounded by grandchildren, with problems and frustrations they could not have then imagined, provides a basis for reflection on the ephemerous and changing nature of human existence.

With the passage of time my relations with old friends tend to be slightly more formal, although without loss of cordiality and good will. In contrast, the social distance is more accentuated between the young people born after my long stays and me. With those who were my "pals" and best informants our relations are very similar to those we enjoyed in former times. As an example, on my most recent trip to Chan Kom in February, 1975, my conversations with 80-year-old "D. Eus" were much like those of 40 years before when I cited him frequently in my field diary. In general, his world-view had changed little: He spoke of the same grandiose projects as then to improve the town, and he exhibited the same attitude of leadership and even the same political preoccupations. With much younger friends, in the 45–60-year age bracket, memories of different incidents once again awoke the camaraderie which earlier existed among us. Return visits to Chan Kom of a few days or a few weeks are extremely enjoyable for me; currently I am entertaining the idea of returning for six months to carry out a systematic study of the basic changes that have occurred since Redfield was first there in 1930.

CONCLUSIONS

By way of conclusions I wish to discuss briefly some of the more general points that have emerged from my studies, particularly as they bear upon the strategy of long-term or longitudinal studies. In general I have found long-term research to be more profitable and meaningful than short-term research. Familiarity with the people being studied and time to reflect unhurriedly on the materials gathered, allow a better understanding of reality and, at the same time, lead to greater refinement of hypotheses as well as revealing gaps in data. Although it is probably useful to formulate, in general outline, plans for long-term research, any such plans should be sufficiently flexible to permit changes dictated by the discovery of new problems or new data. *The factor of serendipity, which, accidentally or unexpectedly, leads us to new problems or discoveries, is one of the best allies of any good researcher* or, at least, of all those who remain alert in their work.

Although I have not discussed group efforts in which I have participated, I have had over the years a good deal of experience in working with and advising younger colleagues. I have found that the best way to incorporate them into developing programs is to assign them special topics appropriate to their training, and then allow them a sizable degree of freedom and initiative in carrying out their work. It is important to know how to create *rapport* with beginners, to help them avoid inhibitions, to comment constructively on their research, and to stimulate them to express their ideas fully, in an atmosphere of mutual cordiality. The best example I can cite of this approach has been that of Evon Vogt and his students and young colleagues during the many years he has directed Harvard University's Field School in Chiapas. Superb investigators, whose training I have observed from the first stages, have come out of this training center.

In contrast, Malinowski was difficult to get along with because of his arrogant and sarcastic disposition. The short time I accompanied him in his fieldwork in Oaxaca allowed me to come to know both sides of his personality: on the one hand, undeniable genius, and on the other hand, acerbic critic. His relationship with Julio de la Fuente, his immediate assistant, was always negative.

When feasible, I think it important that younger colleagues be brought into one's work, in part so that they can continue the work and, if they wish, "inherit the mantle"—notes included—of older colleagues and, in part, because as one grows older there are fewer opportunities to form contact with younger people who like dancing, hunting, traveling, and other activities that require great energy. At the same time I have found that the capacity to create rapport can be maintained into old age, particularly if one has cultivated tolerance and shown a sense of humor. Some social grace, such as playing the guitar or sleight-of-hand skills are also very helpful; personally, the latter has been very useful to me in dealing with peasants of all kinds.

One of the most notorious faults I have observed in beginning investigators is their limited ability to promote relations of interest and empathy with the people among whom they hope to work. This art, which is so well developed among politicians, salesmen, and other professionals who have direct dealings with people, is not a quality that distinguishes anthropologists. With time some learn it, but often in exchange for serious failures. Personally I have always believed it to be one of the most important things to be taught to anthropologists about to begin research. In addition, the importance of the local language should be stressed in such training, as well as ethnohistory, demography, and social statistics.

In conclusion, I would suggest that despite the diversity of interests reflected in long-term studies, it is becoming more and more urgent that minimal common frameworks be agreed upon, to guide data collection, to facilitate comparisons and, particularly, to permit more controlled testing of hypotheses. But here again we must maintain flexibility so that such guidelines can always be adjusted to the diversities of interests that will inevitably characterize long-term research.

BIBLIOGRAPHY

Eggan, Fred
    1934 The Maya kinship system and cross-cousin marriage. *American Anthropologist*
        *36:*188–202.
Harman, Robert C.
    1974 *Cambios médicos y sociales en una comunidad Maya Tzeltal*. Mexico City:
        Instituto Nacional Indigenista. Colección Sep/Ini, No. 28.
Redfield, Robert
    1950 *A village that chose progress: Chan Kom revisited*. Chicago: Univ. of Chicago
        Press.
Redfield, Robert, and Alfonso Villa Rojas
    1934 *Chan Kom: A Maya village*. Washington, D.C.: Carnegie Institution of Washing-
        ton. Publication 448.
    1939 *Notes on the ethnography of Tzeltal communities of Chiapas*. Washington, D.C.:
        Carnegie Institution of Washington. Publication 509. Pp. 105–119.
Siverts, Henning
    1969 *Oxchuc: Una tribu Maya de México*. México City: Instituto Indigenista In-
        teramericano, Ediciones Especiales, No. 5.
Villa Rojas, Alfonso
    1934 *The Yaxuná-Coba causeway*. Washington, D.C.: Carnegie Institution of Washing-
        ton. Publication 436. Pp. 187–208.
    1945 *The Maya of east central Quintana Roo*. Washington, D.C.: Carnegie Institution of
        Washington, Publication 559.
    1946 *Notas sobre la etnografía de los Indios Tzeltales de Oxchuc*. Chicago: Univ. of
        Chicago Library, Microfilm Collection of Manuscripts on Middle American Cul-
        tural Anthropology, No. 7.
    1947 Kinship and Nagualism in a Tzeltal community, southeastern Mexico. *American
        Anthropologist 49:*578–587.
    1963 El nagualismo como recurso de control social entre los grupos mayances de
        Chiapas, México. *Estudios de Cultura Maya 3:*243–260.
    1964 Barrios y calpules en las comunidades Tzeltales y Tzotziles de México actual.
        *Proceedings of the 35th International Congress of Americanists 1:*321–334.
    1968 Los conceptos de espacio y tiempo entre los grupos mayances contemporáneos. In
        Tiempo y realidad en el pensamiento maya. Miguel León-Portilla, ed. Pp. 119–167.
        Mexico City: Universidad Nacional Autónoma, Instituto de Investigaciones His-
        tóricas. Serie de Culturas Mesoamericanas, 2.

3

Thoughts on Twenty–Four Years of Work in Perú: The Vicos Project and Me

William Mangin

INTRODUCTION

The Vicos project or, as it was formally called, the Cornell–Perú Project (in Perú, the Proyecto Perú–Cornell) was conceived by Allan Holmberg in 1949 after a chance visit to the Callejón de Huaylas on a field trip with San Marcos University students. The project was begun in 1951 with the support of Carlos Monge, a Peruvian anthropologist and medical doctor. It had been planned for 5 years, during which time it was hoped to demonstrate how long-term anthropological research and action could lead to improvement in the lives of down-trodden and exploited peoples. The scope of the project grew far beyond original plans. It lasted until 1964 in the case of Cornell and until 1974 in the case of the Peruvian government.

Since colonial times Vicos had been a hacienda of about 100 square miles, located in a North Central Andes valley known as the Callejón de Huaylas. Like many other Peruvian haciendas it was the legal property of absentee owners—in this case the Public Benefit Society of the nearby town of Huaráz—which leased it for 5-year periods to the highest bidder. Vicos conformed to the Peruvian "manorial system" according to which

Long-Term Field Research in Social Anthropology

adult males living on the hacienda owed 3 days of work a week to the lessor, in return for which they had their houses, small gardens, and a few domestic animals. In 1951 the lessor was the Santa Corporation, which exploited the hacienda for flax processed in a small linen factory which, at the time, was in financial difficulties. Some peons worked flax and others were taken off the hacienda for other work.

The inhabitants of the hacienda were by no means the poorest in the region; they were, in fact, considerably better off than many people in so-called "free" or self-governing communities. Nevertheless, in absolute terms Vicos was a very poor place, and many of its residents, exploited by mestizos and the richer Vicosinos themselves, were underfed, underhoused, and illiterate. But, contrary to what Holmberg and others have written about the docile "feudal" fifteenth-century Vicosinos, the hacienda had a reputation in the valley of being rebellious and hard to manage. Thus, in 1951, the Santa Corporation was glad to turn over the remaining years of its lease to Cornell University and the Peruvian Indian Institute.

In general, the community has prospered since 1951. As the result of expropriation and subsequent purchase from its owners, it is now legally a free Indian Community. The hostile, fearful, and obsequious behavior frequently noted in the early 1950s has given way to a much more open, matter-of-fact way of dealing with outsiders. People are better fed, better housed, and far better educated than under the old system. The project, judged by its results, has both admirers and critics. Even the latter, for the most part, agree that the standard of living has risen in Vicos more than in surrounding haciendas and communities and that the rise is probably due to the project; a few argue that the improvement is due simply to the transfer of money from the United States and that other communities would have prospered in similar fashion with such infusions of aid. It is true that most Andean Indians have experienced similar improvements in their lives during the past generation, but I—a critic of the project in many ways—think Vicos moved faster than other communities, and that the improvement is due, at least in part, to the project.

In this chapter, I describe something of the history of the Vicos project and analyze personal and policy decisions and actions as they bear on the wider methodological problem of long-range studies in anthropology. There is a problem of presentation in dealing with such a complex series of events as the "Vicos Project," and I tend to bog down in a sea of names, identities, places, and interrelationships. I will try to check that tendency, but it is impossible to understand what really happened at Vicos without knowing something about the personalities involved and the chance events and unanticipated consequences of project and personnel actions that influenced the course of Vicos history. There is considerable variation in the analysis and interpretation of the events in Vicos by those who have participated in and those who have studied the project. There is even disagreement among observers who were present at the same time over what happened and what sequence events took. The following is my account of what I consider some crucial events in the project's life, though it benefits from hindsight. My view of a 1975 visit to Vicos has already been changed by conversations I had in Perú in 1976.

THE AIMS OF ALLAN HOLMBERG

The Vicos project can be understood only against the background of Allan Holmberg's personality and social philosophy. He came from a Minnesota farm environment and, like others born and raised under similar conditions, he felt that midwestern American farm and small town life was a desirable model for many other societies. Although mildly Protestant in personal outlook, he was a great believer in secularity. He also strongly opposed the Catholic Church in Perú, which he felt historically had aided and abetted racism and exploitation, which he passionately opposed. Not surprising in a man with these views, he was a dedicated Democratic Party liberal. Hence, genuine as Holmberg's interests in research were, I think his interest in improving the lives of the Vicosinos was even more important to him. He wanted the anticipated results of the Vicos project diffused throughout Perú and the world, for he felt he was developing a model that would aid greatly in solving universal problems of poverty, exploitation, and racism. Basically, the project represented to him the opportunity to demonstrate the capacity of the "common man" to assume the responsibility for his own life and well-being, given the opportunity to do so. His thinking, as we shall see, conformed closely to that of other social reformers of the time, especially those concerned with community development. But he differed from them in a very important way: The key to the problem, as he saw it, lay in the combination of applied research and political action.

Holmberg's basic plan was to achieve his goal by introducing changes in agriculture, health, and education, and to do so in the protected atmosphere of the Cornell lease, under the auspices of the Peruvian government. In this he was supported by high Peruvian officials, who assured him that the Vicosinos would be given every opportunity to buy the hacienda for themselves.

THE FIRST STEPS

The first step in initiating the project began even prior to leasing the hacienda when, in 1950, Mario Vásquez, a Peruvian anthropologist and native Quechua-speaker from the Callejón de Huaylas, made a baseline study of Vicos. The project proper began in 1951. At this point Holmberg found himself in a new and unusual anthropological role: For better or worse, he was the new *patrón* of the hacienda, with all of the traditional responsibilities inherent in the role, as well as the new responsibilities of conducting and guiding simultaneous research. Not surprisingly, as matters turned out, he himself had very little time for personal research, but he was always open and supportive in encouraging research by others.

Holmberg, his wife, and two children, moved to Perú in the summer of 1951, accompanied by four Cornell students: Richard Patch, Joan Snyder, Norman Pava, and William Stein. The inevitable problems of fieldwork began almost immediately. On his initial visit, in 1949, he stayed at a pleasant hotel at Chancos in the beautiful valley between Vicos and the mestizo town of Marcará. At that time the hotel was operated by a Swiss couple; it was clean and comfortable and the food was good. Subsequently, the hotel had been taken over by a Peruvian couple, relatives of a local politician, and it was no longer clean or comfortable and there was no food at all. Consequently, the logistics involved in initiating the project were far greater than anticipated. Not only did Holmberg have to provide transportation in his Jeep station wagon between Chancos, Marcará, and Vicos itself, but at least every third day he had to drive the difficult 20 miles to Huaráz to buy food.

Since the hotel was obviously impossible, Holmberg rented a house on the plaza of Marcará owned by the sister of a man named Enrique Luna, the mestizo overseer of Vicos, who was to play an important role in the success of the project. Mario Vásquez had returned from Cornell where he had spent a semester, and settled at Vicos itself, while Humberto Ghersi, a Peruvian anthropology student who had been studying Marcará as part of the project, was in the town itself. All this was essential in the interim until a project residence could be fixed up on the hacienda itself.

My own association with the project began when I arrived in early October 1951. By then things had settled down somewhat, and I lived with Pava in a room in a house on the plaza and ate with the Holmbergs. The food was bought by Holmberg, mostly in Huaráz, and cooked by the servants of the house. Stein was living in Carhuaz with Patch, until he found a community that suited his fieldwork needs, called Hualcán, which was about 10 miles outside of Carhuaz. Patch had begun his study of small industries in the Callejón. Snyder moved in with a family in Marcará and about a year later moved to the Indian commune of Recuayhuanca, across the river from Vicos. Pava, a recent graduate of Cornell, had no special goal, but he made himself very useful and was the first of us to move in with a Vicos family.

My first few weeks were spent getting acquainted with the valley, which was facilitated by being able to ride around with Holmberg. A few months later, Holmberg offered to drive Enrique Luna's sister to Lima for an emergency operation. The Cornell contract with the Huaráz Public Benefit Society for the Cornell lease was not yet signed (and was not to be for another 2 years) and Holmberg wanted to see if he could expedite it in Lima, since he had been assured that there was no problem. It was not the ideal time, and it turned out that he had to return within a month, but public transportation would have been difficult for the sick woman. I went along to help out and to get to Lima. We had a serious breakdown on the way and after a long series of rides and mechanics the sick woman got to Lima in a taxi and Holmberg and I arrived at 3 A.M. The point of this long story is that something very similar to it could be written about practically any 3-month period of the project. I remember wondering then if, when Holmberg conceived of this controlled cultural change, participant intervention project to improve human productivity of Andean peons, he had had any idea of the hours he would spend driving, negotiating, planning construction of houses, taking students and friends to hospitals, counselling, doing psychotherapy, buying food, stoves, saddles, and so forth.

About this time the decision was made to reconstruct the old hacienda house as a project headquaters, and Holmberg began an almost endless taxiing of carpenters, masons, and materials from Huaráz to Carhuaz to Vicos. As he began to buy materials for the house and to contract for work on it, many of the local mestizos got the idea (partially correct) that here was an easy-mark gringo who would buy anything. Even today some of the toilet fixtures Holmberg bought from one of these unscrupulous men in Carhuaz in 1951 sit unused next to the Chancos hotel. Although we made many friends, there was always suspicion of our motives and some hostility was displayed; inevitably we were seen as sources of easy money. Some incidents were really critical: Holmberg once had to pay for the funeral of a young girl said by her father to have been killed by Norman Pava with the evil eye at a fiesta!

As if these chores were not enough, it was about this time that a stream of visitors began to arrive, an influx that peaked in the mid-1960s, but that continues to this day. Holmberg had to entertain and deal with Peruvian officials and visiting foreigners, many of whom had hidden agendas. He was involved in negotiations to get teachers for the school in Vicos and in long efforts to get Vicos incorporated into some of the agricultural and health programs sponsored by the Peruvian government, the United States, and the United Nations. He continued to be heavily involved in construction details, family and project personnel matters, and ceremonial duties as patron of both the hacienda and the project until he left at the end of the summer of 1952. He never again returned for as long a time, but he did come back frequently, including most of the summers of the next 9 years. Practically every time I saw him after that he was about to "bring Mario to Cornell," and they were going to write the Vicos book. Mario Vásquez did go to Cornell a few times but they were both busy, complex men with large amounts of loyalty, affection, and ambivalence for one another, and they never did write the book.

PUBLICATIONS AND ARCHIVES

Nevertheless, although Holmberg's book was never written, a great many wide-ranging studies have been done in Vicos, mostly with endorsement from the project. The separation of research from applied work was never seriously attempted. Many of the direct-hire "applied" people did excellent work on census collection (five censuses were made between 1951 and 1963), nutrition and health surveys, and general record keeping. Many of the "researchers" had no intention of getting involved in the applied work but did. The first, and probably the best, ethnographic work on Vicos was Mario Vásquez' report on his preproject study (Vásquez 1952).

Most of the Vicos studies have been published in Spanish, English, or both languages. The project record is also good in terms of training local people in skills and training Peruvian and American anthropologists, sociologists, agronomists, and others. Many articles and reports have been written about the project as well as several M.A. and Ph.D. dissertations. Wood (1975) and Dobyns and Doughty (1971) have published reports and bibliographies. The Dobyns and Doughty book, basically a reworking of articles by Holmberg, Vásquez, Dobyns, Doughty, and others, which first appeared in the March 1965 *American Behavioral Scientist,* can be considered the "official" description and evaluation of the project. It is interesting although, in my opinion, it suffers from the imposition of some inappropriate and rather silly categories designed by Harold Lasswell, an American political scientist. Himes (1972) has written an interesting outsider's view of the project.

Several surveys and questionnaires were administered at different times, including one by Bryce Ryan in 1954 that he described as a questionnaire with "no content." Deborah Wood (1975) has published a guide to the Vicos material in the Cornell Library which lists the censuses, field notes, photos, records, and reports available. In is all easily accessible and it contains a considerable amount of personal information about Vicosinos and other Peruvians as well as North Americans. My own field notes are not there, except for some photographs and captions, and there is no report of the rather extensive archaeological work done by Gary Vescelius. William Stein has searched for, but has been unable to find, the original contract between Cornell and the Public Benefit Society but it may be available in the smaller, disorganized file still at Vicos.

The ethical problems involved in having data banks were known in the early 1950s, but I do not think any of us anticipated the kinds of possibilities that exist today for abuse through control of information. Land tenure information within the manorial system, for example, could make some Vicosinos vulnerable, for it is clear that some control more land than others. At one point it seemed useful to have such information so that the community might ration out tasks more fairly once the hacienda was bought by them. Now, under the new revolutionary government, a person with a few small fields might be labelled as an exploiter of peasants and be made to leave the community. This has not happened and I do not think all the land tenure information in the Cornell file is in the Vicos file, but the possibility of harmful use is there.

MY INVOLVEMENT IN THE VICOS PROJECT, 1951–1976

In the summer of 1951, I had been working for some time at the Yale University Center for Studies of Alcohol. I was interested in cultural factors involved in drinking, drunkenness, and alcohol addiction. While there was information available on abstainers and on addicts, there seemed to be none about people who had a high incidence of drinking, a high incidence of drunkenness, and a low incidence of alcohol addiction. In looking through the literature, it appeared that highland Middle and South America might have cultures reflecting such a pattern, so I began to look for field research money. In the course of my search, I saw Harry Tschopsik at the American Museum of Natural History. He told me Holmberg had just received a grant to work in Perú and he called to tell him of my plans. Holmberg said they sounded good. After calling on him, he agreed to pay my expenses in the field. (The Institute for International Education paid international travel expenses.) My plan had been to study alcohol use in the Andes. Upon arrival, with almost no Spanish and two or three words of Cuzco Quechua, I decided to concentrate on the Spanish-speaking mestizos of Marcará. A few months later I decided to compare their behavior with that of the Quechua-speaking Indians of Vicos, because the Indians seemed to fit my original model group. For reasons as capricious as Tschopsik's chance call to Holmberg, I was asked by Holmberg to be the field director (more aptly, the caretaker) of the project and to stay a second year in residence in Vicos. I accepted and, because of graduate student anxiety (since many people seemed to think it was peculiar to study alcohol), I expanded my thesis research to a functionalist study of the fiesta complex, dropping the mestizo comparison.

My sympathy for the applied aspects of the Cornell–Perú Project was not strong, but at the same time I was convinced that it might do some good and that it was highly unlikely that it would do any harm. I kept the books, supervised construction of a school building, and maintained a log of daily events from July 1952 until I was replaced as field director by William Blanchard from Cornell in July 1953.

As I rode out of the Vicos plaza on that July day, to get the bus to Lima, I thought (with mixed feelings) that I would probably never see the place again. I reflected on how chance had committed me to Vicos to a far greater extent than I had ever anticipated. Initially I planned to remain 8 or 9 months; then a Social Science Research Grant came through, and I was able to extend to 15 months. Then, because Holmberg was unable to get any of his first three choices for field director, I remained on for another 11 months, a total of 2 full years.

This uncertainty as to how long I would be in the field had certain deleterious consequences for me, principally linguistic. I told myself the need to concentrate on Spanish justified putting off serious study of Quechua and I have regretted this ever since.

I also could never make up my mind about "studying" the project itself. My subsequent visits, with the exception of 2 months in 1960 when I worked with a group of psychoanalysts in Vicos, have been just that, "visits," and I have spent much more time during the last 15 years interviewing and just talking with project people, both Peruvians and North Americans, than with Vicosinos. I have also had many opportunities to discuss the project and attitudes toward the project with government officials of Perú, the United States, the United Nations, and other Latin American countries. As to the Quechua problem, I have found that in my short visits I have been able to learn many things because of the increasing number of Vicosinos who have learned Spanish, mainly through their time in the Army.

While field director of the project, I had to go to Lima several times on project business. Particularly, Vásquez and I negotiated for teachers and tried to get the 5-year lease with the Huaráz Benefit Society signed. I became interested in the impact of news of the Vicos project and in the political problems of the project within Perú. I also became interested in migrants from the region around Vicos to Lima. I met Peruvian social scientists and politicians as well.

I returned to Yale and wrote a dissertation on fiestas and alcohol use. The following year I took a job at Syracuse, about 40 miles from Ithaca, and had the chance to get information about the project from Vásquez and other anthropologists at Cornell connected with the project.

A Second Period in Perú: Informal Ties with Vicos

My second trip to Perú in 1957, financed by the National Institute of Mental Health, involved a study of rural migration to Lima. Before leaving, I saw Holmberg in Ithaca. I had not seen him since Vicos in 1952 and, speaking frankly, our relationship had become strained during my time as field director. There was no specific incident that led to the strain and I attributed it to a "lack of communication." In view of the strained relations he had with the subsequent field director and other project personnel, I had the impression that he had begun to look on me more favorably as the years went by. We spent a pleasant afternoon talking about Perú. When I asked about Vicos, he assured me that the expropriation was moving right along but that Cornell no longer had any connection with Vicos, that it was now totally a Peruvian Indian Institute operation.

When I arrived in Perú a month or so later, I went to the Indian Institute where I was told that Vicos was in fine shape, although the Institute no longer had anything to do with it and that it was totally a Cornell operation. I continued to Vicos where I found Vásquez and Luna. They told me that *both* Cornell and the Institute had pulled out and that they had had to advance the money to operate the hacienda out of their own pockets and were hoping to get it back out of the potato harvest profits.

During the same summer (1957), I gave a talk about Vicos drinking at a conference on alcohol use, which was reported in the Lima papers. At the time I was staying at the Pensión Morris, a favorite of many American anthropologists, I had a phone call from Carlos Monge. Monge, now deceased, was an extremely powerful and important man in Peruvian politics and the major protector and promoter of Vicos, Vásquez, and Holmberg with the Peruvian government. He was highly respected and survived in power from one administration to the next. Under normal conditions, had I wanted to see Monge I would have called on him, so I was surprised at the call. I was further surprised when he said he was coming over to see me immediately. Upon arrival at the pension, he told me a group of people from the Benefit Society of Huaráz were pressuring the Ministry of Indian Affairs to return Vicos to them and that they were spreading hostile stories about Vásquez and the project in the Callejón and in Lima. There was no time to wait for Holmberg's arrival later in the year because an immediate decision was needed, at least to extend the lease, since immediate expropriation seemed out of the question. Monge arranged a meeting with the Minister of Indian Affairs and presented me as a recently arrived member of the Cornell project to show that Cornell's interest and involvement were still real. It was a short meeting and clearly a minor matter for the Minister who fortunately owed more favors to Monge than to the Benefit Society of Huaráz. Monge could probably have managed without my help. I suspect I was just one of many cards he played, but I was glad to be of assistance to him and to Vicos. I will also add an extra complicated thread: I was delighted to administer any needle I could to the Benefit Society of Huaráz.

A few months later, a United Nations–International Labour Organization grant came through for the Indian Institute whereby Vicos and four other Andean Indian communities were to become sites of action-research projects for community development based, in large part, on the Vicos model. Holmberg was an advisor on the grant and William Blanchard, who had replaced me as field director of Vicos in 1953 and was in Lima on his way to a Fullbright assignment in Chile, was talked into accepting a job with the project as field director with a base in Puno, but in charge of operations in all of the sites including Vicos. A new Peruvian agency, the *National Plan for the Integration of the Aboriginal Population* (PNIPA) was established. I spoke with Holmberg and the executive secretary of the Institute, and each assured me that Cornell and the Peruvian government had never been out of Vicos and that the expropriation was imminent.

Richard Adams and Charles Cumberlord (1960) have published a rather gentle account of some of these events in an early history of the project that is considered by most informed people with whom I have talked as, at least, mildly favorable. But Holmberg told me that he considered it "a stab in the back." I report this to indicate that he was becoming extremely sensitive to criticism of, or indeed anything less than praise of, the project. In hindsight, I attribute this to his uneasiness about the possibility that the hacienda might never be expropriated, since he felt that both the future of the Vicosinos and professional judgments about his own involvement with the project depended on the Indians securing control of Vicos.

By 1959, hundreds of foreigners, mostly North Americans, and hundreds of Peruvians (I would guess over 500, including commissions) had worked in Vicos for differing periods of time. In 1959, the Peruvian government established a central school at Vicos to serve the larger region. The school personnel and their families moved into a house built by Cornell out of hacienda profits and with hacienda labor. Mario Vásquez and his wife, Aida Milla, also an anthropologist, lived in Vicos for much of the time from 1960 to 1963 working for PNIPA. A group of four United States universities started a summer field school program. One of their sites during the years 1960, 1961, and 1962 was Vicos. The Vicosinos were getting used to outsiders and, I think, were generally more entertained by and friendlier with the foreigners than with the Spanish-speaking Peruvians with the exception of Vásquez and a few of the teachers in the school. In my three visits during the 1957–1959 period I felt very welcome and had the impression that Vicos was relaxed and stable compared to the first years of the project.

Vicos in the 1960s: Toward Independence

A stable year for the Vicosinos and one of their best economically was 1960, until an incident occurred in late summer that had later repercussions. During the time the four-university student group was there, an unhappy event occurred in Huapra, a hacienda across the river from Vicos, with which it has very close ties of friendship and kinship. The peons of Huapra combined several of their own fields within the hacienda and were trying to emulate Vicos by buying insecticide and fertilizer and farming their own fields together. The owner, a resident of Huaráz, angry about a decision of a Huaráz parish (inspired by Mario Vásquez) to terminate a seven-generation land grant that he assumed was forever, and to return the hacienda to the peons (rather than to his sons after his death), called the police to stop the peons. The police came through Vicos on foot; when they arrived at Huapra, frightened, they ordered the peons to stop farming. They refused and, apparently, shook their farm implements. The police fired, killing three men and wounding several others. The act was witnessed by many Vicosinos (as well as most of the Americans) and the fear and resentment which it caused lingered for some time.

By 1961 the project had become quite well known among anthropologists and specialists in "international development." There was considerable criticism of Holmberg and the project (and all of us connected) in the United States and Perú, and once again some Huaráz businessmen were threatening to have the Public Benefit Society take the hacienda back (a headline in a Lima magazine, Caretas, quoted one of them as saying he had plans to rent it himself and turn the school into a potato storehouse). Henry Dobyns, an anthropologist who had begun to work on the project about 1960 and who played an important role in project affairs until the mid 1960s, was trying to push through the exproriation which, for the first time in more than 10 years, had the support of some United States embassy officials.

In late summer 1961, Senator Edward Kennedy visited Perú with a small group of American advisers. He wanted nothing to do with the embassy, but its officials (and Dobyns, too) wanted him to go to Vicos. A Cornell anthropologist, Paul Doughty, met the senator's plane when it arrived at the Huaylas airport and, by chance, found that one of Kennedy's advisers was an ex-Cornell professor whom he knew. Kennedy rode with Doughty through the valley, where not surprisingly many thought he was the president of the United States. Upon arrival in Vicos, Senator Kennedy heard a very emotional speech by an accomplished Vicosino orator describing past abuses—including the Huapra killings of the year before—and was much moved. When he returned to Lima, he had an audience with President Prado of Perú and later told embassy officials that Prado had never heard of Vicos. Kennedy reportedly asked the president how Perú could ask for a several million dollar land reform loan when his government had been unable over a 10-year period to expropriate this small property. Prado said he could indeed do it, and he called the two ministries involved (Public Health and Labor and Indian Affairs) and so ordered.

But even with this chance intervention of the brother of the President of the United States, it took Carlos Monge another year of maneuvering with the help of Vásquez and Cornell University to get the "final" decree of expropriation. Incredibly, until that time only one hacienda in Perú had ever been expropriated, a small place taken by the national police for a horse farm; and the owner had successfully sued and gotten it back! The Prime Minister of Perú had told an American Embassy official that Vicos would never be expropriated and just to forget about it. Monge got out of a sickbed when he heard that the military were about to depose President Prado (to assume power to prevent Rafael Haya de la Torre, the likely winner in the forthcoming 1962 presidential elections, from becoming president). He knew that with a new government the Prado decision would be meaningless. Miraculously the papers were signed the day before the coup and the Hacienda Vicos became a free community—more or less. The formal event was celebrated with Holmberg and Charles Kuralt and a CBS-TV crew present to shoot a film ("So That Men Are Free"). It was not all according to the original plan, but at least Vicos had achieved a new status.

VICOS AS A FREE HACIENDA: THE PEACE CORPS ERA

Visitors poured in at an accelerating rate. In early 1962 the Peace Corps arranged with PNIPA to provide volunteers for their projects, including Vicos. One project director, Peruvian anthropologist Oscar Núñez del Prado, told me in wonder when the volunteers arrived, "Some fellow named Sargent or something like that [Sargent Shriver, first Peace Corps Director] asked me if I wouldn't like a carpenter and an agronomist here." After several near disasters during training, eight volunteers were sent to Vicos. On the basis of recommendations by people who knew more of my work in urban areas and universities than in Vicos, I had been hired as deputy director of the Peace Corps in Perú. Paul Doughty also was hired to study the impact of the volunteers in the five sites of PNIPA. I had very little to do with the volunteers in Vicos beyond driving up to introduce them and staying 2 days while they settled in. I had assumed that they, like the summer field school students, would live with families in Vicos. I found out later that they resented me very much for that suggestion. They all lived together in a house on the plaza and their main contacts were with the mestizo school teachers rather than with the Vicosinos themselves. Considerable tension developed between PNIPA staff members and Aida Milla, on the one hand, and the volunteers, on the other.

The volunteers were active people with very little to do. One—we will call him Smith—saw a dramatic possibility to change the economy and culture of Vicos by refurbishing the old hotel in Chancos. Chancos adjoins Vicos and was in fact at one time a part of the hacienda. The government had split off some of the best land along with some of the families and assigned them to the hotel. The hotel was popular because it featured some of the best and most famous mineral hot springs in the country. Its baths are said to cure arthritis, syphilis, mental disease, and other ills. Through favoritism, corruption, and incompetence, the hotel had deteriorated badly, but it still drew people who even brought their own food—as in the case of the Holmbergs when they first arrived in the valley. Smith wanted the Vicosinos to negotiate to get the hotel, but he found out almost immediately that most of the men involved in running Vicos wanted nothing to do with the scheme. They did, however, want to get the land and the people back. Smith called the latter fact to the attention of the Lima Peace Corps staff. The director arranged a personal, no-interest loan to the Vicosinos. With it they bought the fields of Chancos and also got back the people who had gone with it. (Until the present government, renters of haciendas rented the people along with the property. In the Vicos contract, they were named in the same paragraph with the plants and mineral resources.) Had it all stopped here it might have been the best thing the Peace Corps could have done for Vicos.

The Case of the Chancos Hotel

But Smith still wanted the hotel. He arranged several meetings between the representatives of the Benefit Society and the owner and interested them in a trade off of Peace Corps involvement in an airport for Huaráz in return for selling the hotel to Vicos. He even persuaded volunteer engineers to visit the Callejón on their vacation to scout a site and the United States Embassy air attaché, a nice man with almost nothing to do, to buzz the potential site in a C-47 transport to show how easy it would be to land. He then let it be known in Lima that the Vicosinos had decided to buy the hotel at Chancos. In a way not yet clear to me, he managed to induce two of the principal authorities of the Community of Vicos to sign a paper for the Benefit Society stating that Vicos would buy and operate the hotel, pledging the hacienda as security. In fact, Smith's father sent him a few thousand dollars and the only risk was his, since he never gave the paper to the Benefit Society. Instead it was filed in Vicos; Smith's goal was for the community to feel committed to a project that he thought would be to their advantage.

Aida Milla had been feuding with Smith for over a year. She looked through the file, certain that the Yankees were doing something bad but not hoping for anything like what she found: the paper pledging the hacienda as security for the hotel. Milla, through a mestizo employee of PNIPA named Ramírez who worked in Vicos and spoke Quechua, denounced Smith and the Peace Corps at a public meeting. Some people, friendly to Doughty, Holmberg and myself, stalled a vote on throwing out the Peace Corps until the next meeting.

I had been absent in the United States while this was going on. When I returned to Lima, Doughty told me there was trouble in Vicos and that we must go there. We left early the next day and arrived just in time for the evening meeting. During the interim, Milla and Ramírez had spread the story of the contract. Both were very angry with the volunteers based on previous association, but, at least in the case of Milla, resentment and suspicion because of the contract was genuine. If the Benefit Society had had such a contract in its possession, it would have justified the worst fears of the Vicosinos who had long been accustomed to seeing Indians cheated of their lands through the signing of mysterious papers. The meeting was very tense and we tried to stall a final vote until Vásquez returned from the United States. Our local friends had been threatened and pressured and did not support us. Although our Quechua was poor, we could still understand how bad the situation was. It was the first time either of us had heard of the contract and we thought Milla and Ramírez were making it up. Smith was noncommittal, but encouraged us to believe this. A school teacher, a Quechua speaker who had been friendly with the volunteers, defended them and suggested waiting for Vásquez, a very powerful man in Vicos, as everyone knew. The emotional pitch was high and a vote was taken to throw out both the Peace Corps and Cornell University. The vote was a recommendation to the whole community from the elected governing body, the *junta,* and was to be presented at a mass meeting outside the school the next day. During the night, we talked with members of the *junta* and they said they would just throw out the Peace Corps and not Cornell or Doughty or me. We explained that we were now with the Peace Corps but they said no, that we were with Cornell.

The next day the meeting was held. When Vicosinos meet they drink, and the drinking started early. By mid-morning a large crowd had gathered and the meeting was held with the *junta* and Smith (serving as accountant of the *junta*) sitting at a table on a raised terrace. The volunteers, Doughty, and I were scattered around in the crowd. Ramírez denounced the Peace Corps and the contract, and the Peace Corps was voted out by a unanimous shout. People yelled ''Kill the gringos,'' but everyone seemed friendly and smiled at all of us.

Unknown to any of us, a disgruntled, discharged teacher from the school had called the police, mainly to embarrass the school director who had fired him and who was not even in the area at the time of the meeting. Because of the Huapra shooting and other incidents in the past, the arrival of armed police caused the already tense meeting to explode. Doughty and I assured the police that all was well and that it was just an ordinary democratic meeting. They were frightened and were glad to leave. After they left another almost unanimous voice vote was taken to throw out the Peace Corps. After a series of surrealistic and bizarre incidents during the rest of the day, culminating in Smith's tearing up a paper that we said was the contract, we all left.

The teacher was also a stringer for *La Prensa,* a Lima paper, to which he phoned a garbled version of the story. It was picked up in Mexico by TASS and the United Press International and was further garbled by them. Finally, Vásquez returned and saved the situation by persuading the Vicosinos to denounce Ramírez. To save face, the Peace Corps was invited back with the understanding that we would solve the hotel problem, but would not send any more volunteers. Smith was hired by the Peace Corps in Bolivia and Peace Corps officials finally solved the hotel problem 5 years later, in 1968. To everyone's surprise, the one thing that worked out was that the airport was actually built. When I went back in 1964, a young Vicosino I had known since he was in grammar school asked me, I hope jokingly, "What are you doing here? I thought we threw you all out."

Later Events

Vásquez realized that something had to be done about the anomalous status of Vicos. He arranged to have it inscribed as an official *comunidad indígena,* a legal entity with certain protections and advantages in Perú. In order to do that a price had to be agreed upon. As part of the Chancos settlement with the Benefit Society, two appraisals were made of Vicos. One set a high, but reasonable price; the other a price over twice as high. In order to get it over, the elected representative of Vicos agreed to pay the higher price. The holder of the mortgage, however, was to be the National Agricultural Bank, not the Benefit Society, since the mortgage involves PNIPA as signatory. Although they do not want full owner's rights, the Vicosinos technically do not have them and cannot sell the property.

At this time potatoes brought a high price and the Vicosinos were harvesting crops and marketing them easily. They had converted the ex-hacienda fields to communal ones and to one variety of large, tasteless, high priced potato. Many had converted their own personal fields to the same use. The crops were now dependent on insecticides, fertilizers, and an outside market. By this time, the road to Vicos was good enough for trucks to reach the plaza, and they still had their own truck. By cutting out the middlemen, they hurt the mestizo town of Marcará, but they were doing well themselves. We (the Vicos project) have been criticized for the impact of the project on the local mestizo economy, since it was so dependent on exploiting the Vicosinos. Subsequent to these events, the Vicosinos have made regular payments on the mortgage and, for a few years in the late 1960s, they were quite prosperous. They also showed other communities how to get the new potato seeds and how to take advantage of the government's supervised credit, rather than to rely on local mestizo usury. With A.I.D. support a few Vicos men went to the United States on a Farmer's Union project to spend a summer on a small farm in Colorado. As a result of Vásquez' efforts many young men went into the army, where they learned Spanish and a trade and saw some of the outside world. Army veterans constitute the only effective nonkinship group in Vicos today.

The PNIPA team in Vicos, later the Nuclear School team, usually had an agronomist or partial agronomist, plus some teachers. With the help of the teachers, Vicos built an expensive feed lot for cattle, and bought some expensive cattle that cannot survive foraging on the puna, as the local cattle can. I heard about that but did not see it until 1975. I was against it, having been always conservative about the prospects for radical technological changes in Vicos. As with the objections I had had earlier to the new potato technology, it seemed at first that I was wrong. Later it turned out that the cattle were sick and, when the government pulled out the Nuclear School in 1974, the Vicosinos lost the advice of the agronomist. In January of 1975, they were very upset by the prospect of having to continue to pay for the defective cattle that were dying off. The problem was finally resolved when the government said they did not have to pay. The years 1975–1976 have been the first 2 years since Vásquez lived there in 1950 that no outsiders have resided in Vicos. An army major once came through representing the new land reform agency and told the Vicosinos the government was going to "reform the structures." They were angry at him and told him to get out and he denounced them. Occasional representatives of SINAMOS (the acronym for another government agency for political promotion) arrive and ask questions or give orders. They seem to have caught the ear of some of the younger men, but it is hard to see much effect of their activities.

Vásquez was the head civilian in the action arm of the Peruvian land reform program and has had to be careful about appearing to favor Vicos. The new land reform and communities law, if carried out in Vicos, would threaten the one thing people are most frightened about—the fields that, under the manorial system and the present system, belong to each family. They have been willing to experiment with the ex-hacienda—now communal—fields, but are very familistic in the ownership of the household fields. Vásquez is now out of the government and the land reform agency has become more conservative so probably the new law will not be enforced in Vicos. If so, it will represent another "victory" for what I see to be the main response of Vicos to the outside, "Be suspicious. Say what they want. Drag your feet, keep doing what you have always done."

CONCLUSION

Vicos is a very important part of my life, and I feel concerned about what happens there. My subsequent views of the Peruvian scene owe much to seeing it all through perspectives developed among Indians and poor Mestizos in and around Vicos. I am frequently asked to comment on the project and I find that, if the questioner is friendly to Vicos, I am apt to criticize the project and stress the importance of the contribution of the

Vicosinos themselves to the subsequent changes. That is invariably a surprise because the public image presented by Cornell and the Peruvian government is that the project saved the Vicosinos from feudal serfdom and showed them the way to twentieth-century prosperity and United Nations freedom. I feel somehow disloyal (to whom?) when I criticize the project, and hypocritical when I praise it. It has gone up and down in 25 years and my own attitudes have gone up and down in the same period. I was convinced in 1953 that Holmberg and Vásquez were endangering Vicos. When I was pressed for criticism of Holmberg by several Andeanists after returning to the United States in 1953, I defended him. Shortly after, I saw Vásquez as "good" and Holmberg as "bad." Then for a period in the late 1950s, when Vicos seemed to be prospering, I saw myself as wrong, too conservative, self-serving, and thought that perhaps Holmberg was right after all and that I had not been activist enough during my year as field director.

Each time I think about writing something about the project (this is, in fact, the first time I have done so), I think how important my most recent contact is in changing my previous view. Then I think, will my next contact change what I am thinking now? Now would be a good time to do an evaluation of the project. But the evaluation should be repeated every few years to get some historical perspective on current political changes.

One of the valuable things about the long-term nature of the project is that one sees there is no end, no conclusion, no success or failure. Some years things look good, some not so good. Many of the changes are national changes not connected with the project. Many of the apparent crises look unimportant over time, or prove to have important spin-offs. For example, Vásquez' making it easy for Vicosinos to join the army has turned out to be important because of the power of the veterans in the community.

In the light of hindsight, with the exception of putting more effort into learning Quechua during my first field trip and sending fewer and different Peace Corps volunteers to Vicos, I am not sure what I would do differently. The project tensions seem to me to have a very similar ring to those I have heard described for the projects of the Leightons in Nova Scotia, of the Navajo, of Harvard University in Chiapas, and other long-term studies. I have never been too pleased with the "applied" aspects of the project, but, since the late 1960s, a great many anthropologists have been castigating the profession for not having undertaken projects or actions that would "benefit" the people studied and Holmberg certainly had that intention. I believe that if we had had more money and greater local resources we might have done *more* damage. The budget was never high and we were constantly forced to operate within the Peruvian system in such things as getting technical assistance from local agencies and teachers from the ministry. We played our favoritism cards when we could (e.g., Monge, being foreigners) but that is also in the local tradition. Chance events, outside forces, personality changes, personal relationships, and ambitions would probably have played the same central role whatever Holmberg's original plan had been. No government in Perú since the coming of the Spanish has been willing to allow Indian communities autonomy and none is in sight that will. The Vicos–Cornell project was one of many outside interventions in Indian local affairs and, unlike most, it is hard for me to see that the community is worse off for it.

Some of my colleagues have asked me, "What do these stories have to do with long term research?" My answer, not always satisfactory to the asker, is "Everything." Until now, the project exists in different forms in different people's minds. There is no definitive work. There are boxes of documents, field notes, reports, photographs, and letters at Cornell University and in individual files. There are at least a dozen Peruvian and American anthropologists who have been connected with the project for many years who have reasonable access to the files, to each other, and to Vicos. Unfortunately, no Vicosino seems to be inclined to study the project but there are many smart and articulate people there who would be willing to give their versions. These incidents that I have reported seem to me to be important and seem to be typical of what went on each year. I do not present them as an exposé or as a criticism of Holmberg. I am convinced from informal conversations over the years that similar incidents have governed the lives of many other short- and long-term anthropological projects that have generally been publically described in formal, impersonal terms. I would call for more personal reactions and more relating of unplanned incidents, political events, and personal animosities when they are important in explaining what has happened.

There is still time for a good assessment of the Vicos project and what has happened to the community since Holmberg's first visit.

BIBLIOGRAPHY

Adams, Richard, and Charles Cumberland
1960 *United States university cooperation in Latin America*. East Lansing: Michigan State Univ.
Dobyns, Henry, and Paul Doughty, eds.
1971 *Peasants, power, and applied social change: Vicos as a model*. Beverly Hills, Calif.: Sage Publications.
Himes, James R.
1972 The utilization of research for development: Two case studies in rural moderniza-

tion and agriculture in Perú. Ph.D. dissertation, Department of Anthropology, Princeton Univ.

Vásquez, Mario C.
1952 La antropología cultural y nuestro problema del Indio: Vicos, un caso de antropología aplicada. *Perú Indígena* 2(5–6):1–157.

Wood, Deborah A.
1975 Directed cultural change in Perú: A guide to the Vicos collection. Department of Manuscripts and University Archives, Cornell Univ. Libraries.

4

Hungarian Ethnographers
in a Hungarian Village

Tamás Hofer

INTRODUCTION

In this chapter, I report on some of the findings and implications of fieldwork carried out by Edit Fél and myself over a period of more than 20 years in the Hungarian village of Átány. The reader will find that the aims and methods of this research have been rather different from those of American cultural and British social anthropologists. My first task, therefore, is to put the work here described in its cultural context.

In central Europe the distinction between the anthropologist and the ethnologist is of critical importance. The anthropologist is, primarily, a person interested in somatology and, secondarily, a person who goes to far lands to study the way of life of exotic peoples. The ethnographer, on the other hand, studies the folk culture of the rural areas of his own country. Consequently, fieldwork for the central European ethnographer is substantially different from that of the anthropologist. For the ethnographer, the field is near; it is easy for him to get there and return home again in a short period of time. There is, in fact, hardly a distinction between what is field research and what is not. From the anthropologist's point of view, the ethnographer is almost always in the field, since he lives

Long-Term Field Research
in Social Anthropology

within the cultural system he explores. This is true whether he is visiting a small village, or is working in an ethnographical museum which is, after all, an institution within the same cultural system.

Both the research methods and the goals of central European ethnography are distinct from those of social/cultural anthropology in other parts of the world. As for research techniques, it is relatively easy for the national ethnographer to adapt himself to his field situation and to begin his research upon arrival. The "culture shock" mentioned in manuals of anthropological field methods is for him largely missing. The "natives" speak the same language as the researcher and the social type of the researcher is not unknown to them, since they generally have had experience with similar people of the urban intelligentsia. Thus, the ethnographer can shorten considerably the "introductory period" of research, during which the connections needed for beginning his research and for collecting baseline data on the village are established. From published sources and statistical data, the ethnographer can obtain the basic information in advance.

In Hungary, the norm of fieldwork of at least a year in one community has not been established; repeated short stays of a week or a fortnight are the general practice. By making repeated short visits to the field, a "national" ethnographer during his lifetime is able to study a number of regional units within the territory of his national culture, or within the area where his native tongue is spoken. At the same time, most "national" ethnographers—often without fully realizing what is happening—are simultaneously engaging in a kind of long-term research. Most of them have a favorite village or town, often the one in which they were born, with which they maintain close contact over a great many years, and from time to time, write articles or monographs on this community. To some extent, Edit Fél and I have followed this pattern in that we have visited all major groups of Hungarian peasants in addition to our work in Átány. Our pattern has differed from that just described because Átány was carefully selected to meet specific research criteria and the fieldwork there was more continuous and systematic. Because Hungarian ethnographers usually have these "favorite" villages, when they speak on general questions their colleagues recognize the extent to which their experiences in these villages have influenced their views.

As to the purpose, the main function of Hungarian ethnography (in common with much other central and eastern European ethnography) has been to contribute to the self-image of Hungarian society and to define and investigate the cultural symbols encompassing its identity by examining the peasant components within it. Ethnographers convey this image of peasant culture not only with scholarly books and popular publications, but also through exhibitions and museums. In fact, the first organized foundation of national ethnography was provided by museums, which at that time fulfilled research and educational functions, in addition to their collection and display roles. Two-thirds of the approximately 150 Hungarian ethnographers are presently affiliated with museums. The image which ethnographers have shaped concerning peasant culture has had an important cultural role: In the process of national integration, it provided national symbols and articulated the connection between the peasantry and other social strata. Not surprisingly, ethnographers have been expected primarily to provide cultural symbols, and possible practical information about the society that might be put to use has not been emphasized.

In focusing on these traits, ethnographers almost inevitably became experts in specific areas of peasant culture, such as ploughs, carts, argricultural practices, folktales, and the like. They visited villages to collect data and objects for their special needs, interpreting their materials from a historical and philological perspective. Community studies in a single village are relatively rare in national ethnography, and they have followed a model that reflects a "textual" rather than a "contextual" approach (Bailey 1964; Devons and Gluckman 1964:193–196). Ethnologists have felt that the sum of the traits they have studied constitutes a basic inventory for the ethnography of the peasant component of society, in the same way that literary historians utilize texts and biographies as a basic resource to help obtain a picture of a national literature. Consequently, most "village studies" have been joint products. The experts on fishing, agriculture, architecture, popular beliefs, and the like join forces, each writing a chapter on his special field, to be included in a single volume.

Since its beginning, then, ethnography has been seen as a part of history and the humanities (Hofer 1968) rather than a social science, and only in very recent years have a few ethnographers initiated research involving extended periods of residence and participant observation in a single community. It should not be necessary to say that, to make my point about the basic characteristics of national ethnography, I am guilty of some oversimplification. Since the 1920s, interesting combinations of the textual and contextual approach have emerged. Traditional themes in ethnography were investigated for the purpose of gaining insight into the cultural and structural mechanisms of peasant society. Researchers examined, for example, the attire worn in a village from a perspective of how the apparel expresses social status, the relationships between village members, various everyday and ritual situations, and personality differences. In this way, a transformation in the quality of data was begun in European (and Hungarian) ethnography; a process which might be equated with the effect Malinowski's work had on anthropology. Concrete cases were described in their context and a genuine attempt was made to analyze their meaning in depth. In the past 20 years, methodological experiments have been conducted in many parts of Europe, using models from social anthropology and sociology.

RESEARCH IN ÁTÁNY

The research here described in Átány reflects both traditional and contemporary approaches to ethnography. Considering the fact that Hungarian ethnographers have been systematically investigating peasant culture in Hungarian villages for over 100 years, it might be said that the fieldwork at Átány is part of a long-term research program which has been pursued by numerous researchers for several generations. While no significant fieldwork had been done in Átány previous to that discussed here, such research had been conducted in the surrounding area. Ethnographical information collected in other Hungarian villages, both near and far, was used extensively in the planning and preliminary research for fieldwork at Átány. It was the primary intent of this research, in fact, to add to this body of national ethnographical literature—and it was only later that it was decided to publish the bulk of the material in foreign languages. In addition to ethnographers, scholars in the fields of history, literature, and linguistics, for example, have been exploring the same population from their respective positions and exchanging views for many years. The degree of interaction among researchers and the intensity of their studies might give the impression that the work of investigating Hungarian life in the Carpathian Basin is an ongoing project being conducted by an interdisciplinary team.

Átány is a peasant village about 110 km. from Budapest on the northern edge of the Great Hungarian Plain. When Edit Fél first went there in 1951, it had a population of about 2500, the overwhelming majority of whom were peasant farmers whose main crop was wheat. It was not, however, until after a second visit in 1953 that Edit Fél decided to begin intensive research. In making plans, she had in mind what she felt were the limitations of earlier ethnographical research. For, although a tremendous amount of data on different cultural traits had been amassed, peasant family organization, the social structure of villages, and the system of relationships between families and persons within Hungarian villages had hardly been analyzed. Virtually no attempts had been made to reveal the order and structure peasants see in their own cognitive domains and what they knew about the world surrounding them. From the outset, then, research in Átány emphasized the notion of "world-view" (*Weltbild und Wesensschau*); today, we would speak of the cognitive map, value system, and moral code of the villagers.

This kind of research obviously required longer and more intensive fieldwork than was usual in Hungarian ethnography. It also involved a search for a special kind of village. As a part of the process of "modernization" in Europe during the past century, Hungarian villages have undergone an accelerating process of change that has made them less and less "peasant." An increase in social stratification and the growth of wage labor both in the country and in cities have contributed to the disintegration of the peasant way of life. Edit Fél initially was attracted to Átány because these change processes had produced less cultural disintegration there than in most Hungarian villages, and therefore it preserved a great many peasant features essential to the plan of research.

Systematic fieldwork began in January, 1954. I had recently completed my ethnographic studies at the University of Budapest and had the good fortune to be invited to join Edit Fél in this enterprise. Research began under rather unique historic conditions. In Hungary, 1948–1949 was the "year of the change," when the socialist transformation of the country's society began. In the early 1950s (the years of Stalin and, in Hungary, Rakosi), this policy was realized by violent and rash methods, which are recognized as distortions today. Increasing pressure was applied on the peasantry: the compulsory delivery of produce, which often deprived the families even of the foodstuff they needed, the designation of wealthier peasant strata as kulaks, whose property was confiscated, internments, and the like. In both ideology and scientific life, the "hard line" came to the fore. At Budapest University, the chair of sociology was eliminated; officially no sociological research was conducted at all.

During our work in Átány, we have been affiliated with the Budapest Museum of Ethnography. Fieldwork, of course, is one of the routine tasks of museum workers and several annual field trips of a week or two, partly intended for collecting museum specimens, was the pattern of the museum. By concentrating our "field time" on Átány, Edit Fél and I were able—in "good" years—to spend from 50 to 60 days in the village; in years with greater pressure from other tasks, we spent but a fraction of this time in residence. Fortunately, the museum accepted our unusual research style and, later, it even put at our disposal a major sum for collecting museum specimens.

Either together or separately, we were able to spend 6 to 10 days at a stretch at Átány and, occasionally, even longer periods. Following a rather strict schedule, we utilized our time most intensively in the village. The notes were typed and the photographs identified in Budapest; the typing of the notes always took at least as many days as the time spent at Átány. The fieldwork always had a definite purpose and theme, such as the observation, description, and photographing of certain kinds of agricultural work or of holidays, or the collecting of material by means of interviews on different themes. In addition, we went to Átány several times to attend weddings or funerals in the families of our friends.

Between 1954 and 1956, we conducted intensive research to survey in general the village's way of life. Then, for a few years, we were engrossed in other tasks, but from 1959 until about 1968 we again conducted intensive fieldwork at Átány with the intent of completing the material for the books we were writing. Meanwhile, the socialist reorganization of the country's agriculture had taken place and collective farms came into being throughout the country between 1959 and 1961. Only a small, insignificant part of the peasant family holdings survived. The effect of rapid industrial development and urbanization made itself more and more strongly felt and the peasant–worker form of life became increasingly common. All of this had greatly transformed Átány too, although, according to the 1970 census, the people of Átány and of villages in its vicinity still made their living by agriculture to a much greater extent than the majority of Hungary's rural population. However, in the books we were writing, we adhered to a depiction of the peasant way of life which had been observed between 1951 and 1959 and that of the earlier period in which our informants had grown up. Thus, our research at Átány was not a genuine longitudinal study and we did not consider the recording and analysis of changes its chief aim. As a matter of fact, we have made extensive observations on processes of change and are planning to write a work in which change and the personal alternatives of adaptation to it will be represented in multigenerational family histories dating from the second half of the nineteenth century.

When we began our research, we had in mind no concrete plan of topics and publications. We vaguely considered an initial community study, a sort of background study for the "more profound" explorations we hoped to carry out. But by 1956, our data were growing so rapidly and the possibilities of Átány were obviously so rich that we felt forced to concentrate on more strictly demarcated themes. For various reasons, we decided to study peasant agriculture: the analysis of the "population of tools and implements" on the one hand and on the other, the mapping of the principles and knowledge applied in everyday decision making in husbandry. Unfortunately, of the long manuscript that resulted from this work, only a few passages could be published in Hungary.

In those years, Sol Tax visited Budapest several times. We showed him a series of maps on which different movements of people and animals

were represented along with the spatial aspect of various social relationships. He suggested to us that an account of Átány be published in the
Viking Fund Series. The book should include many maps and diagrams
and a brief text. After several years of preparation and correspondence,
this plan underwent significant modifications. Further fieldwork on some
basic institutions of the society of Átány allowed completion of the
Hungarian manuscript in 1965. It was then translated into English and
printed in Hungary (Fél and Hofer 1969). In the following years, two other
volumes on peasant farming and household management were completed
and published in German with the aid of European ethnographic institutions. Professor Gerhard Heilfurth (Institut für mitteleuropäische Volks-
forschung, Marburg) published the volume in which the knowledge and
measures used in everyday decision making in farm- and household-
management are systematized (Fél and Hofer 1972). In cooperation with
the Publishing House of the Hungarian Academy of Sciences, Professor
Axel Steensberg (International Secretariat for Research on the History of
Agricultural Implements of the Danish Royal Society) brought out the
study on the tools and implements of Átány and their human and social
significance. (Other publications include Fél and Hofer 1973 and 1974.)

OUR RELATIONS WITH THE PEOPLE OF ÁTÁNY

The stereotyped view of the relationship between the cultural anthropologist and the people he studies is that of a (relatively) wealthy
person who lives among poor villagers or tribesmen. At the very least the
anthropologist will be expected to distribute favors among those with
whom he works and, not infrequently, he will be asked to pay for information. The anthropologist is seen, by the people he studies, as a person of
power and importance, someone to be envied and emulated.

Among Hungarian land-owning villagers the picture was quite different:
By no means did they see a Hungarian ethnographer as someone who
unambiguously stood socially higher than they. Átány peasants were well
aware of the independence granted them by their ability to earn their
livelihood from their own lands, and they not infrequently expressed pity
for us because we did not "eat bread grown on our own soil," because we
had to earn our living by "going from door to door," and because we were
"ink-lickers" who could be ordered about by our administrative
superiors. This compassion probably helped us in gathering information.
It must be confessed, however, that we could sometimes help them by
getting medicines and medical assistance through loans, or in arranging
higher education for some of the children.

The very nature of field research and the gathering of museum specimens also solidified our ties. Since we took many photographs, it became a regular custom to give enlargements to villagers. In cases of death, they would ask for, and receive, enlargements of earlier photographs of the deceased. The collecting of museum specimens also facilitated village connections. For the items we acquired, we paid fair prices, prices at which the objects could have been replaced had the family wished to do so. During hard times this extra income helped many families with daily necessities, as well as with the purchase of prestige items during ordinary times: tombstones, propane stoves, and iron gates that had recently become very fashionable.

We maintained close village ties, even during long absences: Like other relatives and neighbors in Átány, we often were sent a "taste" in Budapest on the occasion of a pig butchering. And, just as we attended the funeral of friends close to us in Átány, so did they come to Budapest when there was a death in either of our families.

Of course, throughout our research, we maintained official connections with the village administration. Initially, these ties were nominal, since appointed officials came from outside the community, rarely stayed for long, and were uninterested in our work. Fortunately, from the late 1950s the man who served as head of the Village Council was sympathetic with our work and we maintained amicable ties with him. Above all, in the first difficult years, it was the pastor of the Reformed Church of Átány who, by "authenticating" us and our work, made it possible to gain the trust of the villagers. Although in recent years the social role and prestige of the Church have greatly diminished in Átány, we nevertheless have maintained friendly connections with the now-elderly pastor and with the Church's elders, all peasants, and the parishioners. For example, at the Sunday service on Whitsuntide, 1975, we presented a copy of our third book on Átány to the villagers.

ETHICAL OBLIGATIONS

The ethical responsibilities felt by anthropologists from industrially developed countries among poor tribal and peasant peoples seem quite different from those experienced by "national" ethnographers. The former feel—or should feel—responsibilities for possible harmful effects of their research on the peoples studied. Sometimes they feel an obligation actively to intervene in situations in which they feel their subjects' well being is threatened by national policies. Consciously and subconsciously, such anthropologists sense a line between their scientific obligations to their professional colleagues and their moral and ethical obligations to the people who have welcomed them and made their scientific studies possible.

In the case of the national ethnologist, this line can hardly be said to exist, for the ethnographer is a member of the same complex social system as the subjects being investigated. If he wants to better the social conditions in which his villagers live, he has to work to improve his own society. Presumably his writings contribute to a greater understanding of his own society, and an honest and humanistic portrayal of peasant life will demonstrate his sympathy for them and perhaps make better known their special problems. But, since his role is viewed as akin to that of a historian or a literary scholar—and not a social scientist—he is not expected to be a social activist, an outright advocate on behalf of the group he has studied (for an exception, see Daun 1972). In all probability, the information he has gathered and published will have little if any direct social or political impact on the group he has examined.

In another way, however, the national ethnographer has impact on the people he studies. The people of Átány know that we are affiliated with an important institution of Hungarian national culture and they were anxious that, and pleased by the knowledge that, in the overall picture of national ethnography, Átány was to be strongly represented. We rarely needed to use pseudonyms, since the people of Átány were proud to have books published on their village and happy to see their parents and their own photographs, with their names in the captions, in these books. In the course of fieldwork, we gave several lectures at Átány, particularly about data on the history of the village which we had discovered in archives and which the villagers had not known about. These lectures, repeated several times, reached practically the whole population of the village. In 1962, in the newly built Cultural Hall of Átány, we exhibited the finest pieces—carefully cleaned and restored—which we had acquired for the Budapest Museum. On the same occasion, the school choir sang old folk-songs we had collected in the village. These local cultural elements brought back from the capital exerted a great effect on the people of Átány; while listening to the songs, some of our informants burst into tears.

All this did not influence the process of ongoing change, but it confirmed the local identity of the Átány people, heightened their appreciation of the peasant culture they had abandoned, and contributed to the shaping of a positive cultural self-image. It enriched their consciousness of the past. On our initiative and supported by the county's organization of museums, a small local museum is now being established at Átány: It is a peasant house and a farmyard. The museum is now intended, first of all, for foreign visitors arriving by car. It brings some financial returns too: In the stable, elderly men, no longer fit for hard work, will produce wickerwork, plait straw or make carvings. However, for the people of Átány, this peasant house is also a symbol of their own past and their cultural traditions.

SOME ADVANTAGES OF LONG-TERM RESEARCH IN ÁTÁNY

When we began our Átány research, we did not know how long we would work there, and we were unable to plan systematically to take advantage of what ultimately became a very lengthy study. Over the years, however, we have found that a number of important topics could not have been researched in the traditional fashion, in a shorter period of time, and with fewer visits to the village. I would like to give a few examples of these findings.

Numerous processes in a peasant society—I am not referring here to irreversible processes of change—take place in cycles longer than a year or two. At Átány we were able to observe such processes. One of them is the domestic group development cycle. Edit Fél, for example, could observe how the family of her hosts watched their teenage daughter to see whether a young man would join her during the village girls' Sunday afternoon walks. She could observe how, on the emergence of the suitor, the girl's dress and behavior changed and how the talks preceding marriage were conducted. She was able to see the wedding and follow the young couple's married life. By now, the granddaughter is marriageable. We could observe how neighbours developed a difference of opinion or held a grudge against each other, and how, after attempts for several years at smoothing things over, a solemn peace-making occurred. Also, the norms of production and consumption could be determined for both lean and fat years. Along with the peasants we experienced the lean years resulting both from the pressure put on the peasantry and from unfavourable weather conditions; but we were also with them when they were well off. The system of allocation and economizing in different periods could be outlined by analyzing them together. We could observe directly the processes of social mobility: How, for example, the son of one of our informants, born at the beginning of our fieldwork, studied and graduated as a hydraulic engineer, how he adapted to his urban surroundings, and how his parents also became more or less urbanized.

Thanks to these years of experience and the information on Átány families and persons, we have achieved a particular sensitivity in understanding everyday occurrences. The village people themselves will interpret every event in connection with what they know about the ancestors, relatives, merits, and secret guilts of the persons concerned. Even if the ethnographer is unable to reach this level of knowledge, he can approach it and thus, as it were, know in advance the context in which certain processes take place.

However, not only do researchers mature, their informants also mature. The combination of long years of association and the long talks many peasants have had with us have enabled them to formulate evaluations and opinions they would not have expressed verbally before. But, in this instance, it is difficult to distinguish the effect of the radical transformation that has taken place in the peasant way of life—a process which obviously encourages more conscious reflection on the former way of life—from the stimulation of contact with the ethnographers.

In the course of our longer visits to Átány, we established such close connections with some families—particularly with families whose guests we have been—that we practically acquired the status of a member of the family. This has ensured for us vantage positions of observation (e.g., in certain family rites) which we could not otherwise have acquired.

Virtually up to the present time, the custom of lamenting over the dead has survived at Átány. The deceased person is laid out in state in his or her home, and the bier is surrounded by the nearest female relatives who, seated there, keep a vigil and sing religious songs. When visitors arrive, these women stand up and lament over the deceased person, singing or reciting improvised texts. Rites around the dead are the ritual summit of the whole of human life. On such occasions all social connections of the deceased and of the family are dramatically expressed. Several hundred people will visit the dead person and give expression to their connections and feelings in an elaborate code of gestures, words, and attitudes. In an elevated and often poetic manner, the lament formulates the fate of the deceased and of the bereaved. In the course of fieldwork, we attended a great many wakes and funerals as acquaintances, as honored friends of the deceased, or as strangers—but in every case as visitors arriving at the house for a definite and limited time. However, when Edit Fél's hostess died, she was present for the 2 days before the funeral, each time for 16 hours, among the nearest kin "in the second place from the head of the dead person." By this experience our former fragmentary knowledge (which we believed to be complete and described as such in *Proper Peasants*) was enriched. Edit Fél noted all of the visitors who came to the room of the deceased, some several times. She observed how the girl who was lamenting over her dead mother's body repeated the same or similar words to each group of visitors, thus organizing and moving the several hundred relatives, neighbors, and friends who had come. Wakes have been thoroughly explored in Hungarian ethnography and an impressive collection of texts and tunes of laments has been published. But of about 600 recorded texts, almost none were made when the deceased was laid out in state. The overwhelming majority were recorded after the ceremony.

REFLECTIONS ON OUR EXPERIENCES

In reflecting on our experiences in Átány, which have extended over more than 20 years, it is not always possible to separate the two principal factors that have led to our present understanding of the community. On the one hand, the simple passage of time and the accumulation of data enabled us to identify connections and perceive systems initially unknown to us. On the other hand, the stimulus of external sources, the writings of anthropologists in other countries, broadened our theoretical framework and heightened our sensitivity to the meaning of data. From the beginning, we found methodological encouragement in the works of such European ethnographers as Weiss (1959) and Maget (1953) who were interested in improving empirical research methods and in interpreting cultural traits as parts of coherent systems. Detailed ethnographies on distant peoples also aided us in approaching certain themes, such as the use of the home; Lebeuf's book on the Fali (1961) is a good example of this help.

Simultaneously anthropologists in other countries were showing much greater interest in peasant societies, including those of Europe, and from their writings we learned much. At the same time, there was emerging from the works of Hungarian historians a new, dynamic picture of the changing stratification of our peasantry and its economic connections, and of the contradictory processes of modernization in the country (e.g., Hának 1972). Economists among our friends and collaborators also gave useful advice on the interpretation of our economic data (e.g., Berend and Ránki 1969). All these influences threw new light upon the observations we made in Átány. In short, Átány was a living laboratory in which it was continually possible to test new hypotheses. Our only regret is that time did not permit us to exploit these opportunities as often as there were incentives for us to do so.

The question has been asked: Is the point of diminishing returns reached after many years of research in the same community? I would ask the question in a different way: When does the *researcher* reach the point at which he has no new theoretical ideas, when he cannot formulate new questions? In Átány, my regret is that I have been able to do less research than the questions and themes that occur to me require, not that I am reaching a point of diminishing returns. Looking to the future, I see many new research possibilities; research on them can be done more expediently at Átány than in other villages, because it can be based on data already acquired and on our personal ties to the villagers.

SOME METHODOLOGICAL CONTRIBUTIONS TO HUNGARIAN AND EUROPEAN ETHNOGRAPHY

I now turn to some of the ways in which, I hope, Edit Fél and I have gone beyond traditional European ethnographic goals, thereby contributing to this discipline and to anthropology in general. One such example is the "implement population" of the village. First we drew up a map of native categories embracing a number of the groups, or "domains," of common cultural traits traditionally described in national ethnographies. We were astonished to find how rich was the corpus of agricultural tools and implements in the village, how many kinds of formal and functional variants of implements existed, how many components and spare parts could be found in a single farm (in a few instances, more than 1000!).

In trying to find a system in the implement "population" of the village, we examined the principles and criteria according to which the people of Átány separate the different types from one another, demarcate the limits of acceptable variation, and eliminate the variants considered to be inferior or improper. A taxonomy of tools and implements was developed. We examined how, in different family farms, the equipment, the sets of implements, are gathered and organized, and also what the structural principles guiding their collection are: What principles of loans, of renting, and of joint ownership guide the circulation of tools among different farms.

In implements and their use, a tremendous amount of experience and knowledge about materials, the soil, plants, animals, and the human body are incorporated. Indeed, the population of implements and tools can be described as a system of knowledge in itself. We explored the life-cycle of implements, the system of their replacement, recycling and discarding, which again led to the system of their acquisition or production, and further, to characteristic developmental cycles of family equipment. From the point of national ethnography, these studies not only contribute to the interpretation of peasant tools and implements preserved in Hungarian museums, but also to the interpretation of peasant agricultural technology and husbandry practices in general. They can also contribute to a theory of artifacts as a cultural system. When we consider what an archaeologist finds in the "artifact population" of a paleolithic site and what far-reaching conclusions he draws from this evidence, it is surprising that so little information on material culture is included in most studies of peasant villages.

A second major theme, which stemmed logically from the above, had to do with peasant farm decision making, or the ways in which families appraise their resources and decide to what ends they will be allocated. We began, in traditional ethnographic fashion, by observing and recording the different operations performed in a number of households, which enabled us to delineate several types. Included in these observations were routine, everyday allocations of food, clothing, money, and manpower, as well as the planning and strategies of larger economic transactions. The Átány notions of "enough," "scarce," "insufficient," and "too much" gave us a frame in which very diverse pieces of information about economizing with the land, with the fertility of the soil, with food and drink, with the space inside the house, as well as the rationing of work and rest, or the division of time, all found their place. A picture emerged of the economic theory of Átány peasants and of the moral code or philosophy of their farming activities.

By using this approach, we were able to find and describe structure in a mass of data usually treated only in descriptive fashion (Fél and Hofer 1972). This work represents a cognitive map of the people's views about economic resources, the natural and social forces limiting their use, and the requirements of consumption. Since the economic activities of Átány peasants embrace many different plants, animals, ways of utilizing labor, and the like, the book inevitably contains a great deal of detail. But from this mass, there emerge theoretical conclusions that appear to coincide with some of the theoretical statements of Chayanov on peasant farming (Chayanov 1966), of Sahlins on the "domestic mode of production" (Sahlins 1972), by Foster on Limited Good (Foster 1965), and by Ortiz on peasant decision making in Colombia (Ortiz 1973). At the time we were writing, however, in 1965–1966, we were not primarily interested in testing these hypotheses. Rather, we wanted to work out in detail the rules by which decisions are made in Átány, the knowledge on which these rules rest, and the possible effect of differences of individual temperaments, of those of a generational nature, and differences among members of the several social strata. We worked, it might be said, at a level midway between the everyday situations we observed in Átány and more general, abstract statements about decision making.

There are limitations of various kinds in our work, partially stemming from the nature of national ethnographic research. For example, we have few quantitative data. In the beginning, external circumstances rendered it impossible to set up files on all families, and to collect monetary data on crop or market transactions. In line with the character of most national ethnography, we described—to use Berreman's terms (Berreman 1962)— the "front region" of culture rather than the conflicts and deviating forms that constitute the "back region." After the first 10 years we began to obtain more "back region" data, in part because of our growing awareness of this distinction, and in part because of the close relationships we had developed with many families. One man particularly, whose son became an "educated man," was, because of our close ties, primarily responsible for aiding us in these matters. On the other hand, we have done little in the area of power relations between political organizations, and between the village and the external world, in part because these themes have had no tradition in European ethnography.

CONCLUSIONS

In both history and the history of science, the period during which the Átány investigations were carried out was one of transitions. In addition to political and social changes, it was a period when European national ethnography was endeavoring to become more of a social science than had previously been the case. When I ask myself whether, in hindsight, we might have worked differently than we did, these circumstances must be taken into consideration. Obviously, with our growing professional maturity and our increasing awareness of ethnography as a social science as well as an historical discipline, we now see additional kinds of data we would have attempted to gather and new research techniques that we might have used. Yet in retrospect, the important thing is not that we knew less about research design and data gathering than we do now, but rather that, in spite of our limitations, we began at all and carried forward our work through many years to its present stage of completeness. My major concern is not with the way we worked, but rather how our findings can be preserved and be made available to other people, researchers, and interested laymen alike. Unfortunately, no younger colleagues, who might be expected to continue the work and maintain our files, took part in our investigations. Only a small part of what we have learned and gathered is likely to appear in books. In addition to our basic corpus of thousands of pages of field notes, there are more than 10,000 photographs, as well as about 3800 ethnographic specimens in the Budapest Museum, the material evidence of the native "domains" that we have explored. Our long-term research in Átány has resulted in both "longer" data (i.e., data bearing on the longitudinal problems of process and change) and "thicker" data (Geertz 1973), with their many layers of meaning and possible interpretation. How is the best use to be made of this unusually complete body of data? Present forms of publication cannot begin to make available the basic data. This, of course, is a problem common to all long-range studies that result in voluminous materials; it is not limited to Átány alone. If only theoretical conclusions, our distilled insight up to a given moment, are published, the basic data—from which later generations may learn new lessons—are apt to be lost. European countries have experimented with ethnographic archives, but data preserved in them tends to remain "frozen." And finally, there is the methodological problem of interpreting the records of earlier researchers. Our notes, taken a few years ago, today tell us much more than appears in the records themselves; but this additional knowledge is not in the notes, it is in our minds and memories. There is no obvious answer to the problems here raised.

BIBLIOGRAPHY

Bailey, F. G.
  1964 Two villages in Orissa (India). In *Closed systems and open minds: The limits of naïvety in social anthropology*, edited by Gluckman, Max. Pp. 52–82. Chicago: Aldine.
Berend, T. Iván, and György Ránki
  1969 *Közép-Kelet-Európa gazdasági fejlödése a 19–20. században (Economic Development of East Central Europe in the 19th and 20th Century).* Budapest: Közgadasági és Jogi Kiadó.
Berreman, Gerald D.
  1962 *Behind many masks: Ethnography and impression management in a Himalayan village.* The Society for Applied Anthropology, Monograph No. 4.
Chayanov, A. V.
  1966 *The theory of peasant economy.* D. Thorner, B. Kerblay, and R. E. F. Smith, eds. Homewood, Ill.: Richard D. Irwin for the American Economic Association.
Daun, Åke
  1972 Some new trends within European ethnology in Sweden. *Ethnologia Europea* 6: 227–238.
Devons, Ely, and Max Gluckman
  1964 Conclusion: Modes and consequences of limiting a field of study. In *Closed systems and open minds: The limits of naïvety in social anthropology*, edited by Gluckman, Max. Pp. 158–261. Chicago: Aldine.
Fél, Edit, and Tamás Hofer
  1969 *Proper peasants: Traditional life in a Hungarian village.* Viking Fund Publications in Anthropology, No. 46.
  1972 *Bäuerliche denkweise in wirtschaft und haushalt: Eine ethnographische untersuchung über das Ungarische dort Átány.* Göttingen: Otto Schwartz.
  1973 Tanyakert-s, patron–client relations and political factions in Átány. *American Anthropologist* 75:787–801.

1974 *Geräte der Átányer Bauern*. Budapest: Akadémiai Kiadó, Kommission der König-
lichen Dänischen Akademie der Wissenschaften zur Erforschung der Geschichte
der Ackerbaugeräte und der Feldstrukturen, Brede.
Foster, George M.
1965 Peasant society and the image of limited good. *American Anthropologist 67*:293–
315.
Geertz, Clifford
1973 *The interpretation of culture*. New York: Basic Books.
Hanák, Péter, ed.
1972 *Magyarország története 1849–1918*. Budapest: Tankönyvkiadó.
Hofer, Tamás
1968 Anthropologists and native ethnographers in central European villages: Comparative notes on the professional personality of two disciplines. *Current Anthropology
9*:311–315.
Lebeuf, Jean-Paul
1961 *L'habitation des Fali Montagnards du Cameroun septentrional*. Paris: Hachette.
Maget, Marcel
1953 *Guide d'étude direct des comportements culturels*. Paris: Civilisations du Sud.
Ortiz, Sutti R. de
1973 *Uncertainties in peasant farming*, London: Monographs on Social Anthropology,
No. 46.
Sahlins, Marshall
1972 *Stone age economics*. Chicago: Aldine-Atherton.
Weiss, Richard
1959 *Häuser und Landschaften der Schweiz*. Zürich and Stuttgart: Eugen Rentsch Ver-
lag.

Part II

GENERAL ETHNOGRAPHIC STUDIES

Most contemporary anthropologists accept the implicit premise that all data have potential value for understanding a sociocultural system. Thus, even when they enter the field with a specific problem focus, anthropologists routinely gather data considered irrelevant by many other social scientists interested in the same problem. Moreover, anthropological fieldworkers are expected to master and employ a wider range of data collection procedures than are nonanthropologists. This is especially true of the lone ethnographer who sets out to study a society never studied previously.

As the essays in this section demonstrate, a series of fieldtrips to a specific community or population offers many advantages over short-term, one-shot studies when the anthropologist's goal is a general description of contemporary life and modernization. In fact, we believe that a single ethnographer who conducts, say, 60 months of field research over 20 years will learn more about a given population, and thus make a greater contribution to ethnographic knowledge and ethnological theory, than would a team of five fieldworkers studying the same group for a single year. This is even more likely to be true when the "loner" also has field experiences in a variety of other societies, as have all the authors represented here.

Long-Term Field Research
in Social Anthropology

Convinced by his experiences in New Guinea and Spain of the advantages of long-term field research, Meggitt argues that anthropologists who limit themselves to single short-term projects run the risk of making "increasingly formulistic and dogmatic statements" about the societies they study. He believes that a series of revisits prevents fieldworkers from being blinded to alternative explanations of behavior and constantly reminds them of human variability. This viewpoint is particularly striking in the face of Meggitt's training in the tradition of British functionalism. When he began fieldwork among the Mae Enga of New Guinea in 1955–1957, he was predisposed to assume that he could learn what was necessary about their way of life in a finite period of time. Thus, he made no commitment to long-term research among this group. He soon realized, however, that shifts in many domains of Mae Enga society needed to be charted over time. He is now committed to "returning to the Mae at fairly regular intervals to record the general patterns of sociocultural changes." His general ethnographic approach touches so many topics (e.g., the structure and dynamics of the lineage system, religious organization, patterns of political leadership, and the resurgence of intergroup warfare), that he is far from reaching the point of diminishing returns in his fieldwork among the Mae Enga. This generalist perspective leads Meggitt to believe, if not prescribe, that anthropologists should gather a wide range of "basic geographical, meterological, and census data, detailed material on the economy and technology, on the kinship system, and on the organization of social groups, ranks and classes." Unfortunately, this is an ideal achieved by too few fieldworkers.

In his study of Tirolean peasants in Austria (as in his earlier study of a New Guinea tribal group), Pospisil illustrates the value of this general approach to ethnographic inquiry. In the peasant village of Obernberg, he has systematically collected an immense quantity of data since 1962: more than 1600 detailed interviews concerning the villagers' social, economic, political, and religious activities; transcripts of some 7000 official records related to the community's economic and sociopolitical structure; detailed maps showing year-to-year changes in land utilization for over 1500 village plots; exhaustive case materials on some 700 economic transactions; and 450 cases of nonlegal conflict and life-cycle incidents, as well as 168 "trouble" cases and several hundred court cases.

This remarkable body of ethnographic data permits Pospisil to present a "portrait of cultural dynamism" among the Tirolean peasants just as he had previously for the Kapauku Papuans of New

Guinea. In both cases, his general studies form part of his effort to arrive at a "valid, comparative, and dynamic theory of law and social control." Unlike Meggitt, Pospisil has consciously followed Kluckhon's example of continous study from the outset. This comparative, long-term perspective permits Pospisil to test a wide range of hypotheses within an holistic context.

In addition to his theoretical interests in comparative legal systems, he believes that he is on the verge of a major breakthrough with respect to what he terms the processes of acculturation and urbanization in the contemporary world. His conclusions, he argues, could not be obtained by social scientists who narrowly restrict their inquiries through prematurely conceived "analytical models." Thus, he echoes Meggitt's call for broad ethnographic empiricism as an adequate foundation for anthropological theories.

In contrast to Pospisil's early commitment to long-term field studies, Helm considers her research among the Dogrib and other Dene people of Canada to be a "continuing afterthought." For more than 25 years her research has led her to examine many topics, bringing some to completion, abandoning others after a brief period, and still pursuing several unresolved questions. Far from being predetermined, her fieldwork seems to be "continually creating itself," as she moved from her initial study of a tiny contemporary community to a broader interest in historical and regional problems affecting all Dene.

Helm argues that long-term fieldwork is appropriate for studying both variations and alterations in sociocultural systems. The transformation of contemporary Dogrib society through external forces and internal responses is well illustrated by the set of case histories she presents.

The final chapter in this section deals with Foster's three decades of fieldwork in the Mexican peasant village of Tzintzuntzan. His research is known not only for its ethnographic richness, but also for its theoretical incisiveness. It is noteworthy, therefore, that he believes his earlier work (conducted in 1945–1946) to be of much less theoretical value than his work carried out annually since his return in 1958. He also makes a strong case for the importance of serendipity, or what he calls "trigger mechanisms," in focusing his attention on particular aspects of the Tzintzuntzan way of life. He is convinced that the longitudinal perspective has permitted him to benefit from chance observations and, as a result, to reflect the magnitude of recent changes in Tzintzuntzan and Mexican society at large.

Foster also argues that his experiences in Tzintzuntzan suggest that anthropological theory emerging from short-term research too often "is based on a relatively static view of the community." He cites the controversy over his concept of "limited good" as a primary example. He not only illustrates his awareness of the importance of long-term research, but also disarms his critics with his statement, "It is possible that, had I begun my research in Tzintzuntzan in 1970, the idea of limited good would never have occurred to me."

The experiences of Foster, Helm, Pospisil, and Meggitt all reflect their commitment to basic ethnography as the cornerstone of subsequent theoretical innovations. Their pursuit of long-term research in widely dispersed communities involves a common thread: the belief that an intimate view of modernization at the local level provides crucial data for broader models of sociocultural transformation. Their contributions to anthropological methods and theories are touched by a humanistic perspective only found among those who have spent a lifetime to learn about another way of life.

5

Reflections Occasioned by Continuing Anthropological Field Research among the Enga of Papua New Guinea

M. J. Meggitt

INTRODUCTION

The Enga-speaking people, who today number more than 150,000, reside in the western highlands region of what was formerly the Territory of New Guinea, which was administered by the Government of Australia at first under a mandate from the League of Nations and subsequently as a trust territory of the United Nations Organization. In September 1975, Papua New Guinea became a self-governing nation, although it continues to maintain some economic links with Australia.

The Enga are sedentary horticulturalists who practice an intensive mode of long fallow cultivation well adapted to tropical high altitudes to produce their staple crop, sweet potatoes, which also supports their numerous pigs. Population densities, 300 to 400 persons per square mile in some localities, are considerable by Melanesian standards. All central Enga are members of named and territorially anchored patriclans that ideally are exogamous, politically autonomous, and self-sufficient in terms of subsistence. The clans are also elements of localized hierarchies of agnatic descent groups. Postmarital residence is normally viripatrilocal and inheritance patrilineal. Traditionally, magico-religious beliefs and

107

Long-Term Field Research
in Social Anthropology

activities were mainly concerned with propitiating ancestral spirits and domestic ghosts and with ensuring the continuing material welfare of clans and families. In the past, intergroup warfare over land was rife. Clan leadership was in the hands of the Big Men who achieved their power and influence primarily through their dealings in the frequent public exchanges of valuables (notably of pigs) in which descent groups were engaged. In many respects, Enga society could be regarded as being typically Melanesian. Since the 1940s, however, the people's contacts with Europeans have led to significant changes in certain local institutions.

My field research, which has been especially concerned with the Mae Enga division of these people, was carried out during the years 1955–1957, 1960, 1961–1962 (all three sojourns financially supported by the University of Sydney), 1967 (supported by the University of Michigan), 1970 and 1973 (supported by the Wenner–Gren Foundation). Joan Meggitt, who has accompanied me on all but one (1960) of these field trips, has devoted her energies to pursuing investigations among Mae Enga women, as well as to making archival inquiries and to the logistics of field subsistence.

Before undertaking my initial fieldwork in New Guinea, I had completed two field studies (1953–1954 and 1954–1955) among the Walbiri Aborigines of Central Australia. The advantages accruing from a second visit to the same people were immediately apparent to me. Accordingly, I determined that in my next field research, wherever it was to be, I would try to ensure that I spent more than one period in the chosen area. Nevertheless, when the opportunity arose to work in the New Guinea highlands, I did not have any clear cut intention of following a long-term program of investigations there. Indeed, I was predisposed by my training in the tradition of British functionalism to assume (however tacitly and naively) the feasibility of discovering in a finite period of time what I needed to know about "the society," taken as a bounded and somehow stable entity.

Analysis of the results of the first Enga fieldwork (1955–1957) demonstrated to me that an understanding of the man–land ratio, the use of the land, and the popular attitudes held about it was crucial to any reasonable explanation of many important features of Mae society—such as the segmentary lineage system, political arrangements, the organization of ceremonial exchanges of valuables, religious beliefs, and rituals—and that these relationships of men to land were not as fixed or as static as Enga ideology might suggest. Their shifts through time had to be charted in terms not only of demographic fluctuations but also of the over all effectiveness or adaptability of the intensive system of horticulture. Accordingly, I managed to return to the Mae in 1960 and 1961–1962 to make restudies of land holding and residential distributions in the sample neighborhood of clan groups.

By that time, obvious changes (from the 1955–1957 situation) were occurring in response to governmental policy, the activities of Christian missions, and the tentative entry of the people into cash cropping and the world market for primary products. It was clear, even to a British functionalist, that continuing, albeit intermittent, investigations would be necessary in order to discover and to analyze the effects of these changes, as well as to keep testing the interim hypotheses that earlier data had generated concerning the systematic interconnections (or their absence) of a wide range of variables.

It was at this point that I explicitly committed myself to returning to the Mae at fairly regular intervals to record the general patterns of sociocultural changes which were taking place and also to examine in sequence specific loci of changes. To date, the main problems I have tackled have concerned the structure and dynamics of the lineage system, religious organization, the pattern of leadership, the complex of ceremonial exchanges, Mae involvement in the western economy, and, most recently, the resurgence of intergroup warfare (see Bibliography). Problems still to be investigated in depth include the inception of local government councils and their changing role in the context of national independence, the impact on local and regional political and economic aspirations of the growing number of Enga who have received secondary and tertiary "Western" education, the status of women in the new circumstances, the apparent revival of traditional rituals, the novel reliance on sorcery in disputes, and the increasing importance of indigenous curers in the face of the extension of western medical facilities.

As I look back on the history of this research, I am struck afresh by the shift from my original assumption that successful prosecution of field inquiries would in some manner necessitate only two or three sojourns among the Mae to the recognition that in a real sense there is no end in view. This belated insight, of course, raises the question whether it would have been better to have planned right from the start for the second alternative. That is, would such an approach have led to the establishment of a different scale of priorities that in turn would have proved more productive of results, more economical of time and money spent in the field? On balance, even with the benefit of hindsight, I do not think so. Whether 1 trip or 20 was envisaged, the investigations of fundamental social structural arrangements, land use and population figures would have to be undertaken first, as indeed they were, whereas the subsequent examinations of modes and loci of particular social, economic, political, and religious changes would in any case have been dependent on what was in fact happening to and among the people; that is, on the historical order of events as they occurred. The latter sequence could hardly have been predicted at the outset of the field research, even in the light of what was then already known about changes in other parts of Melanesia and in other colonial areas.

SITUATIONS SUITABLE TO LONG-TERM RESEARCH

Obviously, a program of long term research has been, and will continue to be, particularly appropriate in attempts to understand Mae Enga society and culture. Here we are concerned with a people who saw Europeans for the first time in the mid-1930s, became colonial wards in the late 1940s, have had a peasant economy overlaid on their tribal polity, and are now citizens of a newly independent country that is struggling to define its identity and national goals and to protect its autonomy from the economic encroachments of the major Pacific powers, especially of Australia, Japan, and the U.S.A. Events at every stage of this known, albeit brief, history have much to tell anthropologists and can be drawn on to provide direct empirical tests of their hypotheses and assumptions (often tacit) about social and cultural change and stability. Clearly, similar kinds of situations have occurred or still persist elsewhere in Oceania and Africa; situations posing problems that are equally suitable for long-term investigation. Moreover, my research experience among other peoples (that is, the Walbiri in 1953–1954, 1954–1955 and 1959–1960 and the Andalusians of southwestern Spain in 1968, 1969, 1971, 1972 and 1975) persuades me that here, too, real advantages accrue from pursuing field inquiries over a number of years. Indeed, the fact that repeated sojourns among three peoples whose social circumstances are markedly different have in all cases been undeniably productive suggests that long-term field investigations are probably the ideal to be aspired to in most anthropological research.

THE CONTINUED CHALLENGE IN LONG-TERM RESEARCH

However, even if we grant the assumption that continuing field research is in most cases a consummation devoutly to be desired, should we not remain alert to the possibility that such inquiries inevitably reach a point of producing diminishing returns to the extent that further investment is no longer warranted? The investigator may be blind to the fact that this point is already passed.

It is true that there may be certain sociocultural phenomena (e.g., kinship terminology or "ethno-categories") about which the anthropologist gains less and less new knowledge with each successive field trip. If this is the whole point of fieldwork, it would be hard to make a case for devoting yet more time and money to this preoccupation. An investigator may also reach the stage where there seems little more to discover about, say, the "traditional" mode of stock raising in a given community, whether in terms of allied social arrangements, economic returns, or ecological consequences. But it would be a rare, indeed a bizarre, society that was not changing in some or many of its elements during the period of those investigations; changes, whether in the very mode of stock raising itself or in residential distribution, rules of recruitment to groups, or systems of exchange, are likely to be in just those social fields of prime theoretical interest to the anthropologist. It is by trying to understand observed variations in particular social phenomena that the "essential" features of the phenomena emerge and it becomes possible to trace out their patterns of interaction and disjunction.

Obviously, the magnitudes, rates and significance of such changes, even in what purport to be the same institutions, will differ from one society to another, if only because societies find themselves in different situations *vis-à-vis* their physical environments, their neighbors, metropolitan powers, and so on. But the fact remains that in most, perhaps all, societies many of the variables critical to anthropological understanding of social systems will manifestly be changing. The fieldworker faces the problem of accounting for these changes, both retrospectively and predictively. To this extent then, the work is never done and the anthropologist's inquiries, *over all,* do not reach a dead end or a point of diminishing returns. In effect, little or nothing continues to be wholly familiar—there is no stepping twice into the same stream. The very mutability of the data prevent the fieldworker from taking them for granted.

Indeed, it seems to me that the real danger of familiarity breeding contempt, or at least leading to dulling or obfuscation of perception, attaches to the situation of the anthropologist who makes but one sojourn in an alien society and then spends the rest of his academic career sorting and resorting the one collection of data. Such an anthropologist is much more likely to make the mistake of believing that he has seen all there is to see of significance in that society and in the data and that, in some osmotic way, he really understands all about them. Having no comparative evidence drawn from changed situations observed later in time with which to test ideas about the original material, he may well go on to make increasingly formulistic and dogmatic statements about the latter without perceiving all of its significant aspects and covert interconnections.

The anthropologist himself undergoes complex changes during a continuing series of field investigations. One obvious fact is that most fieldworkers (even the many slow learners among us) do become more proficient with practice. In the most pragmatic terms, a summer field trip of 2 or 3 months among people with whom one has already worked several times is basically economical of time and money. In such a period, an experienced investigator can not only carry out quickly and effectively the necessary repetitive studies of essential areas of inquiry (for instance, census taking; making land, residential, and occupational surveys), he can simultaneously look into specific problems (such as the impact of the introduction of cash crops or of adult suffrage). A newcomer to that society would be hard put to it to secure a comparable range of pertinent and reliable data in the same time.

The returning fieldworker, unless he has trodden on his hosts' toes earlier, is likely to have little difficulty in reestablishing friendly relations provided that there has been no radical change in the total political and economic situation during his absence (and it is the obligation of the anthropologist to inform himself about such changes). People know who he is; they have by now a fair idea of what it is that he does. They can, on his return, probably accept him without any great anxiety as a more or less cogenial and basically harmless and trustworthy adjunct to the community.

Also to be considered are the observable changes that the investigator undergoes through his own process of aging during this period. He may have begun his field inquiries as a fresh-faced, exuberant bachelor, exhibiting social and personal characteristics likely to lead his hosts into placing him in a particular social category. That placement in turn probably affected the degree to which they were willing to divulge to him information, whether religious, political, or economic, that they considered to be of strategic value. Five or six field trips and 20 years later during which the people have seen the anthropologist gradually turn into a grey haired and restrained head of a family, he may be regarded as a more appropriate repository of such knowledge. Indeed, as I have found, a surprising number of his hosts may now turn to him for counsel not only about modes of dealing with "foreigners," but also about ways of operating profitably within their own community.

Finally, if the anthropologist is halfway intelligent, then throughout professional life his research interests or emphases are likely to shift to the extent that he is conversant with developments in his own and cognate disciplines—so much so that he may no longer be concerned with the kinds of inquiries that preoccupied him at the outset of his field career (for instance, the meaning of kinship terms or the categorization of types of firewood) and instead concentrate successively on other issues, such as indigenous adaptations to Western economic demands or the rise of local political parties. Such transformations, in my opinion, make him at least a more interesting anthropologist and, hopefully, a more productive one as well. Not only is he now more likely to be able to generate a better balanced and more exhaustive account of that society, past and present, but also he is in a position to make a wider range of intellectual contributions to his discipline.

COMMON QUESTIONS FOR LONG-TERM STUDIES

My assertions about the inevitability of changes in both fieldworkers and the societies they study may well have given the impression that each instance of long-term research, while being potentially or ideally a good thing, is nevertheless wholly idiosyncratic, being as much an existential experience for the investigator as it is a means of substantially advancing the development of the discipline. Am I implicitly ruling out the possibility, let alone the desirability, of any kind of standardization? Obviously, if I believe, as I do, in the need for some degree of intersubjectivity in the presentation of the results of research in anthropology, I cannot reply with an unqualified affirmative. Anthropologists may not be "scientists" in any significant sense of this term, but they are bound at least by minimal canons of rigorous inquiry into, and rational definitions of, the problems that attract them.

At the same time, I see no particular virtue in any attempt to establish rigid guidelines or formulas within which every fieldworker, whether working on a long-term basis or not, should operate and according to which he should order his research priorities—even if this were a feasible requirement. It seems to me better, in general, that each individual's intelligence and common sense be trusted and personal interests be respected.

However, I do believe that there are certain kinds of essential information that the fieldworker, whatever his own research concerns may be, has a real obligation to gather and later to publish for the benefit of his colleagues, including those whose specific interests may differ largely from his own. This information includes, for instance, basic geographical, meteorological, and census data, detailed material on the economy and technology, on the kinship system, and on the organization of social groups, ranks, and classes. Clearly, most investigators, whether they plan one field sojourn or many, do try to secure such information early in their inquiries, for the obvious reason that, without the presentation somewhere at some time of such "contextual" data, anything else they publish (no matter how elegant the analysis) will remain for their readers very much in a vacuum and to that extent be largely unintelligible—or at least be not especially useful for comparative purposes.

But, whereas I can perceive that reference to *Notes and Queries* or to the *Ethnographic Atlas* may remind the fieldworker of areas of social and cultural significance that would repay investigation, I would not wish to see our discipline become one in which every anthropologist sets off for the field with a standardized and temporally arranged check list in hand through which he plods laboriously at the expense of seizing on whatever unexpected, interesting, and perhaps much more illuminating events and situations that are burgeoning around him.

Whatever it is we are as anthropologists, we are not "hard scientists" routinely setting up wholly controlled and infinitely replicable laboratory experiments. Rather, I think we are more or less sensitive social historians. Our hypotheses and explanations and their imaginative (and essentially nonrigorous) testing are the products of our personal capacities to respond both to the changing field situation and to ideas (old and new) current in our own discipline and in others such as history, political economy, and human geography.

In sum, any standardization of field research (whether this is short- or long-term) should, it seems to me, be limited and compatible with common sense notions of personal independence, moral responsibility, and the need to maintain flexibility of inquiry in the face of varying or newly appearing problems.

ORGANIZATION OF RESEARCH

Another question arising from the assumption that continuing field research in a given society is likely to be worth pursuing concerns the extent to which such an undertaking should be carried out in concert or successively by several anthropologists. A particular issue would be that of specifying the ways in which the initiator of the research program makes provision for the incorporation of younger colleagues into the venture.

I have never participated in an organized "team" situation in the field, nor have I had colleagues, other than my wife or assistants, formally involved in my work. I am not sure that I am competent to comment on such matters. However, it does seem obvious that, where joint, repeated research is envisaged, a real problem exists in devising efficient and ethically acceptable procedures for fitting additional investigators into an established or even a nascent program. Such an arrangement must demand delicate handling to ensure that the effectiveness and productivity of the inquiry are not impaired, while at the same time the individual egos (and some anthropologists appear to cherish remarkably tender psyches) remain unbruised and the actors' perceptions of their own integrity are not rudely contradicted. It is no doubt difficult for a "recognized" initiator of an ongoing field study to treat later arriving junior colleagues as full partners with their own independent ideas and different orders of research priority, and not merely as assistants bound to examine solely those problems (or even only aspects of them) that the senior person regards as significant or urgent. Nevertheless, it is patent that equity and humility must prevail if the undertaking is not to dissolve into dissension and back biting.

A further issue, perhaps the converse of the above, is whether or not some form of special training must be provided for students of anthropology to prepare them for participation in long-term research projects. On balance, I do not think that such preparation has to differ significantly from that which, ideally, any prospective fieldworker should receive. For instance, whatever the particular research interests with which a student may begin, it is unlikely nowadays that the society in which he chooses to pursue them will be one about which nothing of consequence is already known. The student does not select a field locality at random or simply out of ignorance. Accordingly, whether the student plans to make one sojourn in that society or ten, he will prepare himself in much the same manner—by familiarizing himself with every scrap of information already available for that society, by immersing himself in the literature relevant to the region, by reflecting on everything already written on the research issues he has in mind, and, in the light of all this knowledge, by trying to sharpen the theoretical rationale for the inquiries he proposes to make.

Once in the field, the investigator will probably find that much of what he thought he knew is factually incorrect or misleading, and that much of what he does discover is a function of the shifting field situation itself and of the changes his ideas undergo in response to it. Obviously, the anthropologist who contrives to return several times to that society is in a better position to make his amendments and adjustments than is the fieldworker who can count only on one visit there.

Finally, some comment should be made on the obligations devolving on the individual who chooses to undertake a course of long-term fieldwork on his own in a given society. This is the situation in which I find myself. The important consideration here, it seems to me, is that such a "loner" must from the start accept the responsibility of disseminating his results and his ideas promptly as he proceeds, so that other anthropologists with common research interests, whether topical or areal, can quickly assess the validity of his work and draw his attention to any deficiencies or apparent errors of interpretation. Indeed, his critics, if they are markedly dissatisfied with the quality of his research or are unconvinced of the tenability of the proffered hypotheses and explanations, can themselves go to that area to make their own inquiries.

Naturally, an investigator who has initiated a continuing program in a particular society may expect others who also wish to work there to offer him some professional courtesies, such as discussing the advisability or practicality of making related inquiries among the same people. But, whatever his personal feelings of annoyance at what he may view as an intrusion, he has no right to stake a claim in perpetuity to a people, society, or community and to try for no other compelling reason to discourage other anthropologists from going there. Unfortunately, some egotists attempt to do just that.

My own experience in this regard has been that, following my initial research among and publications about both the Walbiri and the Enga, others have worked with these people, both to test some of my formulations and, more importantly, to assay their own, different ideas. Without exception, this situation of multiple, independent investigations in the same area has proved to be mutually stimulating and profitable. An important consequence is that the discipline does not have to rest content with the one picture of the society, filtered through the mind, biases, and preconceptions of only one anthropologist.

RESEARCH RESULTS

As I have always regarded myself primarily as an ethnographer, I am reluctant to suggest that my field research has produced theoretical results of any great moment. However, I firmly believe that a significant personal benefit stemming from my being able to observe several communities over periods of time has been that I have become more and more aware of the importance of temporal changes and of the need for the anthropologist to be an historian or at least an historiographer (in the more restricted sense of chronicler of events). Time and again I have seen my own and other investigators' predictions and explanations overset because they did not take sufficient account of historical processes and trends affecting the society being studied.

In support of this assertion, I give here an example of the kind of error into which the ethnographer may fall when, early in the course of his investigations, he hits upon what then appears to him to be a satisfactory functional (and probably static) "explanation" for the existence of a particular state of affairs. Subsequently, it may be years later, the situation changes in such a way as to reveal the magnitude of his misconception and, no doubt, the extent of his former naivete. But, if the fieldworker had not been able to sustain his inquiries over the long-term, he might never have been confronted with the evidence of his mistake. I refer here to my own attempts to grapple with the fact of the relative unimportance of sorcery, both in belief and practice, among the Mae Enga when I first encountered them in the 1950s.

On the basis of my observations, as well as of the reports of various missionaries, I was satisfied (I still believe rightly so) that there was a fundamental homogeneity in Enga world view, cosmology, and religious assumptions. Everywhere people made much the same statements about the constitution and significance of sky beings, ancestral spirits, ghosts and demons, and they all drew on elements of a common corpus of ritual techniques. In the sphere of magic, including sorcery, one could also perceive general similarities in the views they held about the nature of such phenomena. Nevertheless, there were marked differences from area to area in the range of popular knowledge about magical procedures (again including sorcery), in the emphasis placed on their efficacy, and in the frequency with which they were employed—and it was among the Mae that recourse to magic seemed to be the most limited.

This is not to assert that the Mae at that time did not on occasion acquire and utilize magic. A few men, notably Big Men, procured from foreign trade- or exchange-partners spells and materials, which they used to supplement their own exertions in the hope of achieving success in material transactions. But, compared with, for instance, the Laiapu Enga, Mae men and women scarcely bothered with, and indeed knew little about, the kinds of magic intended to promote the growth of crops or of pigs, to trap eels or cassowaries, to stop rain, to prevent thefts, and so on. Whenever I pressed men on this matter, their reply was that hard work, expertise, and good weather were necessary and largely sufficient to ensure adequate returns in subsistence activities. Given the application of these factors, it was unnecessary to call on magic as well—whereas without them the employment of magic alone would not produce rich crops or big pigs. Indeed, some men were equally skeptical about the utility of deploying magic in public presentations or in warfare, arguing that all such magic did was to augment the confidence of a man who already had reason to trust his own negotiating or military skills.

Moreover, although it was generally believed that a few Mae men (again usually Big Men) purchased from foreigners spells and information about modes of sorcery, not only were these rarely, if ever, thought to be employed but also most men were ignorant of, and incurious about, such devices.

> Yes, [they said] we know these techniques exist, and we have heard that some Enga, especially the Saui and the Laiapu, use them frequently; but we don't bother with them. There is no need to do so. If we [the men of a clan] are angry with an outsider or with an enemy group, sooner or later we contrive to kill our adversaries in ambush or in battle. Using an axe or a spear to avenge wrongs or insults is much more dependable than performing sorcery and, besides, it is personally more satisfying to cut down an enemy at close quarters. [In that way one can also magnify his reputation as a "killer of men".]

By the 1950s, the officers of the Australian Administration had succeeded in persuading most of the Mae that recourse to violence, whether murder or interclan warfare, was not the best way to settle the disputes that so often convulsed local clans, in particular those which arose over land and other property seen to be in short supply. In place of bloodshed, the Administration offered the opportunity to litigate in the Courts for Native Affairs, whose judgments were given essentially in terms of British justice and rules of evidence. The Mae, by and large, were willing to put up their axes and bows and to try the new system. Litigation appeared to them to be a useful way of achieving their ends, one that economized on time, energy, and blood and would allow them to get on with their all important gardening and exchanges without the interruptions posed by war.

Thus, from about 1952 to about 1962 Mae men became active, enthusiastic, and increasingly knowledgeable litigants, and the rate of homicide obviously declined. During this decade, I was impressed by what appeared to be the neatness with which intergroup litigation, in both formal and informal courts, was serving as an effective sociocultural alternative to traditional forms of murder and warfare. In particular, it seemed to me that one could not maintain in a simple manner the view that covert expressions of aggression or hostility in the guise of sorcery or witchcraft are probable, if not inevitable functional substitutes for physical violence when the latter is suppressed by external, superior forces. More had to be known about other alternatives, such as the characteristics of the legal system available to the people in question and how they perceived them.

Meanwhile, I was satisfied that for the Mae, at any rate, the Courts for Native Affairs provided an acceptable arena in which disputants could resolve matters that formerly impelled them to violence—and that the people could look forward with some confidence to a relatively peaceful future.

I was wrong, of course. In partial exculpation of my own error, I may say that the Mae also took some time to understand that, in fact, given their circumstances, reliance on the modes of British justice could not in itself be a solution to the real and pressing problems exercising them. The basic issue still facing the central Enga was that of continually adjusting the boundaries of, and titles to, specific tracts of land to meet the changing needs that corporate descent groups experienced as their actual populations increased or decreased. Because such local demographic variations were not always unidirectional and could be relatively rapid, flexibility and a degree of equivocality were necessary for the effective exploitation of events. That is, a clan wanted to be able to keep its options open in holding or obtaining the land it required. The way to do this was, depending on circumstances, variously to employ duplicity, overt threat, or physical violence (culminating in all-out warfare) with the aim that, win, lose, or draw, the group could return once more to the struggle with its equally rapacious neighbours and try again to retrieve lost land, to keep existing land, or to acquire more land. Short of complete dispossession and dispersal of a militarily defeated group, no outcome was accepted as precluding further action by either contestant.

It was precisely in this respect that recourse to western courts was unsatisfactory. The judicial decision of a magistrate concerning the definition and location of a land boundary was ideally unequivocal, final, binding, and publicly recorded for future reference, a state of affairs that suited neither plaintiffs nor defendants. The losers in a land case naturally wanted an opportunity to reopen the issue when it pleased them, in the hope of recovering the tract in question; the winners, confirmed in their opinion by their victory, did not want to be prevented from going on to secure even more land from adversaries whose "weakness" had been exposed by defeat. Without reactivating the matter through a legal appeal to a higher court or lands commissioner (which was not easy to do), neither party could press on with that particular battle in court and, in effect, had to turn to the old forms of chicanery and forcible disseizement in order to achieve its ends.

In consequence, by the early 1960s the Mae were less and less inclined to litigate over such important issues as possession of land, trees, or pigs, and the incidence of violent confrontations between groups increased. But, although the people were once again ready to fight in old ways over old issues, the total situation had in many respects deteriorated and their problems had in fact become exacerbated by other changes that had taken place during this decade of relative peace.

On the one hand, there had been a substantial growth in the population of the central Enga (of the order of 2% per annum). This stemmed in part from the peace itself, which saw a decline in deaths from murder, in war, from wounds, or as a result of forced flight, and in part from dietary additions; but mainly it reflected the significant extension of health services throughout the region with concomitant reduction of the mortality of mothers, of infants, and, also important, of pigs. On the other hand, the introduction of cash cropping (for instance, of coffee, pyrethrum, and exotic vegetables) and of cattle projects not only removed certain areas from subsistence cultivation but also redefined and increased the worth of land. In short, the ratio of people to land was now worse than it had been before the imposition of peace—and the Enga were becoming very much aware of this.

Together with this recognition of increasing pressure on critical resources went a perceptible heightening of tension in intergroup relations. Disputes over land and pigs quickened, brawls became more frequent, as did homicide and arson, and by the end of the 1960s, notwithstanding vigorous countermeasures on the part of the central authorities, interclan warfare was recurring among Laiapu and Mae Enga. Despite the appearance of technological innovations such as the use of steel axes and motor transport (but not guns), the fighting was carried on very much as it had been in the past—raids, ambushes, full-scale attacks, and set-piece battles—and the casualty rates were of the same order as before. This state of affairs has persisted well into 1975.

Given the obligation of the police and riot squads of the Administration to halt such hostilities, often the combatants are dispersed and some arrested before the engagement runs its "natural" course whereby the stronger force defeats its opponents and secures at least part of the coveted land. A period of uneasy peace follows as the frustrated aggressors await the return of their warriors from jail and plan another attack.

What is striking nowadays is that not only do both groups undertake the activities traditionally appropriate to a temporary truce, such as looking to their defences, mounting patrols, evacuating noncombatants and pigs, courting potential allies, and seizing opportunities to waylay unwary members of the enemy clan, but they may also implement novel interim measures to strengthen their respective positions. In particular, the Mae have turned to the practice of sorcery to protect clan interests. However, as far as I could determine, they do not display any great interest in utilizing "coastal" forms of sorcery, even though it is evident that some men now know about these, either from their contacts with coastal Papuans and New Guineans working in Wabag or from their sojourns on the plantations and in towns "down below."

Instead, there is an explicit (and I think growing) reliance on the kinds of sorcery that the Mae have always believed to be used by other Enga, especially by the Laiapu and the Saui. Now, when two clans have been fighting or are poised ready to resume the struggle, some of their members (often at the behest of their Big Men) exploit the communication network linking their extraclan relatives and exchange partners to ascertain from whom among the eastern Enga they can procure the necessary spells and other objects to use against their enemies. Then some of these men take the opportunity surreptitiously to visit the likely vendors, with whom they secretly bargain for the appropriate advice and material, generally on the understanding that, when the sorcery proves efficacious, the seller will be paid in cash, pigs, or pork.

Such evidence as I have (and this is not an easy matter to investigate, given that dabbling in sorcery is a crime) indicates that buyers are usually not especially concerned to obtain the kinds of sorcery that aim to injure or kill one particular victim. Rather, they prefer any of the forms that have a shot-gun effect, whereby the enemy group is thought to be assailed in several different ways simultaneously or in quick succession—suffering deaths, illnesses, accidents, house burnings, and loss of crops. That is, the current Mae view of the value of "total" sorcery against the opposed corporate group accords well with their traditional notion of "total" warfare as the best way to deal physically with such opponents. Apparently, the occurrence within a reasonable time of any of these misfortunes among the enemy is sufficient evidence of the efficacy of the sorcery and a warrant for the payment of the vendor.

In discussions with Mae men, I asked why they were now buying and using sorcery when in the past they did not attempt to do so. The answers were always much the same.

> Times have changed, and for the worse. Our enemies are stronger, more aggressive and more cunning. Our land is in danger and we might fight to keep it. Maybe sorcery will help in this, maybe it won't. But now that we travel about more and can more readily procure sorcery, we would be fools not to try it. And, if it doesn't work, we still have our axes. [Times may indeed have changed, but the essentially pragmatic attitude of the Enga has not.]

The point of this brief history is that, at each stage in the flow of events, it is all too easy for the ethnographer to believe that he has the explanation for what he sees then and that this view has some general validity that he does not have to question further. Thus, until the 1950s the Mae did not bother with sorcery because physical violence, including warfare, appeared to solve their problems. From the 1950s to the 1960s, with warfare suppressed, the Mae still had no need of sorcery because litigation was feasible. Although simple "functional" explanations may appear to be appropriate up to this point, they seem to me to fail in the face of the post-1960s situation, when not only was warfare substituted for litigation but sorcery was added to the people's repertoire of political activities.

To argue more generally, I believe that the great danger in reliance on synchronic investigations is that insensibly they may impose on the anthropologist a synchronic analysis, a theoretical set or predisposition that confirms him in an uncritical acceptance of factitious equilibrium or stability in the sociocultural complex he is observing. In consequence, as we see displayed repeatedly in anthropological monographs, stability is taken to be the norm and change the problem to be explained, whereas, if anything, the assertion should be the other way around.

Moreover, even if the anthropologist is alert to this trap and genuinely wishes to analyse the society diachronically, dependence on the results of a single field sojourn handicaps him unmercifully in this endeavor. I do not believe that the undertaking of a long delayed second restudy offers any automatic solution to this problem. Too often this procedure simply generates two synchronic studies, effectively separated in time and not essentially connected through time. The anthropologist is then landed with the further problem of having to explain how it is that his people (often the same individuals) have moved from (tacitly assumed) equilibrium position 1 to (tacitly assumed) equilibrium position 2.

In short, I am asserting that, especially in the study of societies for which there is a paucity of archival or other written historical records of depth, the average anthropologist really needs to be able to observe the same society or community frequently over a long period if he is to avoid the sterile, static scientism that too often characterizes our discipline in favor of a communicable and illuminating explanation of how and why that human society, as a people and as a more or less integrated system, exhibits both changes and continuities, which may be in marked conflict with each other. Finally, I believe that the undertaking of long-term, repeated investigations in a society enables the ethnographer to meet in an important way part of his obligations to the people, especially if they are still in the process of acquiring a culture of literacy. By this I mean that the anthropologist is in a position to compile a social history of the events that have occurred during the period of his acquaintance with that society. In this way he is not simply acting as a folklorist intent on salvaging popular traditions, he is also providing a reasonably objective record (that is, one less biased in the direction of "Western" interests and assumptions) on which the indigenous historians of the future can base their own interpretations of their society's past. This, I would argue, is one of the most valuable returns that we as anthropologists can make to the people who have helped us.

IMPACT OF RESEARCH

The anthropologist's continuing or intermittent presence within a community, whatever the duration of this social and personal interaction, must have effects on expectations and attitudes. The consequent alterations in behavior must in turn generate feedback responses in the total situation. However, given the ego involvements of both anthropologist and hosts, it may not be easy for either to assess in any clear or objective fashion the extent, the permanence, or the ultimate significance of these induced changes. Perhaps only a third person, a less committed outside observer, could successfully make such an evaluation. Certainly I do not regard myself as being competent to specify, let alone to judge dispassionately, the outcomes of the ongoing interchanges in which many Mae Enga men and women and I have been engaged over the years.

Nevertheless, I will venture a few observations based on my field experience that may be of passing interest. Clearly, one must distinguish between the impact of the investigator's presence on the particular community or neighborhood in which he lives from that on the society at large—and this raises the issue of the "scale" of both the category of the hosts and of the guests. No doubt long-term inquiries carried out by a fieldworker (and especially by a team of anthropologists) among a small society such as the Walbiri could well have pervasive effects on the whole people, even though the outsider does not readily perceive them. On the other hand, it may be that when an ethnographer visits, however frequently, a populous society those of its members who do not reside near the neighborhood(s) in which he usually works remain largely unaware of his very existence. This seems to have been the case with respect to my own research among the Enga, who number well over 150,000 and live in a series of high valleys. Moreover, some people, such as the Enga or the Andalusians, appear to be relatively incurious (at least overtly) about the status and activities of an outsider whose presence does not directly impinge on them, whereas the reverse is true of rural (and perhaps also of urban) Aborigines, who habitually categorize every individual with whom they have even the slightest acquaintance and consequently commit themselves to some kind of real response to his existence.

To deal more specifically with the question of my estimation of the effects of my activities on the neighborhood of Enga clans, within which I have dwelt intermittently since 1955, is also not easy. I have to distinguish between those clanspeople on whose territory I in fact lived (and their fraternal clans and political allies) and those clans with whom "my" people are generally at odds.

With respect to the latter, the answer is clear enough. They identify me as a member in some basic sense of my host clan, regard me in the same unfavorable light as an enemy, and, by and large, avoid having any dealings with me. They make it obvious to me that I am unwelcome in their domains and, were I to try to enter them, I should probably be attacked physically. To become the target of such opprobrium is the price the long-term investigator pays when working in a number of societies in the highlands of New Guinea; his acceptance by some groups automatically entails his rejection by others, their political adversaries, and this response has of late been exacerbated by the swelling tide of intergroup violence that is, for eminently understandable reasons, washing through these regions.

There is no doubt that over a long period any anthropologist of ordinary sensitivity finds this unrelenting hostility unpleasant, even wearing, but he must learn to tolerate it if he is to continue working in that society. Parenthetically, I may remark that it would be as well if more students in training for field research were warned of the possibility that they too may find themselves in similar circumstances, and that these conditions will not dissipate with the simple effluxion of time or with repeated visits to that area. If anything, they may become more pronounced. Visitors are not necessarily loved simply because they smile a lot and mean well.

Conversely, I believe that among the people who have initially accepted the anthropologist as harmlessly neutral or, more positively, have responded to him with helpful amity (for whatever altruistic or manipulatory motives), his frequent sojourns among them (always assuming he is not basically socially inept or myopic) are of some significance on at least two grounds. On the one hand, the people are given multiple opportunities to decide about their own feelings toward the outsider, and they can feel that they are freely deciding on abundant evidence whether or not they really do want him in their midst. On the other hand, the return visits of the anthropologist to the same people may (but do not always) persuade them that, for various reasons, he does want to be there, and that, in an important sense, he finds their company congenial and rewarding. He is not a casual visitor, a transient who went there once and never returned with the implication that he did not care for what he encountered in that community.

However that may be, the one apparently dependable conclusion that I have reached, one that I think worth emphasizing, is that over the long haul as the anthropologist and his hosts come to know each other more intimately (and on both sides this personal awareness can become almost alarmingly intense), a basis can emerge for the unforced growth of a mutual but unsentimental trust, with all the pressing moral obligations and serious practical responsibilities that such a relationship entails for both the visitor and his hosts. Not only is each often in a position to help the other achieve his explicit goals, but also each generally wants to do so.

BIBLIOGRAPHY

Meggitt, M. J.
1956   The valleys of the Upper Wage and Lai rivers. *Oceania 27*:90–135.
1958a   The Enga of the New Guinea Highlands. *Oceania 28*:253–330.
1958b   Salt manufacture and trading in the western highlands. *Australian Museum Magazine 12*:309–313.
1962a   The growth and decline of agnatic descent groups among the Mae Enga. *Ethnology 1*:158–165.
1962b   Dream interpretation among the Mae Enga. *Southwestern Journal of Anthropology 18*:216–229.
1964a   Male–female relationships in the Highlands of New Guinea. *American Anthropologist 66*:204–224.
1964b   The kinship terminology of the Mae Enga. *Oceania 34*:191–200.
1965a   The Mae Enga of the Western Highlands. In *Gods, ghosts, and men in Melanesia*, edited by Lawrence, P. and Meggitt, M. J. London: Oxford Univ. Press.
1965b   *The lineage system of the Mae Enga of New Guinea.* Edinburgh: Oliver and Boyd.
1967a   Some uses of literacy in New Guinea and Melanesia. *Bijdragen tot de Taal-, Land- en Volkenkunde 123*:71–82.
1967b   The pattern of leadership among the Mae Enga. *Anthropological Forum 2*:20–35.
1971   From tribesmen to peasants: The case of the Mae Enga. In *Anthropology in Oceania*, edited by Hiatt, L. R., and Jayawardena, C. Pp. 191–209. Sydney: Angus and Robertson.
1974   Studies in Enga history. *Oceania Monograph, 20*. Sydney: Univ. of Sydney Press.
1977   *Blood is their argument.* Palo Alto, California: Mayfield.

6

The Tirolean Peasants of Obernberg: A Study in Long-Term Research

Leopold Pospisil

INTRODUCTION

It is often assumed that ethnographic research is the focus of the academic endeavors of the anthropologist and that its locus represents his first choice of geographic area, selected on the basis of a long-lasting interest in the country and its people. Undoubtedly, this is true of most of the area specialists. In my case, the fieldwork happened to be a corollary to my theoretically oriented inquiry into the nature and function of law. Selection of the cultures I have studied depended on practical considerations and the requirements of my theoretical work rather than on my ethnographic interest in a given area. Indeed, if I had had my choice, my study would have led me either to the Tarim Basin of Central Asia or into the Ruwenzori Mountains of Central Africa.

After studying law in Czechoslovakia and anthropology at the University of Oregon and at Yale, I developed, on the basis of library research, a comparative theory of law, which I wished to test in the field. Because I was impressed by Malinowski's work, I wanted to follow his example. However, I also realized two of his shortcomings: He relied too much on the analysis of one culture (his fieldwork outside the Trobriand Islands

Long-Term Field Research
in Social Anthropology

was certainly not impressive) and he failed to study his Trobriand Islanders over a long enough period of time to allow him to analyze the dynamism of their culture. In this latter respect, I preferred the example of Kluckhohn's continuous study of the Navajo. In order to develop a comparative and dynamic theory of law and social control, I decided to study a series of societies of varied types and complexity. Accordingly, after a brief initial period with Edward Dozier among the Tewa Pueblo Indians of Arizona, I went to New Guinea and conducted my second and, this time, long-term research (1954–1955, 1959, 1962, 1975) among the Kapauku Papuans of the Wissel Lakes region; I used an opportunity to visit the Nunamiut Eskimo of Alaska (1957); and finally I decided upon a prolonged study of the Tirolean peasants of Austria (1962–1963, and summers 1964–1975).

Whereas the Eskimo had been nomadic hunters and gatherers without well-defined leadership, the Kapauku were sedentary people with a formalized hierarchy of headmen, who practiced shifting and mound cultivation. The Hopi–Tewa, for my purposes, were classified as transitory between a farming "tribal" society and an emerging civilization governed by formal chiefs. This series of increasingly complex societies is concluded by the Tirolean peasants who, as members of the European community, simultaneously practice informal customary settlement of village conflicts and are subject to formalized Austrian law which derives from the famous legal code of 1811. Thus I have tried to achieve the two research objectives: comparative data from societies of different evolutionary types and true portraits of cultural dynamism.

THE RELEVANCE OF THE LONG-TERM STUDY

One may ask whether a long-term study, with its expenditure of time and money, is not counterproductive. Most social anthropologists seem to have needed only 1 or 2 years of work in a single field to be able to write penetrating analyses. But where are the quantitative or detailed qualitative data on which their generalizations and intriguing conclusions are based? If, because there was too little time to master a complex language, the fieldworker used an interpreter or the lingua franca, are we not falling back into pre-Malinowski practices?

Irrespective of these questions, long-term investigation has several definite advantages. Other things being equal, a longer research period allows for both greater depth and the coverage of a wider field of inquiry, both leading to the accumulation of more data. I believe that long-term study is essential to good anthropological research which, even in a study as specialized as law, should be solidly based upon a knowledge of the culture as a whole. Unlike sociology, economics, or political science, anthropology does not rule out parts of the culture as "irrelevant" for a specialized inquiry. Anthropological research is thus radically different from that of an economist, for example, who in a Tirolean village would inquire only into economic matters and neglect matters which may be crucial to understanding the economic processes (e.g., political structure or the education of individual farmers). Obviously, a short-term research period precludes an initial holistic anthropological study, followed by specialized inquiry. One can also make predictions that can be verified later, as I was able to check predictions made on the basis of a study of the internalization of values (Pospisil 1958b; 1971:214–232). Thus the observation of long-term changes approaches in significance the experiments of natural scientists. In sum, the heuristic value of a true science is its ability to predict.

Long-term research also opens new areas of information to the worker. In all cultures there are important items which are either taboo in any discussion or are shared with only close friends and relatives. Among Kapauku Papuans, for example, practice of black magic, knowledge of witches, one's personal savings and profits, and political plans and aspirations are not discussed. Among the Tirolean peasants personal income, savings, smuggling to Italy, and political intrigues are kept secret. But for an analysis of the economy, say, these facts are indispensable. People are willing to surrender this information only to good friends. To make such friends in a short period is hardly possible. In many societies it may take several years. Long-term research is the obvious answer in this respect.

Short-term research precludes observation of the annual round of seasonal events and work, if shorter than a year. An anthropologist spending even 1 year in the field may fail to witness rare events or rituals which take place only at long intervals—a funeral, initiation, war, magical rites, a pig feast, or even a wedding. Any report on these events will rely solely upon the memories of informants—his data will be secondary and less reliable than those from direct observation. Some events, processes, and even types of attitudes and structural relationships vary in cycles, sometimes of several years' duration. To study just a segment of that cycle would invite distortion. The Kapauku pig feast is repeated in a given lineage approximately once in 6 years. If a scholar studied this society the first year after such a feast or the last year before it, his research would yield radically different results that would affect his economic interpretation. Similarly, to study the function, role, and behavior of an American president necessitates a 4-year study at a minimum because this happens to be the term of office though in many instances 8 years are needed. The behavior of the president prior to election, after election, or during his terminal year of office is marked by profound differences. To acquire a background for an adequate analysis of the presidency requires, therefore, coverage of all these phases of the tenure.

Short-term research cannot allow for a systematic study of a process as it happens (acculturation, borrowing, urbanization, etc.). It allows the anthropologist only to record the resultant change—in other words, it may provide the answer only to the question "What happened?" The answers to how and why it happened have to be provided again by reliance on informants' memories, and informants usually answer not in specifics but in convenient generalizations. The anthropologist thus cannot find out, for example, who conceived of a given idea, how this person influenced others to accept it, and how the idea was realized through specific actions. In this predicament, Durkheimean and Marxian jargons, with their denial of the importance of the individual, come as a blessing. All one has to do is to blame the change on the group, on "group will" and "public opin- ion." In this kind of ethnography, we sometimes read such obviously impossible statements as the "group decided," "the clan as a whole punished the offender" (as if the babies, the sick, and all the old men and women were involved). How much more precise and specific are the primatologists who study and identify particular actions of specific indi- vidual animals. Their generalizations are true abstractions, drawn from (*abstractu*) individual specific instances. Only prolonged research allows the actual study of a process in progress and provides the specifics.

Further, I take a categoric stand and claim that all social phenomena are dynamic in nature. Culture change does not imply a disturbance of any structural equilibrium that is normal to a society. Indeed, such an equilib- rium would be a highly abnormal phenomenon. Therefore, static models of a society are unrealistic. Sociocultural change need not be explained apart from the structure of a society—it should be part of it. As a consequence, study of a society ought to be done for a prolonged time to record properly the cyclical, repetitive, or one-directional changes in the observed behavior of the people. Thus it is not long-term research that needs justification and clarification, it is the brief *ad hoc* research, which, unfortunately, is growing practice in much of anthropology, that needs to be justified.

BACKGROUND AND HISTORY OF THE RESEARCH

I have been conducting two long-term investigations. Since part of my work on the Kapauku Papuans of West New Guinea has been published in several books and a series of articles, I have decided to outline in the following paragraphs my research among peasants of the North Tirol in Austria (see also Pospisil 1969).

Initially, for a period of 1 year (1962–1963), I studied Obernberg, a small secluded village of 350 inhibitants in a valley of the same name, near the Brenner Pass. The 11 years of follow-up research provided me with a unique opportunity to record a process of rapid transformation of a religious Central European peasant community, with its traditional culture and economy based on mountain farming and cattle breeding, into a secular settlement with a diversified commercialized economy based largely on tourism. This transition, whose onset and progress I have observed since 1963, has not been confined to the economy. The influx of many tourists, opportunities for employment other than farming, improved communication with the outside world, and an increasing supply of cash have stimulated further adjustments in the people's value system, social organization, religious attitudes, and social controls. Moreover, these changes have produced almost a political revolution within the power structure of the Obernberg society.

Despite the fact that the valley lies only a few miles west of one of Europe's most important communication arteries (the Brenner Pass road and railroad), until 1963, the time of my first research, Obernberg was still a peasant community in which much of the traditional Tirolean life was preserved. Its relative isolation was caused by the fact that its only communication with the outer world was a narrow winding road that climbed through a precipitous gorge. This precarious access discouraged automobile traffic. As a consequence the inhabitants of Obernberg maintained an economic and political conservatism, religious fervor, and village endogamy. The monolithic, political leadership derived its rather excessive power from the peasants' firm conviction that village disputes and problems ought to be settled within the village and not brought to the attention of state authorities.

Owing to the construction of a relatively wide and safe paved road, begun in 1964 and completed in 1967, the economic, social, and political life of Obernberg changed radically. The full impact of cultural change did not come until 1967 when the road was completed. Since then the ever-increasing flow of tourists has provided a large amount of cash which the farmers have reinvested mostly in the tourist trade. Only a part has been spent on farm machinery. The secluded, placid rustic Alpine valley attracted as many as 1500 cars over the weekends in the summers of 1970–1973. To accommodate the ever increasing flow of tourists, 4 new hotels have been built and guest rooms established in 24 farmhouses. In 15 of these flush toilets were installed, while in 12, complete bathrooms were added. Although the population of the valley has remained static, 12 new, modern villa-like houses have been built, and an additional 6 were under construction in 1975. To accommodate tourists during the summer mountain climbing season and the winter skiing, shelters (Alme) for cowherds and shepherds have been remodeled as guest cottages.

Since catering to tourists has proved more profitable than the meager mountain agriculture and the time-consuming production of hay, the acreage in grain and potatoes has been reduced and several of the steep mountain meadows have been changed to pastures or abandoned to forest. One of the meadows of the fertile valley floor has been planted with spruce trees. As a consequence the number of livestock has had to be reduced and cattle are kept and sold almost exclusively for breeding purposes. Sheep, ducks, and geese have disappeared completely.

The reorientation of the Obernberg economy toward tourism led to increasing dependence upon trade and the importation of food. Thus the traditional subsistence economy has given way to an open market-oriented system, dependent primarily upon cash derived partially from the sale of cattle and increasingly from services rendered to tourists. The city visitors brought young Obernbergers into contact with members of the opposite sex from the outside, thus contributing to the breakdown of the valley's endogamy. The villagers began to dress like townspeople and, in 1966, virtually all the girls and young women cut off their long braids and adopted "more fashionable" hair styles.

In the legal sphere, the amazing lack of dependence upon courts of law, which was so manifest in the years 1962–1963, gave way to reliance on state authorities and state courts for the settlement of local conflicts.

The influence of tourists is also being felt in the spheres of religion and politics. The once omnipotent local parish priest, although still retaining his religious prestige, has lost almost all influence in secular matters, with the exception of those involving education. Even in marital affairs his influence has slipped, and most of the villagers would not consider going to him for counseling and advice—a fact documented in the case studies. The peasants have begun to question their traditional conservatism; they have developed religious tolerance (toward Protestant tourists) and many of them have challenged the traditional clique that, virtually unopposed, had dominated the political life of the village until 1965. The progressive farmers, who had already elected several of their members to the village council, in the fall of 1969 scored their greatest victory (as predicted in my paper of 1969) by electing an able young farmer as mayor of the community. The next elections will most probably see the political power shift completely to the progressives of the Christian Catholic Party (*Österreichische Volkspartei*).

The progressive farmers followed up their political success by a systematic insistence upon accelerating the process of economic and social urbanization. They have already established a unified electrical supply for the village, derived from a single outside company (many of the inefficient, old, small electrical turbines of individual farmers have been abandoned) and have constructed a temporary ski lift. Two dirt and two paved roads leading into two steep side valleys of Obernberg have been constructed. The progressives were behind the building of the four new hotels, financed by local as well as outside capital.

At present, many new economic ventures are being planned: a unified water supply, a permanent large ski lift combined with a small tourist lodge on top of one of the mountain ridges, repair of dilapidated old watermills which are tourist attractions (two of these have already been designated "historical sites"—*Denkmalschutz*), and an extension of the paved road through the village to the end of the valley. However, the greatest project underway is construction of a dirt road up to the grass-covered mountain ridge on the north side of the valley, coupled with large-scale reforestation of the neighboring mountain grasslands which were denuded of their forests more than a thousand years ago. This is a consequence of the decline in need for marginal land for hay production, since cattle breeding now takes second place to the tourist business. These projects will not only change the landscape, but will also effect important and beneficial climatic changes in the usually cold and windy valley.

Obernberg has thus acquired political democracy, a commercialized economy, and a tolerant religious attitude at the price of abandoning its unchallenged and unified leadership and the tranquil economic and political life of the past. The mayor ceased to be the leader of the community and is becoming more and more a mediator between competing economic associations and political factions. His decision-making activity no longer reflects the single set of values of the traditional Tirolean peasantry. The urbanization process and the commercialization of the economy have been further accelerated with the completion of an exit off the newly constructed Brenner Autobahn. The effect of the influx of tourists upon the economy and social life of the community is tremendous. Thus traditional Obernberg Valley has become one of the fastest-growing tourist resorts in the Alps.

THE DATA AND THE SCOPE OF THE ANALYSIS

During the past 12 years, I have been engaged in an intensive, systematic, virtually uninterrupted investigation of the economic and sociopolitical changes that have transformed Obernberg. To achieve this continuity, I added to the initial 1-year research period in 1962–1963 10 successive summer field sessions (each of 3 months' duration). During my absences from the village, quantitative records and case data have been collected by two resident field assistants—one a member of the border guard, the other one a local school teacher and nowadays an assistant professor at the State Teachers College in Innsbruck. A massive body of continuous quantitative data covering the 12-year period has been collected and this is combined with qualitative data on relevant aspects of the culture. The completeness of the information on Obernberg culture has been ascertained by reference to the *Outline of Cultural Material* (Murdock *et al.* 1961). My formal analysis of the Tirolean laws of inheritance may serve as an example of the kind of cultural data collected (Pospisil 1971:323–324).

The quantitative data for the economic and sociopolitical study are derived from official records, extensive personal observations (as a participant observer), and a large number of private interviews (about 1600). In addition, detailed economic questionnaires were submitted to members of all the households in the village. The data from interviews and questionnaires and observations of actual behavior give me insight into the overt behavior of the villagers working in the fields, at home, or interacting at formal meetings, in elections, and during disputes. They reveal the inner structure of the community's economic and sociopolitical organization, which was hidden from outsiders behind a facade of officialdom and lofty idealism.

Transcripts of official records include a total of about 7000 items covering yearly financial budget statements of the community and of the several incorporated associations, and land register and district court records.

I have information on land ownership and detailed inventories of livestock, machinery, and financial resources for each farm for a consecutive 10-year period. For each of 5 consecutive years, sets of maps were drawn showing the Obernberg territory with its landholdings and the individual fields with their various crops. These maps, each of which includes over 1500 land plots, are an excellent tool for the quantitative study of the community's agricultural production and the actual crop rotations used by various farmers. The data show changes in the proportion of specific crops and their relationship to corresponding changes in the areas of pasture, meadows, and woods. These data will be compared with what farmers said they did and with their statements of what "ideally" should have been done about the crop sequences. Thus, what happened can be compared with informants' ideas about their behavior and with their ideals of good husbandry.

Consumption and the distribution of goods were studied through obtaining household shopping lists, records of the sale of livestock and agricultural produce, tax payments, bank loans (for purchase of machinery or modernizing), and savings. These were recorded over a 10-year period for specific households as well as from such pertinent institutions as the bank, community office, Office of Internal Revenue, and the like. Income derived from farming and tourism, tabulated for every farm, shows the increasing financial importance of tourism in the village's economy. Since it is the farmer's wife who takes care of the tourists and, consequently, collects the money from them and regards it as her own (although she still pools it with her husband's resources), her economic importance has been enhanced. Her elevated status has been recognized by her husband and has had important economic and social consequences well documented in the data.

I have also recorded other effects of the hundreds of German, Scandinavian, and other tourists who come directly into the village from the Brenner Autobahn. The advantageous changes in the economy and social customs of the Valley have been accompanied by what my informants regard as the undesirable effects of urbanization. These include pollution from the exhaust fumes of hundreds of cars and from papers, cans, and bottles discarded by tourists in the woods and pastures. The declining moral standards of the young Obernberg citizens are reflected in the legal infractions of several local boys and girls. One boy was even convicted for conspiracy of armed assault and robbery.

With the increase of serious criminality, the focus of settlement of conflicts shifted from village authorities to formal litigation in the courts at Steinach and Innsbruck. My legal assistant and I have secured several hundred transcripts of legal decisions from the records of the District Court of Steinach and the Appellate Court in Innsbruck. However, the informal settlement of disputes has by no means been superseded; I collected 168 troubles cases (in addition to the nonarbitrated conflicts mentioned above) which include decisions informally rendered by the village authorities (e.g., mayor, heads of local clubs and associations, teacher, priest), and several prolonged grievances that have not yet erupted into open conflict. These cases now await analysis, tabulation, and comparative evaluation.

A substantial amount of material has been gathered on political intrigues and alliances that will illuminate the substructure of the political organization of the community and permit the description, in a precise and often quantitative way, of the political changes that have occurred in the village and have often influenced its economy directly.

Thus the account of culture change is based neither on a reconstructed "zero level of acculturation," nor is it only qualitative and speculative.

RESEARCH PROCEDURE AND OBJECTIVES

The data on the Obernberg economy and its changes during the last decade are being analyzed and related to sociopolitical data to enable me to examine the processes of commercialization and urbanization and changes in values and social control.

To achieve these objectives, an assistant and I are tabulating and computerizing the numerical material, drawing analytical maps of land-holdings and cultivation, formally analyzing qualitative data wherever pertinent, and checking my conclusions in the field. The results will provide quantitative figures for total production, distribution, and con-sumption within this Alpine valley and on its individual farms. Thus, a "gross community product" can be calculated for each of the 10 years and for each farm, trends in income, commercialization, "moderniza-tion," and entrepreneurship can be determined. Factors responsible for variations in the production of crops and livestock can be identified, whether they are of environmental, economic, or sociopolitical nature (e.g., climatic changes, field plot locations, soil quality; household composition—sex, age, health, industry, and education of the members; variant forms of land title; and the financial status of the farmers). Differ-ences in distribution of goods on individual farms (sales of farm produce and of services to tourists and purchases of goods and services) and changes in volume over time are being examined and will be correlated with sociopolitical factors such as education and personality attributes of the farmers (their progressiveness or conservatism, degree of decisive-ness and commercial aggression, willingness to experiment, etc.), formal membership in the various economic and sociopolitical associations, kin relationships, and involvement in a network of friendship and partnership within and outside the valley. Since time requirements and work calen-dars were recorded for the various kinds of manual labor during the first field session as well as for subsequent years, the time-saving factor of newly introduced modern machinery can be exactly determined.

Analysis of legal and informal dispute cases will add a further dynamic quality to the account of the peasants' ownership of the means of produc-tion, to the way they distribute goods, labor, and services, and to their patterns of consumption.

Because I have studied noneconomic aspects of the culture of Obernberg (the sociopolitical structure, religion, mythology, etc.), the economic analysis does not take place in isolation from the important sociopolitical factors of economic change. Because economic data are being correlated with these other data, a more definitive judgment can be passed upon various hypotheses such as those that concern peasant conservatism, the efficiency of the peasant economy, the role of rural entrepreneurship, surpluses, and the politics of investment and consumption. It is possible to examine how individual farmers change their economic strategies with opportunities for mechanization, new commercial potentials such as the tourist trade, and fluctuations of prices of various farm products.

SIGNIFICANCE OF THE RESEARCH

In contemporary anthropology it appears not to be enough to describe and analyze ethnographic data. One is required either to be a "model builder" or to write a book which centers around and proves a single hypothesis, no matter how simple or vague it may be. There seems to be a compulsion to present a new theory in every article or book, though data to support the theory are often incomplete and usually are regarded as of secondary importance. In contrast, I have studied the Tirolean and Kapauku societies in order to fill gaps in knowledge, not gaps in a system of models or hypotheses. Thus my intent seems to be closer to that of the natural sciences, in which the aim is to discover something new, than to the model-builders in social science. A brilliant logical exegesis without all the relevant data (or a representative sample thereof) to support it, which we often find in our social science periodicals, is for me not of paramount interest. As a natural scientist stated: "Pure logic is the safest way to go wrong with confidence." I may add—a preconceived theoretical conclusion, supported by some few carefully selected data, is even worse. Therefore my fieldwork in New Guinea and in Tirol, together with my other work, has not been confined to the test of one anticipated model, or to verification of a hypothesis, or to illustrating a political creed. It addressed itself to a series of theoretical problems pertaining to social control, and it provided the test and modification for a theory of law originally conceived from library research which deals not only with important legal attributes, with change of law, and with legal morphology, but also designs a formal method for cross-cultural comparison and analysis of substantive law (Pospisil 1971). The theory as well as the method have been shown to be applicable to "tribal" as well as modernizing peasant societies.

The long-term field research, and my analysis of Tirolean material, represents a continuation and extension of studies I have pursued in economics, law, and culture change. It parallels in scope as well as in method (quantification and use of computers) my work among the Kapauku Papuans of West New Guinea in the years 1954–1955, 1959,

1962, 1975 (see especially Pospisil 1958a, b, c, 1963a, b, 1965a, b). Among the Papuans, rapid acculturation was made possible by construction of an airstrip in the Kamu Valley (Pospisil 1961, 1964); in the Tirol the fast pace of urbanization was also triggered by a means of communication—a paved road and an exit from the Brenner Autobahn. The comparison of the acculturation of the Papuan society and the urbanization of the peasant culture has yielded an insight into the nature of the two processes and highlights the role the economy (especially the transition from subsistence to a commercialized economy), cultural values, politics, and legal and informal social controls play in the two types of culture change.

The final analysis of the Tirol material is expected to shed light on the relationship between socioeconomic change and psychological factors such as the ability to internalize new values. The combination of the study of individuals (their internalization processes and specific actions initiating culture change) with the analysis of changes on the societal level is expected to demonstrate the paramount importance of psychology in anthropological research. It combats the Durkheimean tradition of "sociological solipsism" in the study of human society. It was possible to predict changes in Kapauku society, which I could verify in subsequent research periods, because of the use of the internalization tests. Thus, the results of the analysis should support the latest tenets of Murdock, who holds that only a combined effort of psychology and anthropology can bring about a true science of human behavior, a science with valid generalizations, replicable tests, and predictability (Murdock 1971).

In my comparative, long-term work on the processes of economic and sociopolitical changes that characterize the Kapauka Papuan and Obernberg situations, I have arrived at some tentative conceptualizations on the nature of acculturation and urbanization processes and their consequences for various aspects of society—a conceptualization which must be further tested in other societies. My data indicate that the two processes may be conceived as effecting changes in two different spheres of social relations. While urbanization affects primarily the structure of the basic interpersonal relations that are Ego-centered (which I have called "social structure"), acculturation during the first two decades of the Kapauku exposure to the West affected primarily their "societal structure." It altered the relations as well as the nature of Kapauku social groups, such as political confederacies, alliances, lineages, sibs, and villages.

Thus urbanization in Tirol affected the cultural ordering of Ego's relations with other members of his society (the structure of Ego's social relations). These changes affected only the relations with individuals and aggregates of people for which Ego is the point of reference and which do not constitute discrete units within the matrix of the society (e.g., kindred, kin relations, friends, partners, networks). The change left intact the structure of Tirolean society (societal structure), which has to be viewed as an organized conglomeration of its constituent groups with absolutely defined nonoverlapping membership (as contrasted with the relatively defined overlapping membership of kindreds, Ego's friends, and Ego's allies, etc. of the "social structure"). Accordingly, urbanization altered profoundly such relationships as those between parents and children and husband and wife, whereas it left unaltered the composition and function of the Tirolean family. It changed the patterns of Ego's friendship and political networks while it has not altered the structure and function of the Obernberg community, of the political parties, and of the numerous economic, social, and religious associations.

To become urbanized meant to the Obernberg people not only to change one's outer appearance and behavior, it meant also, and especially, profound changes in interpersonal Ego-centered relations and attitudes. Economically, the young people became independent of the *patria potestas*—father ceased to play the role of the logical employer and provider. With this change also came the waning of father's prestige and influence over his children, an influence which in the old peasant days lasted sometimes until the son was in his middle fifties! Similarly the income of the wife, which formerly was limited to that derived from the sale of milk, butter, and eggs, was increased astronomically by proceeds from lodging and catering to the tourist, making the wife less dependent on and subservient to her husband. As a consequence, it can no longer be claimed that most families are patriarchal. Indeed, in several instances matriarchy has become the rule, and in many marriages sharing the decision making has become an accepted reality.

In contrast, the Kapauku acculturation has meant that the society and its segments (groups) are under attack. Their political confederacies have disappeared, their lineages and sublineages have lost their important functions and *raison d'être*, and their traditional alliances and political cliques have been dispersed. New groups with new functions have come into being. For example, under Indonesian influence the village (*kampong*) became a politically and administratively meaningful group, whereas formerly it was just one of several places where members of a lineage resided. If there were several villages per lineage, the leadership rested with the lineage, the lineage headman having jurisdiction over all villages of his lineage irrespective of his own residence. The traditional Kapauku village had no economic, political, or ceremonial function whatsoever.

Thus the Tirolean and Kapauku material shed new light on the two processes which often have not been distinguished or, if differentiated, then only on the basis of the type of situation in which they occurred: acculturation resulted from contact between a "tribal" culture and a "civilization," while urbanization was regarded as the effect of a contact between city dwellers and peasants. The comparison of the Kapauku "tribesmen" and the Tirolean peasants, however, shows that the two processes differ more profoundly—namely, in their effect on structures: the first primarily producing changes in the nature and relationship of the society's segments (societal structure), the second affecting the structuring of Ego-centered relations (social structure). Whereas the acculturated Kapauku are still Kapauku as individuals, although their traditional society is gone, the urbanized Obernbergers are a new breed with new interpersonal attitudes and Ego-centered relations, although their Obernberg society persists with little change in its subgroup system.

CONCLUSIONS

Long-term research is the proper method for scientific study of culture processes. There is no substitute for ongoing direct observation, recording, and analysis of culture change. The *ex post facto* study of changes on the basis of a reconstructed zero point of acculturation through the use of old historical (e.g., archival) sources, or by two widely spread field research sessions, is far inferior to the direct observation of actual change and long-term study and should be resorted to only when prolonged field research is impossible or impractical.

Moreover, I suspect that because of the brevity of the current single period of ethnographic research some anthropologists have produced chimeras of "static primitive societies," "structural equilibriums," and false typologies of social groups (households, families, bands, hunting groups) which if studied over time would appear only as temporary phases of a single type of a dynamically viewed group. Indeed, our traditional relatively short synchronic analysis may be responsible for the current distorted popular portrait of "primitive tribal" societies.

Research even of 1-year duration is inadequate for investigation of a culture foreign to the fieldworker. Learning the language takes at least half a year, if not more. As a result, pidgin English or an interpreter is substituted even in projects dealing with semantic, philosophic, cognitive, and sociopolitical problems where a thorough knowledge of the language is a *condicio sine qua non*. An anthropologist studying a Bantu-speaking group and using Swahili could be compared to a Chinese ethnographer studying a college community in New England and communicating with the American students in pidgin German. Strangely enough, work of such quality is generally taken seriously in our discipline.

I do recognize that the duration of the fieldwork of our graduate students is not of their choice but is made brief by our "modern" educational policy to mass-produce Ph.D.'s. No matter how much our conscientious students object and how much our knowledge expands, we comply with the request of our graduate schools to "expedite" and do not protest.

In order to study the processes of social control and the relationship between the dynamism of law and the rest of the culture in my two chosen societies, I had not only to master the Kapauku language and the local Obernberg dialect of Tirolean German, but in both cases I first studied systematically the two cultures in their totality to find out how law and social control related to their particular parts. A thorough quantitative analysis of both the "tribal" and peasant economies became a prerequisite, as was also a detailed study of the two people's sociopolitical structures. Indeed, since Tirolean peasants participate actively in the national life of Austria, I had to study the national and regional institutions that affect their lives. Only after having established a broad base did I concentrate on law and culture change. My conceptualization of the difference between acculturation and urbanization is but one of the theoretical rewards for the painstaking recording, tabulation, and analysis of the data. Of course, even without these, the data themselves are of importance. How many reliable, quantitative, and encyclopedic (as called for by Firth 1965) economic analyses of a "tribal" society or of a peasant valley do we have for comparative work?

The long-term study of the two societies has made me seriously doubt most of the theoretical conclusions concerning the static nature of "tribal" societies and the conservatism of peasant societies. Indeed, in both types of society, I have found a readiness to embrace new, proven methods of agriculture or new ways of maximization of profits. However, neither the Kapauku nor the Obernberg peasants indulge in wild experinenting with unproven methods and theories. As a farmer of Obernberg put it to me succinctly: "Has it really been worthwhile to force on the Russian people communism and in the process to kill over 20 million of them for the sake of a type of economy which has still to steal inventions from the West, be fed by the surplus capitalist wheat, and have Fiat build their automobile factories, and all that after well over half a century of the blessings of communism?" Accordingly, the people of Obernberg accepted modern machinery—but not until it was shown to be efficient and economical in their particular mountain situation. They also reacted with surprising speed to the demand for tourist lodging, and the male farmers willingly surrendered their economically dominant position to their wives.

What can be more revolutionary than this in a population where the old proverb solemnly and categorically states, "Pity the males dominated by women!" But while catering to the tourists, they refused to dismantle their farming economy, in spite of the well-meant advice of economists and social scientists from the city. "Who knows what may happen to the European prosperity! We remember the Depression and only a fool would forget its lesson." Thus, unlike the urban wizards, they are prepared at any time to switch back to a subsistance economy should circumstances demand it.

There are many other generalizations about peasants based usually on brief research, which do not stand the test of long-term precise investigation. These generalizations often become doctrines for students following their masters. Nothing is more antiscientific than automatic and unquestionable acceptance of other people's theories. Therefore, to eliminate hero worship for one's academic mentor the ethnographer should not be expected to bring students as "understudies" into his or her own fieldwork. This practice not only prevents the young people from acquiring important language skills, but, in the long run, makes them disciples rather than scholars. Any young anthropologist is entitled to his or her own independent research and theoretical framework, both of which may be negated by participation in a mentor's research. We should be producing scholars and not followers. I have always admired great revolutionary thinkers, such as Newton, Freud, Einstein, and Marx. Because I wanted to be like Marx I could not be a Marxist. The progress of our discipline needs independent research workers and thinkers, but we can do very well, as a matter of fact, far better, without the disciples.

It seems to me that most of us in anthropology became disciples at least in one respect: In our field work we have tried to follow Malinowski. Indeed we tried to emulate him in aspects in which he excelled, and, unwittingly, we have committed often the very same errors he did. Many of us mastered the language of the people we were studying, we became diligent participant observers, thus advancing over the pre-Malinowski era of superficial and often ethnocentric research. Unfortunately, we have also subconsciously treated culture as a static entity whose nature could be elucidated in one solid research. Our lip service to culture change has not often been matched by corresponding adequate research. As I have tried to show, the nature of culture is dynamism. If our model of culture and society were a correct one, there would not be a need for appendage chapters on "culture change." Since the *essence of culture is change,* the word does not have to be reiterated, and change would become simply a part of any structural and functional analysis. Thus there seems to be only one way to get necessary data for an adequate anthropological analysis:

through the long-term research. There is no equally good substitute in the study of culture for a record of the dynamic data as they happen, no matter how onerous and expensive this procedure may be.

BIBLIOGRAPHY

Firth, Raymond
　　1965　Review of Kapauku Papuan economy, by Leopold Pospisil. *American Anthropologist 67*:122–125.
Murdock, George P.
　　1971　Anthropology's mythology (The Huxley Memorial lecture). *Proceedings of the Royal Anthropological Institute of Great Britain and Ireland for 1971*. Pp. 17–24.
Murdock, George P., Clelland S. Ford, Alfred E. Hudson, Raymond Kennedy, Leo W. Simmons, and John W. M. Whiting
　　1961　*Outline of cultural materials*. New Haven: Human Relations Area Files.
Pospisil, Leopold
　　1958a　*Kapauku Papuans and their law*. Yale University Publications in Anthropology, No. 54. New Haven: Yale Univ. Press.
　　1958b　Social change and primitive law: Consequences of a Papuan legal case. *American Anthropologist 60*:832–837.
　　1958c　Kapauku Papuan political structure. In *Systems of political control and bureaucracy in human societies*. Proceedings of the 1958 annual spring meeting of the American Ethnological Society. Pp. 9–22.
　　1961　Culture change resulting from changes in native legal systems and from imposition of European legal code. In *American Philosophical Society yearbook for 1960*. Pp. 343–346. Philadelphia: American Philosophical Society.
　　1963a　*Kapauku Papuan Economy*. Yale University Publications in Anthropology, No. 67. New Haven: Yale Univ. Press.
　　1963b　*The Kapauku Papuans of West New Guinea*. New York: Holt, Rinehart and Winston.
　　1964　Culture change resulting from changes in native legal systems as well as from imposition of European legal codes. In *American philosophical society yearbook for 1963*. Pp. 453–457. Philadelphia: American Philosophical Society.
　　1965a　A formal analysis of substantive law: Kapauku Papuan land tenure. *American Anthropologist 67*(5:2):186–214.
　　1965b　A formal analysis of substantive law: Kapuku Papuan laws of inheritance. *American Anthropologist 67*(6:2):166–185.
　　1969　Political and legal change in a Tirolean village. Unpublished paper, part of application for National Science Foundation Grant for Scientific Research. 25 pp.
　　1971　*Anthropology of law*. New York: Harper and Row.

7

Long-Term Research among the Dogrib and Other Dene

June Helm

INTRODUCTION

A brief trip to the field in August of 1976 marked my twenty-fifth year of research among the Dene Indians of Canada's Northwest Territories. Although I stress Dogrib studies in this chapter, I have also worked with Slave and Hare populations and have had brief field contact with Chipewyan and Mountain–Bearlake groups. Despite dialectic divergence and certain variations in other aspects of culture (e.g., kin-term systems), these Athapaskan-speaking populations of the central subarctic may profitably be viewed by the social anthropologist as a single people, especially when their common cultural, environmental, and historical context is taken into account. More important, the people collectively perceive themselves as "Dene." Except for the Loucheux (Eastern Kutchin), whose linguistic and cultural affiliations lie in Alaska, I have worked with all major divisions of the Dene of the Northwest Territories. As hunters and fur-trappers, the N.W.T. Dene range over approximately 450,000 square miles of muskeg, boreal forest, and edge-of-the-tundra (see Figure 7.1). In 1970, their population was about 6500.

In my research, I have pursued some themes (e.g., socioterritorial

145

Long-Term Field Research
in Social Anthropology

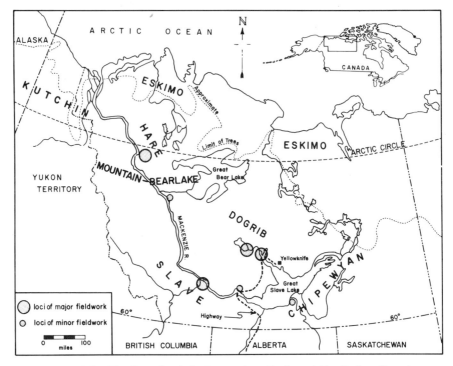

Figure 7.1. The Dene lands in the western Northwest Territories, Canada.

organization) through to a reasonable state of resolution, have brought some (e.g., comparative kin-term systems) only partially to completion, and have abandoned or lost interest in others (e.g., personality and culture). I have also encountered several unforeseen opportunities that have directed me to new interests (e.g., the Dogrib hand game, described in Helm and Lurie 1966) or turned me back to earlier ones. From the time of my initial exposure to Dene life in 1951, there have always been emergent or unfinished ethnological questions, so that my research has been continually creating itself. As a result, the methodological and theoretical implications of my long-term fieldwork with the Dene have been reconstructed after the fact for this paper.

In terms of human groups, I moved from an initial study of a tiny Slave Indian community of 56 persons to an interest in the regional and tribal dimensions of Dogrib life. I have also pursued a broader comprehension of the entire Dene population of the Mackenzie Basin from the south side of Great Slave Lake to the north side of Great Bear Lake. Just as my geographical range of interest has expanded, so has my temporal perspective. My first field project of 1951–1952 focused on contemporary community life. But it led me into ethnohistorical research on the Northern Dene, a pursuit which has been greatly stimulated by Dogrib oral history. And since 1973, my temporal orientation has extended to the future, through service as a resource person to the Indian Brotherhood of the Northwest Territories, a group dedicated to placing future control of Indian life into Indian hands.

FIELDWORK AMONG THE SLAVE: LYNX POINT

Married and living in Canada, I went to the Northwest Territories for dissertation fieldwork in 1951 because it was maritally and financially feasible to do so. Scotty MacNeish, to whom I was then married, had obligingly scouted the ethnographic lay of the land for me in his 1950 archaeological survey of the Mackenzie River region. From him I learned that the men of the Slave Indian community of "Lynx Point" (a pseudonym) were engaged in a joint economic enterprise that by all accounts was a unique venture for "atomistic" northern Athapaskans. This promised to give a topical focus to my ethnographic work in the Northwest Territories, an area that had at that time attracted only modest attention from field ethnologists (namely, J. Alden Mason in 1913, Cornelius Osgood in 1928–1929, and Richard Slobodin in 1938–1939 and 1946–1947).

Teresa Carterette (then graduate student in anthropology, now professor of psychology) joined me as co-fieldworker. As with later field partners, field interests and data were fully shared. In return for serving as amateur schoolteachers to the monolingual children, the people of Lynx Point provided us with a tiny log cabin, occasional firewood, and an accepted role in the community. In this, as in similar small settlements, there were several adults who had varying degrees of fluency in English. Simplified English (with a dash of fractured Athapaskan) became my field language, and so, without long-term plans for continuing Athapaskan fieldwork, it remained.

By the end of my stay at Lynx Point, three explicit questions had been generated by the field data. One was a problem in the Slave Indian kin-term system: Why did a few Lynx Point informants employ Iroquoian cousin terminology rather than the Hawaiian system more commonly used in the community (and reported for the Slave by Morgan [1871] and Honigmann [1946:68])? A second question was whether the domain and style of leadership at Lynx Point was comparable to traditional patterns of Northern Athapaskan leadership. Allied to this question was a third: Was the small kin-community of Lynx Point—whose families were linked by multiple primary ties—a unique and/or recent development in northern Athapaskan socioterritorial organization? If not, how could this structure be reconciled with Steward's (1936) formulation of the large composite band, composed of "unrelated families," to which he had assigned the northern Canadian Dene?

The kin terminology question led me to gather more kin-term data from Slavey at Ft. Providence and Ft. Simpson in 1955 and to seek comparative data through interviews with Chipewyan informants in 1954 at Camsell Indian hospital in Edmonton, Alberta, and in fieldwork among the Hare Indians in the summer of 1957 (MacNeish 1960). The question of patterns of leadership led to a search, during the winter between the field seasons at Lynx Point, of the historical as well as the ethnographic literature on all aspects of leadership through time among the Arctic Drainage Dene (MacNeish 1956). That search of the literature, combined with data on Hare Indian socioterritorial groupings from the 1957 field season, also began to clarify levels and patterns in northern Athapaskan socioterritorial organization; later data from the Dogrib confirmed the picture (Helm 1965).

A more general, less precisely defined line of interest emerged as well, as it does for almost all ethnologists working in circumpolar regions: the human ecology of the subarctic. I began to think of the ecology of the Arctic Drainage Dene in terms of the changing intercultural environment and resource definition since contact, as well as come to awareness of regional variations in resources and socioterritorial adaptations in the Mackenzie basin.

FIELDWORK AMONG THE DOGRIB: LAC LA MARTRE AND RAE

My first fieldwork among the Dogrib was in the "bush" community of Lac la Martre. The research, funded by a division of the Northern Affairs branch of the Canadian government, was framed by that division's interest in the native subsistence economy (Helm and Lurie 1961). I also brought to the field continuing questions on change and continuity in Northern Athapaskan socioterritorial organization and leadership patterns. In addition, I was interested to see if the Dogrib, a group which had been affected later and rather less by contact with white institutions than had other Dene in the Arctic Drainage, had the Iroquoian kin-term system which my previous comparative work (MacNeish 1960) indicated might be the general precontact form.

Before embarking on a 3-day canoe trip to Lac la Martre, my field partner, Nancy Lurie, and I provisioned at Rae, the major trading center of the Dogribs. That week's stopover planted the idea of eventual fieldwork there. I already knew from my Slave friends that the chief of the Rae Dogribs held a unique reputation for effective "tribal"-level leadership. Moreover, at Rae I would have the opportunity to investigate socioterritorial entities greater than small, nucleated territorial groups ("local bands") such as Lynx Point and Lac la Martre—specifically that entity which I came to term the "regional band" (Helm 1965). So, several ongoing ethnological questions were waiting to be pursued when I "settled" at Rae in 1962.

At Rae, I eventually collected enough interviews among the Dogribs to falsify my expectation regarding their kin-term system and vitiate my broader argument, but by then other anthropological questions were at hand. This was the first time, with the exception of my brief stay among the Hare in 1957, that I had resided in a major tribal center, rather than in a small isolated bush community. Being at Rae meant that many more potentially knowledgeable and interested informants were available to aid on the problems that had come to engage me. I began for the first time to work regularly with paid informants. The most notable of them is Vital Thomas, who became key informant, interpreter, friend, and landlord of the "shack" which he keeps available for me.

From informants like Vital Thomas I was able to tap a rich oral tradition—the Dogribs' perceived ethnohistory—regarding many topics, including leadership and socioterritorial organization. In 1962, traditional attributes of leadership had living form in the Head Chief, Jimmy Bruneau, then 80 years old. From Chief Bruneau and the regional band leaders chosen consensually for traditional virtues and abilities, the line of Dogrib folk history led back to events that, as documented by European explorers, took place in the 1820s.

I continued to return to Rae in pursuit of other evidence on sociocultural continuity and change from an ethnohistorical perspective. But it was apparent that, through the forces of government-*cum*-"development," massive changes were underway in the 1960s with a speed and impact unparalleled in the Dogrib past. Reluctantly, I recognized I must also attempt to keep up with the snowballing course of introduced changes at both the local and the Territorial level.

CHANGE: VARIATION AND ALTERATION IN SOCIOCULTURAL SYSTEMS

Long-term field research almost surely confronts the ethnologist with evidence of change. In everyday (and dictionary) usage, variation is one kind of change. Three dimensions of sociocultural variation are: unique or nondistinctive features (in the linguistic sense) in the repetitive occurrence of the "same" phenomenon; the succession of events within a closed cycle, such as a people's yearly round; and customary alternatives in belief, knowledge, and action. The first two forms of variation occur within the bounds or limits of a constant total state or condition; they are nondirectional. Alternatives, however, hold through time the potentiality of directional change or alteration. Alteration is irreversible "movement" from one state or condition to another. As a rule, anthropologists speak explicitly of change only when addressing alteration, whether as cumulative drift or, at the opposite extreme, radical redirection. To deal with "directional processes" Vogt (1960:29) called for "long range field projects giving us up to 20 years of continuous year-round readings"—vide the Chiapas project. The solo ethnographer perforce does not spend 20 continuous years in the field. But, as my years among the Dene illustrate, through continuing though intermittent fieldwork the single researcher can monitor processes of both variation and directional change beyond what the one-time field experience allows.

Variation

Variation may be conceived—and perceived—in terms of three kinds of "events": short-run recurrent events; longer-run normal events or cycles; and paranormal events, by their nature uncommon. Short-run events recur relatively frequently and the time span of each is relatively brief—a few hours, days, or weeks. Among the Northern Dene, short-run events include such sets of processual activities (collectively, an event) as the household daily round of wood chopping, food preparations, net and snare tending, etc.; women's monthly menstrual sequestrations; the cycle of seasonal economic pursuits—fall fishing, winter trapping, spring "ratting," etc.; and observances marking culturally defined stages in the individual life cycle, for example, menarche, childbirth, marriage, death. A single field period may not expose the ethnographer to the full compass of short-run events: During 1951–1952 no one got married at Lynx Point; in 1957 the Hare were not setting snares for hare because the species was at the nadir of its population cycle. The ethnographer relies on informants to "fill him in" on such "missing" events and, as well, to help him ascertain the more common or unalterable features of events observed but once or twice.

Longer-run normal events—constitutional events if we follow Bohannan (1958)—may occur at regular or irregular intervals, but barring disruption or transformation, they can be expected to occur from time to time over the long-term. The people themselves anticipate such events and often can forecast them within some time range. The processual span of the total event-run may, however, extend over years. As the following account of succession to Dogrib chieftainship illustrates, commitment to long-term field research offers the possibility of timing one's field presence for the critical or climactic stage of such an event and the opportunity of arranging at least intermittent exposure to segments of the event-run.

A Case from the Dogrib

The Old Chief, Jimmy Bruneau, had acceded to office in 1934 as designate of the dying chief Monphwi. The latter had been the designate in 1902 of the Old Chief's father, the great trading chief Ekawi Dzimi, who had been a prime leader for 35 years. The "passing of the mantle" by a sort of paramount leader—a role established at least two long generations before it was transformed into "government chief" by the Treaty of 1921—had, by all evidence, simply reinforced, rather than replaced or conflicted with, the essential process of consensual male decision by which leaders of any level or duration have traditionally been selected. With my continuing interest in conditions and criteria of leadership and leader selection, I was concerned to follow the course of succession to office of head chief. Would the "designate"-by-consensus tradition be maintained, or would the Rae Dogrib at last resort to the alternative elective method that most Canadian Indian groups now practiced?

In 1962, I heard comments that the Chief was getting old (he was 80), but that he had not yet said what he "had in his mind" concerning his successor. When I returned in 1967 the comment was, "We've been talking about a new chief for 2 years now." The Old Chief was now extremely deaf; although he had expressed the desire to step down, he had not designated a successor. One man prominent in community discussion for successor (but not by the chief) was a leader from another regional band, the *et'at'in*. In 1968, the Old Chief was still in office and the issue of land rights and Indian reserves, introduced by government officials at the annual Treaty payment that summer, seemed to have flooded out other concerns from the people's minds. In 1969, I again arrived at Rae in time for "Treaty." This would be the occasion when a new chief would formally take office; if there was to be a change, the decision would be made shortly before Treaty.

After a meeting on other issues with a Territorial official a few days prior to Treaty, a group of men formed outside the Old Chief's house. Discussion ranged widely as to who should be the new chief. Some expressed the opinion that it should be someone who could speak English and read and write. Some younger men's names were mentioned, as well as illiterate but well-regarded older men. There appeared still to be a push on the part of members of the *et'at'in* regional band to place one of their important men in the office.

Sunday, the following day, word went out to the older men of Rae to gather at the house of a respected band leader, who had been a central participant in the previous day's discussion. Although there had been some talk of a formal election, the parley and mode of decision making followed traditional lines. ("Not very democratic," commented a young Indian activist whose generation had not figured in the decision making.) As a compromise to the Old Chief, who was manifesting reluctance to retire, some men of consequence approached him with the proposition that he step down in favor of his son, a 60-year-old monolingual. Also in an effort to induce him to relinquish his office voluntarily, they pointed out that one of the most respected band-councilors had stated his intention to retire. The Old Chief accepted the proposal.

No one, except the new chief, seemed happy with the compromise. Although respected as a hard worker in the bush, he was not seen to have other attributes, either traditional or modern, desired in a leader. Within 2 years a movement to select another chief climaxed. In order to avoid outright rejection of the incumbent, the strategy was to hold for the first time a formal election, with the incumbent running against three other men (one the *et'at'in* candidate), but there seemed to be a general understanding as to which one was likely to emerge the winner, a respected monolingual of the band of the Old Chief and Ekawi Dzimi. His pride wounded, the incumbent chief refused to run. The election brought the anticipated man to office by a two-thirds majority. Their polity defined and rigidified by government fiat for 50 years, the Dogribs had at last retreated from their principle of the consensual political community. Subsequent events have demonstrated that this step instituted an irreversible alteration of their political processes.

In contrast to short-run recurrent events and longer-run normal events, paranormal events are those which emerge along side of, or aside from, the usual, ordinary, and predictable course of a people's affairs. As defined here, they are not impositions from outside the system, although they may arise in response to them. Although "aside from" the normal, paranormal events partake of preexisting values and understandings and cultural and social forms. Revitalization movements are paranormal event-runs that are "conscious, organized efforts to . . . create a more satisfying culture [Wallace 1956:279]"; if successful, by definition they bring about significant alteration. Bohannan (1958:11) sees a different function for a kind of paranormal event that he terms "extra-normal" or "extra-processual": It serves to "reestablish fluidity in the [constitutional] power system'' and disappears once its equilibrating function is accomplished. Imputed functions aside, the definitive quality of paranormal events is that their emergence is not ordinary, routine, or confidently predictable by either the folk or the ethnologist.

A paranormal event-run of cultural significance, either as a quasi-cyclical surge of tension and its subsidence or resolution or as an ultimately transformational process, takes time to build and run its course. The one-time field trip gives little chance to encounter such events. The repeat visitor may miss the inception of a paranormal event, but recurrent contacts with the group allows him at minimum to sample slices of the run and compass of the total process.

The northern Dene, like many North American Indians, have in their cultural repertoire the ''prophet'' (*nate*, 'dreamer') as a potentially mobilizable role. The following account sketches my exposure to the peaking and partial subsidence of a manifold paranormal event among the Dogrib, the prophet movement of the 1960s.

A Case from the Dogrib

During the winter of 1966–1967, a letter from Rae informed me of three drink-induced deaths among the people. On my return the following summer, distressed concern still loomed large. I learned that a Slave Indian prophet from Northern Alberta, invited to Rae by a leading Dogrib elder and moral arbiter, had visited at Christmas and again at Easter to preach adherence to Catholic virtues and especially against the destructive effects of drink. His preaching had been welcomed; Dogribs emphasized that people were no longer drinking as they had before. Furthermore, one Rae Dogrib had become the charismatic disciple of the Alberta Prophet and was preaching and holding services on the ''Alberta model,'' which in paraphernalia and ritual features seemed to be ultimately derived, at least in part, from the Northwest Prophet Dance of the previous century. Addressed by some as ''*Gota*'' ('Our Father,' as for the Christian God), he called on the Dogribs to abjure alcohol and certain other white-introduced indulgences such as card playing.

Although the Rae Prophet followed an anti-white theme of the Alberta Prophet in his preaching, in the summer of 1968 Dogrib friends invited me to the prophet's night-long ceremony held at a small bush settlement (Helm 1968a). By this time some of the Dogrib were expressing their overt rejection of the Rae Prophet: He was too arrogant, demanding, and usurpatory of the authority of the Old Chief and the Catholic priest. He had, however, in the preceding and following winters led dog-team expeditions to Fort Franklin, some 300 miles as the crow flies, and brought word of the Bear Lake Prophet, an elderly expatriate Dogrib.

During Easter of 1969, the Bear Lake Prophet and the Alberta Prophet had visited Rae and, so a letter informed me, "beat" the Rae Prophet in preaching. An elderly Dogrib I had known at Lac la Martre in 1959, now a prophet too, had also been at the gathering.

During Christmas week of 1969, a Dogrib friend telegraphed me (per request) that the Bear Lake Prophet was on his way to Rae. By December 27, I was with the Rae Dogribs. For 10 days I attended sessions with the Bear Lake Prophet, taping his stories and moral and religious exhortations. (He had no cultic rituals.) I also interviewed the Lac la Martre Prophet, also in Rae.

To summarize, exceedingly briefly, the situation since 1970: The Lac la Martre Prophet, experiencing doubts about the supernatural legitimation of his calling (as he had explained to me in the interview), ceased to be active. The aged Bear Lake Prophet died in 1974, and was greatly mourned. The Rae Prophet continued to hold some adherents from his regional band, the *et' at' in* (the same group that attempted to swing the chieftainship succession to one of their members). Most Dogribs, however, rejected or lost interest in him as a prophet. By the mid-1970s, his drive for moral dominance had found a fresh outlet as a community activist in the political program of the Indian Brotherhood.

The prophets had impact only among older, largely monolingual Dogribs. On the critical issue of alcohol abuse, which stimulated the initial enthusiasm for the Alberta Prophet, the younger generation has not sought a religious solution. The Rae Prophet's redemptive goals for the larger Dogrib society have failed, but only in the still-longer run can we know if he has established a moral nucleus for a sect or other group divergent from the mainstream.

Alteration: Irreversible Change in Dogrib Society

Isolated and insulated by their subarctic domain, the Dogrib and other Dene had, until after World War II, little involvement with the Eurocanadian world except through the narrow and selective channels offered by the fur trader and the missionary. The 15 years that followed the war saw the inception of sustained government intervention in northern native life with the introduction of effective medical services, and social assistance and welfare measures.

During the 1960s, the Dogrib were confronted with additional forces for change of an unprecedented magnitude. Of these, three were of greatest significance in transforming Dogrib lifeways:

1. In the early 1960s, the opening of an all-weather gravel road (the Mackenzie Highway) that connected Rae with Yellowknife (a White mining town that in 1967 became the Territorial capital) and with southern Canada

2. During the 1960s, the exposure for the first time of the majority of the Dene children to Eurocanadian schooling
3. In the late 1960s, the interest of multinational oil-gas consortiums in the construction of a pipeline to transport natural gas from Alaska and the western Canadian arctic the length of the Mackenzie River Valley to southern markets

The highway was an immediate lure to involvement in the wider world. Regular and chartered bus service took Dogribs to new experiences in the south, for example, to visit the Alberta Prophet. Every day Indians travelled the 70 miles between Rae and Yellowknife with unaccustomed ease. The easy access to alcohol in the urban center brought increased anxiety about drinking problems to the Rae people.

The program of universal schooling for the native children of the territories brought complex and equivocal adjustments to the Dogrib and the other Dene. Sedentarization at the settlements, such as Rae, increased; families spent less time out on the land as primary-grade day schools were built and school attendance required. Loathe to leave wife and family in the settlement so the children could attend school, men were less inclined to go into the "bush" for extended trapping and hunting. This placed more reliance on welfare and other kinds of income subsidies, since opportunities for wage work did not meet the financial needs of town-dwelling Indians. Another consequence of the mass education program became apparent when the young men who had spent years in urbanized living at distant secondary-school hostels returned home. Few were inclined to take up traditional "bush" life; the older people complained that without the aid of strong young men it was no longer possible to go out to live off the land.

In the late 1960s, I began to meet young Dogribs and other Dene who had a level of education and urban sophistication I had not conceived of 15 years before. Some young men and women had completed twelfth grade; a few had been to a university. Some had returned with a commitment to Indian rights movements that were burgeoning throughout Canada and the United States in this period.

Although oil and gas exploration had been underway in arctic and subarctic regions in earlier decades, only in the late 1960s did the fact of northern oil and gas reserves become a potentially critical force affecting northern native life. At the annual Treaty payments in the summer of 1968, government agents raised with the Dogrib and the other Dene of the N.W.T. the question of their accepting "reserves" (reservations) under the provisions of the Treaty signed in 1921. As I attended the Treaty session at Rae, I wondered why the Canadian government, after 47 years, was asking the Indians either to take reserves or accept some other form of settlement of the government's outstanding treaty obligations. However, within a few months one consequence, at least, became apparent: The acceptance of reserve lands or equivalent compensation would fulfill the government's treaty obligations to the Indians, thereby complete the extinguishment of aboriginal title to the lands of the N.W.T., and thereby eliminate Indian land claims as a factor in negotiations around the development of a Mackenzie Valley pipeline.

Historically, the Indians of this inaccessible and, in white terms, largely unusable northern land had escaped the extremes of stress and demoralization experienced by more southerly Indian groups. That some of those processes are underway today is evident. Increasing alcohol-related problems, increasing dependence on government income subsidies, a widening gap between the experiences, outlooks, and desires of the newly urbanized youth and the old people and, especially, the threat to the land base of native society—these are the threats to societal and cultural morale and integrity that have come in the wake of imposed "development."

THE HISTORICAL DIMENSION OF LONG-TERM RESEARCH

The individual anthropologist can perhaps achieve a 40-year span of research among a single people (vide Mead and Manus), but even this is too brief for a full appreciation of not only what and how and why changes occurred, but what and how and why continuities have persisted. One means of extending one's perspective is to tap the oral history and "memory culture" of the people. True, these generally provide a weaker corpus of data than direct ethnographic observation; however, native insights and emphases often open new dimensions of thought and inquiry to the ethnographer. Unlike the use of documentary materials, field research on the past allows the ethnographer to generate answers to his questions; he is not completely constrained by the interests and viewpoint of a prior recorder. For the deeper push into the past, historical documentation, of course, becomes the prime source.

When in 1959 I went to the Lac la Martre Dogrib, I found a community essentially comparable to the Lynx Point Slavey community of 1951. During the 1950s, the Canadian government was introducing changes throughout the north (e.g., day schools, the Old Age Pension) that were affecting even bush communities. Still, in their isolation from most of the daily impact of the "modern" world—no roads, no television, little or no command of English, infrequent contacts with Whites—these bush communities had retained much of a way of life that had endured for 100 or more years. With the perspective gained from the historical literature, I realized that I was seeing the end of a sociocultural era, which I came to term "contact traditional" (Helm and Damas 1963). In subsequent years, comprehension and delineation of the lifeways in this era (Helm and Leacock 1971; Helm *et al.* 1975; Helm *et al.* in press), was deeply enriched by the oral history of the Dogribs with whom I worked at Rae during the 1960s.

The pursuit of social anthropological questions has gained much from this historical perspective. In my first foray into historical reconstruction (MacNeish 1956), I surmised that early epidemics might have irreversibly altered Dene socioterritorial organization (cf. Service 1962:88). But continuing assessment of ecological imperatives and the historical literature, interpreted in light of the specificities gained from contemporary field evidence, oral history, and mission records, has allowed me a substantial degree of confidence that the reconstruction of groupings within the 20th century holds in basic outline and principles for aboriginal socioterritorial organization as well. I have argued that the traditional socioterritorial organization of the Mackenzie Dene took the form, not of a single kind of "band" (cf. Service 1962, Steward 1936), but of three analytically distinguishable kinds of groups organized on the principle of bilateral primary kin links between constituent conjugal pairs, a system which yielded fluidity and flexibility in membership (Helm 1965). I have attempted a quantitified measure of uni-versus-bilocal links in residence (Helm 1969) and have lightly explored the implications of the Dene data for the socioterritorial organization of other hunting–gathering societies (Helm 1968b). Moreover, Reynolds (1968:214–215) has found that the Dene data have bearing on the socioterritorial organization of the chimpanzee as well.

LONG-TERM RESEARCH AND APPLIED ANTHROPOLOGY AMONG AMERICAN INDIANS

Throughout the history of Americanist fieldwork, ethnologists have, as individuals, made intermittent efforts to call for redress of wrongs or to present grievances on behalf of the groups of their field research. Beginning in the 1950s, litigation under the Indian Claims Commission Act of 1946 saw scores of anthropologists testifying as expert witnesses for U.S. Indian groups (as well as for the federal government) regarding aboriginal land occupation and use and the circumstances of federal treaty making and implementation. But, as Lurie (1970) has noted, governmental and legalistic perceptions of the issues, rather than Indian perceptions, dominated. However, at about the same time, Indian groups began to call directly on anthropologists to carry out research in the interests of the group *on a topic defined by the group* (e.g., Slotkin's work [1952] for the Menominee Native American Church). As a further development, Indian associations and tribal groups are now commissioning anthropologists as resource persons and technical advisors to assist in research and writing conceived and executed by the members of the Indian group (e.g., Walker with the Nez Perce [Slickpoo 1973]; Lurie with the Menominee [Shames 1972] and Winnebago). The call by American Indian groups for applied anthropological work on their behalf becomes especially pertinent to those who have been conducting long-term research among Indian peoples. I suspect that it is those anthropologists best known to a group through sustained contact and commitment who will most frequently be called to serve as resource persons or technical advisors.

In my own case, years of field and library research preadapted me for applied anthropological work for the Dene. In the late 1960s, I became acquainted with some young Dogribs and their white co-workers who were instrumental in forming the Indian Brotherhood of the Northwest Territories in 1969. The Brotherhood's "crash" goal was to develop an informed and united Indian stance *vis-à-vis* governmental and other white pressures stemming from the massive "developments" proposed for the Territories. My long standing research on Dene socioterritorial groups and their land use and deployment past and present matched the research needs of the Indian Brotherhood for the emerging politico-legal contests.

Thus, in 1973 the Brotherhood asked me to serve as an expert witness in its efforts to establish a *caveat* on land development in the Territories. I testified before the Territorial Supreme Court regarding the nature of Indian land holding and land use through the historic era to the present day, as well as my understanding of the natives' comprehension (or, rather, their lack of comprehension) of the implications for land alienation in the treaties signed in 1899 and 1921. My student–colleague Beryl C. Gillespie, as the other anthropologist–witness, presented evidence from the earliest European documentaion of tribal deployment over the land of the Northwest Territories.

The next step in our applied work moved us, in the following year, from role of expert witnesses based on prior, nonapplied research, to that of "advisors" to the Land Claims Research Project of the Brotherhood. I provided a design for field research to be carried out by local Indians. The Project's aim is to establish the facts of native land use and deployment as part of the Brotherhood's effort to maximize Indian control over land use and development through negotiation and/or judicial process.

THE NEXT GENERATION: STUDENT–COLLEAGUES AND
LONG-TERM RESEARCH

For the senior anthropologist, it is more often a matter of other scholarly involvements and of academic and personal commitments rather than unavailability of funding that tend to inhibit continuing fieldwork. At least, this has been so in my case. For this reason and because I could not profitably use additional field seasons until accumulated data were analyzed, close involvement with the fieldwork of two students has been especially rewarding.

In 1968, I brought north as graduate students Beryl C. Gillespie and David M. Smith. After an orientation week at Rae, Gillespie went to the so-called "Yellowknife Indian" community of Dogribs, at Detah, to pursue the historical question: "What happened to the Yellowknives?" (Gillespie 1970); with two older Dogribs, Smith and I flew to Ft. Resolution, an important contact-traditional fur transport post on the south side of Great Slave Lake. There, the "old timer" Metis and Chipewyan acquaintances of our Dogrib friends eased Smith's entry into the community. Besides Gillespie's charge to pursue the "Yellowknife question," I asked from both of them data relevant to my interest in kinship systems, socioterritorial groups, and leadership patterns past and present. Beyond that, I encouraged them to pursue whatever rewarding topics might come their way.

In the following years, Gillespie (1975) pursued archival research in the Hudson's Bay Company microfilms in Ottawa, a resource I had yearned after but knew I would not be able to immerse myself in. Smith returned for additional seasons at Resolution, continuing to enrich his oral tradition material on contact-traditional life (Smith 1973) and to analyze the course of culture contact and change from an ecological perspective (Smith 1975). Their duplicate field notes are in my files, enlarging my resources on the historical and ethnographic dimensions of northern Dene life.

FIELD PARTNERS

For simplicity in exposition, I have used the first-person s'ngular when speaking of periods in the field, yet, in several field seasons, a colleague was with me (see Table 7.1). Increased ethnological productivity aside, those seasons have always been the most pleasurable. Like Indian trapping partners, my field partners and I have worked in easy concert or divided our efforts as circumstances warranted (but always with notes in

TABLE 7.1

Ethnographic Field Periods [a]

Months	Year	Location and tribe: Helm	Co-workers
6–9	1951	"Lynx Point", SLAVE	T. Carterette, colleague: She remained through winter for 15 months total
3–7	1952	"Lynx Point", SLAVE	
6	1954	Camsell Hosp., Alta., CHIPEWYAN	
7	1955	Providence and Simpson, SLAVE	
7	1957	Good Hope, HARE	
7–12	1959	Lac la Martre, DOGRIB	N.O. Lurie, colleague
7	1960	Lac la Martre, DOGRIB	S. Messerley, assistant
7–8	1962	Rae, DOGRIB	N.O. Lurie: Most of season at LLM
6–7,11	1967	Rae, DOGRIB	N.O. Lurie
6–7	1968	Rae, DOGRIB	D.M. Smith, student: Resolution, CHIPEWYAN B.C. Gillespie, student: Detah, DOGRIB
6–7	1969	Rae, DOGRIB	BCG: Detah; DMS: Resolution
1,7	1970	Rae, DOGRIB	
7	1971	Rae, DOGRIB	BCG: Rae, Detah; Norman, BEARLAKE (3–5) DMS: Resolution (9–12)
	1972		DMS: Resolution (2–4) BCG: Detah; Norman (9–11)
6	1973	Rae, DOGRIB	
2,3	1974	Simpson, SLAVE: Norman, BEARLAKE*	BCG: same (2,3)[b]; Ft. Smith, CHIPEWYAN[b] (7) DMS: Snowdrift[b], Resolution, CHIPEWYAN[b] (7)
8	1976	Rae, Lac la Martre, Rae Lakes, DOGRIB	

[a] Between 1970 and 1975, linguistic field research among subarctic Athapaskans was carried out by linguist Robert Howren and graduate students in linguistics under NSF Grant GS–3057, June Helm and Robert Howren, Co-principal Investigators. Archival and other documentary research in Dene ethnology was pursued as well.
[b] Indian Brotherhood Land Claims Research.

duplicate). More important, the mind's companionship born of intense common interest forestalled the psychological malaise that is apt to arise during extended tours alone. On the other hand, I am temperamentally incapable of enacting daily the role of mentor or spouse while pursuing fieldwork, so students or husband must busy themselves elsewhere.

The imperative partnership in fieldwork is, of course, that between the ethnologist and those members of the host group who aid, guide, instruct, and create the data for him, and it is so manifold that I can only make simple acknowledgment of it here. Had I not found the Dene of the north so temperamentally compatible there would be no long-term research to record. Of all the admirable and congenial attributes of the Dogrib and their neighbors, I shall single out one: the disinclination to type-cast whites solely according to stereotyped ethnic or status definitions; rather, to assess them in terms of their individual humanity. Thus, a trading post manager is not automatically assigned to a "liked" or "disliked" category on the basis of white-ness or occupational status. It is by his individual character and personality that he is ultimately judged "a good Hudson's Bay man," "a poor Hudson's Bay man," or—as my Dogrib friend Vital Thomas summed up the dour Scot who cast a disapproving eye on all persons of his acquaintance, Indian and white alike—"that's a *real* Hudson's Bay man!" As a white ethnologist, one hopes that one's final personal reputation is "good," though I cannot but wonder what the full implications will be if someday a Dogrib exclaims, "That's a real anthropologist!"

BIBLIOGRAPHY

Bohannan, Paul
    1958 Extra-processual events in Tiv political institutions. *American Anthropologist* *60*:1–12.
Gillespie, Beryl C.
    1970 Yellowknives: Quo iverunt? In *Migration and Anthropology. Proceedings of the 1970 annual spring meeting of the American Ethnological Society*, edited by Spencer, R.F. Pp. 61–71. Seattle: Univ. of Washington Press.
    1975 Territorial expansion of the Chipewyan in the 18th century. In *Proceedings of the Athapaskan Conference*, Vol. 11, edited by Clark, A. M. Pp. 350–388, National Museum of Man, Mercury Series, Canadian Ethnology Source Paper, No. 27. Ottawa.
Helm, June (see also MacNeish, June Helm)
    1965 Bilaterality in the socioterritorial organization of the Arctic drainage Dene. *Ethnology* *4*:361–385.
    1968a An annotated description of a Dogrib prophet cult ceremony: Part of 1968 final report to National Museums of Canada. Manuscript, Ethnology Division, Museum of Man, Ottawa.
    1968b The nature of Dogrib socioterritorial groups. In *Man the hunter,* edited by DeVore, I. and Lee, R. Pp. 118–125. Chicago: Aldine Press.
    1969 A method of statistical analysis of primary relative bonds in community composition. Bulletin of the National Museums of Canada, No. 228, *Anthropological Series* *84*:218–239.

Helm, June, T. Alliband, T. Birk, V. Lawson, S. Reisner, C. Sturdevant, and S. Witkowski
  1975 The contact history of the subarctic Athapaskans: An overview. In *Proceedings of the Athapaskan Conference,* Vol. 1, edited by Clark, A.M. Pp. 302–349. National Museum of Man, Mercury Series, Canadian Ethnology Service Paper, No. 27. Ottawa.
Helm, June, and David Damas
  1963 The contact-traditional all-native community of the Canadian North: The upper Mackenzie "bush" Athapaskans and the Igluligmiut. *Anthropologica, n.s., 5:9–22.*
Helm, June, and Eleanor Leacock
  1971 The hunting tribes of subarctic Canada. In *North American Indians in historical perspective.* edited by Leacock, E.B., and Lurie, N. Pp. 343–374. New York: Random House.
Helm, June, and Nancy O. Lurie
  1961 *The subsistence economy of the Dogrib Indians of Lac la Martre in the Mackenzie District of the N.W.T.* Ottawa: Northern Coordination and Research Centre, Department of Northern Affairs and National Resources.
  1966 The Dogrib hand game. *National Museum of Canada Bulletin* No. 205. Ottawa.
Helm, June, E. S. Rogers, and J. G. E. Smith
  press Intercultural relations and cultural change in the shield subarctic. In *The Subarctic,* edited by Helm, J. *Handbook of North American Indians,* Vol. VI. Washington: Smithsonian Institution.
Honigmann, John J.
  1946 Ethnography and acculturation of the Fort Nelson Slave. *Yale University Publications in Anthropology, No. 33.* New Haven: Yale Univ. Press.
Lurie, Nancy O.
  1970 Anthropologists in the U.S. and the Indian Claims Commission. Paper presented at the annual meeting of Northeast Anthropological Society, Ottawa, Canada, May 7–9, 1970.
MacNeish, June Helm
  1956 Leadership among the Northeastern Athabascans. *Anthropologica 2:131–163.*
  1960 Kin terms of arctic drainage Dene. *American Anthropologist 62:279–295.*
Morgan, L. H.
  1871 Systems of consanguinity and affinity in the human family. *Smithsonian Contributions to Knowledge,* Vol. 17. Washington, D.C.
Reynolds, Vernon
  1968 Kinship and the family in monkeys, apes, and man. *Man (n.s.), 3*(2):209–223.
Service, Elman
  1962 *Primitive social organization.* New York: Random House.
Shames, Deborah
  1972 *Freedom with reservation.* Madison: Impressions, Inc.
Slickpoo, Allan P., director
  1973 *Noon Nee-Me-Poo (We, the Nez Perces),* Vol. I. Lapwai, Idaho: Nez Perce Tribe of Idaho.
Slotkin, J. S.
  1952 Menomini Peyotism. *Transactions of the American Philosophical Society* (n.s.), 42, Part 4.
Smith, David M.
  1973 *Inkonze: Magico-religious beliefs of contact-traditional Chipewyan trading at Fort Resolution, N.W.T., Canada,* National Museum of Man, Mercury Series, Ethnology Division Paper, No. 6.

1975   Fort Resolution people: An historical study of ecological change. Unpublished Ph.D. dissertation, Department of Anthropology, University of Minnesota, Minneapolis.

Steward, Julian
1936   The social and economic basis of primitive bands. In *Essays in honor of A. L. Kroeber*, edited by Lowie, R. Pp. 331–350. Berkeley: Univ. of California Press.

Vogt, Evon
1960   On the concepts of structure and process in cultural anthropology. *American Anthropologist 62*:18–33.

Wallace, Anthony F. C.
1956   Revitalization movements. *American Anthropologist 58*:264–281.

8

Fieldwork in Tzintzuntzan:
The First Thirty Years

George M. Foster

INTRODUCTION

Tzintzuntzan is a Spanish-speaking peasant community of 2500 people, on the east shore of Lake Pátzcuaro, 230 miles west of Mexico City on a good paved highway. The lake, perhaps the most beautiful in Mexico, lies at an elevation of 7000 feet, surrounded by extinct volcanic peaks rising to 12,000 feet. At the time of the Spanish conquest of Mexico, beginning in 1519, Tzintzuntzan was the capital of the Tarascan Empire, the most powerful cultural and political group in west central Mexico. Its importance is still attested to by five circular pyramids rising above the village. Briefly, during the early colonial period, Tzintzuntzan was slated to be the seat of the bishopric for west central Mexico, but the church fathers soon thought better of such ambitious plans. Still, a major Franciscan monastery functioned there for well over 2 centuries, and colonial church buildings cast their distinctive stamp on the village. Spaniards and their Mexican-born descendants—increasingly mixed with the indigenous peoples of the areas—have lived in the village since the 1530s; church registers, well into the nineteenth century, distinguish entries as *Ciudadano* (of Spanish descent) or *Yndio* (Indian, Tarascan speaking).

165

Long-Term Field Research
in Social Anthropology

Although Tarascan appears to have been the dominant language until after 1850, for the past century Spanish has been the principal language. Today the 10% of the population that can speak Tarascan represents recent migrants from adjacent Indian villages. Tzintzuntzan is a pottery-making and trading village, in which farming is of secondary importance, best characterized as mestizo by race and peasant in cultural typology.

THE FIRST VISIT

My association with Tzintzuntzan and its people began in a fortuitous fashion. It was only after 1959 that I realized I was making a personal long-term commitment to the community. My wife, Mary, and I first passed through the village in early 1940, as tourists, at a time when I was engaged in doctoral research in another part of Mexico. The thought that I was being given a prescient glimpse of a large chunk of my professional career did not cross my mind. In the spring of 1944, Julian Steward, founder and director of the Smithsonian Institution's new Institute of Social Anthropology, sent Donald Brand, a geographer, and me to Mexico to teach at the National School of Anthropology. The formal agreement between the Smithsonian Institution and the Mexican National Institute of Anthropology and History specified that during half of each year we would meet classes and, during the other half, we would train students in field methods and conduct research in the Tarascan area, carrying on "The Tarasca Project" (Rubín de la Borbolla and Beals 1940) initiated in 1939, at that time still a high research priority in Mexico. Thus, I had no choice in selection of the research area; acceptance of the Smithsonian appointment committed me to work in Michoacán.

In June 1944, Brand and I made a brief survey of the Tarascan area in order to pick a site at which to initiate research in late December. We visited Tzintzuntzan but did not seriously consider it because it seemed no longer Tarascan. Instead, we selected Ihuatzio, an extremely conservative Tarascan fishing community three miles distant in the same *municipio* (a political unit similar to a small United States county).

There we arrived, Brand and I, accompanied by six students from the National School of Anthropology, and there we learned an important lesson. Although we had cleared our research with the appropriate state and local authorities and had visited the village and secured a pledge of cooperation from the priest, we were greeted with reserve that verged on hostility. After 3 days, we found it prudent to leave. Eight strangers dropped into a conservative community were seen as a major threat and no official instructions or orders would induce people to accept us. Consequently, we split our group, so that, on January 5, 1945, I found myself in Tzintzuntzan with Pablo Velásquez and Gabriel Ospina, both students at the school. Pablo was a native Tarascan from a village in the high sierra to the west and Gabriel was a Colombian on a fellowship in Mexico.

We lived and worked together in Tzintzuntzan for the first 6 months of 1945, Velásquez concentrating his attention on the adjacent Tarascan hamlet of Ichupio, leaving the village for Ospina and me. In June, Velásquez and I returned to Mexico City; I to resume my teaching obligation. Ospina remained in Tzintzuntzan until March, 1946. During these additional 8 months, I returned on average for about a week each month. Later we returned on several occasions, the last in September, so that our observations spanned 20 months. Ospina's continuous presence in the village for 14 months and his superb qualities as a fieldworker spelled the difference between average and exceptionally good baseline data.

In retrospect, Tzintzuntzan proved to be a far happier choice than I could have foreseen—preferable, I am sure, to Ihuatzio. As *cabecera,* or chief administrative town of the *Municipio* of Tzintzuntzan, the village is the site of the municipal archives and of most political activity as well. As the first Christian community in Michoacán, because of the long residence of Franciscan monks, and because of the continuous presence of priests since the Franciscans' departure in the 1770s, Tzintzuntzan, in 1945, had a more complex religious and ceremonial life than Ihuatzio. Again, with a major pottery home industry, as well as farming, fishing, and tule reed weaving, Tzintzuntzan had a much more varied economic base than the latter village, whose economy was based largely on fishing. Finally, Tzintzuntzan turned out to be among the first communities studied by anthropologists of the type we have come to call "peasant." My thinking about the nature of peasant society was stimulated well beyond what would have been the case had my theoretical orientation continued to be traditional, Tarascan Indian, and historical, as would certainly have proven true had we remained in Ihuatzio. The bulk of our findings on this initial project are found in Foster and Ospina 1948.

RETURN IN 1958

In spite of my satisfaction with the Tzintzuntzan experience, I did not, in 1946, think seriously of maintaining research continuity. A return to Washington, D.C. in 1946 as Director of the Institute of Social Anthropology, a year of field research in Spain 1949–1950, removal to Berkeley in 1953, and consulting applied anthropological activities in other parts of the world in 1952, 1955, and 1957, all turned my mind from continuing research in Mexico. Then, during the summer of 1958, Mary and I made a leisurely trip through Mexico to select a research site, with

Tzintzuntzan a top candidate among the several possibilities we considered. When we returned to the village, we found that in spite of a 12-year absence we were remembered and well liked. The evident pleasure expressed by old friends and the presence of Gabriel Ospina and other professional friends at UNESCO's CREFAL (Fundamental Education Training Center for Latin America) at nearby Pátzcuaro quickly tipped the scale in favor of a return to Tzintzuntzan. From 1958 to the present, we have made at least one trip and sometimes two trips annually to the village, spending from 1 to 4 months each year in residence.

In renewing my studies, I had in mind as models Lewis' restudy of Tepoztlán (Lewis 1951) and Redfield's restudy of Chan Kom (Redfield 1950). Initially I did not realize I was embarking on a very different type of project, a longitudinal study with frequent repeat visits more comparable to Kluckhohn's work among the Navajo. In the 1950s, the distinction between a restudy and a longitudinal, or long-term, study had not yet emerged. Methodologically, this distinction is important. A restudy, particularly if the time spent in the field is relatively brief, inevitably draws attention to change. In contrast, longitudinal study affords opportunity both to study change *and* to delve more deeply into the culture itself.

The 12-year gap between my early and later observations suggests that my Tzintzuntzan research resembles both a restudy and a longitudinal study. To a certain extent, this is true. Actually, however, the "gap" is much less than the dates suggest, since Gabriel Ospina had returned to Pátzcuaro in late 1952 as one of the first staff members of newly established CREFAL. Because of his earlier residence in the village, his friendships with the people, and his knowledge of the local scene, Tzintzuntzan became one of the major communities for CREFAL's training programs and planned culture change projects. Rare was the week, from late 1952 until his departure from CREFAL in 1960, that Ospina did not spend several days in Tzintzuntzan. From long discussions with him, from CREFAL censuses and other records (e.g., Ospina 1954), and from reports of shorter studies by other anthropologists (e.g., García Manzanedo 1955, Willner 1958), I obtained a very good picture of what had transpired during the second half of the period I was absent, leaving a gap of only about 6 years for which we have no firsthand information other than from villagers themselves.

Living Arrangements

During the initial study, Ospina, Velásquez, and I lived first in the school building (during the long vacation) and then in a small house at the pyramids designed to be a museum, our cooking and cleaning needs taken care of by *compadres* and close friends. In both places we were in the village, but slightly removed from the center of things. We were unable to look out into the street and see who passed by, who interacted with whom, and we were unable quietly to observe from within how a household functioned. In beginning our new work, Mary and I hoped to live much closer to the villagers, to be participant observers to the greatest degree possible. Here it was that an old friend, Doña Micaela González, her second husband Melecio Hernández, and her grown daughters, Dolores and Virginia Pichu, rose to the challenge. With great apprehension, Micaela subsequently told us, and in response to Ospina's urging, she agreed to put a glass window and a cement floor in a room for our use, to accept us into her home, to prepare our meals, to wash our clothing, and to answer our questions.

The arrangement has more than met the expectations of all parties and since 1959 we have lived in Doña Micaela's home. With each succeeding year, we found ourselves accumulating more and more field equipment, file boxes, local arts and crafts, and clothing so that by 1970 we had outgrown our small room. Simultaneously, Micaela—who was one of the first villagers to abandon the traditional noncompetitive stance—had reached the point where, to keep up with two or three other villagers, she felt compelled to build a second story on her house. Here again our interest coincided with hers: We designed and paid for a second story apartment which we have furnished to our taste and where we keep sufficient field equipment and clothing so that we can arrive with no more than a brief case and live in great comfort. We have no equity in this property; when we no longer need it, it reverts to the family. Meanwhile, we have comfortable and attractive quarters, loving care from the family members while we are in residence, and superb informants within hailing distance.

The research advantages of living with a family, and of observing it in its most intimate moments, can scarcely be overemphasized. Chance remarks overheard and chance events observed—"trigger mechanisms," I call them—have been among the most important sources of my theoretical ideas. There are many field situations where it is not feasible to live intimately with informants; where it *is* possible, there is no substitute for it. The rich data obtainable in this fashion simply cannot be duplicated in any other way.

RESEARCH RESULTS: THE CORPUS OF DATA

Physically, the corpus of data I have acquired over the years fills 10 file boxes with 5 × 8 inch sheets of paper. Three boxes contain basic data of many types, classified according to the HRAF indexing system, which I have used from the beginning of my Tzintzuntzan work, and which I feel is the most logical system for community studies. A fourth file contains nearly 400 dreams from more than 40 informants, while a fifth holds TAT protocols, all taken from tapes, of 20 informants. A sixth box contains data, much of it taped, on health and medical practices and beliefs. Two more boxes are filled with nearly 200 years of vital statistics, a near 100% sample of births, marriages, and deaths drawn from the parish archive and, since 1930, from the municipal civil registry as well. I have hand-transcribed from the original sources half or more of these data, a process requiring hundreds, and possibly thousands, of hours. This is a difficult process, not easily left to an assistant, since the Tzintzuntzan records are interspersed with those of the entire parish and *municipio,* and represent only about a quarter of all entries. Often the community is specified; but frequently it is not. Then only the researcher's knowledge of family lines and their communities makes possible reasonable certainty in assigning provenience. Just when the task of hand-copying the parish records seemed to be hopeless, Father Isidro Huacúz gave permission to take the oldest, most precious, and most difficult to read records to Guadalajara, 200 miles away, for xeroxing. There, for three summers, over a hot and balky Xerox, I copied about 10,000 pages from which a research assistant in Berkeley is extracting the pertinent data.

Finally, two boxes are filled with over 3000 slips, each of which contains basic data on a single person, all people whose names appear on any of the three 100% complete censuses taken in 1945, 1960, and 1970. These individual records have been extracted from the original family census sheets (which I keep bound in 9 × 14 inch post binders), and have been added to regularly from vital statistics and many other sources of information. The data include, in most cases, birth date, place of birth, parents and grandparents, siblings, spouse or spouses, children (in rank order of birth), and the place of residence, keyed to a map showing all households, for each census year that the person's name appears. These individual records have made possible the reconstruction of family genealogies going back from four to six generations. Particularly in the analysis of interpersonal relationships, and in sorting out the constitution of the guest list at a wake, a baptism, or a marriage, to be able to identify every participant as to home location, possible kin relationship to hosts, and the like, individual genealogical records are treasures of the highest order. The work involved in making and updating more than 3000 individual records, only part of which can be entrusted to research assistants, is an extremely time-consuming activity.

I have described my research corpus—if only in the sketchiest terms— to document the obvious: With time to gather data *and* time to create or fall into the conditions essential to obtaining data, repeat visits make possible the accumulation of a wealth of information that cannot be obtained, even with a team approach, in a traditional short-term project. As one example, the elderly priest in Tzintzuntzan at the time of my arrival, a good friend until his death in the early 1960s, would not give permission to copy from the parish archive, much less authorize removal of the records for copying. This opportunity simply had to await the arrival of the younger priest, with whom I have a closer personal relationship, and who appreciates the importance of historical as well as anthropological research in Tzintzuntzan.

HYPOTHESIS FORMULATION

What theoretical or other considerations have guided me in amassing these data? Why have I emphasized some areas, and perhaps neglected others? Formulation of hypotheses in Berkeley, to be tested by data specifically gathered to test these hypothesis has, I confess, played a very minor role in guiding my work. This is not to say that I work without a sense of problem. When I returned in 1959, I assumed—with the "restudy" model in mind—that the principal justification for continued work was to exploit a detailed cultural baseline in order to measure subsequent changes and to analyze these changes to learn more about the processes of change. Consequently, I spent much time trying to identify innovators and in determining how—in education, travel experience, work, and the like—they might differ from less innovative personalities. I have maintained this interest and, in addition to systematic updating of censuses, vital statistics, and similar data, I have taken pains to note the growing numbers of young people who leave the village to continue higher education, the numbers and destinations of emigrants, the widespread acceptance of television, of cars and trucks, gas stoves, and other signs of "modernization."

But as time passed, I also realized that the original Tzintzuntzan research barely scratched the surface of the cultural reality and that in *all* areas of life there was still much to be learned. As a student of Kroeber and Lowie, I was taught that all forms of behavior, all data, have meaning, and that they are relevant to interpretation and explanation, even if this relevance is not apparent at the time they are noted or recorded.

Consequently, I have been happy to continue with my earliest research habits of trying to record as many data as possible on everything that occurs to me. When I become aware of data "out there," I want them, even if I have no plans for their immediate use, and even knowing that some of what I record will never reveal (to me) their real significance. I began recording dreams, for example, in a very casual fashion. It was not a topic that had previously interested me and I felt deficient in the psychological training necessary to the interpretation of dreams. Still, when a relative lull came in the gathering of other data, it dawned on me that this was a rich and untapped source of information about many aspects of village life and that through manifest content analysis I should be able to learn a great deal about personality, world view, and perhaps other things. So, without definite plans, I plunged into the task, asking friends to tell me their dreams. I simply assumed that I was a sufficiently good anthropologist to be able to draw something meaningful—to recognize basic patterns—from a sizable collection of dreams. The result was "Dreams, Character, and Cognitive Orientation in Tzintzuntzan" (1973). Ultimately, I hope to publish the entire corpus of dreams, with pertinent information about the dreamers, so that others can make use of this rich body of data.

In some instances, I have waited 20 or more years before realizing the significance of behavior that, at the time noted, fit into no current research interests. For example, while doing doctoral research among the Popoluca Indians of southern Veracruz state 1940–1941, I was intrigued by the fact that people—Indians and mestizos alike—when approaching each other on a jungle trail, would exchange greetings with *Adiós* ('Goodbye'). Sometimes they would pause briefly for a few more words, and sometimes they would pass without further comment. Subsequently I realized this is a common Mexican practice, not limited to any group or geographical area. Still, I puzzled: Why should "Goodbye" be used as a greeting?

During my initial and subsequent Tzintzuntzan research I recorded many observations, including speech forms, having to do with how people interacted with each other, without specific ideas as to what these data might mean. I was particularly impressed by the fact that friends, when separating, when "Goodbye" seemed appropriate to me, were careful to say, "We will not say goodbye." Only in 1963 did these, and many more data, suddenly coalesce into a plausible pattern, as a result of a "trigger mechanism" experience. One night, after having seen Doña Micaela kick the dog out of the kitchen for perhaps the thousandth time, it dawned on me that she simultaneously used the respectful third person singular form in her verbal command. "Speech Forms and the Perception of Social Distance" (1964a) was the result of this final observation. A mass of earlier observations on verbal interaction, including *Adiós* and "We will not say goodbye" flooded into my mind, and almost immediately I knew what they meant: That perception and manipulation of social distance are expressed through an elaborate system of verbal forms. It was almost as if I had punched the computer button and received the printout, for within half an hour I had assembled most of the illustrations used in the article.

The "trigger mechanism" also accounts for "Cultural Responses to Expressions of Envy in Tzintzuntzan" (1965b). Over the years I had observed and recorded odd bits of behavior: the universal rejection of compliments, the *remojo* gift given to friends by someone who acquires something new of importance, the concealment of pregnancy, the *bolo* (copper coins thrown by the godfather to village children immediately after the baptism of an infant), the way in which, at family fiestas, there is no clear idea as to how many guests will come, and the like. Then, on one occasion, 50 or more children came to Doña Micaela's house for a "school breakfast." To my astonishment, they ate in absolute silence. "They're taught to eat in silence," was Micaela's response to my question as to why. That children would eat noisily in a group was as astonishing to her as that they could eat quietly was to me. Something said to me "envy!", and these behavioral forms, and many others as well, almost instantly came to mind, falling into what now seems like predestined places; within an hour the paper was blocked out. Eating in silence, I realized, and many other forms of seemingly unrelated behavior have one important thing in common: Symbolically or in fact, they are devices useful in reducing the likelihood of envy from persons not fortunate enough to have food, a new possession of value, or a healthy new descendent.

An important methodological point emerges from these experiences. Once the trigger mechanisms had given me the basic idea, I was then able to ask myself, "What other situations may there be in which this model might predict behavior?" In both instances I was quickly able to think of, and then ask specifically about, situations which proved to conform to the model. Through this heuristic process, additional data were discovered and fitted into place. Another anthropologist might well have made these social distance and envy observations during a single field session and come to similar conclusions. Still, in my case it was the slow accumulation over the years of observations not related to specific hypotheses or topics of primary interest that made possible the final products.

In other instances, I have been unable to identify the precise moment and manner in which new hypotheses or models first occurred to me beyond recognizing that masses of data slowly acquired made them possible. The dyadic contract articles (1961a, 1963) are illustrative. The ideas in the first paper developed in an unplanned fashion, as I was drawn into village reciprocity networks. Eventually, I realized that there was a significant pattern in exchange relationships, which I interpreted in the form in which they are published. Only after writing the first paper did it occur to me that people interact with patrons, including supernatural beings, in essentially the same manner as with fellow villagers.

The model of Limited Good (1965a) represents a combination of a "trigger mechanism" and a slowly growing awareness of what behavior means with respect to a cognitive outlook. From the time of my first Tzintzuntzan work, I had speculated that the economic world view of the villagers, and perhaps that of peasants in general, was marked by what I came to call the "Image of the Static Economy." The "economic pie," I argued, quite realistically was seen as constant in size and unexpandable. Consequently, "If someone is seen to get ahead, logically it can only be at the expense of others in the village [1960–1961:177; see also 1961b, 1964b]." I saw the problem, however, only in economic terms. The integrating theme of "implicit premises," central to the complete argument, developed during a 6-month community development assignment in Northern Rhodesia (now Zambia) in 1962. There I was struck by how different were Britishers' assumptions about people, character, and culture from my own, and how different both of our assumptions were from those in Tzintzuntzan. I began thinking about the static economy in the wider context of implicit premises, but still I did not have the final key to Limited Good. This came—the idea was "triggered"—when I chanced to read an article by John Honigmann about a village in West Pakistan. Three sentences in a footnote caught my eye:

> One dominant element in the character structure [of the villagers] . . . is the implicit belief that good of all kinds is limited. There is only so much respect, influence, power, and love in the world. If another has some, then somebody is certainly deprived of that measure [Honigmann 1960:287].

This "trigger" caused all of the elements in the model (including such diverse things as treasure tales and the nonregenerative quality of blood) to fall into place. Limited Good thus owes its formulation to three major activities or events: the slow accumulation through field research and reading of information on peasant economic behavior; my exposure to a drastically different culture (British colonial society) that contributed an element critical to the model; and a "trigger," in this case the published observations of a colleague. The lessons I draw from this is that the anthropologist, however strongly committed to a single community or people, should actively seek out other cross-cultural experiences as a source of pertinent ideas and that general, as well as specialized, reading is essential for the widest exposure to potential stimuli.

These examples should illustrate why, given my approach to field research, I have found repeat visits to Tzintzuntzan so valuable. In a sense, one can say that personal and research maturation have been the most important results of this strategy. Leisurely trips over a long period of years, with time to reflect between visits, opportunity to try out ideas on students, to write papers, in full realization that gaps in data can be filled in at a future time, have proven to be exceedingly important factors in my research. Equally important to this maturation process and to my research results has been the companionship of my wife, who has been with me during most of the work since 1958. Her primary research interests have been linguistic, based on the nearby Tarascan hamlet of Ichupio, from which has come her doctoral dissertation (M. L. Foster 1969). We have, however, lived the same life in Tzintzuntzan, attended the same fiestas, heard the same things, and observed the same behavior. She has noted points that have escaped me and has had access to situations from which I, as a man, have been excluded. The discussions we have had in the field, the speculations about the significance of this or that act or event, and her perceptions as a woman have played a major role in my research and writing.

EQUILIBRIUM MODELS

In reflecting on my experiences in Tzintzuntzan, I am struck by a point which has received little attention in the literature. Theory that emerges from short-term research, however stimulating, consciously and subconsciously is based on a relatively static view of the community. Historical reconstruction, ethnohistory, and the memories of elderly informants simply cannot convey the full meaning of rapid change in a community and the influence of such change on the development of anthropological theory. The magnitude of changes during 30 years in Tzintzuntzan are described in some detail in Kemper and Foster (1975). During this period, the community has changed from a very "closed," "uptight," fearful, suspicious traditional community to an "open" community, very much a part of modern Mexico.

In considering critiques of the Limited Good hypothesis, for example, it seems to me that the importance of time perspective is not fully apparent. The model is accurate for traditional Tzintzuntzan, perhaps to about 1965, although with a decreasingly good fit during a few years preceding that date. But changes in behavior, in attitudes, and above all in relations with the outside world—due particularly to radio and television, education, and emigration—have in significant measure modified the traditional Limited Good outlook and masked many of its manifestations that still survive. In other words, the kinds of evidence that led to my initial formulation, while by no means gone, are much less obvious than they were 15 years ago. It is possible that, had I begun my research in Tzintzuntzan in 1970, the idea of Limited Good would never have occurred to me. It would be entirely possible for a young anthropologist to study Tzintzuntzan today and, on the basis of his findings, argue that even in Tzintzuntzan the Limited Good hypothesis is inappropriate. To a degree he would be correct: In *contemporary* Tzintzuntzan it explains behavior much less satisfactorily than in *traditional* Tzintzuntzan. But such an argument, because of lack of time depth, in no way denigrates the model. It merely confirms what we already know: World views can and do change.

SOME METHODOLOGICAL QUESTIONS

If, in 1945, I had realized that my commitment to Tzintzuntzan was to be life-long, would I have done things differently? Are there additional kinds of data, and other approaches to gathering data, that I would have sought or used? In hindsight, I feel fortunate that I emphasized data rather than theory in the initial study. My regrets have to do with data I might have, but failed to gather, not with hypotheses I might have, but failed to develop or test. Theories come and go but good data are timeless, grist for the anthropologist's mill when least expected.

Time permits the accumulation of vast masses of data. Time also presents a special problem: familiarity with the community. Behavior which, at an earlier period in my research, would forcibly have struck me, now seems ordinary and normal, so that significant facts and clues go unrecorded. For the same reason that anthropologists often are insensitive to critical items in their own societies, after many years I have become insensitive to the implications of some of the things I observe in Tzintzuntzan. Age, too, undeniably cuts me off from increasing bodies of data. When working on the question of euphemisms a few years ago, I formulated a series of questions on sexual usages (1966a). I cut short my questioning when I realized villagers were beginning to ask themselves if I had become a dirty-minded old man. Thirty years earlier this problem would not have arisen.

I am also worried by the fact that during recent years I have had fewer new, fresh ideas than in earlier years. I sometimes wonder if I am reaching a point of diminishing returns. If so, to what is this due? In part it is certainly a question of age. Past 60, I simply do not have the same drive and enthusiasm that characterized my earlier work. I am no less anxious to be in the village; in fact, I appreciate it more than ever and hope in the future to spend more time in it than during very recent years. But trigger effects are rarer than formerly, and I doubt that I will come up with another dyadic contract or Limited Good model.

Yet, fortunately, each time I panic for fear the well is running dry, rich new lodes appear. Recently, I have concentrated on health and illness beliefs and practices. Five years ago I thought I knew all there was to know on the subject; in reality, I knew almost nothing. Even more recently I have realized that the possibilities for symbolic interpretations of ritual behavior are far greater than I had assumed.

THE ROLE OF STUDENTS

Over the years, about a dozen graduate students have accompanied me to the Pátzcuaro area, some more than once. Most of these have been placed in nearby communities where we have had easy access to each other, but where they have been on their own. I have favored this arrangement not only because I have been apprehensive about cluttering up Tzintzuntzan with outsiders, but also because of the feeling that students enjoy having a community to themselves. As a result of our unpleasant experience in Ihuatzio early in 1945, which can be attributed largely (but not entirely) to the size of our group, I have been hypercautious about bringing additional workers, students included, into Tzintzuntzan. Consequently, only three have spent significant amounts of time in the village, and, until 1977, never simultaneously. Melissa Kassovic, just now completing her doctoral dissertation, has spent nearly 2 years in Tzintzuntzan since 1972. Stanley Brandes, who completed doctoral research in Spain, has spent about 7 months in the village since 1967. Robert Kemper has spent short periods of time in Tzintzuntzan since 1967, as reported separately in this book. His doctoral dissertation and subsequent research on Tzintzuntzeños in Mexico City stem directly from my data base. William Iler accompanied me to Tzintzuntzan during the summer of 1959; subsequently he has turned to other interests.

All students, whether in Tzintzuntzan or adjacent villages, proved to be fine fieldworkers. Their skill in winning the friendship of the people with whom they have worked has been notable. Such success suggests I have been unduly cautious in my approach to student training. On the other hand, it may be because of caution and great care in picking students that things have gone so smoothly. Then too—as far as Tzintzuntzan is concerned—there is the question of the ideal number of students to be introduced into a community. I feel there is an optimum number of outsiders at any one time, and I prefer to err on the low rather than the high side.

My students and I have never really worked on a joint project in the field, so we have had no problem with integration of, or rights to, field data. The only joint publication to date is Kemper and Foster (1975) and that developed as an afterthought, when we found that our independently gathered data lent themselves to a specific problem. With all students I have had a formal, but simple, agreement that spells out their expectations (or rights) and mine. All give me copies of their field notes, which remain in my files. When I am dealing with comparative topics where their data are pertinent I may cite their findings, with appropriate credit and with their permission. The data, however, belong to them, and can be used in any way they wish. Students, in turn, have had full access to my files and have comparable reciprocal rights with respect to publication. This system has worked well and has resulted in no disagreements.

I have, perhaps naturally, wondered what will happen to my files when I am no longer able to use them. Fortunately, Brandes, Kassovic, and Kemper have all expressed interest in carrying on research in Tzintzuntzan or on former Tzintzuntzeños. To them will fall the task of deciding how the materials can best continue to be used in the interests of science and of the villagers. I cannot imagine better hands in which to leave a scientific legacy.

IMPACT ON THE PEOPLE STUDIED

Our impact (and that of my students) on Tzintzuntzan has been varied and significant. I believe no one is worse off, for our presence, and I know that some are better off. A few, without our intervention in medical crises, would almost certainly be dead. We have never paid directly for information in Tzintzuntzan, but there have been important material advantages for those people with whom we have worked most closely, and to whom we have felt most indebted. Every year we arrive in the village with from $100 to $200 worth of presents: cloth for dresses, clothing for children, kitchen equipment, clocks and watches, and the like. We have supported promising young people through secondary school, and beyond. The largest sums of money have been for medical attention, including not a few surgical operations. We have loaned money on occasion; some loans have been outstanding for many years.

There are also negative aspects to a policy of substantial help given to relatively few people. This help and the ever-present possibility of future aid have affected relationships for the worse between some of the families that have benefited most from our presence, and between them and other families that feel they might have benefited more. We are, after all, a limited good and our largesse, though considerable, is not inexhaustible. Many families would have appreciated, and benefited by, medical, educational, and other forms of help. Just as village families traditionally see themselves in competition for scarce "good" of all kinds, so do those that benefit, or aspire to benefit, from us see themselves competing for our favors. The resulting envy and jealousy are fairly well suppressed during our stays, but in at least a few instances they have resulted in strained relationships among village families.

Micaela and her family are probably the most envied people in the village. Their remarkable economic progress during the past 20 years is seen as almost entirely due to our help, a perception far from the mark. Nonetheless, it can be argued that, had we not come to roost with Micaela, she and the other members of her family would have more intimate ties with more villagers than is now the case. It can also be argued that there would be little difference, for the few other families that have made major economic progress during the same period also find themselves increasingly distant from their fellow villagers.

I have been concerned with the moral and ethical questions surrounding the relationships between anthropologists and informants. Clearly, I have profited enormously from this relationship. In a large measure, my position in anthropology is due to the people of Tzintzuntzan. If the village had the equivalent of a United Crusade, it would be easy to assign royalties from books to it. But there is no village mechanism whereby money can be given for the benefit of the community at large. I contribute substantially to such things as public lighting and school funds and my name routinely is found on the list of "cooperators," or contributors, to any village function in which individual citizens are approached. Each year I leave with the village priest a substantial sum of money to be distributed at his discretion among the village needy. Altogether, my continuing contributions have far exceeded any monetary profit to me from publications. Some people obviously have benefited more than others; others, whom I feel have little real call on my resources, have also benefited.

In a wider sense, and for the village as a whole, I think our major impact has been to give villagers a sense of *ésprit* that would otherwise be lacking. They used to look upon themselves as humble villagers, people undervalued and ignored by their own more elevated countrymen. Prior to our arrival, no one had shown interest in their major occupation: pottery making. The fact that we return year after year and are obviously delighted to be there has led to a feeling that Tzintzuntzan must be something special. After all, no other Michoacán village can boast a resident anthropologist (much less two). *Que bueno que no nos olviden* is the standard greeting of villagers on each return, "How good that you don't forget us." And when we leave, it is always ¿ *Pourque se vayan tan pronto?,* "Why are you leaving so soon?" The phrases are ritual, but I believe they express the feeling that the presence of *el doctor* and *Mariquita* is tangible evidence that Tzintzuntzan is not an ordinary village.

Many of my undergraduate students visit Mexico, pass through Tzintzuntzan, and stop to buy pottery or other arts and crafts in the roadside stands. Some ask the vendors if they know me and all seem pleased—say returned students—to acknowledge their friendship. Other Americans who have read the 1967 book on Tzintzuntzan display a flattering knowledge about the village. Tzintzuntzeños have come to take it for granted that their home is widely known in the United States, more so than other Michoacán villages. They are pleased that this is so.

A related problem has to do with anonymity. Many—perhaps most—contemporary studies use pseudonyms for community and informants. With literate people who will read what we write, this is a basic precaution to protect the people concerned. When I began work in Tzintzuntzan, however, it was still considered the mark of a careful anthropologist to identify his informants by name and to tell something about them. North American tribal research, of course, could not be done without clear identification of peoples and places. So it never occurred to me to conceal the true name of Tzintzuntzan, nor to use other than the real names of informants (except in a few obvious instances). By the time I realized the ethical implications of my policy, it was too late to turn back. Calling Tzintzuntzan *Tarasca* would have fooled no one. Also, the villagers would have been furious. They are delighted to see my publications, some of which are in Spanish, to see their photographs, and to see their names in print. They would feel cheated if I had to tell them, "It says 'Informant B'; that's really you."

Obviously I do not use real names in every case; for example, in matters having to do with crime I change names and disguise circumstances. But, my students tell me, the principal criticism of those few villagers who have read my work is that I have not given them and their families sufficient exposure.

I have always enjoyed fieldwork and feel that the mark of a true anthropologist is to be able to relate to people, not simply as informants, but as friends who share much more than an immediate concern with data. In Tzintzuntzan, after an initial period of several months of suspicion and doubt, rapport and friendship developed quite naturally. The friendship relationships we enjoy with the villagers in some ways are like those we enjoy in Berkeley. Tzintzuntzeños, like most Mexicans, have a finely honed sense of humor, an appreciation of the subtleties of every situation, which readily crosses cultural boundaries. Our ability to share the same jokes, to appreciate the ridiculous in ourselves and others, is one of the bonds that tie us together. We converse easily, we gossip, we discuss events of the day or the past year, and we ask each other questions. In short, in one way we interact on a level of *collegiality* that parallels friendship within our own society.

But for all the close ties I believe exist, I am still a *patrón,* a wealthier, more powerful, more important person in their eyes than they themselves. To some extent, I have maintained equality in my relationships through meticulous observation of the courtesy rules of address. From the beginning I have addressed all villagers near my age, and older, with the formal *usted.* I have used the informal *tu* only for children and young people up to about age 18. Friends whom I first knew as children, some of whom are now middle-aged, continue to be addressed informally, but when addressing young adults I have known only as adults, I always say *usted.* This courtesy is, I believe, greatly appreciated, for many outsiders, and particularly government officials, routinely address all villagers as *tu.*

On the other hand, except for a handful of very elderly people, whom I address as *Don* or *Doña,* followed by their given name, I use first names in addressing everyone. A very few people call me *Don Jorge,* but none says *George.* Almost universally I am known and identified as *el doctor,* and addressed as *Doctor.* Had I entered the community as a lone young anthropologist, this pattern might not have developed. But with students addressing me as *Doctor* from the day we entered the village, it was probably inevitable that villagers would take their cue from them. Also, it may be noted, *any* male with a claim to a profession—carpenter, mason, weaver, or teacher—is addressed as *Maestro,* so the term *Doctor* conforms to standard usage.

To some extent, this linguistically emphasized distance is mediated by my wife, Mary. During 1945 and 1946, she visited the village only occasionally, remaining most of the time with our small children in Mexico City. When I spoke of her forthcoming visits, I used the form María, so from the beginning the villagers identified her in a less formal fashion. After 1958, María quickly became *Mariquita.* Use of the diminutive is common for older women and it serves two functions. On the one hand, it is affectionate. But it is also a device whereby a person perceived to be more important or powerful than the speaker can be approached on terms of intimacy. Depending on the speaker, the use of *Mariquita* expresses either, or both, subtleties. Most villagers certainly feel they can approach Mary more easily than they can approach me. In a sense, I am boxed in by a verbal formality that has no out. Through the presence of *Mariquita,* this formality is eased considerably. I doubt that greater informality would have produced better data or closer friendship ties. After all, the villagers deal with a large part of the world on a fairly formal basis. To them formality is neither unnatural nor undesirable, and often they prefer it.

CONCLUSIONS

In summary, I turn to the major question that underlies this collection of essays: Why long-term research? The justifications I have found, professional and personal, fall into three principal categories:

1. I have had an intimate view of change at the microlevel, a view that could not be obtained in any other way. I know the people who are confronted with change possibilities, and I can place them in a sociocultural and economic context in assessing the reasons that underlie their acceptance or rejection of these possibilities. I can also ask them *why* they have made the decisions they have made. In addition to a more thorough understanding of microlevel processes of change, the Tzintzuntzan experience has impressed upon me the static bias that characterizes most anthropological models, including change models. When this point is more fully appreciated many of the anthropological disagreements found in the pages of our journals will be found to stem from the fact that conclusions were drawn on the erroneous assumption that yesterday's community is also today's community.

2. The total time available has vastly widened the spectrum of behavioral situations I have been able to observe. My data are "thick." Theoretical insights do not come to me in one massive package; they develop slowly, over time, as I turn from one theme to another. Many, as I have pointed out, have been purely serendipitous. The patient accumulation of masses of data, the lack of a sense of urgency, the ability to hold off on a "hot" idea, secure in the knowledge that another field season will permit gathering of additional critical data—all have been advantages to me. As a consequence of the research pattern that developed in Tzintzuntzan, I have been able to consider and write about a much wider variety of topics than would have been possible had I limited myself to one, or a few widely separated, visits.

3. A long-term commitment to Tzintzuntzan and its people has on a personal level been highly rewarding. I have come to understand myself, my motivations, my inner conflicts, to a degree I doubt possible had I spread my research efforts over several projects. The personal satisfaction and emotional fulfillment that comes from residence in Tzintzuntzan is now a more important pull than the expectation of dramatic new

research findings. I have learned what friendship really means and what is involved in a long-term friendship tie. When, in 1960, I found that quite unconsciously I was putting our Tzintzuntzan photographs in the family photograph album, I knew that our ties with the village would be permanent.

BIBLIOGRAPHY

Foster, George M.
1960– Interpersonal relations in peasant society. *Human Organization 19:*174–178.
1961
1960 Life expectancy of utilitarian pottery in Tzintzuntzan, Michoacán, Mexico. *American Antiquity 25:*606–609.
1961a The dyadic contract: A model for the social structure of a Mexican peasant village. *American Anthropologist 63:*1173–1192.
1961b Community development and the image of the static economy. *Community Development Bulletin 12:*124–128.
1963 The dyadic contract in Tzintzuntzan II: Patron–client relationship. *American Anthropologist 65:*1280–1294.
1964a Speech forms and the perception of social distance in a Spanish-speaking Mexican village. *Southwestern Journal of Anthropology 20:*107–122.
1964b Treasure tales and the image of the static economy in a Mexican peasant community. *Journal of American Folklore 77:*39–44.
1965a Peasant society and the image of limited good. *American Anthropologist 67:*293–315.
1965b Cultural responses to expressions of envy in Tzintzuntzan. *Southwestern Journal of Anthropology 21:*24–35.
1966a Euphemisms and cultural sensitivity in Tzintzuntzan. *Anthropological Quarterly 39:*53–59.
1966b World view in Tzintzuntzan: Reexamination of a concept. In *Summa anthropológica en homenaje a Roberto J. Weitlaner.* Pp. 385–393. Mexico City: Instituto Nacional de Antropología e Historia.
1967 *Tzintzuntzan: Mexican peasants in a changing world.* Boston: Little, Brown.
1968 El cambio cultural planificado y la irrigación en la cuenca del lago de Pátzcuaro. *Anuario Indigenista 38:*45–51.
1969 Godparents and social networks in Tzintzuntzan. *Southwestern Journal of Anthropology 25:*261–278.
1970 Character and personal relationships seen through proverbs in Tzintzuntzan, Mexico. *Journal of American Folklore 83:*304–317.
1973 Dreams, character, and cognitive orientation in Tzintzuntzan. *Ethos 1:*106–121.
Foster, George M., assisted by Gabriel Ospina
1948 *Empire's children: The people of Tzintzuntzan.* Smithsonian Institution, Institute of Social Anthropology, Publication No. 6. Mexico City.
Foster, Mary L.
1969 The Tarascan language. University of California Publications in Linguistics, Vol. 56. Berkeley: Univ. of California Press.
García Manzanedo, Héctor
1955 Informe sobre la cerámica de Tzintzuntzan. *Instituto Nacional Indigenista, Serie Mimeográfica,* No. 7. Mexico City.

Honigmann, John J.
1960 A case study of community development in Pakistan. *Economic Development and Cultural Change 8:*288–303.
Kemper, Robert V., and George M. Foster
1975 Urbanization in Mexico: The view from Tzintzuntzan. *Latin American Urban Research 5:*53–75.
Lewis, Oscar
1951 *Life in a Mexican village: Tepoztlán restudied.* Urbana: Univ. of Illinois Press.
Maccoby, Michael, and George M. Foster
1970 Methods of studying Mexican peasant personality: Rorschach, TAT, and dreams. *Anthropological Quarterly 43:*225–242.
Ospina, Gabriel
1954 Plan de rehabilitación cultural y económica de Tzintzuntzan. Manuscript, Centro Regional de Educación Fundamental para la América Latina (CREFAL), Pátzcuaro.
Redfield, Robert
1950 *A village that chose progress: Chan Kom revisited.* Chicago: Univ. of Chicago Press.
Rubín de la Borbolla, Daniel, and Ralph L. Beals
1940 The Tarasca project: A cooperative enterprise of the National Polytechnic Institute, Mexican Bureau—Indian Affairs, and the University of California. *American Anthropologist 42:*708–712.
Willner, Dorothy
1958 Report on an evaluation of a community development project of CREFAL in Tzintzuntzan. Mimeographed manuscript, Centro Regional de Educación Fundamental para la América Latina (CREFAL), Pátzcuaro.

Part III

PROBLEM-ORIENTED STUDIES

In recent years, problem-oriented research has largely supplanted general ethnographic studies as the dominant approach in anthropological fieldwork. The current popularity of hypothesis testing and model building reflects this fundamental shift in methodology. Unfortunately, problem-oriented studies often assume that sociocultural systems are homeostatic. In contrast, as the essays in this section demonstrate, a longitudinal perspective encourages the investigator to treat human societies as dynamic, open-ended phenomena. This orientation is especially important for anthropologists studying urbanization, industrialization, and economic development.

For example, Kemper's research among Tzintzuntzan migrants in Mexico City shows the potential of examining urbanization longitudinally rather than cross-sectionally. Although this investigation has been going only since 1969, the prospect of continuing the fieldwork into the next century offers a rare opportunity for analyzing what happens to people during an era of unparalleled demographic and economic development. In this regard, a major problem confronting Kemper involves the growth of the migrant population beyond a size that a single fieldworker can handle. It is likely that, in order to keep

Long-Term Field Research
in Social Anthropology

track of the changing careers of these migrants, he will eventually have to convert this one-man project into a team effort.

Unlike the other studies discussed in this volume, Kemper's research represents a direct extension of another long-term study: Foster's research in Tzintzuntzan. This development of a problem-oriented project out of a general ethnographic study suggests that younger anthropologists should consider the advantages of similar follow-up fieldwork before striking out on their own. It also shows the importance of having a set of core ethnographic data, especially household censuses and family histories, as the basis for problem-oriented studies.

This concern with "minimum core data" is evident in Epstein's research in the Indian villages of Wangala and Dalena. When she completed her initial fieldwork in 1956, she had no plans to return. In fact, she did not revisit these communities until 1970, when she received an unexpected invitation to conduct a 5-week restudy from a German political sociologist doing doctoral research there. Her earlier focus on the impact of irrigation on local economic and social organization was expanded in the restudy to encompass a broader range of economic development problems. She makes clear that the comprehensive ethnographic census and detailed household surveys from the previous fieldwork were vital to the restudy's success.

As a result of her reexposure to Indian village life, after more than a decade of research in the Pacific and in New Guinea, Epstein became interested in the policy implications of her research findings. She got involved with translating theory into action-oriented programs to improve the people's way of life. She also came to appreciate the value of prediction in studies of socioeconomic change. Through a related cross-national project, she is putting some hypotheses derived from the Indian research to a comparative test. Finally, she discovered that returning to Wangala and Dalena profoundly influenced her personal values and career priorities. She is now committed to revisit these communities and to involve her students in what has become an ongoing research interest.

In contrast to Epstein's late commitment to longitudinal research, Colson and Scudder began their joint work among the Gwembe Tonga as a long-term study of the effects of relocation caused by the construction of Kariba Dam. Since their initial fieldwork in 1956, they have expanded and modified the project in several ways. While they still maintain time series data on the demographic, economic, and social dimensions of four relocated Gwembe villages, they have added new samples of fishermen, labor migrants, and secondary school leavers to the original sample populations. Thus, their interest has shifted from relocation to the study of the Gwembe's participation in the modernization of the new nation of Zambia.

This shift in perspective has important implications for the continuing theoretical and applied relevance of this long-term project. Colson and Scudder now realize that the initial scheme for their research—involving at least two stages of fieldwork within a time gap of from 5 to 10 years between stages—was inadequate because it wrongly assumed that Gwembe communities traditionally existed in a stable adaptation within a stable ecological context, that the relocation represented a temporary disruption, and that the post-relocation period would see the emergence of a new stable solution within a social and physical environment also marked by stability. Two decades of work in Gwembe District has convinced them that human systems do not move mechanistically toward adaptive states. On the contrary, they argue that anthropologists deal with "people making decisions through time in contexts which change both because of their own actions and because of changes in external conditions which often neither they nor we are able to anticipate."

Fahim's research among the Nubians is also concerned with the consequences of resettlement. Beginning in 1963 as a member of a team studying Nubian life in the previously relocated village of Kanuba, Fahim has continued his work as an adjunct of a regional study on development. Unlike the Colson–Scudder study of Gwembe, Fahim initially had no formal plans to conduct a systematic longitudinal investigation in Kanuba or its region, but the initial ethnographic study of Kanuba has been drawn upon in Fahim's long-term involvement with the region. He has several times been able to tackle specific practical problems in very brief field seasons because he already had considerable data on one community and had good rapport with its people. In this manner, he justifies blending this long-term study with his regional, cross-sectional research devoted to making policy recommendations to various governmental agencies.

As an Egyptian, Fahim is concerned not only with publishing his research results for an academic audience but also with making them available to governmental officials and to the Nubians themselves. In this regard, he faces problems similar to those of Hofer and Villa Rojas. He also realizes that the "fame" of Kanuba, which has received more than the usual amount of assistance from external sources, has a feedback effect on its socioeconomic development. Thus, it has become necessary to develop a flexible research strategy that allows the longitudinal changes in Kanuba and its region to be understood as a blend of internal and external forces.

The lesson of all these problem-oriented studies is clear: a solid, holistic ethnographic data base is essential and of great utility in developing theoretical contributions and policy recommendations. An additional similarity among these projects concerns the technical problems of maintaining the core data files; processing, analyzing, and publishing huge quantities of data; dealing with changing field conditions, populations, and personal circumstances; and—ultimately—ensuring that the fieldwork goes on.

9

Fieldwork among Tzintzuntzan Migrants in Mexico City: Retrospect and Prospect[1]

Robert V. Kemper

INTRODUCTION

In 1967, while writing up the results of summer research on the peasant marketplace in Pátzcuaro, Michoacán, I became interested in the participation of local communities in Mexican urbanization. Subsequent discussions with George Foster, then my graduate adviser at the University of California (Berkeley), led me to undertake fieldwork for the doctoral dissertation among Tzintzuntzan migrants in Mexico City. I have now spent on that project about 20 months of field research spread over 7 years (17½ months in 1969–1970, 2½ months in summer 1974, 5 days in November 1974, 3 days in November 1975, and 2 weeks in August 1976). Plans for future research include year long revisits on a decennial schedule in addition to a number of shorter trips. The goals of the project are to understand how a specific population of rural emigrants adapts to urban living and to develop a comparative theory of urbanization.

[1] Fieldwork in Mexico City and analysis of census data and ethnographic materials have been supported by NIGMS Grant GM–1224 and by grants-in-aid from the Wenner–Gren Foundation for Anthropological Research, Inc. Their assistance is gratefully acknowledged.

189

Long-Term Field Research
in Social Anthropology

In this chapter, I shall examine the development of the project so far, discuss the plans for further fieldwork, and consider the study's theoretical and methodological implications for other anthropologists and social scientists interested in comparative urbanization research and theory.

HISTORY OF THE RESEARCH

From the outset, my research has been a continuation of Foster's long-term fieldwork in Tzintzuntzan. Our decision that I should carry out this fieldwork for a dissertation was due primarily to the availability of substantial data on the migrants' home community. Complete village household censuses for 1945, 1960, and 1970 would provide me with superb demographic and socioeconomic data, while detailed genealogies and voluminous fieldnotes would provide in-depth background information on the migrants and the families to which they belonged. Thus, I would be able to concentrate on a single phase of what for other ethnographers is usually a time-consuming two-stage project. Just as Oscar Lewis had followed migrants from Tepoztlán to Mexico City, so I would go from Tzintzuntzan to the capital. Indeed, my decision to do the project was influenced by Lewis' long-ignored suggestion (1952:41) that follow-up studies of migrants from villages like Tzintzuntzan (i.e., communities already subjected to intensive ethnographic fieldwork) would yield valuable comparative data on Mexican urbanization. Thus, from the beginning my objectives were longitudinal and comparative.

FIELDWORK IN 1969–1970

Mexico City was selected as the field site because Tzintzuntzan emigrants share with many Mexican peasants, including those of Tepoztlán, a preference for settling in the capital. Thus not only would I find enough migrants to make the study worthwhile, I would be able to compare my findings directly with those of Lewis and other scholars while avoiding the arduous task of locating Tzintzuntzeños in a number of Mexican cities. Under these conditions, I conducted fieldwork in Mexico City, with several brief trips to the village, from April 1969 to August 1970.

In retrospect, I see that the fieldwork among the Tzintzuntzan migrants in the capital fell into three phases, punctuated by short trips back to the United States to renew tourist papers every 6 months. In the first phase, I faced three main problems: finding accommodations for me and my wife, locating the migrants in a city of over 8 million people, and beginning the process of data collection. During the second phase, marked by a transition from "passive" to "active" research strategies (Freilich 1970:24), I conducted a detailed ethnographic census of as many migrant households as could be located. The concluding phase was devoted to gathering life histories, household budgets, and social network data and to administering projective tests and questionnaires about migrant experiences. Thus, as the fieldwork progressed, the problem orientation became more specific and the data collection procedures more structured.

Since the methods, techniques, and preliminary results of the 1969–1970 research have been reported in detail elsewhere (Kemper 1974), I will discuss here only a few issues as they relate to my long-term fieldwork among the Tzintzuntzan migrants. Of course, much of what I say also applies to short-term field research, since my work was geared to the immediate goal of completing a dissertation. Only in retrospect have I become aware that my decisions and actions during 1969–1970 have had an important impact for continuing the project.

Selecting a Place to Live

All anthropologists face the problem of finding accommodations compatible with their field situation. In my case, after two weeks of living in hotels and rooming houses, we rented a furnished apartment near the center of the city. Having an apartment independent of all of the migrants had immediate advantages and disadvantages for the 1969–1970 fieldwork: On the one hand, it gave us a place away from the constant demands of fieldwork in an unfamiliar setting; on the other, it denied us the intimacy of participant observation common to anthropologists who work in village settings. As it turned out, this separation gave me a neutrality which preserved the opportunity for future research. If we had made a commitment to reside with a particular family during this first fieldtrip, it might have adversely curtailed our future options. Thus, from the perspective of planning to conduct a long-term project, I made a fortunate decision in selecting our initial residence in the capital.

Studying a Dispersed Population

When I arrived in Mexico City, I had a list of about 20 migrants' names and just two addresses, which I had obtained in a hurried search through Foster's data files before my departure from Berkeley. So, my immediate goal was to locate as many migrants as possible, as quickly as I could, so I might get on with the real fieldwork. It took me about a year to slowly develop a social network which included nearly all of the migrants; in fact, my network became so much wider than that of any of the Tzintzuntzeños that they used to ask me where one of their fellows lived or worked. I found that the migrants were spread among more than 40 neighborhoods in the metropolitan area, with a preference for peripheral zones on the northern part of the city where many of the men worked in factories. A few people, usually relatives, lived next door to one another; many more were separated by miles of urban traffic. Nor did the Tzintzuntzeños have a village-based voluntary association which might have compensated for their geographical distribution in the capital.

In retrospect, I know that such an association (or greater propinquity in the migrants' residential pattern) would have saved me months of trekking across Mexico City looking for people. On the other hand, having to go from household to household made me aware of the importance of the Tzintzuntzeños' mutual assistance arrangements with kinsmen, other ex-villagers, and other urban residents; I came to appreciate first-hand the impact of urban distances on the social and economic situations of people without cars or phones; and I eventually realized why the migrants seemed to lack a sense of "community."

Had I known from the outset that the Tzintzuntzan migrants were so numerous (483 persons living in at least 74 households, rather than my original guess of about 100 persons in 20 households) and so dispersed (spread over the metropolitan area, whereas I had hoped that they might live in one or two neighborhoods), and that I would log some 9000 miles driving in and around Mexico City in doing the fieldwork, I would have thought about electing another dissertation topic. Thus, my ignorance of the field situation was a blessing insofar as my long-term commitment to the project is concerned. When I consider what I went through to do the initial fieldwork, and think of how few other anthropologists have pursued long-term field research under such circumstances, I realize that the investment of time and energy must not be wasted.

Establishing a Satisfactory Role in the Field

My affiliation with Foster provided the credentials necessary to conduct the fieldwork and also to participate in Mexican anthropological activities. Since most of the migrants were aware of his work in Tzintzuntzan, they were willing to accept me as a student interested in their past, present, and future. Especially in the beginning, Foster's name (and through his connections, the names of certain well known villagers) opened doors for me which otherwise might have remained closed.

In terms of my professional relations, Foster gave me letters of introduction to the directors of the several anthropological institutions based in

Mexico City. In addition, because the Society for Applied Anthropology was holding its 1969 meeting in Mexico City, he came down and introduced me to a number of leaders in Mexican anthropology. Later on, he sponsored my membership in the Sociedad Mexicana de Antropología.

At this suggestion, I audited a course at the National School of Anthropology and History during my first months in Mexico City. Toward the end of the fieldwork, through a contact which he made possible by providing my transportation to the 1969 AAA meetings in New Orleans, I taught a graduate seminar on urban anthropology at the Universidad IberoAmericana. In both cases, I made contacts with Mexican anthropologists that will be valuable throughout my career.

The implications of my role situation among the Tzintzuntzeños and among Mexican anthropologists are clear. Under the auspices of a well known patron, whose guidance placed me on the right path of do the dissertation research, I was able to establish my own contacts among both the migrants and the Mexican social science community so that my research could continue. Following his lead, I maintained a neutral stance toward the political side of Mexican anthropology; as a result, I have had no difficulty so far in receiving permission to do fieldwork among the Tzintzuntzan migrants.

Collecting Field Data

Following Foster's example, I adopted the widely used HRAF system for coding and filing field notes. Information was typed onto 5×8 inch sheets and filed in two sets: one arranged topically in the HRAF numerical categories; the other by households. A third copy was mailed periodically to Berkeley, where Foster read the notes, wrote comments to me regarding points of special interest, and then filed them for safekeeping.

A number of times I wrote to him that I needed background data on a certain incident or on a specific individual. Within a week or so, depending on the mails, photocopies of the information I sought would arrive. I was spared a great deal of fieldwork, especially having to take down genealogies, because the data already existed in Foster's files. Moreover, we were each so familiar with the HRAF system and with the specific information in the files that it was quick work for me to ask for a piece of data, for Foster to retrieve, photocopy, and mail it to me, and for me in turn to use it to further my inquiries among the migrants. In addition to making his data files available, Foster also made a point to follow-up on any leads related to migration when he was in Tzintzuntzan doing his own research.

In recognition of our common interests and in partial reciprocity for his efforts in my behalf, I collected some data on topics which I knew interested Foster. For example, I administered Thematic Apperception Tests (TATs) to 15 migrants to provide comparative data for his sample of about 20 respondents in the village. In addition, I also gathered extensive information on *compadrazgo* (fictive godparenthood) relations among the migrants. In both cases, I used this comparative data to examine villager–migrant differences and similarities in my dissertation. Neither of us, however, have treated these topics in detail in subsequent publications; this collaboration remains to be done.

The most important common element to our research efforts was the 1970 ethnographic census. We asked for almost identical information and gave the census at about the same time. Whereas Foster was able to obtain a 100 response rate in the village, I censused only about 70% (51 of 74 household units) of the migrants firsthand. Although in nearly all of the remaining cases I was able to get reliable second-hand information, I knew that circumstances in the city made a 100% census virtually impossible. Because of my work among the migrants, Foster was careful to inquire about the whereabouts of all villagers who had been in the community at the time of the 1960 census and were no longer present. This additional data made it possible for me subsequently to discern the total pattern of emigration from Tzintzuntzan as a complement to my data on the migrants in Mexico City.

In retrospect, it is fortunate that I did my initial fieldwork among the migrants at the same time that Foster was administering a census in the village. Because of this coincidence, I now have a good set of demographic and socioeconomic "core" data on the Tzintzuntzeños in the capital and in the home community. Moreover, because the Mexican national census was conducted in February 1970, I can relate the ethnographic census data for migrants and villagers to the broader regional and national situation.

Analyzing Field Materials and File Data: 1970–1973

Upon returning to Berkeley in September 1970, I began to organize my field materials into a format suitable for a dissertation. In accord with my original plans, I also examined Foster's data files for background information on the migrants' situation before they went to Mexico City. I soon realized that, although Foster had done considerable analysis of his materials, the information I sought was not tabulated according to my needs. Therefore, we went to considerable effort and expense to convert his

1945, 1960, and 1970 census materials into a format amenable to computer data processing techniques. After several months' work, I was able to generate a substantial body of comparative cross-tabulations which showed how markedly Tzintzuntzan had changed during the 25 years of Foster's work there. This material eventually served as the basis for a joint article (Kemper and Foster 1975) on the impact of Mexican urbanization on Tzintzuntzan.

In addition to devoting considerable time to analyzing the census data and comparing the results with those of my census of the migrants in Mexico City, I also depended heavily on the continually up-dated information sheets kept on each person who has resided in the community during the past quarter-century. By close examination of this data file, which contains personal data on more than 3000 individuals, I ascertained that more than 700 villagers had emigrated since the late 1930s. Furthermore, because of the systematic detail of the data sheets, I could specify the type (and often, the place) of destination for each emigrant as well as the overall sociodemographic patterns of migration from the community. Then, by correlating these data with the computerized household census files, I demonstrated that the migrants to Mexico City were "positively selected" (i.e., came from households with higher living standards, better educational levels, and more innovativeness than nonmigrant households), but that this selectivity had declined in recent years as the number of emigrants increased. Thus, I was in a position to support the demographic hypothesis of migrant "regression toward the mean" (cf. Browning and Feindt 1969) through a combination of my census data on the migrants in Mexico City and Foster's file data on the entire natal community. This is a use to which Foster would probably not have put his own data, since his current interests were far removed from migration theory.

There are several lessons to be learned from my analysis of Foster's data files in conjunction with the analysis of my own field materials. First, comparability should be built into a study from the beginning; it is difficult to agree on definitions of, say, household and family types after investigations are completed. Second, using another scholar's data files requires an understanding of what the data "mean"; that is, the ambiguities in the fieldnotes and census materials must be explicable either by the original scholar's direct explanations or through his annotations in the data files. Third, the most useful data from another anthropologist's field materials are often those of lesser importance to that person's current interests. Their analysis by a student or colleague may thus be a valuable service to the original investigator. Finally, there must be an agreement as to what data may be used and to what purpose they may be put; otherwise, the original fieldworker's plans for subsequent publication may be interfered with.

After a year of analyzing my own field materials and those from Foster's files, I rapidly completed the writing of the dissertation. Subsequently, I have written several papers based on these materials, but always with the realization that constant changes in the migrants' and villagers' situations soon render these publications obsolete. This awareness continues to cause me considerable frustration. I know that each year in which I fail to return to the field because of other commitments represents a year in which significant events are not recorded.

By late 1973, this sense of frustration had reached a point that getting back to Mexico City had become a top priority. To this end, I received a small grant-in-aid from the Wenner–Gren Foundation for Anthropological Research, to carry out a 10-week ethnographic survey among the Tzintzuntzan migrants in Mexico City during summer 1974. This fieldwork was intended, as I wrote in the grant proposal, to provide important mid-decade information on the changing migrant population and on the urban conditions in which it lived. As such, it represented the second phase of my long-term commitment to conduct research among this group.

The research involved re-establishing contact with those migrants whom I had known in 1969–1970, discovering which migrants had left Mexico City either to return to the village or to settle elsewhere, and censusing those newly-arrived in the capital since 1970. In short, I was more concerned to up-date my demographic and socioeconomic "core" data than to test specific hypotheses. Of course, I did expect to gather additional data, beyond the census itself, on such topics as family and household developmental cycles, socioeconomic mobility, and intra-metropolitan geographical movements. All of these topics needed more study before I could summarize in monograph form the migrants' adaptations to urban life during the early 1970s.

FIELDWORK IN 1974

The most important aspect of the summer 1974 field season was that I accomplished almost as much in 10 weeks as I had before in as many months. The "costs" of the research, both in money and personal effort, were substantially reduced during this second field trip. Not only did I know much more about the population I was studying, I was also a more mature, more effective ethnographer. A number of circumstances made the 1974 research especially productive; I treat these in the following in terms of the same general categories as I discussed the 1969–1970 fieldwork.

Selecting a Place to Live

On this occasion I went alone to Mexico City and lived with a migrant family. This particular family had been our closest friends among the migrants in 1969–1970; furthermore, the household head was the half-brother of the woman in whose home Foster lives while in Tzintzuntzan. They thus had a good idea of the needs of an anthropologist and were willing to attend to mine. In short, the situation was ideal for getting maximum work done in a short time.

More important than having a place to live was the chance to observe first-hand on a daily basis the interpersonal relationships within a migrant home. In addition, the family's entrepreneurship (they had opened two small stores) gave me an insider's view of how migrants try to improve their economic situation in the city. And, finally, the family served as willing key informants on a wide range of topics. Since the family and I both were pleased with the arrangement, it appears that I have a place to which I can always return while doing fieldwork. I know that few urban anthropologists live with the families they study; following Foster's model in this instance may give me unique insights into problems of migrant social organization that others can not resolve.

Studying a Dispersed Population

Based on my earlier fieldwork, I knew that it would be impossible, in 10 weeks or in 100, to locate and survey every Tzintzuntzan migrant in Mexico City. I did hope to canvass, with some field assistance, about 75% of the population; in fact, we were able to gather firsthand data on more than 70 households and got reliable secondhand data on most of the remainder, out of a total of about 110 households. I had expected that the older or more affluent migrants who owned homes would still be living where they had in 1969–1970, whereas the younger, poorer, more recent arrivals would be more geographically mobile. I discovered that, although about half of the migrants had changed residences at least once since 1970 and some were no longer in the capital, this proposition held true.

Since I had no car on this fieldtrip, I depended on the excellent public transportation system of taxis, jitney cabs, buses, and subways. In addition, the family with whom I lived took me to visit other migrant households on weekends and in their spare time. The large number of recent arrivals forced a strict rationing of time and effort. Although it would have been pleasant (and perhaps ethnographically profitable) to pass time with old friends, I was determined to gather the "core" data on people not already listed in my files. That also forced me to visit Tzintzuntzan to check on the dozen or so "return migrants" and to ascertain who else had left the village since the 1970 census. In the process, I confirmed the emigration of villagers to Mexico City and also to many other destinations, including the United States.

For studying a dispersed population, a series of visits has many advantages. This time I knew what faced me and how to plan my available time to see as many migrants as possible. I did not have to build a social network family by family; I already had one which enabled me to cope with the migrants' geographical distribution in the metropolis. Moreover, the second visit to the Tzintzuntzeños made me aware of continuities and changes which I had not observed on the first fieldtrip.

Changing Roles in the Field

Previously I had been a student, now I was a professor. Nevertheless, because of my age (28), I continued to introduce myself as "Roberto" and asked that people so address me. I continued to use the formal *usted* rather than the informal *tu* in all conversations except with age mates (and children) whom I knew well and who used it first in speaking with me.

When I had been a student, I could plead poverty when unusual requests for assistance arose. Now this was more difficult, and as I continue the research my social debts to the migrants and villagers will have to be repaid with interest. Additional burdens of reciprocity also accrue with professional colleagues in Mexico City. As an anthropologist hoping to carry out research in Mexico for the rest of my career, I feel responsible to lecture in local universities, to publish papers and books in Spanish in local journals and monograph series, and to assist in training local students. This is an obligation I incur in exchange for the privilege of continuing my fieldwork.

Collecting Field Data

Since my primary goal was to survey as many migrant households as possible, and I knew that there would be more than I alone could visit, finding field assistance was one of my first tasks. One of the young men in the home where I was living served as an interviewer; the son of an anthropologist at the National University also worked with me. After several training sessions, both of them proved to be superb census takers.

I soon discovered, of course, that they could not be expected to pursue potentially rich sources of information outside of the interview schedule; no assistant can provide much detailed information on topics which demand careful probing over a number of visits.

The productivity of the summer of 1974 fieldtrip shows that revisits are not only economical, they also encourage an ethnographer to go to the field with a set of specific queries which he hopes to resolve. Turning over a share of the "core" data collection to assistants gave me time to concentrate on these topics of special interest. Having my field notes arranged topically by HRAF categories and also by family group meant that I could daily see the depth and breadth of my sample grow. Let me give a brief example.

During the 1969–1970 field research, I had gathered a substantial body of data on the *compadrazgo*. I had discussed these data briefly, in comparison with those gathered by Foster for Tzintzuntzan, in my dissertation, but had not analyzed them fully. In returning to the field in 1974, the gathering of additional data on *compadrazgo* was crucial. I was particularly eager to find out the variety of occasions (e.g., baptism, marriage) on which *compadres* can be chosen, since the anthropological literature is very sketchy on the urban *compadrazgo*. Data collected in the summer of 1974, presently being analyzed for a paper in preparation for publication, will demonstrate the ways in which urban migrants use the *compadrazgo* as a mechanism for improving their socioeconomic mobility, for strengthening ties with relatives and friends dispersed throughout the metropolitan area, and for maintaining ties with the village.

Analyzing Field Materials: 1974–1976

Since the summer of 1974, I have visited the migrants in Mexico City only briefly: 5 days in November 1974, 3 days in November 1975, and 2 weeks in August 1976. These brief visits have helped to keep current my knowledge of the migrants' situation. Most of my recent work has been dedicated toward compiling my materials into two monographs: the first published in May 1976 in Spanish and the second issued in Spring 1977 in English. The Spanish-language monograph is somewhat shorter and less technical, but still conveys the general results of my work on the urban adaptation of the Tzintzuntzan migrants in Mexico City. The English-language monograph will be more theoretical and, therefore, of broader interest to professional social scientists interested in comparative research on urbanization in developing countries.

These monographs represent the end of the first phase of my involvement in long-term research among the Tzintzuntzan migrants. In a sense, they are the first of a series of interim reports which I hope to issue about once every decade. This first phase of my research does *not* represent a baseline study; for scholars interested in urbanization and rural–urban migration, there can be no such studies. If I were forced to abandon my research among the Tzintzuntzeños tomorrow, the publications based on the first 7 years of research would retain whatever value they now have as "short-term" documents. In continuing the project, I am intent on substantiating or invalidating my current findings in the light of future fieldwork and new results in the comparative literature.

PLANS FOR FUTURE RESEARCH AMONG
THE TZINTZUNTZAN MIGRANTS

Senior scholars often reflect on their careers; few junior scholars predict the path of careers still unlived. Nonetheless, a commitment to study the migrants from Tzintzuntzan is high among my career priorities. Much can happen during the next 3 decades to change my current plans, so a flexible approach to the project is more likely to succeed than will a rigid scheme.

Since my interests are broadly comparative, the case of the Tzintzuntzan migrants holds my attention because it provides data for developing a model of the urbanization process that will include the interaction of individual, community, regional, national, and international sociocultural systems. All of the research that I have done, or contemplating conducting in the near future, is oriented toward this same goal. I have worked in a "new town" near Dallas, Texas; have studied the impact of tourism on urban–regional development in Taos, New Mexico; and plan to investigate Mexican American migration and socioeconomic mobility in Dallas. Thus, my commitment to the Tzintzuntzan migrant project is tempered by involvement in related comparative urban research.

In continuing the project beyond the work already completed, I expect to concentrate on two principal domains: first, to keep up the file of demographic and socioeconomic "core" data on the migrants in Mexico City; second, to explore a series of topics likely to yield significant theoretical results.

Maintaining the "Core" Data File

The Tzintzuntzan migrant population in Mexico City is already fairly large, with more than 600 persons living in more than 100 household units. It includes nuclear families, joint households, widows/widowers with children, and single persons (e.g., students, maids, bachelors). The migrant group, as I have defined it, is composed of persons born in Tzintzuntzan (and the neighboring hamlets, insofar as these individuals are linked to Tzintzuntzan by kinship ties), as well as spouses, children, and friends born elsewhere who reside in their households. Given the bilaterality of the kinship system and the diffuseness of urban social networks, it is virtually impossible to limit the potential size of the population under study. This situation will become geometrically more complicated as the years pass and today's children marry, have children, etc.

To maintain the demographic and socioeconomic "core" data file means, at minimum, to conduct an ethnographic census each decade (i.e., 1980, 1990, and 2000). Even better would be to update the census in mid-decade, as I was able to do in 1974. If the population continues to increase (both through the arrival of more migrants and the birth of children to those migrants already in the capital) as it has during the last ten years, it will become increasingly difficult for me, as a single fieldworker, to keep up close contacts with a broad spectrum of the migrant population. Finding good field assistants, or bringing students and/or colleagues into the project, will become critical to the success of this component of the long-term research enterprise. Ultimately, I feel that a commitment to maintaining the "core" data file will convert me from a "loner" into a "team" ethnographer. The population will soon become too large, too dispersed, too varied in its demographic structure for me to continue alone.

The Problem of Computerizing the "Core" Data File

In contemplating the maintenance of substantial demographic and socioeconomic data files for 3 decades, I have already thought seriously about computerizing all of the personal and household information in order to aid in storage, retrieval, and analysis. The many advantages of computers for rapid counting, sorting, and analyzing cannot be ignored; on the other hand, possessing a "data bank" increases problems of preserving the confidential relationships which I have established among the Tzintzuntzeños. This problem is made more severe as other investigators are drawn into the project.

Computerization also means that I must improve my own skills in statistics and electronic data processing. Although I expect to hire someone to do the coding and keypunching, I will have to check the work for errors. But more important, the questions which I will want to ask of the "core" data file will require that I can manipulate a variety of available programs (e.g., the Statistical Package for the Social Sciences) and also design special purpose programs.

My limited experience already shows that gathering "core" data is not as difficult as analyzing these materials on a systematic basis. Time spent on the "core" data files is time that cannot be devoted to pursuing other activities; this is one of the liabilities of longitudinal research which must be faced by all investigators.

Generating and Testing Hypotheses

I believe that long-term studies, like short-term research, have as their primary goal the generation and testing of hypotheses about human behavior and cognition. If the research I am doing on the Tzintzuntzan migrants in Mexico City is worthwhile, it is because the data already in hand and yet to be gathered will meet this goal. The project is suitable for testing hypotheses generated from my own data files or from the comparative social science literature. I have already mentioned how hypotheses related to migrant selectivity were tested on the basis of Foster's data files; now I would like to give two other examples from my own field materials. The first, which involves intra-metropolitan geographical mobility, is based on data gathered among the Tzintzuntzan migrants; the second, which involves cognitive mapping, is based on ideas derived from the comparative literature.

Intrametropolitan Geographical Mobility

Until recently, few ethnographers have tried to explain the patterns and processes of intra-urban residential movements. Most studies of geographical mobility have been short-term, but attempt to compensate by emphasizing a life history approach. Nonetheless, the dynamics of decision making among migrants tend to be obscured, particularly since migrants make choices in the context of changing metropolitan environments. As cities expand, their peripheries enlarge, and so do the options of migrants who seek to have their own homes rather than renting a place to live. It is this process which I expect to examine for the case of the Tzintzuntzan migrants in Mexico City.

My first fieldwork in 1969–1970 generated migration histories for more than 40 families and individual migrants. The overall pattern was that the earlier arrivals (in the 1940s and 1950s) had settled in slum zones near the center of Mexico City. As they improved their socioeconomic circumstances, they tended to move to the periphery, especially in the northeast quadrant of the metropolis. Later arrivals (1960s) tended to move directly to the periphery with the assistance of those who had already located there. These migrants have tended to move even farther out from the city's center, as the metropolitan zone expanded and new peripheral zones became available for settlement (through legal subdivisions, quasi-legal neighborhoods, or illegal squatter settlements). The most recent arrivals (1970s) have settled in Mexico City in these present peripheral zones and also in the formerly peripheral, now intermediate areas. Still, in almost all instances, the Tzintzuntzeños come to Mexico City with the assistance of those who came before them.

As a result of this process and of the patterns of job search after arrival, I hypothesize that a series of "enclaves" are now developing among the Tzintzuntzan migrants. Some evidence for this was gathered during the 1974 field season. In one case, I discovered that while in 1969–1970 only two families (related by marriage) lived in a certain northwestern-sector neighborhood, in 1974 some 11 families resided in this neighborhood. Every family drawn into this "enclave," which covers an area within 5 minutes' walk, shared ties of kinship, *compadrazgo,* or urban working place. As the "enclave" develops, the ties among the families are strengthened at the expense of ties with the remainder of the Tzintzuntzeños in the capital.

What are the elements of this "enclave" hypothesis which are directly related to long-term research? First, it took a second fieldtrip to see the pattern of intra-metropolitan geographical mobility of the Tzintzuntzan migrants develop in this manner. Second, I believe that these "enclaves" are likely to be transitory mechanisms of urban adaptation which will endure only until their members are able to break away in the search for their own homes. Third, as I continue the fieldwork, I will be in a position to test the "enclave" hypothesis by collecting information on the choices made by the continuing flow of Tzintzuntzeños to the capital.

Cognitive Mapping and Urban Adaptation

Social scientists from several disciplines are now interested in the field which is usually called environmental psychology or cognitive geography. So far, only a few anthropologists have done fieldwork in urban areas on this topic. My work among the Tzintzuntzan migrants offers an ideal situation for exploring the dynamics of individuals' perceptions of the urban environment. Given the substantial background data that I have for the migrant population, I believe that a sample can be selected for testing the hypothesis that a person's cognitive map of Mexico City provides a measure of his urban adaptation. By asking a sample of the migrants to draw maps of the metropolis and to answer a series of questions about their maps, I expect to show:

1. That recent arrivals have narrower perceptions of the city than do migrants with longer exposure to city life
2. That less affluent migrants have narrower mental maps than do more affluent migrants, regardless of the length of urban experience
3. That children of migrants have broader mental maps than do recently arrived adults

A series of subsidiary hypotheses will also be examined, but they too will deal with the cognitive dimensions of urbanization. This sample will be examined several times over, say, a 5-year interval to ascertain if individuals' cognitive maps change as urban circumstances are altered. Thus, I will do a longitudinal panel study within the broader research project on the Tzintzuntzan migrants in Mexico City. If the panel study yields the expected results, it should be possible to add a psychological component to my model of urban adaptation.

This research on cognitive mapping can be conducted at relatively little expense of time and money because it draws upon the available demographic and socioeconomic "core" data on the migrant population. The panel study method ensures that the dynamics of urban adaptation are considered; other studies of mental mapping have been limited to single queries of populations for which adequate "core" data are lacking. Finally, the proposed research demonstrates how hypotheses generated from other sources (in this case, teaching a course on urban problems) can be tested by anthropologists involved in longitudinal research projects.

Other examples of hypothesis generation and testing could be given here, but these two should show how topics of current debate in the urbanization and migration literature are amenable to investigation within the context of a long-term study. I expect that new topics will emerge in the next 30 years, with the result that a series of theoretical contributions will emerge from this research project.

PERSONAL DIMENSIONS OF LONG-TERM RESEARCH

I feel a considerable personal investment in the fieldwork among the Tzintzuntzan migrants in Mexico City. As a partner in reciprocal relationships, I believe that I have a responsibility to assist them (within my limited resources) in exchange for their continuing cooperation in my research. But above all, my wife and I like nearly all of the people with whom we come in contact and we hope that they achieve the success that they seek. The migrants are generally literate, highly motivated, and hardworking; they are as colleagues in a common research enterprise, not laboratory subjects upon whom instruments are tested. And even when a few of them refuse to talk with me, I respect their desire for privacy.

I have good friends among both the older and younger Tzintzuntzeños in Mexico City. Within a decade or so, many of these people will be pensioned, while others will reach middle age. This demographic shift will occur as I, too, grow older. It is likely that an interest in life cycles and in the development cycles of domestic groups will become important in my future research as I begin to work among the second and third generation of Tzintzuntzeños in the capital.

In addition to my changing ties with the migrants, I am aware of a changing relationship with Foster, my mentor during the 1969–1970 dissertation research and my continuing guide to the intricacies of life in Tzintzuntzan. His commitment to long-term research obviously provides the model for my own. I feel that he would be disappointed if I were to abandon the research among the Tzintzuntzeños; this awareness furnishes an anchor keeping me on course. In addition, my relationship with Foster suggests that "passing the mantle" to students or colleagues is a critical dimension of long-term studies which can begin by offering them opportunities to do research on special topics (e.g., migration) related to the theme of the original project.

THEORETICAL AND METHODOLOGICAL CONSIDERATIONS

Nearly all studies of urbanization conducted by anthropologists have stressed the "community" as a natural unit of analysis. The dispersion of the Tzintzuntzan migrants in metropolitan Mexico City suggests that populations also can be studied in "nonplace" situations. This raises the issue: Who or what are we studying in long-term research? How long is sufficient to conduct research among particular groups? In my case, I have taken a pragmatic stance. The unit of analysis is the set of persons affiliated with households in which Tzintzuntzan migrants reside. The period of research is 3 decades, which seems long enough to describe and analyze the processes of urbanization in terms of intergenerational mobility. In sum, my definition of the problem to be studied is rather open-ended in the belief that this minimizes the chance of missing important data.

Ultimately, the signal advantage of long-term research on urbanization is that no amount of cross-sectional research yields satisfying diachronic results. Slices of time, no matter how carefully selected, fail to attain the richness of field materials drawn from repeated visits among a well studied population. These statements will not surprise many economists, psychologists, or political scientists; panel studies have long been a principal component in their methodological repertoires. Anthropologists lately come to urban research are only beginning to explore the merits of short-term and long-term studies. The decisions made now will influence the quality and quantity of our contributions to comparative urban theory for years ahead.

Fieldwork among the Tzintzuntzan migrants suggests that anthropologists should not undertake a long-term study without developing or building upon a strong data base from which subsequent changes can be measured. When considering the investment of time and effort in long-term research, perhaps anthropologists might employ an approach used by many archaeologists: survey potential field sites, assess the merits and demerits of each site, conduct preliminary fieldwork in the most promising sites, perform initial data analysis, and then decide where further research is justified. But, in contrast to archaeologists, social anthropologists seem to have few guidelines to tell them when enough fieldwork has been done in a particular place.

So long as individual fieldworkers are the primary agents of anthropological research, their ability to establish rapport and maintain good relations with particular populations will be the foundation of long-term field projects. They will have to be aware of their own changing professional and personal development—and be able to continue field research in the face of changing family circumstances, jobs, health, and theoretical inclinations. And they will have to be sufficiently productive as scholars to garner continuing support for their field research from funding agencies and from their social science colleagues. The value of any long-term study, whether among the Tzintzuntzan migrants in Mexico City or among the Eskimo, will not be fully measured in the short-run. Long after today's theoretical fads and methodological innovations have been tossed aside, the data collected carefully and patiently over several decades in key ethnographic settings will continue to provide a basis for testing new ideas.

ACKNOWLEDGMENTS

The research project is possible because of the continuing cooperation of the Tzintzuntzeños, the encouragement of George M. Foster, and the assistance of a number of Mexican scholars and institutions, especially the Instituto Nacional de Antropología e Historia.

BIBLIOGRAPHY

Browning, Harley L., and Waltraut Feindt
   1969   Selectivity of migrants to a metropolis in a developing country: A Mexican case
          study. *Demography 6:*347–357.
Freilich, Morris, ed.
   1970   *Marginal natives: Anthropologists at work.* New York: Harper and Row.
Kemper, Robert V.
   1974   Tzintzuntzeños in Mexico City: The anthropologist among peasant migrants. In
          Anthropologists in cities, edited by Foster, G. M. and Kemper, R. V. Pp. 63–91.
          Boston: Little, Brown.
   1976   *Campesinos en la ciudad: gente de Tzintzuntzan.* Mexico, D.F.: Ediciones Sep-
          setentas, No. 270.
   1977   *Migration and adaptation: Tzintzuntzan peasants in Mexico City.* Beverly Hills,
          California: Sage Publications.
Kemper, Robert V., and George M. Foster
   1975   Urbanization in Mexico: The view from Tzintzuntzan. *Latin American Urban
          Research 5:*53–75.
Lewis, Oscar
   1952   Urbanization without breakdown: A case study. *Scientific Monthly 75:*31–41.

10

Mysore Villages Revisited

T. Scarlett Epstein

INTRODUCTION

In the course of taking my first degree in economics as an adult student at the University of Manchester (England, 1950–1953), I was taught by W. Arthur Lewis. I suspect that this accounts for my becoming interested in the problem of the economic development of less developed societies. However, unlike my eminent supervisor, who analyzed the development process from the heights of a macroeconomist, I was more interested in the social aspects of development. I soon began to appreciate that here I would have to turn for inspiration to social sciences other than economics. It was this search for enlightenment on the social dimensions of economic development that brought me into social anthropology.

Fortunately for me, there was at that time a team of outstanding social anthropologists gathered at Manchester including Max Gluckman Elizabeth Colson, Victor Turner, and others. Their research in Central Africa and subsequent analysis of field material seemed to me to provide just the sort of insight into social processes that is necessary in trying to understand the full implications of the development of less developed societies. Accordingly, as soon as I graduated in economics, I decided

209

Long-Term Field Research
in Social Anthropology

Copyright © 1979 by Academic Press, Inc.
All rights of reproduction in any form reserved.
ISBN: 0-12-263350-4

that I wanted to conduct a lengthy intensive study of a locality and, by means of participant observation, examine economic development at the micro-level.

By way of fortunate coincidence, M. N. Srinivas happened to be Visiting Professor at Manchester just about the time I had to finalize my Ph.D. research outline. I discussed my research interests with him and he suggested an area in south India, where he himself had done research and which seemed to present the very problem I was particularly keen to study. The literature on Indian village life, supported by M. N. Srinivas' personal accounts, exerted a powerful influence on me, so much so that I decided to become a nonconformist of the Manchester School and do my fieldwork in India rather than in Africa. In doing so I followed in the footsteps of F. G. Bailey, another Manchester student, who had just completed his fieldwork in India when I was ready to start mine. I drew up a research proposal for a study entitled "Economic Development and Social Change in One South Indian Village." With Max Gluckman's support, I managed to get a Rockefeller Research grant which financed my study.

MICRO-STUDIES

I began my fieldwork in south India in November 1954 when I settled in a village I subsequently named Wangala, which had a population of 985 individuals residing in 192 households. Wangala is situated in Mandya District of what was then Mysore State but has since become Karnataka State. The village is multicaste with peasants as the "dominant" caste (Srinivas 1959). The villagers speak Kannada, a Dravidian language. Mandya District is part of the semiarid tropics. Farmers had depended on irregular and scarce rainfall for the necessary water to facilitate cultivation of subsistence crops. Two millets, ragi (*Sorghum vulgare*) and jowar (*Eleusine coracana*), had been grown as staple crops and provided the staple diet for most villagers. The advent of canal irrigation in Wangala prior to the outbreak of war in 1939 enabled farmers to venture into cash cropping. The specific reason for selecting Wangala as a research site was my interest in studying the impact of irrigation on village economic and social organization.

I was fortunate in being invited to live in a Brahmin home in Mysore city where I spent 3 weeks prior to moving into Wangala. During this brief spell, I managed to learn the rudiments of Kannada. I also engaged Suri, my research assistant, a graduate in statistics from the University of Mysore. He came with me to Wangala and helped me throughout my 2 years of fieldwork. As a Brahmin and a vegetarian he could find no place to live in the village, as there was not a single Brahmin household. Therefore, we shared a house and I kept a vegetarian kitchen.

Originally, I intended to study only one village. However, after I had been in the field for some time I began to appreciate the difficulty of studying post facto changes. I wanted to be able to see what Wangala society had been like before village lands had become irrigated so as to be in a better position to gauge and understand the changes that had taken place. Accordingly, I tried to discover a village in the same culture area, reasonably near Wangala, but with only dry lands. I reasoned that a study of such a village would enable me to see what Wangala must have been like before irrigation. To put it briefly: I wanted to recreate Wangala in its preirrigation state. I did find a village, not too far away from Wangala, whose lands lie above canal irrigation level and therefore remain dry. The village, which I subsequently called Dalena, had a population of 701 individuals residing in 153 households. In my innocence, I expected Dalena to have continued fairly unchanged throughout the years that neighboring villages had come to enjoy the benefits from irrigation. It did not take me long to discover, after I had started fieldwork in Dalena, that no village remains static while surrounded by a changing environment. Irrigation in the area had aroused out of their almost stagnant conditions not only villages, like Wangala, that benefited directly from canal water, but also dry-land villages, like Dalena, where men sought new opportunities outside the borders of their own village. Thereby, Mandya, a small but rapidly growing town, became the center of an integrated regional economy.

In 1956, on completion of my 2 years fieldwork in south India I returned to Manchester, wrote my thesis, and published it in 1962 as a book. I hoped that some day I would be able to restudy Wangala and Dalena, but because of financial constraints saw little chance of ever being able to do so. None of my village friends were literate in English and only a few could write the vernacular. Thus I could not correspond with any of them and lost touch altogether. Subsequently I changed my regional interest to the Pacific and conducted research in New Guinea.

Quite unexpectedly at the beginning of 1970 while I was at the Australian National University, I received an invitation to return to south India from a young German sociologist. He and an Indian student, both attached to the University of Nürnberg, had used my earlier publication as base data and conducted a follow-up study in Wangala and Dalena. They volunteered all possible help and even offered to make available to me their experienced research assistants. I immediately began to make arrangements to take advantage of this rare opportunity. I managed to return to "my" south Indian villages in July 1970—14 years after I had left. Before going on to evaluate my own experience of a restudy I want to discuss the advantages and disadvantages of different types of comparative research of which long-term studies are only one.

Types of Comparative Micro-studies

Anthropological micro-studies are frequently criticized for their parochialism by other social scientists outside the profession, in particular by economists. By focusing on one small society, which is never randomly selected, a micro-study fails to produce data which lend themselves readily to large-scale generalizations. It may be very interesting to know the specific characteristics of one small-scale society, but what insight can be discerned from this for a better understanding of at least some aspects of society in general? Though anthropological research is essential to gain an insight into social processes and culture patterns, the narrow horizon of micro-studies is a serious drawback. Comparative micro-studies provide one way to overcome this. There are different types of comparative micro-studies. These are by no means mutually exclusive, but in fact would produce best results if one were conducted to reinforce the others. In what follows, I draw mainly on my own research experience as exemplary material. However, I suggest that many of the propositions I discuss lend themselves readily to generalizations over large numbers of anthropological micro-studies.

Meso-regional Studies

My own earlier micro-studies, like so many others of their type, were conducted in isolation from other ongoing fieldwork in India or anywhere else. Because of time and resource limitations I could focus on only a few aspects of the problems I had set out to study. For instance, I know now that it is impossible to analyze fully the impact of irrigation on the socioeconomic system of villages in Mandya District without research in the town of Mandya itself. To study the development of an integrated regional economy necessitates an integrated regional approach. O.H.K. Spate rightly warns anthropologists of the dangers of regarding as microcosms the individual villages studied: "It is sometimes forgotten that any number of traverses do not add up to a triangulation . . . why is the useful concept of meso-regional analysis so often overlooked? . . . but for this too a firm basis of detailed local studies is necessary [Spate 1973: XIV]." Spate thus stresses the need for a number of complementary studies to be conducted in the same region. This is precisely what I now think ought to have been done when I began my fieldwork in South India. My own village studies would have been much more meaningful had they been set within the context of a broader research scheme focusing on economic development and social change in the Mandya region. The comprehensive data that are likely to emerge from such an exercise would provide a much sounder basis for restudy at a future date than is the case with my own isolated micro-studies. Moreover, if in the first instance my own research had been conceived of as part of or leading to a meso-regional study, I would have viewed irrigation in its wider setting and would never have been so foolish as to believe it possible to find a village economy that had remained static while neighboring areas developed. I would have been better prepared than I was to study Dalena, the dry-land village, the development of which symbolizes the process of regional integration of villages in Mandya District. I have been advocating for some time now the advisability of studying Mandya town. So far, I have not been successful in getting this research off the ground, but I am still trying.

There are available some examples of meso-regional studies: The Rhodes–Livingstone Institute encouraged studies in Central Africa with such objectives in mind; Douglas Oliver had a team of students working in the Solomon Islands. Two such programs are covered in this volume: the Ramah Project organized by Kluckhohn and described by Lamphere; and the Harvard Chiapas Project organized by Vogt. The considerable difficulties involved in organizing meso-regional studies readily account for their paucity to date. First of all, there is the serious problem of finance; then there are the difficulties which are part of all team efforts; and, possibly most important, is the danger of providing a straitjacket for researchers. Though these are serious considerations to bear in mind, I suggest that they do not represent insurmountable obstacles: Financial support can be found, personal animosities and/or differences among team members can be ironed out, and researchers can be expected to collect at least a minimum of required core data, over and above which each can and should be encouraged to follow his/her own particular interests in the course of fieldwork. The more different social facts are brought to light, the more comprehensive the overall analysis is likely to be. The object of meso-regional studies is to analyze the different interrelationships among economic, political, and general social variables in a regional context. The emphasis here is on the *region* and it is therefore not surprising that it is Spate, a geographer, who advocates such studies. Meso-regional studies are not necessarily appropriate for all or even most of anthropological research. They are relevant, though, to research topics like the one I undertook to study in 1954. I should have expected that a large canal irrigation scheme would affect not only the intravillage organization but would also change the total environment of villages in the area. Alas, at the time I was oblivious to the importance of village externalities. Furthermore, I was not in a position to tackle a meso-regional study single-handed.

Cross-cultural Comparative Micro-studies

Cross-cultural comparative micro-studies are another possibility for comparative research. Such studies, by their very nature, are problem—rather than region—oriented. With hindsight, I now think it would have been wiser had I focused my investigation on a topic, such as, for instance, the process of monetization of rural economies, which had already been examined in Africa (e.g., Watson 1958) and other developing societies. This would have helped to consolidate our understanding of one particular aspect of socioeconomic change. Instead I ventured into a relatively new field of inquiry. However, since canal irrigation is a widespread phenomenon in less developed countries it should have been easy for micro-studies similar to my own to be conducted in other cultural settings. Such exercises would have helped to test my hypotheses that (a) irrigation helps to perpetuate the traditional socioeconomic system and makes farmers more village-introverted (which characterizes developments in Wangala) and (b) diversification of economic roles and relationships increases the rate of social change (which is based on Dalena's experience). I am aware of only two attempts to test these hypotheses systematically: one was conducted by a team of German geographers attached to the University of Heidelberg who studied irrigation in Sri Lankan villages and the other by Kaja Finkler in Mexico (verbal communication). Their findings support my hypotheses. Obviously, many more studies in different cultural contexts are needed before these hypotheses can be regarded as fully verified. Probably, what is likely to emerge is that they will need refining to fit different circumstances. I find it tantalizing not to know what sort of refinements may be necessary.

There have been many attempts at cross-cultural analysis of the findings produced by anthropologists who conducted their research in different cultural settings. Very rarely though do researchers start by trying to test the same hypotheses in different cultural settings or put to the test a hypothesis resulting from the study of one society by conducting fieldwork in a different part of the world altogether. In this context my ongoing cross-cultural study of population growth and rural poverty may represent an interesting exercise (see the following discussion).

Long-term Micro-studies

Such studies can be of different types:

1. Continuous research in the same small society over a number of years
2. Periodic restudies at regular or irregular intervals
3. Reexposure after a lengthy interval of time has elapsed since the original research

My own restudy of Mysore villages falls into the third category, for as mentioned already I had lost touch with the villages after completing my first spell of fieldwork in 1956 and returned only in 1970. On the basis of my own experience I find it difficult to speculate whether all situations lend themselves equally well for reexposure—my own certainly did.

Several considerations apply to all three types of long-term micro-studies.

1. Research focus: If the restudy focuses on the same social phenomena as the earlier research and the emphasis is placed on examining change over time, there is every reason to believe that the project would encounter little difficulty. However, research interests, just like societies, rarely remain static, even for the same worker. A restudy is likely to emphasize the importance of variables not emphasized in the first inquiry. This may create difficulties insofar as the base findings do not provide the data for comparison, but it may be possible to extract the necessary data from the earlier field notes or other unpublished material. Even if this should be utterly impossible, I suspect that it is far better to have at least some related data available for an earlier period than to come to a society as a complete novice.

2. New versus old researcher: One of the first questions which arises in the context of a restudy is whether to encourage the original worker to go back or to arrange for one or more younger investigators, well versed in the earlier findings, to take a new look at the "old" society. There are pros and cons for both these approaches.

A different researcher brings new ideas and a new personality to the restudy, which may help to neutralize any personal bias in the findings. Moreover, a younger generation of workers may approach the restudy from a completely new angle and use different methods of investigation, resulting in an account so different from the earlier findings that it may appear to bear no relation to the original research. By this I do not mean to imply that it would not be a desirable exercise to have earlier research results tested by a younger generation of investigators. This, however, is possible only if there is continuity in approach and the restudy starts from similar premises and uses methods of inquiry similar to those of the initial research.

On the other hand, a new worker, even though knowing the society's social history, yet faces the problem of having to establish rapport.

It is important in this context to remember the human concern involved in micro-studies. The researcher who spends at least 1 year living with a particular small group of people not only learns about their lives but also becomes an important individual in their eyes. Many informants establish a firm personal attachment to the first investigator they encounter who shared their lives for a period of time. They are not readily prepared to transfer their allegiances to another individual. The mutual trust and respect established between the initial researcher and informants provides a favorable climate for a restudy. Most social anthropologists experience an increasingly marginal rate of data collection for a considerable part of their studies which means that the restudy conducted by the original investigator need not take anywhere near as long as if a new researcher is involved.

The above points can be readily illustrated by my own experience in restudying Mysore villages.

REEXPOSURE TO MYSORE VILLAGES

The overall focus of my own interests hardly changed over time; in my initial study I concentrated on examining the interdependencies between economic and social developments and this is still my continued concern. Thus, when I returned to South India, I went equipped with copies of all the material I had collected during my first spell of fieldwork (sketch maps, census forms, field notes, genealogies, household budgets, photographs, etc.). Much as I would have liked to spend another 2 years in the villages, personal circumstances made a long spell of fieldwork impossible. I could spend no more than 5 weeks.

My German colleague, Mr. Schönherr, at whose invitation I ventured back to South India, had told the villagers of my impending return. They had been convinced all along that he was my son, and therefore were not too surprised to learn of my revisit. In fact, they superimposed their own custom of categorizing relationships in genealogical terms and regarded as my kin every researcher who visited their village after I left. It emerged that at least seven or eight people had come to ask them questions of one sort or another, but none had stayed as long as I did and none was accepted by them as I had been. The warmth of their reception was overwhelming and remains one of my most treasured experiences. I had no problem whatsoever in reestablishing rapport and began to collect data from the first moment of my return. As it so happened my first day back in the Mysore villages coincided with the wedding in Dalena of the daughter of one of the headman's younger brothers. It struck me immediately that there had been a change in wedding practice among peasants: Whereas previously the groom's people met all expenditures, now it was the bride's family that paid it all. Pursuing this line of enquiry led to a lot of other interesting material. Data were flowing in at such a pace that I often typed my field notes until the early hours of the morning and was up again at 5 A.M. ready to collect more information.

Like most other anthropological fieldworkers, I too had made a number of special friends in the villages I studied. They were my best and most trusted informants. Most of them were about 5 or more years older than myself. By 1970, some of them had died; the rest of us had aged; some had become ill or otherwise disabled. On my return, my old contacts were quickly renewed. It meant that now that I was older myself I also had closer links with an older age group of informants than I had had during my first spell of fieldwork. I discuss the impact of my changed social role on our relations in what follows. Here it suffices to say that as a female fieldworker, who played down the fact of her sex—I never wore a sari in the villages either in 1954–1956 or 1970, so as to differentiate myself ostentatiously from village women and so avoid being identified with them—I was readily accepted by male villagers and also obviously had no difficulty in securing access to female society.

I began my fieldwork in 1954 by collecting a 100% socioeconomic census of the village households, which provided the basis for the compilation of a stratified random sample. Each of the sample households was then subjected to intensive qualitative as well as quantitative inquiry. With the aid of my earlier residential sketch maps of the villages—an invaluable help to restudies—I was able to identify most of my original sample households. In 1970, my time back in Mysore was too brief to allow me to repeat the exercise of collecting a 100% socioeconomic census, and therefore I lacked the basis for compiling another stratified random sample of all the households. I could, of course, have randomly sampled the villages by selecting one household out of every fifth or tenth house in the village streets, but I decided that this would not be a satisfactory procedure either. I considered it more meaningful to reexamine some of the households in the original study.

In the intervening years, the "case study method" had been developed (Van Velsen 1967). Thus, I decided to concentrate on case studies of individual households. I selected one from each of the different economic strata of the villages: for Dalena, I chose one peasant magnate, one peasant middle-farmer and one of the poor Scheduled Castes; for Wangala I did the same but added one migrant laboring household, a new phenomenon in the village, to cover the full range of economic differentiation. I tried to learn as much as possible about the changes that had occurred in these households and spent many days just sitting with informants asking questions, but mainly listening to what was being said and observing what went on.

These detailed case studies of a few carefully selected households enabled me to give quantitative accounts of the increasing economic differentiation that had taken place in these villages, as well as to indicate the processes by which the rich farmers had increased their wealth and the poor landless Scheduled Castes laborers had become poorer not only in relative but also in absolute terms. By viewing village society as a system, I managed to piece together the different items of information like a jigsaw puzzle and analyze the overall process of social change. I found evidence for the continued village introversion in Wangala and village extroversion in Dalena. I collected enough material to write at least one more book on the restudy besides the one I have already published. Under ideal conditions of restudy, I would have liked to update my 100% village census, compile another stratified random sample and examine in depth as well as to collect case studies. Alas, this was impossible!

Mr. Schönherr was nearing the end of his investigation by the time I arrived in Mysore. He conducted his inquiries with the aid of four indigenous assistants and focused on "political organization and change." He had not attempted to learn the vernacular and conducted his investigations through an interpreter by means of long structured interviews during each of which he tried to complete a questionnaire of several pages. Therefore not only were his research interests not the same as my own, but more important still, his method of collecting data was also entirely different. He made appointments with informants either for them to come and see him or for him to turn up at the time and place they specified. It did not surprise me to hear that villagers frequently failed to keep 'the arrangements they had made with him, which made him feel frustrated. A number of my village friends asked me in confidence why I had not tried to make "my son" follow in his mother's footsteps and join the village life instead of remaining aloof as was his practice.

The data Mr. Schönherr collected were thus of a different type and quality than my own. Since he asked different questions in a different way, his data did not lend themselves for cross-checking with my own. All his material was contained in questionnaires which readily lent themselves to quantitative analysis. During my visit, I shared accommodations with Mr. Schönherr and his research assistants. Every evening after we returned from our investigations I settled down to typing my field notes. Mr. Schönherr regularly watched me doing so with a puzzled look on his face; after about a week he got up enough courage to ask how it was that I had so much correspondence to do, for this is what he assumed I was typing. He was amazed when I told him that I was recording my field notes. I was equally amazed to find out that after more than 1 year's fieldwork he had not collected a single field note. It had never dawned on him that it might be useful to view political organization and change as part of an overall social process. His training in sociology had convinced him that political behavior can be abstracted from other social relationships. Therefore he was sure that he needed only the answers to his questionnaires and no other data. Accordingly, I was not surprised when he kindly sent me a copy of his thesis, which he had submitted to the University of Nürnberg and for which he was awarded his doctorate, to see that his analysis of political organization and change in Dalena and Wangala was very different from the analysis I presented in my follow-up study. Anyone reading the two accounts may not even suspect that they relate to the same places.

It is this experience which convinced me of the need for continuity in the conduct of a restudy. Thus, wherever possible I suggest it is desirable for the same researcher to return to the same field location. If this is impossible, it is essential that the new investigator should at least contact the "ancestor" before embarking on the restudy so as to be initiated competently into the complexities of the particular society which may not emerge fully from the published material. Moreover, such contact may provide a bonafide and acceptable introduction to informants. I am convinced that Mr. Schönherr's relations with villagers in Wangala and Dalena would have been closer and thus his research more fruitful had he managed to contact me before he started his fieldwork rather than when he had almost completed it.

One of my Indian students, who is presently restudying a village near Lucknow which was first studied in the early 1920s by one of Professor R. Mukerjee's students (1929), managed to track down the original researcher. This man is now in his 80s but still alert. This personal contact gave the student important additional insight into the village society before he started his fieldwork. Moreover, the old man's nephew, the present postmaster in the village, helped the student to gain ready entrée to the society. Of course, it may not always be possible for a new worker to contact the original investigator. For instance, another of my Indian students is restudying Rampur, the north Indian village which Oscar

Lewis made famous (1958). Oscar Lewis being dead, she tried to establish contact not only with his widow, but also with one or another of the Indian research assistants who helped in the 1953–1954 village study. Mrs. Lewis gave the student access to her husband's unpublished field notes and photographs, for which we are grateful. One of the Indian research assistants, I. P. Singh, who had in the meantime become a professor of anthropology at the University of Delhi, readily agreed to introduce the student to the villagers and also gave her much unpublished information on the village.

RESEARCH TRAINING FOR STUDENTS

At the start of my first fieldwork, I had little guidance in how to collect various types of socioeconomic data. I had to improvise as I went along. I assume that many colleagues of my own or older generations of anthropologists can recount similar experiences. *The Craft of Social Anthropology* (A. L. Epstein 1967) was a long overdue guidebook for anthropological fieldwork and appears to provide valuable aid to budding fieldworkers.

The great diversity of data collected by the many individual anthropologists, who conducted the large number of micro-studies now available, makes it difficult—sometimes even impossible—to make any meaningful comparisons and/or draw valid conclusions. It is scientifically unsound to assume that a common denominator runs through the many studies conducted by individuals with different academic backgrounds and interests, each using different methods of data collection. This extreme heterogeneity in the studies makes not only cross-comparisons but also comparisons over time a dubious proposition. There seems to be a need to standardize the collection of at least a minimum core of data to facilitate not only cross-cultural comparative studies but also studies over time. This is obviously not easy to do, for it involves encouraging researchers to use standardized procedures at least in the collection of the core data; but it seems certainly worth a trial.

My own ongoing research can be seen as such an experiment in the standardized collection and analysis of cross-cultural micro-data. Eight Ph.D. students (three Indians, two Kenyans, one Nigerian, and two Sri Lankans) are conducting micro-research in their respective home countries as part of my "Cross-cultural Study of Population Growth and Rural Poverty." They are testing the same hypotheses by means of identical, or at least similar, methods. Wherever possible, they are restudying societies for which there are earlier reports available. These studies thus not only have a cross-cultural dimension but four of them also represent comparative investigations over time. Moreover, my own recent experience of restudy motivated me to think in terms of longitudinal research and its implications for field methods. Accordingly, I am encouraging my students to regard their present research as the beginning of long-term studies.

REEXPOSURES AND THEIR ADVANTAGES

The advantages of reexposures over individual, once and for all, micro-studies appear so obvious that it is hardly necessary to outline them in greater detail. Most anthropological studies seek historical depth for their successful exercise, but this is often hard to come by. Restudies provide this important historical dimension. Moreover, they also facilitate the analysis of continuity and change over time. For instance, if I had not been able to restudy the Mysore villages I would never have been in a position to analyze successfully the persistence of the traditional systems of hereditary labor relationships between farmers and resident landless laborers in Wangala and their disappearance in Dalena. Only the time perspective could provide the necessary insight for me to explain the operation of these social processes.

The results of reexposures à la Firth (1959) and Mead (1956) speak for themselves: They offer historical dimensions and theoretical depth that could never be the outcome of a once-and-for-all period of fieldwork.

I do not know whether equally startling results can be claimed for, or expected from, the other two categories of long-term micro-studies, the continuous or periodic restudies. I have never been in a position to indulge in such research activities. I have been able to revisit South India on several occasions since 1970 and always made a point to return to Wangala and Dalena, but my stays were too brief to conduct any serious fieldwork. I am now planning to arrange for a follow-up study by myself or one of my students during the coming year, to be repeated, if possible, at 5-year intervals.

Impact on the People Studied

The study of particular societies inevitably gains them attention they would otherwise have never received. Shrewd informants are quick to grasp this and try to manipulate the fieldworker to their own advantage. For instance, when I first moved into Wangala two of the village magnates tried to get me to intervene on their behalf with the Mandya Sugar Factory so that each of them would be offered a contract for growing cane on 4 acres instead of the 2 acres which was the general factory practice. Some villagers requested me to help bring about the establishment of a health center in Dalena, others wanted me to induce the authorities to set up factories outside their village to provide employment for residents and so on. A common theme seemed to be running through these varied requests: They all aimed at exploiting the advantage of having an outsider live in their midst so as to benefit from developments exogenous to their own society. Needless to say, I could not possibly meet all their requests. However, I tried to help in problems encompassing either the village as a whole (e.g., arranging for immunization at the outbreak of a typhoid epidemic in Wangala in 1955), or affecting large numbers of people (e.g., helping the Untouchable community in Wangala to get funds to purchase materials for a well of its own so that people no longer had to fetch their drinking water from a polluted pond). My interests in Wangala and Dalena, therefore, seemed to have helped broaden the horizon of the villagers and sharpened their awareness of the world surrounding their own society.

On the whole, I think I can claim that the villages have benefitted at least to a limited extent from my connection with them. However, I am also fully aware of the fact that unintentionally I raised aspirations in a number of my informants which I never managed to help them realize and which therefore must have caused them considerable frustration. It is still not clear in my own mind what I could have done to avoid this.

It is difficult to generalize the extent to which a village population's self-image has changed as a result of having been studied. A researcher invariably seems to have had most impact on the closest friends and best informants. The following example indicates the impact my research has had on one such informant in helping to increase his awareness of the social processes of which he is a part and of the acute social problems surrounding him. As mentioned earlier, during my first field study no single villager in Wangala was literate in English and only a few could write the vernacular. By the time I returned in 1970, some of the young boys whom I helped to learn English had become university graduates. One of them, to whom I refer by the psuedonym Rampa (Epstein 1973:224), had just been awarded a first-class master's degree in economics at the University of Bangalore and had been offered a lectureship at a college in Mandya. Rampa had already read my 1962 book by the time we met in 1970. He congratulated me on the way I had managed to describe and analyze rural South India and confessed that he regarded my account as his bible for understanding village life. It was he who first suggested that my book be translated into the vernacular—a task which is now being completed by the University of Agricultural Sciences, Bangalore. Rampa's account of his own experience, to my mind, symbolized the widening gap between rural societies and the trained few resulting from an education which has little relevance to village life. In my 1973 book, I discussed Rampa's case to illustrate that insofar as education is expected to help improve rural living conditions, these young village graduates are a sad disappointment: They turn their backs on the village and look to the towns for their future careers.

I had given my young friend a pseudonym, but anyone familiar with Wangala has no difficulty in identifying his real name. Knowing that Rampa would read my restudy of his village and discover himself discussed in it, I was frankly a bit nervous before I met him again in Bangalore in 1974. However, he soon put my worries to rest; in fact, he told me that after having read and carefully considered my analysis of his life style, he began to appreciate how wrong it had been of him to try and cut his links with his fellow villagers and ignore their plight. As a result, he decided to resign his lectureship in Mandya and join the Karnataka State public service, where he now wants to make his career in the field of development and extension administration. "If my education has not helped my native village, at least it will enable me to be of service to rural societies in general," were his own words on the subject. I was greatly impressed with the way young Rampa had taken into serious consideration my discussion of his attitudes and was gratified to see the impact this had on changing the course of his life. This had been more than I had ever dared to hope.

Rampa may represent the odd case of a "success story." Though this may be so, I am extremely pleased to find that a bright and educated young man, indigenous to the very village I studied, not only agreed with my analysis of the processes of social change I had observed, but was encouraged by it to increase his own commitment to rural development. So far only a few people in Dalena and Wangala have read my books; all of them are young men educated by the English media. My South Indian village studies are now being translated into the vernacular. As soon as they are available in their Indian reincarnation, they will be exposed to a much wider indigenous audience whose comments and criticisms I am eagerly awaiting.

Researcher–Informant Relations

In the time span between my two studies in Mysore, I not only grew older but I also changed my social roles: From being an unmarried girl, I became a married mother of two daughters. I found that this social transformation of my person greatly facilitated my restudy. During my first fieldwork, some of my village friends left me in no doubt that they disapproved of a woman of my "advanced" years being without a husband and children. By the time I returned, I could satisfy them that I had fulfilled my "natural" role. Therefore, many older men and women approved of me more readily than during my first fieldwork. At the same time, I came to be recognized by younger villagers in somewhat of a parental role. I feel certain that this was an important factor in the influence I exerted over Rampa. His own mother had died in the intervening years and he now looks up to me as if I were his mother. Other young villagers displayed similar attitudes toward me. Whereas, on the earlier occasion villagers could not readily fit me into any of their familiar social categories—I was a woman but according to their norms too old to be unmarried and without offspring—and therefore, in particular, the young men of the village did not quite know what to make of me. When I returned and showed the villagers photographs of my husband and children, everyone seemed more at ease with me; they were able to categorize their relations with me according to their own social roles. I still did not fit in completely, because my village age mates were already grandparents while my own children were still far too young to be married, but at least they found it easier to fit me into their system of classification.

Though undoubtedly I feel a great debt to many villagers, I thought it advisable from the point of view of academic objectivity not to get too involved in the lives of individual informants. I have given presents whenever the occasion warranted it (e.g., when a villager has a marriage in the household); I now correspond regularly with Rampa and have renewed my contact with Suri, the research assistant who helped me during my first fieldwork and joined me again in the restudy; I try to meet them every time I travel to south India and also to revisit Dalena and Wangala on these occasions. But I have refrained from helping individual villagers educate their children or meet any of their many specific demands. I did this because I thought it important for me not to become identified with individual households and thereby leave myself open to charges of favoritism. Whenever a specific request was made to me, I tried to explain at great length the reasons for my refusal. The villagers soon learned to accept this and from their continuing friendly behavior towards me I think I am justified in assuming that they have come to respect me for my neutrality.

My reexposure to Wangala and Dalena has had an important effect on me in several respects. First of all, it suggested to me the importance of trying to work out the policy implications of my findings and translate them into action-oriented programs to try and improve the levels of living of the poorest sections in the societies I studied. This accounts for my including a section entitled "Some Palliatives of Socioeconomic Developments" in my 1973 book on South India. Second, I began to appreciate the importance of prediction in studies of socioeconomic change. This is reflected again in the 1973 book where I discuss what the future holds for Dalena and Wangala and other villages of similar types. Only time can tell whether my predictions will be realized, but one thing seems certain: Only by making predictions can we expose our analyses to rigorous testing.

Third, meeting again my village friends after a lapse of 15 years has made me feel much more humble vis-à-vis them and made me change my personal values and sets of priorities. This lesson was dramatically brought home to me when on my return to Wangala I sought to meet again one of my closest village friends who in the intervening years had gone almost blind; when I approached him he fumbled with his hands reaching out to touch me; when I took his hands in mine, he said quietly and with great dignity: "Now that I know you are still alive and have come back to see me again I can die in peace," which made me feel very small indeed.

BIBLIOGRAPHY

Epstein, A. L., ed.
  1967 *The craft of social anthropology.* London: Tavistock.
Epstein, T. Scarlett
  1962 *Economic development and social change in South India.* Manchester: Manchester Univ. Press.
  1973 *South India, yesterday, today, and tomorrow: Mysore villages revisited.* New York: Holmes and Meier.
Firth, Raymond
  1959 *Social change in Tikopia: Re-Study of a Polynesian community after a generation.* New York: Macmillan.
Lewis, Oscar
  1958 *Village life in Northern India: Studies in a Delhi village.* Urbana: Univ. of Illinois Press.
Mead, Margaret
  1956 *New lives for old: Cultural transformation—Manus, 1928–1953.* New York: William Morrow.
Mukerjee, R., ed.
  1929 *Fields and farmers in Oudh.* University of Lucknow Studies in Economics and Sociology, No. 4. Calcutta: Longmans, Green.
Spate, O. H. K.
  1973 Foreword. In *South India, yesterday, today, and tomorrow: Mysore villages revisited,* by T. Scarlett Epstein. Pp. xiii–xv. New York: Holmes and Meier.
Srinivas, M. N.
  1959 The dominant caste in Rampura. *American Anthropologist 61:*1–16.

Van Velsen, J.
  1967   The Extended-Case Method and Situational Analysis. In *The craft of social an-thropology,* edited by Epstein, A. L. Pp. 129–149. London: Tavistock.
Watson, W.
  1958   Tribal cohesion in a money economy: A study of the Mambwe people of Northern Rhodesia. Manchester: Manchester Univ. Press.

11

Long-Term Research in Gwembe Valley, Zambia

Thayer Scudder
Elizabeth Colson

INTRODUCTION

We began our study of the Gwembe or Valley Tonga of Zambia in 1956 when their area was still a relatively isolated region served by few roads, schools, or shops.

Gwembe Valley is that portion of the Zambezi River Valley that lies between Victoria Falls and the confluence of the Zambezi and Kafue Rivers. The valley floor lies at about 1300 feet above sea level, far below the 4000 to 5000 foot plateaus which flank it on either side. Steep escarpments make access to Gwembe difficult. The largest part of its population, in 1956, lived on the north bank of the Zambezi in what was then Northern Rhodesia and is now Zambia. The rest lived in Southern Rhodesia, now called Rhodesia by its settler population and Zimbabwe by its African population. The Zambian portion of the valley is a single administrative district, Gwembe District. It is with the fortunes of the people of this district that we have been primarily concerned.

Beginning in 1956, one or the other (or both) of us has visited Gwembe, at least briefly, on 12 different occasions: 1956–1957, 1960, 1962–1963, 1965, 1967, 1968, 1970, 1971, 1972, 1973 (and Scudder returned yet again

227

Long-Term Field Research
in Social Anthropology

in 1976). We have never been away for more than 3 years and usually the interval between visits has been less. But we did not plan it that way in the beginning. Originally the study was to have a beginning, a middle, and an end. Its purpose was to be an examination of the impact upon Gwembe people of the flooding of their country by the building of Kariba Hydroelectric Dam and how they adjusted to life in new areas.

Kariba Dam and Its Impact

Today Gwembe landscape is dominated by Kariba Lake, impounded behind the 400 foot dam which was begun in 1955 and sealed in late 1958. When the waters reached the reservoir margin in 1963, Kariba, then the largest man-made lake in the world, reached a length of over 170 miles and a surface area of approximately 2000 square miles. As the lake filled, the village sites of approximately 57,000 people (on both sides of the Zambezi) were flooded. Although the villagers were largely relocated within the lake basin, the majority were no longer "people of the Zambezi," their old boast. They were forced back on less fertile soils towards the base of the Middle Zambezi escarpments (see Figure 11.1).

Big dams, for all their negative impacts, are a very effective mechanism for incorporating local populations into a wider regional and often national framework. In the Gwembe case, new roads were built to the dam site prior to the commencement of construction, and feeder roads were extended to relocation areas. Thousands of laborers responded to job opportunities at the site or in such operations as bush clearance around the perimeter of the future lake. Within a matter of months, years of relative isolation were swept away. Prior to the flooding, people were moved to new lands chosen (and in some cases, prepared) for them. The new reservoir created a temporarily lucrative fishing industry which drew immigrants from outside Gwembe, some fishermen originating from as far away as Malawi and Tanzania.

Zambian Independence

The decades of our study also span the end of colonial rule in Zambia and the first decade of national independence. In 1956–1957, Zambia was a member of the short-lived Federation of the Rhodesias and Nyasaland, although the British Colonial Office still held responsibility for African administration in Zambia. Those Gwembe Tonga who lived in Zimbabwe fell directly under the control of its settler government which had very different policies for its African population.

In Zambia, settler political power was broken in 1962. In 1964 the

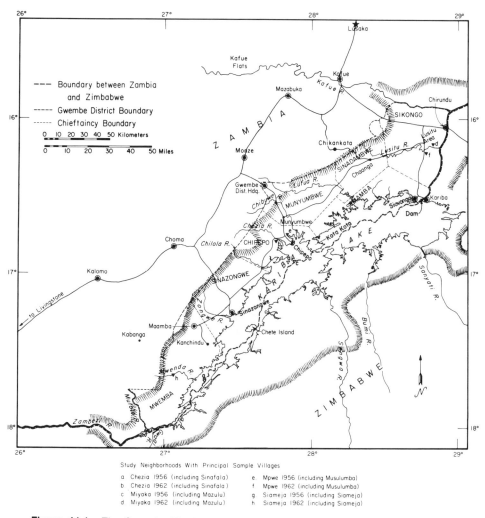

Study Neighborhoods With Principal Sample Villages

a Chezia 1956 (including Sinafala)	e Mpwe 1956 (including Musulumba)
b Chezia 1962 (including Sinafala)	f Mpwe 1962 (including Musulumba)
c Miyaka 1956 (including Mazulu)	g Siameja 1956 (including Siameja)
d Miyaka 1962 (including Mazulu)	h Siameja 1962 (including Siameja)

Figure 11.1. The Gwembe District and the Kariba Lake Basin.

country became independent. Thereafter, deteriorating relationships with Zimbabwe closed off that country to Zambian labor migrants, including those from Gwembe District. Gwembe migrants increasingly sought work in Zambia. This, and the new policies of the Zambian government, accelerated the incorporation of Gwembe dwellers into a wider national polity of which they had been scarcely aware in 1956. Gwembe society, which was intensely egalitarian in 1956, was becoming increasingly stratified. In 1956, few Gwembe Tonga were literate in any language; by 1972 probably every village in Gwembe District could boast of at least one student who had been to secondary school. A few young men and women had taken university degrees either in Zambia or overseas and were employed in Lusaka, the capital, or other cities. Others, who received teacher training, were assigned to rural primary schools where they form a new elite with local businessmen, employees of the local and district administration, and various others.

Gwembe District now has two industrial centers, whereas in 1956 there were only villages and two mission stations. Zambia's only coal mines were opened in South Gwembe in 1965. North Gwembe now has a power installation so that Kariba power, vital for the Zambian copper mines and for industrial development, no longer originates only from generators on Zimbabwe soil. The two industrial centers have recruited diversified work forces, only some of whose personnel originate in Gwembe.

Increased agricultural and veterinary services and the provision of credit in the years since independence have encouraged a diversification of the economic structure of the District's villages: Cash cropping provides new opportunities at home. But migrants continue to exploit opportunities available elsewhere in Zambia. They are to be found in all the towns of Southern Province (to which Gwembe District belongs)—these are strung along the railway line that crosses the plateau some 10 to 20 miles to the west of the escarpment and the district boundary. The largest concentration, however, is in Lusaka, in Central Province. Today Gwembe people maintain both rural and urban bases between which people, messages, cash, and other goods flow with increasing frequency, given the new availability of roads and transportation.

CONTINUITY AND CHANGE IN THE GWEMBE STUDY

During the 2 decades covered by our study, our research has continued to change, partly in response to the changing circumstances of the Gwembe people, partly because of our own changing interests, but also because a long-term study has its own dynamics. As we have attempted to understand continuities and change, the timing and sequencing of events have become more crucial phenomena. We have come to see current practices as coping devices applied to particular situations rather than as stable adaptations which will continue to be invoked. In turn, what is happening at the time of any one visit has the potential for a variety of futures. We find ourselves trying to forecast the probable consequences of the choices people are making, both for themselves as individuals and for the communities with which they identify. We also find ourselves paying more and more attention to the interplay between national resources and policies and the choices open to Gwembe residents. In 1956–1957, although policy decisions were bringing upheaval to Gwembe, we could deal with these as external forces and restrict our attention primarily to what was happening in Gwembe villages and neighborhoods. On our return, we found a people who were increasingly mobile, both geographically and socially, and who used different frames of reference as they moved from situation to situation.

The purpose of this chapter is to show how we have attempted to develop a research design and methods flexible enough to cope with the study of people who are seizing or rejecting new opportunities, using and avoiding new national agencies, rethinking and clinging to old ideologies, and becoming something else while they remain themselves.

Initiation of the Project

In 1955, the government of the newly formed Federation of the Rhodesias and Nyasaland announced that contracts would be let for the building of Kariba Dam. Only a few appalled officials who had worked in Gwembe had any idea of the immensity of the human problems it would create, but Henry Fosbrooke, then director of the Rhodes–Livingstone Institute (now the Institute for African Studies in the University of Zambia), decided to give top priority to a study of the Gwembe Tonga. He saw them as having a unique way of life and wanted it studied before its distinctive agricultural system and social order were altered. Fosbrooke, however, was interested in more than salvage anthropology—this was an opportunity to learn about social change and the relationship between ecology and social order. For such a study, the research would have to be carried out in at least two stages, the second to be timed after the people had settled into their new homes. This implied an interval of from 5 to 10 years between the two stages. The emphasis was to be upon the long-term consequences of living in a new region rather than upon the transition period associated with the disruption. That period was assumed to be aberrant.

This plan was based on a perspective which we would no longer accept since it assumes:

1. A stable adaptation within a stable ecological context
2. A disruption
3. The emergence of a new equilibrium within a social and physical environment also marked by stability

Fosbrooke was inclined to opt for a 10-year interval between visits to give people a chance to change from permanent and semipermanent cultivation of alluvial soils to shifting cultivation and lake fishing, but for logistic reasons he thought it better to plan on a 5-year interval. He hoped that the social anthropologist and geographer appointed to carry out the research might be able to return again for a third visit at the end of a further 5-year period, but he sought financing only for the first two phases of the study. He approached the Federation Government and received a grant of £20,000 ($56,000) to cover both phases of the research.

He then invited Colson to serve as social anthropologist for the project. She had carried out a 3-year study of the neighboring Plateau Tonga (1946–1947, 1948–1950) and spoke a dialect of Tonga. Scudder, a social anthropologist with a background in biology and geography, was recruited to do research on Gwembe ecology.

Our Research Plans in 1956

In planning the initial study, we built on Colson's knowledge of the region. In 1949, she had spent a month in a Zambezi neighborhood in Central Gwembe. In Plateau neighborhoods, she had also talked with many Gwembe emigrants and visitors. Emigrants had settled on the Plateau because it was free of tsetse fly and they were able to have cattle, use plows, and grow cash crops. They also had access to trading stores, schools for their children, and a market for their crops. Most Gwembe villages were on the Zambezi River, a 3- to 4-day walk from the railway, over rough trails dropping some 3000 feet to the river. Schools were few and shops practically nonexistent.

Gwembe migrants walked to the Plateau along paths following the tributary rivers flowing from the escarpment to the Zambezi, each Gwembe neighborhood therefore having links with particular areas on the Plateau. Thus most Gwembe Tonga whom Colson knew in the 1940s came from a chieftaincy in Central Gwembe because she worked principally in Plateau neighborhoods into which Central Gwembe fed. From published sources and discussions with district officials, we knew that the people of that chieftaincy were not representative of the other six chieftaincies in Gwembe District: Both upstream and downstream one would encounter differences in dialect, social organization, ritual, and life style. Again people living in upland valleys between the Zambezi plain and the escarpments differed from Zambezi River people. On the other hand, neighborhoods on opposite banks of the Zambezi, although they were under different national regimes, shared many features and freely exchanged populations.

We believed it made sense to begin by making systematic studies of several communities rather than by collecting survey data on the universe of neighborhoods. To extrapolate from the findings of the systematic studies, we would have to rely on information in the district files, discussions with such visitors as came our way, and quick visits to neighborhoods throughout Gwembe to ask questions about critical features isolated in the detailed work. In other words, we proceeded as we would in a single-period field study except that our choice of villages on which to concentrate was made with the second phase of research in mind and we collected as much specific information as possible to permit us to measure change in quantitative terms when we returned.

In the second phase, we wanted to be able to compare the response to resettlement of Zambezi neighborhoods whose resources had differed. We also wanted to examine the effect on host populations who had to share space and other resources with immigrant communities. Finally, we wanted to follow what happened on both sides of the Zambezi, given the major differences in political philosophy and resettlement policies of Zambia and Zimbabwe. To do all this would have involved intensive studies in some 10 neighborhoods in combination with research on local government, the local court system, and the role of the district administrations; the combing of official records; and a survey of neighborhoods falling outside the intensive sample. It was impossible. Zimbabwe simplified our choice by moving its people before we could arrange to settle in any Zimbabwe village. Our intensive study, therefore, became confined essentially to Gwembe District in Zambia. Given information available in 1956, we opted for intensive studies of river and upland neighborhoods in Chipepo and Mwemba Chieftaincies, in Central and South Gwembe respectively. A second Central Gwembe chieftaincy resembled Chipepo. Two upland chieftaincies would not be involved in the resettlement. The two chieftaincies of North Gwembe had small populations and in 1956 were expected to lose little land to Lake Kariba and to receive few resettled people.

Only as our stay ended did it become definite that Lusitu, in North Gwembe, would receive a substantial number of immigrants from Central Gwembe, including some villages in our sample. Other changes in official plans announced late in 1957 also helped to invalidate the original research design: Our host upland village in Central Gwembe was unexpectedly slated for resettlement. This is only one instance of how unexpected events bedevil the planning of long-term research. We have encountered many others and have learned that a rigid research design becomes a handicap over time.

For strategic reasons, we began work in adjacent neighborhoods in Central Gwembe. This permitted us to hold ecological variables constant, or at least to know where they differed, and we could join forces for such purposes as survey trips and obtaining supplies. Being in different neighborhoods gave us the maximum of independence and minimized the personal tensions which are bound to plague teamwork. We also became dependent upon Tonga neighbors for companionship, an essential feature in good anthropological fieldwork. That we are still colleagues after 20 years speaks to the wisdom of arranging field research by teams, whether short-term, or long-term, in such a fashion that each member has both geographical independence and specialized research interests in addition to a common purpose in the advancement of the general study.

The subordination of our special interests to the general project was handled by an agreement that each would supply a carbon of all field notes to the other and that each had the right to publish independently using the total body of information. This agreement still stands and has worked well. Over the years we have shared ideas as we read field notes, talked, and pooled experience. Today we frequently cannot remember who first had some productive insight or suggested the collection of new kinds of data. Although initially each was to be responsible for a particular aspect of the study, and this still holds true to some extent, we agreed to make notes on subjects which fell into the other's sphere. Thus Scudder took note of disputes, divinations, and clan joking arrangements, while Colson asked about daily diets and field types.

Each of us began a detailed census of one or more villages in our chosen neighborhood and collected the associated genealogies. The census form was adapted from one used by Colson in Plateau Tonga villages (Colson 1954), and that in turn (though at a good remove) was influenced by the form Clyde Kluckhohn had developed in the 1930s for his long-term study of Ramah Navajo (see Lamphere, this volume). The census included the information a social anthropologist needs even for a one-time study, but at the same time it provided a way of comparing the attributes of individuals and villages over time. The form included questions on birthplace, parents, marital history, children and siblings (including current residence), migration histories, ownership of fields and stock, occupation, schooling, bridewealth payments, religious affiliation, participation in cults, observation of food taboos, and other status attributes.

The first 6 months were largely devoted to the systematic study of the two neighborhoods. Then Scudder began a survey of neighborhoods on both sides of the Zambezi, spending a few days in a number of neighborhoods while he made notes on geographical features, agricultural systems, other subsistence techniques, neighborhood history, and the form of neighborhood rituals. He combined this with a continuing study of local fishing techniques and the attempts then being made by the Zambian administration to introduce people to techniques suitable to lake fishing. Colson, who continued a study of local courts and local government, began additional intensive neighborhood studies. She first settled in the upland neighborhood of Central Gwembe which was slated to become host to one or the other of our two Zambezi neighborhoods. Thereafter she lived for 3 months in two Zambezi neighborhoods in Mwemba Chieftaincy, South Gwembe. Time ran out before she could move to an upland neighborhood in that region. Throughout the year, each of us also spent many hours at Gwembe District headquarters copying annual reports and other files and talking with administrative and technical officers about plans for resettlement and district development.

We did not accomplish all we hoped to do during that first year but we had data for a descriptive account of Gwembe life in the period immediately prior to resettlement (Colson 1960; Scudder 1962), and the means whereby we could make more than impressionistic statements about changes in various patterns in the post-resettlement period.

Second and Subsequent Stages: Revamping the Village Studies

The original research design strongly affected later work although recent stages of the study had no place in the original design. Colson's visit to Gwembe in 1960, about 15 months after the final move when people were still short of food and feared the regions into which they had been thrust, also had not been planned. Both of us went back for a year in 1962–1963 in accordance with the original plan and financed by the original grant. Thereafter we have returned when we could, frequently thinking that each visit would be the last. We have financed visits through other assignments, personal and university funds, and grants from the African Committee of the SSRC/ACLS, the National Science Foundation, and the John Simon Guggenheim Memorial Foundation. Over the total period of the study, costs of actual fieldwork for both of us (including travel, salaries, vehicles, research assistants in the field, and supplies) have amounted to about $150,000, though this has been possible only because on occasion we have accepted field salaries well below our regular salaries. In preparing data for publication, we have had additional costs for research assistance and other expenses, supported partially by our universities, but also by grants from NSF, NIMH and the John Simon Guggenheim Memorial Foundation.

In each visit, we have returned to neighborhoods studied in 1956–1957, but we soon found we did not have time to maintain census data on the populations of all seven villages studied intensively in 1956–1957, given the rapid increase in population and the continued in and out migration. Both are problems likely to plague any long-term study that seeks to follow individuals, and we would recommend an early decision be made about the size of the sample that can be maintained. We are left with four cohorts (Mazulu, Musulumba, Sinafala Villages and a section of Siameja Village, each in a different neighborhood) on which we try to maintain time series data on demographic, economic and social variables. The resident population count for these four units in 1956–1957 was 866 men, women, and children; in 1972–1973 it had risen to 1528. The actual sample is larger because it includes those no longer resident for some categories of information.

In 1962–1963 and 1972–1973, we attempted to complete censuses covering both current residents and anyone included in the 1956–1957 census wherever resident. Inevitably some strays were never found, but the data are good enough to enable us to compare changes in individual experience as well as to follow villages through time as social units. We found as the work proceeded that we could carry out the census effectively only if we devised checklists for each village which show all who have lived within it, with enough detail so that each person is easily identifiable. The check-lists also enable us to gather information on births, deaths, marriages, divorces, changes in residence, and present whereabouts of those we follow even when we return for brief visits since we can run through the lists with a few knowledgeable informants from each village. The check-lists are less bulky to transport than computer print-outs. Increasingly, we find them useful when we tabulate data for write-up. Indeed, for simple tabulation purposes on relatively small samples, a check-list is a more useful device than a computer and involves less labor and expense.

Through 1965, we were able to handsort data accumulated over three visits and much of that material has been tabulated and is available in print (Colson 1966, 1971b; Scudder and Colson 1971). Since then, however, the village time series data have become a major problem in two respects:

1. Much field time goes into following strays to their new place of residence and coping with the rapidly increasing population in the sample.
2. Write-up is delayed because research assistants who code the data for computer analysis invariably fall behind the input of the more recent field research.

The old division of work between us persists with respect to the village studies. Scudder is primarily concerned with maintaining the updating of one village for which he has detailed economic information and rather precise dating of births, deaths and other events. Colson follows three villages, on which we have fewer detailed economic data and dating is accurate only to the year. This is a conscious choice on our part. We have considered the advisability of diminishing the village study to a comparison of two villages for which we would have equally rigorous information, but we have decided that the overall variations among the four villages are of such interest that we should try to maintain all four. Whoever is back in Gwembe for a short visit does the check-list on as many villages as can be reached. We are now exploring ways of having secondary school students take over the task of keeping the census up to date on a regular basis. So far, this has proved satisfactory for only one village, but we have hopes that we can continue the time series on at least three villages through local assistants. However, it is only since about 1970 that it has been possible to find assistants of this calibre in Gwembe.

Incorporating New Phenomena in the Study

By the mid-1960s, our interest had shifted from relocation to the response of Gwembe people to citizenship in an independent African nation determined to upgrade the lives of its people. Of course, local communities were linked to the outside world prior to independence in 1964, but during the following 10 years the pace of development accelerated. Construction in the Zambian capital and along the line of rail opened up many jobs for unskilled laborers while the increasing number of people flocking to urban centers encouraged innovative Tonga to hustle a wide range of services. Gwembe people still attempt to exploit the resources of a region, but the region is now the whole of Zambia.

The attempts of government to develop the rural areas also opened up an increasing range of opportunities within Gwembe. Even in its present depressed state, the Kariba Lake fishery continues to play an important role in the development of Gwembe. The fishery is the largest single source of employment, aside from village agriculture, in Gwembe. Close behind are the coal mines which employed a labor force of just under 900 in 1973. The Ministry of Education, the Ministry of Rural Development, and the Gwembe Rural Council also employ hundreds of full-time personnel. While we have yet to estimate the total for 1973, between 1956 and 1970 the total number of government employees working in Gwembe District at other than day labor increased from under 100 to over 500. Whereas in the mid-1950s, men and women were almost exclusively subsistence farmers in the village and men were unskilled labor migrants elsewhere, by 1973 occupational specialization both inside and outside Gwembe District had expanded vastly.

In coping with the new diversity, we have created various special samples in addition to the village samples. In 1962, we began a study of the Kariba Lake fishery which generated its own sample of fishermen from villages throughout the district. Also in 1962–1963, we made a conscious effort to track down all the labor migrants from one of our sample villages at their current places of work, two being traced to Bulawayo in Zimbabwe. It is commonplace in anthropology to assess the impacts of labor migration on home communities. Few fieldworkers, however, have attempted to look at what is happening to the absentees and residents as intertwined. Methodologically, the task is not so difficult if one has the time and patience to track down people wherever they may be. While Scudder has done this at each revisit for the people identified with Mazulu Village, both of us began work among the Lusaka contingents from the sample villages during 1972 and 1973 and expect to spend an increasing proportion of our time with the city contingents.

In 1956–1957, Gwembe population was so little diversified that we could ignore the existence of an elite. By 1962–1963, this could no longer be justified. We began to collect data on those employed in Gwembe at jobs which required some degree of literacy, devising a questionnaire for this purpose which we continued to use in subsequent visits. Shopkeepers formed another emergent category and we have collected information on the background of the shopkeepers, the means of funding the shop, and ambitions for the future as well as details on purchasing. In 1965, 1967, and 1970 we circulated questionnaires to students in secondary schools serving Gwembe to identify them for future study and to discover their background, financing,and ambitions. In 1972, we began a systematic study of secondary school leavers from Gwembe—defined as those who had attended at least one term of secondary school before graduating or dropping out. Although it is not easy to estimate their total number, since they attended at least 20 schools located in both Southern and Central Provinces, we suspect the total did not exceed 600 by the end of 1972. We traced and interviewed 140 of them in 1973. Our sampling procedure was not sophisticated—creating a stratified sample would have increased tremendously the time required for the survey. What we did was to prepare a detailed list of those who had attended the one secondary school located in Gwembe District, founded in 1962, on the assumption that more Gwembe students had passed through this school than any other. We then traced as many students on this list as possible. We also interviewed the majority of all secondary school leavers working in Lusaka and Livingstone, the two major cities of Central and Southern Provinces, our procedure being to ask respondents to name others working in the same locale whom we then interviewed. As a result of this snowball technique, we believe our sample is representative except for the area of present employment which overemphasizes the southern half of Zambia and primary school teachers who were relatively easy to find, especially if they worked in Gwembe.

The extension of the study to urban migrants from the sample villages, to secondary school leavers, and to other elite who do not base themselves on villages, has helped us to visualize the Gwembe people as belonging to a larger national system. The understanding of the phenomena we are examining is not furthered by such concepts as "encapsulation," "compartmentalization," "rural–urban continuum," and "lagging emulation." As we have written elsewhere, villagers are no less "modern" than their urban kin (Colson and Scudder 1975).

Indeed, the same respondents may move back and forth between town and country. In the early 1960s, fishermen on Lake Kariba sold their fish fresh at the lakeside, a practice favored by a number of factors including pricing and location of markets. By the 1970s, comparative advantage lay with the fisherman who sold dried fish in the towns. The better fishermen realized this and transported and sold their catch to urban markets. Cotton farmers in North Gwembe quickly realized that they could save on transport and service costs by shipping privately to the central ginnery in Lusaka rather than through the government marketing system. Small traders and businessmen vary their efforts between rural and urban contexts. One Gwembe businessman first worked as a fisherman and then used his savings to pioneer the hamburger business in Lusaka. From its profits, he built a 14-room house in a low-income suburb in Lusaka and rented out most of the rooms. With further profits he opened two shops in North Gwembe, leaving his Lusaka ventures in the hands of trusted kin. He may have been unusually successful, but the pattern is not exceptional.

The exploitation of both urban and rural possibilities is not confined to businessmen. Young married women often spend the dry season with husbands in town and cultivate village lands during the rains. They may have their babies in town hospitals or, if in the village, they may use local dispensaries for lying-in. Children are exchanged freely between town and country. Older men and women now settled in the village may visit the towns several times a year and some look forward to settling eventually with children in town. Those resident in the rural area at any one moment do not differ from their urban kin in their general awareness of national politics, in their consumption preferences, in their willingness to utilize modern medical and other services, or in their explanations of misfortune. We have been forced to recognize that we are looking at a single universe and that the choices being made and the events which flow from them relate to that totality.

This merging of Gwembe into the wider national context must not be viewed as an end product or as indicating an irreversible trend towards homogeneity based on urban patterns. Conditions can change again. Mobility may become restricted, both geographically and socially, by a shrinking economy and the consolidation of an elite class. Children born and reared in town in time may differ from their rural cousins. Meanwhile even secondary school leavers are closely linked to their villages of origin through regular visits, payment of approximately 10% of their salaries in remittances and goods, and purchase of cattle as a form of investment— cattle which are placed in the care of village kin.

The expansion of the Gwembe arena to the whole of southern Zambia has been a challenge to us as fieldworkers. It has led to a major realloca- tion of field time, as we too move between villages in Gwembe District, the headquarters of the Rural Council and District Government, the towns of southern Zambia, and the offices of national ministries. But at least since 1963, we have confined our efforts solely to Zambia since Zimbabwe has been less accessible and will be so until the political situation changes. Another reallocation of field time has been forced upon us because it now takes longer than formerly to obtain data from official records. With independence, the Zambian Government dismantled the old system of administration which channeled technical and administrative information through district offices. The district office is much less a central archive and no longer produces an annual report containing statistics on popula- tion, livestock, stock and crop sales, trading licenses, schools, health, court hearings, rainfall, and a general comment on the state of the district. Obtaining comparable information after 1964 has involved visits to vari- ous ministries in Lusaka or to local branches of the ministries in several towns in Southern Province. This has happened at a time when the number of government services has greatly expanded and many more agencies are compiling records that we need to consult if we are to understand district and national development.

Over the years, we have accumulated an enormous body of information about events that have taken place in Gwembe or to Gwembe people. What is gradually being deleted from the research under the pressure of other work is time simply to be with friends and neighbors who are willing to help us understand how they view the world and interpret the sig- nificance of events. Colson regrets this more than Scudder and believes that we are sacrificing the possibilities for deepening understanding as- sociated with long-term studies in our emphasis upon the longitudinal study of events. But the very nature of Gwembe life at present forces us away from the villages. We can no longer assume that Gwembe people are villagers who share a common way of life linked to a common symbolic system or that all have the same range of choices available to them, or for that matter that the range of choices open to any of them remains relatively constant.

THE RESULTS OF THE GWEMBE STUDY

Our Own Theoretical Education

Our many revisits to Gwembe have taught us that anthropology, while more complicated than we originally thought, is also more exciting. We are not dealing with systems that move mechanistically toward adaptive states. On the contrary, we are dealing with people making decisions through time in contexts which change both because of their own actions and because of changes in external conditions which often neither they nor we are able to anticipate. Anthropology is still too tied to system concepts derived from biology and the physical sciences even though we chaff against them and criticize them. A major reason why this is so is because of the type of fieldwork most anthropologists still do—the single slice through time which predisposes the investigator to encapsulate findings through terms and concepts that emphasize static as opposed to dynamic qualities and integration as opposed to flux.

We are studying dynamic sets of interrelationships that are highly responsive to the context in which they occur. One of our major findings has been the frequency with which people experiment, test the gains and losses, and decide whether it is worth pursuing a new course. Another is the extent to which they are able to combine great flexibility of action with the maintenance of conceptual frames which appear to be remarkably stable. Though our specific interests vary, we both agree that we are looking at a stream of events which occur in response to and in a feedback relationship with a variety of stimuli, rather than at trends which can be extrapolated from one time to another. We realize that coping is an ongoing process which has to be seen in action to be understood. Whereas originally we were more inclined to look for consequences regarded as stable adaptations, we are now likely to ask, "Under what circumstances can we expect to find people behaving in this fashion on our next return?"

Contribution of the Study to the People of Gwembe

Some of the people involved in the study have come to see our function in life to be the maintenance of their demographic histories and they ask who will undertake that task when we are too old to carry on. Some have seen our books and articles and are pleased to know that books about

them exist. We have published three books and one monograph through
the Institute for African Studies and they are available from the Institute
and in bookshops in Zambia. Royalties have been given to the Institute to
further research in Zambia. We have distributed copies of our books to
the District Office, the Rural Council, and to some chiefs and villagers.
We make a point of sending reprints of articles to the Institute and the
University of Zambia and see to it that reprints of particular articles reach
interested persons in Gwembe. But we would like to be able to point to
more specific contributions to the welfare of Gwembe. This is somewhat
difficult. Here we discount the gifts we distribute or the various services
we have provided while in residence, such as the dispensing of medical
supplies or the provision of transportation.

Although in planning the study, Fosbrooke hoped that our findings
would have an impact upon the resettlement process, we were never
asked to provide a written report or formal advice to those in charge of the
move. Informally district officers and technical officers tried to probe in
1956–1957 for what might be useful to them from our accumulating
knowledge. Neither they nor we thought of ourselves as experts on
resettlement, but we could make predictions about the probable impact of
certain proposed actions. Fortunately, it was accepted that we talk in
general terms. Neither then nor at any other period has either of us been
expected to discuss the actions of individuals with officials—something
we would refuse to do if asked.

We could tell officials that their plan to move social units rather than
individuals fitted well with anthropological theory, but that in Gwembe
the significant social units were neighborhoods rather than villages. We
urged that neighborhoods be moved as units and emphasized the recurrent plea of villagers that if they must move they be allowed to move
inland along the tributaries about whose deltas they were living. They had
old ties of kinship and friendship with those living along the tributary
which would ease their adjustment to the new region. We pointed out that
fear of resettlement was exacerbated when people were asked to move to
an unfamiliar area./With reference to the future lake fishery, we assured
district personnel that Gwembe men were good fishermen given existing
conditions and could be expected to adopt techniques for successful lake
fishing though they would need training and capitalization. We doubted,
however, that they would operate any large-scale enterprise that required
the cooperation of a number of men over time, given the individualistic
nature of Gwembe work organization. We also questioned the optimism
that expected the fishing industry to compensate people for the loss of
arable soils. We predicted a future crisis when the first round of shifting
cultivation had exhausted soils and new fields were not available. We

queried the method of computing compensation for destruction of homesteads which placed a value only on dwellings.

We had no hesitation in querying official plans to allocate land in resettlement areas on a per capita basis to males on the tax rolls. We stressed that land ownership was well developed in Gwembe and that both men and women owned land. We had no evidence that chiefs were regarded as custodians of the lands of their people, who for the most part regarded the chiefs as government officials rather than as hereditary rulers. It seemed unlikely that people would take kindly to any allocation of land by chiefs or district officers.

Finally, we were skeptical of the officials' belief that neighborhood shrines could be transferred to resettlement areas on the ground that shrines represented not the communities that were moving but rather the relationship of these communities to particular known physical environments—the shrines were the media through which the communities tried to influence the natural forces impinging upon their particular locality. We expected shrine custodians to lose their office and indeed that both ritual and political leadership would be undermined by the failure to ward off the taking of land and to counter the government's demand that people move.

Our predictions were based on anthropological theory and the single time study—they required no long-term research. However, the long-term nature of the study sent us back to Gwembe where we had to face our record.

For the most part, the officials disregarded our comments, either because they were helpless to change plans formulated in the capital or because they did not believe us to be correct. They were unable to move all neighborhoods as units, although they tried. Three of the five neighborhoods in our original sample suffered disruption. We chose not to work again in one of the two which moved as a unit, but the other seemed the most contented by the mid-1960s of the four neighborhoods we followed. Those moved inland along their own tributary again found the adjustment easier than those moved to unfamiliar territory. Bitterness against the government was strong because compensation had not been paid for granaries and other homestead structures. But, what we had not realized in 1957 was that the method of compensation would place stress upon family relationships.

Scudder's work on Gwembe fishing does seem to have been influential in the decision to restrict commercial fishing on the Zambian side of Kariba Lake to Gwembe Tonga initially and the early success of the fisheries is evidence of the rightness of the prediction that they would adapt to lake fishing. By mid-1963, when Kariba Lake reached its outer boundary, at least 2000 Gwembe men were fishing in Zambian waters, close to the maximum we had expected to become involved. Furthermore, as we had predicted, attempts by government to introduce larger units than an experienced fisherman working with a few relatives and hired hands were unsuccessful.

By 1964, however, productivity had peaked. Thereafter annual landings and number of fishermen dropped off rapidly until the end of the 1960s when a very gradual rise in both landings and number of fishermen began. The latter reached approximately 1000 in 1973, but by then only half of these were Gwembe Tonga. But while the Kariba Lake fishery had passed its zenith (associated with an explosion in biological productivity during the years when the reservoir was filling), its impact on district development has been tremendous. On the basis of our 1963 research, we estimated · that approximately 25% of gear-owning fishermen (all then Gwembe Tonga) were saving at least $60 on an annual basis, while some were saving over $600. When productivity dropped, many fishermen de-emphasized fishing or stopped entirely. Some invested their savings in rural shops, fishing being the most important single source of capital for store construction and inventory formation since 1964. Many more invested in cattle which are now an important village industry. They also purchased plows and used ox-traction to pioneer the cultivation of cash crops such as cotton, brewing sorghum, and sunflower.

The fishing industry also had other major effects on Gwembe development. During the boom years, an active trade in fish and agricultural products (including beer) went on between the fishermen and surrounding villages, with the fishery playing a major role in drawing the Gwembe Tonga more rapidly into a market economy. Fishing also helped a significant number of Gwembe students to finance clothing and school fees for secondary school. We have yet to analyze all our data on the impact of the Kariba Lake fishery, but the broad outlines are clear. We would have been hard put to learn the varied effects if we had not followed the fishery and its impacts over a 10-year period.

Our predictions with respect to land allocation were also borne out. The people themselves successfully disregarded attempts to parcel out new fields on a per capita basis and the plan was abandoned. In the years after resettlement, we have been struck by the continuity in the formal rules of land tenure, despite the fact that resettlement for the moment revolutionized land holdings. The actual rights that cultivators had in their holdings have varied greatly over the years. Immediately after resettlement when everyone was cultivating newly cleared land, individual freedom to dispose of land was at a maximum. Thereafter, as the original cultivators have died and their rights have been inherited, land again has become subject to lineage claims compromising the freedom of the holder. Such shifts apparently can take place without anyone raising the question of the advisability of reformulating the rules governing land holding. People query particular claims; so far they have not queried the system of tenure.

Tensions linked with differential access to valued land have also varied over the period of our study. They were high in 1956–1957, though not as high as at some earlier periods for which we have evidence. Most instances of long-term hostilities between kin, associated with mutual accusations of sorcery, hinged on quarrels over land. In 1962–1963 with claims to lineage land extinguished for the moment, tension over land was at a minimum. Sorcery accusations appeared to rise from envy over differential holdings of stock and other movable wealth. By 1972–1973 we found sorcery again being attributed to anger over land disputes, although accusations frequently reflected deteriorating relationships between prior residents and the relocated people to whom they had loaned fields rather than quarrels between kin. Sorcery beliefs, incidentally, have not changed greatly over the two decades, but sorcery has been attributed to different motives at different periods and people have been more or less likely to accuse kin, neighbors, and co-workers of being the source of their ills.

We had predicted that resettlement would change the informal power structure of neighborhoods when the land base was destroyed. In 1956–1957, power was diffuse but linked to land ownership. Men with the biggest holdings of inherited alluvial soils were usually well off in food and livestock which gave them influence over the poor. They could also afford to marry a number of wives who both did much of the agricultural work and prepared food for guests. More wives meant more children and since much of a girl's bridewealth was taken by her father, more wealth. When the people moved, the old land base which supported wealth differentials was eliminated at least for the time being, for everyone had an equal chance to claim land in the new region. We thought it likely that younger men able to undertake the physical labor of land clearance would emerge as the dominant members of the community while the older men, deprived of their principal asset, would be reduced in status. Here we had not counted sufficiently on the importance of personal ability in pushing a man to the fore even under the old conditions. Middle-aged men who had influence in 1956–1957 usually succeeded in reestablishing themselves by mobilizing a variety of assets to ensure that they obtained large fields of the best soils available. Those senior to them were for the most part less fortunate.

We had predicted that the local shrines could not be moved. When the lorries moved people in 1958, poles from a shrine might be attached to leave a drag trail for the spirits to follow, but our skepticism about the efficacy of such measures turned out to be well founded. We did not hear of the reestablishment of any shrine until people had been settled in their new homes for at least 10 years and as late as 1973 most neighborhoods still lacked such a ritual focus.

A further prediction, which was borne out in 1962–1963, had been that of the demise of the ritual office of shrine custodian that was associated with the neighborhood rituals of the annual cycle. We argued that this office, like the shrines, was tied to a locality and it would also be discredited when the spirits associated with the office failed to protect the people against forcible removal. The office began to reemerge only some 10 years after the move. We also expected the resettlement to discredit the political order created by the colonial administration. This had been coopted by the administration as an agent for resettlement and throughout 1956–1957 was increasingly regarded as an enemy. In 1962–1963, we found that chiefs, headmen, and officials of the Rural Council had all lost status. Indeed by then, the majority of the people in the district opposed the whole colonial hierarchy and gave their loyalty to the political party which had protested the building of Kariba Dam and their forced separation from their homes. Resettlement had given them a vital interest in the politics of Zambia.

The Formulation of Relocation Theory

The long-term study of the Gwembe people has played a major role in allowing Scudder to generalize about the implications of compulsory relocation for communities involved, regardless of locale.

In 1961–1962, he spent a year in Egypt at the American University in Cairo during which he participated in a study of the Egyptian Nubian population soon to be relocated in connection with the Aswan High Dam Scheme. Subsequently, in the middle 1960s, he had the opportunity to visit the Volta and Kainji Dam Projects in Ghana and Nigeria, both of which together were responsible for the relocation of over 125,000 people. More recently, he has tested a number of hypotheses against the literature dealing with compulsory relocation and through visits to other relocation projects inside and outside Africa. As a result, he came to the conclusion that rural communities undergoing compulsory resettlement respond in the same general fashion irrespective of their sociocultural background and of the policy of resettlement authorities.

The similarity of response is primarily because of the extreme stress which accompanies forced removal (Scudder 1973a,b, 1975). In coping with this stress, relocated communities behave as if they saw sociocultural systems as closed systems, a response which greatly facilitates prediction by the anthropologist. They cling to familiar people and familiar institutions, changing during the initial years following removal no more than necessary to come to terms with the new habitat including its prior inhabitants. Presumably because the level of stress is close to a critical threshold, radical changes from within (revitalization movements, for example) and from without (including attempts by planners to change social organization) are rejected.

It was our careful recording of Gwembe Tonga responses that provided the empirical basis for initial theory formulation. In 1956–1957, we did not pay much attention to the impacts of compulsory relocation as such, since we were more interested in how the Gwembe people would adapt to their new local environment and emphasized this rather than their responses to the relocation process. With the wisdom of hindsight, Scudder regrets not having accompanied any of the Zimbabwe communities which were actually being resettled while we were in the Gwembe Valley, but at that time we set other priorities. Furthermore, in 1956–1957 people did not seem particularly preoccupied by the threat of removal—indeed they seemed to proceed on the assumption that relocation would never occur. Now we realize that this was a coping strategy to alleviate stress: Then we were amazed to see headmen working hard to construct new homesteads at the old site within a year of the time they had been told they would be moved.

By the end of 1963, our observations and Tonga answers to our queries made it abundantly clear that relocation had been accompanied by multidimensional stress which did not appear to come to an end until 1963— approximately 4 to 5 years after the move (Colson 1971b). By then the people were once again economically on their feet; indeed, their standard of living was higher than before. Full funeral ceremonial, which had been greatly curtailed during the period immediately following resettlement, had reappeared. Personal and lineage shrines had been rebuilt or newly initiated. Prophets were again active. Nonetheless, the effects of uprooting continue to an extent, since only in the 1970s are neighborhood shrines and rituals being reestablished.

Because it can be generalized, relocation theory obviously has important policy implications for those responsible for executing resettlement and development programs. As a consultant for the Bandama River Authority in the Ivory Coast, Scudder has made a number of policy recommendations that are based on the theory. Some of these have been accepted, with initial results within the range predicted. Scudder currently is trying to generalize the theory to other situations, including the current conflict between Navajo and Hopi over the Joint Use Area, resolution of which would require the forced removal of hundreds of Navajo families.

Though this major outcome of our study of Gwembe has been of little service to the people on whom the study is based, it does have long-term and long-range implications, which some day they may have reason to invoke.

THE FUTURE OF THE STUDY

We are now in the twentieth year of the study. Despite the fact that long-term research has very real advantages over the initiation of a new project—such as relative economy of costs and a greater ease of obtaining cooperation—further research will depend in part on how satisfactorily we can handle a number of increasingly serious problems.

Problems of Write-Up

Writing-up the results of fieldwork is becoming increasingly difficult. The sense of excitement generated during 1956–1957 and 1962–1963 is hard to sustain; sometimes we are bored with the material and writing is a burden. We cannot assume, for one, that readers have read what we have previously written about the project and the region. It becomes excruciating to have to give once again the same background information before turning to what excites us now. Write-up is complicated also because as the data accumulate (and we submit that only those of us who have carried out systematic long-term studies can visualize the masses of data involved), it is no longer possible to scan notes quickly to prepare a piece for publication. Each topic requires arduous search and analysis of a voluminous source material, much of which cannot be computerized for easy access. Nevertheless, our obligation to publish increases with each revisit—an obligation now not just to our profession and sponsors but increasingly to the Gwembe people who have patiently (and sometimes not so patiently) shared their lives and thoughts with us.

We have tried to publish the results of the research at regular intervals (see Bibliography), though this is less easy as the study proceeds. It was easy enough to envisage our first year's work as complete in itself. We were to describe what we found in 1956–1957 and did so in books on the social organization and ecology of Gwembe (Colson 1960; Scudder 1962). It was also easy enough to envisage the research through 1965 as dealing primarily with the resettlement period and the adjustments forced upon the people (Colson 1971b). Writing up data from either period presented problems not very different from those posed by the single field trip. We also have written essays on particular topics that interested us, such as the Kariba Lake fishery, the frequency of innovation, the stability of formal rules of land tenure, the changing character of possession cults, the appearance and demise of a short-lived enthusiasm for Christianity in one neighborhood, relationships between Gwembe and the line-of-rail, and so on (see Bibliography). It is only now that we are beginning to face the question of how best to deal with time series data to which so much of our research time has been directed in recent years.

We can update censuses, but this does not mean that we know how best to make the material available to others. We believe the time series of core data to be an important research resource, but to date have little to show as a result of recent updatings because we are bogged down in processing the data. The belief that a computer could handle much of the task has been a handicap rather than a help, in part because we have turned coding over to assistants and busied ourselves with other aspects of the material. Part of the problem no doubt also relates to our attempt to pioneer the use of a new experimental soft ware system, REL, developed at the California Institute of Technology by Dr. Frederick Thompson and Dr. Bozena Dostert–Thompson and their colleagues. The system is still experimental and hence not able to meet our needs. We assume that it will all come out right in the end and then we can not only write-up quickly, but interact with our data through the computer in a highly innovative fashion. In the meanwhile, we have relied on qualitative information or done quick handsorts of a few factors germane to a particular topic. We have also begun to backtrack a bit so that we can use conventional computer software systems for processing some of the data. But because we have not been working with the time series data for concentrated periods, it has not generated new questions to be explored.

At least for the moment, we have come to the conclusion that probably the best longitudinal research in social anthropology is done through collecting data on small samples which can be punched and hand sorted in the field; that coding ought to be done by the research workers themselves; and that no mechanical device can match the human brain when fully applied to material which is known in all its detail. This means thinking through what it is one wants to get from a particular body of data and making sure that one does not get swamped in a mass of information which cannot be stored in the mind and thought about.

Our experience also has some implications for how time is to be apportioned among field research, write-up, and the other activities that make up the professional anthropologist's life. When we began work in

Gwembe District, it was impossible to find local assistants who could keep good records for us. Literacy was not that wide-spread. For accurate reporting and dating, frequent return visits were necessary. Probably a visit at least every 2 years was advisable, but we have usually been unwilling to give this routine a priority over competing interests. Such a schedule would also mean sacrificing time for writing and so a falling further behind in publication. Moreover, it is usually the writing which generates new ideas and sends us back to Gwembe with enthusiasm for new investigations. It is difficult to maintain a longitudinal study of the scope of the Gwembe Study with a team of only two anthropologists.

Integrating New Workers

We have considered the possibility of building others into the research. We persuaded C. Lancaster to carry out a study in a North Gwembe chieftaincy that we had been unable to include in our detailed study (Lancaster 1971, 1974). In 1969, we solicited social scientists at the University of Zambia to use our core data base in their own research and, in 1972–1973, included funds for Zambian consultants in our NSF grant. So far, colleagues in Zambia have been involved in teaching and other commitments which made it difficult for them to carry out research and Gwembe appears to be remote from the center of their interests.

We have considered recruiting our own students to work with us in Gwembe, but have faced the probability that they would be unwilling to undertake the drudge labor of maintaining the time series on core data. This would still fall to us while we would lose the precious time we have for other interests in making arrangements for their participation and in supervising their work. They would be doing the things we want to do while we would be left with the things that have to be done. Colson thinks it not worth the effort; Scudder is less certain.

Within Zambia, the situation can be expected to change with time and we intend to continue to look for local colleagues. In the meantime, we have begun to train local primary and secondary school students and graduates to collect microeconomic, demographic, and other types of data for us. Perhaps one or more of them will eventually become social scientists interested in the continued study of their region.

Our Own Involvement

There are personal costs in continuing long-term research. For one, there is the problem of developing tunnel vision—the tendency to interpret anthropological issues too much in terms of one society. We try to handle this by reading widely on other regions and by visits and research in other geographical areas.

Again, while the Middle Zambezi Valley is beautiful, Gwembe villages and the railway townships are not places where we would choose to vacation. Living conditions for the anthropologist are arduous, especially in the most densely settled area where the carrying capacity of the land under the existing system of land use was exceeded as soon as it received 6000 relocated people. Today much of that area, where two of the sample villages are situated, is a dust bowl during the dry season, with cattle dying of hunger in low rainfall years. While the standard of living in Gwembe has risen over the years, the vast majority of the people are still desperately poor, by our standards, and the gap between us has steadily widened (Scudder, for example, has moved from graduate student to professor during the duration of the study). We expect the remaining years of the 1970s to be hard ones, with the gap between aspiration and achievement widening, especially for the majority of primary and secondary school leavers. The expectation weighs upon us, for these are long-term friends who will suffer and we can do little or nothing to prevent it.

We are also watching the aging of old friends who are passing from vigorous maturity into old age and sometimes senility. The fact that we too are growing older and occupy new age statuses opens to us new information and new insights, but closes off other avenues. There are costs in all this to the anthropologist that should not be minimized.

On the other hand, we have gained new respect for Gwembe men and women bcause we have watched them contend over many years with good times and bad. Children have grown to maturity, flirted through early love affairs, married, and accepted responsibility. Some have faced the tragedies of barrenness, the death of children, the desertion or death of a spouse. Some friendly, outgoing young men have become grasping homestead heads and the focus of sorcery suspicions. On the other hand, harassed young wives, beset by many children and with none old enough to be efficient helpers, have later emerged as happy middle-aged women, in charge of their world.

Predictably, a long-term study is likely to diminish the roseate hues in which so much of ethnographic description is couched, while at the same time the people who are the focus of the study become more the product of their own history and less the exemplars of cultural patterns. We have lived too long with the realities that face Gwembe people not to be concerned about what happens to them. It is impossible to go away and forget that their lives go on.

It is this same fact that pulls us back—we want to know what happens next and this means more than checking on various hypotheses.

So far, we have faced no external constraints on return. Funding has not been a problem. Long-term studies are economical in that equipment can be stored and the time needed within which to get significant results on each visit is greatly reduced. We run into normal delays in obtaining research permits, but it is not necessary to establish our bona fides yet once again. In Zambia, we are known as scholars who have a long-term commitment to the country and its people. The Institute for African Studies, the major center for social science research in Zambia, provides both a home-base and a warm welcome; therefore, there is no delay in starting fieldwork immediately on arrival.

One of our Gwembe associates is a teller at the International Airport Office of Barclay's Bank. Even if he is transferred and is not there to greet us on our next arrival and change our foreign currency into Zambian kwacha, he and a number of other Gwembe people live in a Site and Service Township which is within several hundred yards of the Institute for African Studies. Fieldwork and visiting with friends can and will begin almost immediately because of the degree of rapport that has been built up over the years. Even those Gwembe Tonga who do not particularly like us, and they exist, nonetheless see us as known entities—as people with whom they have shared past experiences, both pleasant and unpleasant. In that regard, we are a continuity in people's lives in a world of increasing discontinuities. For that matter, they are a continuity in our lives and help to give them meaning. It is good to go back—to see what has happened to old acquaintances and to the many undertakings that we have followed through time, such as the lake fishery, the local courts, the rural council, Gwembe District development, and even changes in the nation at large.

Our understanding of ourselves and of the nature of human society has expanded in tandem with our research. No doubt it will continue to do so.

BIBLIOGRAPHY

Brokensha, David, and Thayer Scudder
  1968   Resettlement. In *Dams in Africa,* edited by Warren, W. M. and Rubin, N. Pp. 20–62. London: Frank Cass.
Colson, Elizabeth
  1954   The intensive study of small sample communities. In *Method and perspective in anthropology,* edited by Spencer, R. Pp. 43–59. Minneapolis: Univ. of Minnesota Press.
  1960   *Social organization of the Gwembe Tonga.* Manchester: Manchester Univ. Press.
  1962   Trade and wealth among the Tonga. In *Markets in Africa,* edited by Bohannan, P. and Dalton, G. Pp. 601–616. Evanston, Illinois: Northwestern Univ. Press.

1963   Land rights and land use among the Valley Tonga of the Rhodesian Federation: The background to the Kariba resettlement program. In *African agrarian systems,* edited by Biebuyck, D. Pp. 137–156. London: Oxford Univ. Press.

1964a Social change and the Gwembe Tonga. *Human Problems in Central Africa 36*: 1–10.

1964b Land law and land holdings among the Valley Tonga of Zambia. *Southwestern Journal of Anthropology 22*: 1–8.

1966   The alien diviner and local politics among the Tonga of Zambia. In *Political Anthropology,* edited by Swartz, M., Tuden, A. and Turner, V. Pp. 221–228. Chicago: Aldine Press.

1967   Competence and incompetence in the context of independence. *Current Anthropology 8*: 92–100, 108–109.

1969   Spirit possession among the Tonga of Zambia. In *Spirit mediumship and society in Africa,* edited by Middleton, J. and Beattie, J. M. Pp. 69–103. London: Routledge and Kegan Paul.

1970a The assimilation of aliens among the Zambian Tonga. In *From tribe to nation in Africa,* edited by Cohen, R. and Middleton, J. Pp. 33–54. San Francisco: Chandler.

1970b Converts and tradition: The impact of Christianity on Valley Tonga religion. *Southwestern Journal of Anthropology 26*:143–156.

1971a Heroism, martyrdom, and courage. In *The translation of culture,* edited by Beidelman, T. Pp. 19–35. London: Tavistock Press.

1971b *The social consequences of resettlement.* Manchester: Manchester Univ. Press.

1973   Tranquility for the decision maker. In *Cultural illness and health,* edited by Nader, L. and Maretzki, T. Pp. 89–96. Washington, D.C.: American Anthropological Association.

1974   *Tradition and contract.* Chicago: Aldine.

1976   From chief's court to local court: The evolution of local courts in Southern Zambia. *Political Anthropology 1*:15–29.

1977   A continuing dialogue: Prophets and local shrines among the Tonga of Zambia. In *Regional Cults,* edited by Werbner, R. Pp. 119–139. London: Academic Press.

Colson, Elizabeth, and Thayer Scudder

1975   New economic relationships between the Gwembe Valley and the line of rail. In *Town and Country in Central and Eastern Africa,* edited by Parkin, D. Pp. 190–210. London: Oxford Univ. Press.

1979   Growing old in Gwembe Valley. In *Other ways of growing old,* edited by Harrell, S. and Amoss, P. Stanford: Stanford Univ. Press.

Fried, Marc

1963   Grieving for a lost home. In *The urban condition,* edited by Duhl, L. J. Pp. 151–171. New York: Basic Books.

Lancaster, C. S.

1966   Reciprocity, redistribution, and the male life cycle: Variations in Middle River Tonga social organization. *African Social Research 2*:139–157.

1971   The economics of social organization in an ethnic border zone: The Goba (Northern Shona) of the Zambezi Valley. *Ethnology 10*:445–465.

1974   Brideservice, residence, and authority among the Goba of the Zambezi Valley. *Africa 44*:46–64.

Read, J. Gordon

1932   *Report on famine relief, Gwembe, 1931–32.* Lusaka: Government Printer.

Reynolds, Barrie

1968   *The material culture of the peoples of the Gwembe Valley.* Manchester: Manchester Univ. Press.

Scudder, Thayer

1960a Environment and a culture. *Natural History* 1:7–16; 2: 24–31.

1960b Fishermen of the Zambezi. *Human problems in Central Africa* 27:41–49.

1962 *The ecology of the Gwembe Tonga.* Manchester: Manchester Univ. Press.

1965 The Kariba case: Man-made lakes and resource development in Africa. *Bulletin of the Atomic Scientist,* December, 6–11.

1966a Man-made lakes and population relocation in Africa. In *Man-made Lakes,* edited by Lowe-McConnell, R. Pp. 99–108. New York: Academic Press.

1966b Man-made lakes and social change. *Engineering and Science* 6(29): 18–22.

1968 Relocation, agricultural intensification and anthropological research. In *The anthropology of development in sub-Saharan Africa,* edited by Brokensha, D. and Pearsall, M. *Monographs of the Society for Applied Anthropology,* Vol. 10. Pp. 31–39.

1971 Gathering among African woodland savannah cultivators, A case study: The Gwembe Tonga. *Institute for African Studies, Zambian Papers, 5.*

1972 Ecological bottlenecks and the development of the Kariba Lake basin. In *The careless technology: Ecology and international development,* edited by Farvar, M. T. and Milton, J. P. Pp. 206–235. New York: Natural History Press.

1973a The human ecology of big projects: River basin development and resettlement. In *Annual review of anthropology,* edited by Siegel, B. Pp. 45–55. Palo Alto: Annual Reviews, Inc.

1973b Summary: Resettlement. In *Man-made lakes: Their problems and environmental effects,* edited by Ackermann, W. C., White, G. F. and Worthington, E. B. Pp. 707–719. Washington, D.C.: American Geophysical Union.

1975 Resettlement. In *Man-made lakes and human health,* edited by Stanley, N. F. and Alpers, M. P. Pp. 453–470. London: Academic Press for the Institute of Biology.

1976a Social anthropology and the reconstruction of prehistoric land use systems in tropical Africa: A cautionary case study from Zambia. In *Origins of African plant domestication,* edited by Harlan, J. R. *et al.* Pp. 357–381. The Hague: Mouton.

1976b Social impacts of river basin development on local populations. In *River basin development: Policies and planning* (Proceedings of the United Nations' Interregional Seminar on River Basin and Interbasin Development), Vol. 1. Pp. 45–52. Budapest: Institute for Hydraulic Documentation and Education.

Scudder, Thayer, and Elizabeth Colson

1968 Memorandum for possible research workers in the Kariba Lake basin. *Bulletin of the Institute for Social Research, University of Zambia* 3:70–73.

1971 The Kariba Dam project: Resettlement and local initiative. In *Technical innovation and cultural change,* edited by Bernard, R. and Pelto, P. Pp. 40–69. New York: Macmillan.

12

Field Research in a Nubian Village: The Experience of an Egyptian Anthropologist

Hussein Fahim

INTRODUCTION

Kanuba (pseudonym) is the village with which this chapter is concerned. It is one of several villages that Egyptian Nubians established below Aswan in the Nile Valley as a result of the inundation of their lands when the first Aswan Dam (built in 1902) was twice raised, in 1912 and 1933. Prior to the construction of the new Aswan High Dam during the 1960s, Egypt's Nubian land extended along the Nile banks between the city of Aswan and the Sudanese border. Following the inundation of this land, the remaining Nubians moved in 1964 to a new site. They are now settled on recently reclaimed lands in the Kom Ombo area, some 50 kilometers north of Aswan and close to Kanuba. In their new location, which has become known as "New Nubia," Nubians have been provided with schools, health facilities, agricultural services, and a greater opportunity to become part of the larger Egyptian society.

Though all of Egypt's nearly 120,000 Nubians share in their nation's Islamic traditions and have similar social organization and cultural values, they have their own distinct life style and language.

Due to the scarcity of arable land in the old Nubian setting, the migra-

Long-Term Field Research
in Social Anthropology

tion of young men to work in towns and cities had increased over the years preceding the relocation in the 1960s in connection with the High Dam. Because of their reputation for honesty and cleanliness, many were sought as domestic servants. Nearly half of the Nubian population of Egypt presently work and live in major cities and towns outside Nubia.

While the richness of antiquities in Old Nubia attracted students of past civilizations since the early decades of this century, it was the construction of the Aswan High Dam and the necessity to relocate approximately 100,000 Nubians (including some 50,000 in Sudan) that promoted the interest for the study of the contemporary civilization of the Nubian people (Fahim 1972).

SOME ASPECTS OF FIELDWORK IN KANUBA

Initial Stages

My research connection with Nubians began in 1963. I was then a research assistant in the Social Research Center (SRC) of the American University in Cairo. I was assigned for fieldwork with John Kennedy, an American anthropologist who was at that time the chief investigator of the Kanuba study. Several years earlier, the Center had begun an ethnological survey in Old Nubia, under the direction of Robert Fernea, in order to record the Nubian life style prior to relocation in 1964. Funded by the Ford Foundation and undertaken in collaboration with the Ministry of Social Affairs, the survey was also to provide information and recommendations to the government relocation authorities for possible incorporation into the planning and execution of the resettlement scheme. As to Kennedy's study, its objective was to identify and analyze changes in a Nubian village relocated some 30 years earlier, to provide clues to the type of future changes that could be expected in the Old Nubian villages that were soon to be relocated to the Kom Ombo area.

Prior to the selection of the research site, Kennedy, Samiha El Katsha (another SRC research assistant), and I went to Old Nubia in February 1963 for a 2-week field trip to familiarize ourselves with its environment and current way of life. In the spring of 1963, we surveyed those Nubian communities which had relocated themselves in Daraw area following the first and second heightening of the Aswan Dam in 1912 and 1933. Daraw is a little market town located some 35 kilometers north of Aswan. Our task was to choose a village research site. We rented a house in Daraw where the Kennedys (John, his wife, and two children), Samiha, and I stayed for nearly 2 months. When Kanuba was chosen as the research setting, we used to commute daily between Daraw and the village, a distance of some

4 km, until we were able to rent a house in Kanuba. These first 2 months of commuting, in my view, were the most difficult period of our fieldwork. It was then that I encountered the challenge of anthropological training.

It was a tough time, though with many pleasant memories. Kennedy and I used to be received in the village guest room or sit outdoors with a few interested informants. I still recall the afternoon when a hot sand storm blew up and everybody ran inside his house for protection, leaving us alone. We protected ourselves by staying in our Landrover and later drove back to Daraw looking depressed, deeply silent. The next day, we went to the village to proceed with our work hoping that there would be no storm, or, should one occur, that we would be given shelter. Our breakthrough was one week later when, as I recall, a Nubian was courteous enough to invite us to his house for a cup of tea.

In the fall of 1963, we moved to Kanuba, eight of us living in a four-room house. Two more assistants joined us, Ms. Sohair Mehana and Mr. Omar Abdel Hamid. We soon appreciated the convenience of living in the village rather than being daily commuters. Yet that meant more pressure in terms of fieldwork and related sensitivities. We made a good entry to the village in that we succeeded in having the people accept our presence. We had still to prove our goodwill and good conduct. Villagers were surprised to see university people from Cairo willing to share and appreciate their life style. Yet, they had their suspicions and doubts. That was why, as I was told later, we were given a place located close to the village headman's house—so we would be under close observation and possible control. It was a village decision—so I was told. To them, our research team seemed peculiar in composition. Our sharing one house was also puzzling.

Our living together was an experience for me. I shared a room with Omar. The Kennedys squeezed into another room, leaving the third room for Sohair and Samiha. The fourth room was used as a living quarter where we took our meals and held our work discussions. Our cook, who was not a Nubian, came from a nearby village. He was in his late fifties, a kind and honest man. He used to come at eight o'clock every morning and leave in the late afternoon. We all liked and respected him. He always wondered what we were really doing, but he never bothered to inquire. The presence of the Kennedy family, I felt, added a fine family touch to our life in Kanuba.

The team of research assistants was composed of two men and two women, members of the same generation but differing in education and social background. Then there were the Kennedys, representing a totally different culture. Cross-cultural situations emerged, some of which were unpleasant while others were funny indeed. Mehana and El Katsha had their entire education in American schools in Cairo while Hamid and I were educated in national schools. Our knowledge and comprehension of English was relatively limited. That made it difficult in the beginning to communicate properly our field data to Kennedy. We wrote our field notes in Arabic and had them translated for him.

The other problem I encountered arose from my going into the field with very little academic training in anthropological research. My college major was sociology and my graduate work was 2 years of course work in social sciences. Yet my nearly 8 years of work in the field of child welfare provided me with an invaluable training in dealing with practical realities and in learning about life and people from sources other than books and classroom instruction. To make up for my lack of formal training in anthropology, I registered for graduate work in the Anthropology Department of the American University and took anthropology books with me to Nubia. I should mention with gratitude the assistance rendered by Kennedy who discussed with me my readings and field observations.

Kennedy, a foreign anthropologist, by providing an outsider's perspective helped me a great deal by forcing me to verify my observations and interpretations. As a native of the culture, I also often criticized his propositions and conclusions. During the first 4 or 5 months, Kennedy and I used to go together wherever work took us: weddings, ceremonial events, and market days. Later on, I used to go alone to observe particular events and to seek information on specific issues. The entire team used to spend an hour or two every evening reporting on the day's achievements and telling anecdotes; we also used to lay our plans for the following day's work. In the morning, we used to receive small white pocket cards full of further questions that Kennedy had thought of during the night.

In collecting data, we used a variety of techniques, particularly observation and questioning informants. Samiha and I gathered quantitative information on household composition, occupational structure, and villagers' attitudes toward educational and occupational careers for their children. The research team also paid regular visits to New Nubia and observed closely the processes of initial adaptation to the new environment of villages then being resettled.

Subsequent Work in Kanuba

Two years after the completion of this fieldwork in Kanuba, a research team returned to the region for a follow-up survey of continuity and change in New Nubia (Fernea and Kennedy 1967). Kanuba was also revisited. Other than that one return visit, there were no formal plans to conduct a systematic longitudinal study in the village on the part either of the principal investigator or myself. Both Kennedy and I thought, however, that it would be interesting and significant if one of us (or perhaps both) could return to the village for a restudy after a number of years.

Between 1964 and 1966 the letters I received from Nubian friends often carried village news; informants also visited me at home in Cairo and in the office. During the summer of 1966, I made a 2-week field trip to the village in order to fill some gaps in my data for my M.A. thesis on rituals and culture change in Kanuba. In the fall of 1966, I left for 2 years to go to the United States to complete my graduate studies at the University of California, Berkeley. Upon my return, I made a field trip in February 1969, to New Nubia to update my material and to explore new research possibilities. During my 1-month stay, I revisited Kanuba on several occasions.

In 1970, I was assigned as the principal investigator of a 5-year research project to study and evaluate the agricultural scheme in New Nubia, especially as it related to the villagers' social structure and culture. This study has been undertaken by the Social Research Center of the American University in Cairo at the request of the "Egyptian Organization for Land Cultivation and Development" (EOLCD). In the fall of 1970, I returned to New Nubia to design a survey schedule for collecting basic descriptive data on all resettled villages in the Kom Ombo area. In the winter of 1971, survey data were collected in the 43 New Nubian villages as well as in Kanuba, which I added to the survey, by six research assistants from the SRC.

In September 1971, Kennedy and I visited Kanuba for one day (the maximum then allowed foreigners traveling in rural areas), while Kennedy was in Cairo to attend a conference. Constraints on research permits, especially for researchers associated with foreign institutions, kept me from the field for nearly 2 years. In 1973–1974, I went to the United States on a 1-year leave to write up my Nubian material at the California Institute of Technology. Upon my return, I paid a further visit to New Nubia. Then, in February and March 1974, I administered an interview schedule to a sample of 150 land holders in two of the New Nubian villages and also made a quick follow-up check on life and events in Kanuba.

BACKGROUND INFORMATION ON KANUBA

Before I present some methodological issues and research findings from the Kanuba study, it seems appropriate to provide some background information on the village.

When Nubians began to settle in Kanuba in 1934, they planned to preserve their traditional economic and social patterns, yet several changes took place. Their initial efforts to farm the land failed due to scarcity of water for irrigation. They abandoned agriculture and sought work in big cities like Cairo and Alexandria. However, during the 1940s, individuals and families returned to the village to try cultivating the land once more. Some attempted to overcome the water problem by introducing elaborate mechanical means of irrigation. Though once again water proved to be beyond the reach of the pumps, these families decided to stay in the village. They were able to make their living by wage labor at jobs available either in local development projects or in government departments in neighboring cities. As Nubians succeeded in filling many clerical jobs in the region, the number of returnees increased. By 1964, the labor migration rate had dropped.

Since the establishment of the village in 1934, various changes corresponding with the change in occupational structure have taken place. Social organization, for example, is no longer based on lineage and tribal affinity. Nuclear families have become increasingly important. Leadership has shifted from the traditional headman and group of elders to a village association consisting of community representatives with a board of elected officers. Actual leadership is now in the hands of a group of educated young people striving to make Kanuba a model village with high standards of education, health, and economic progress. This group is headed by a village leader who is "modern-oriented" and who wishes to introduce "progress" to the village in the areas of agriculture, education, utilities, health services and the like.

Education, once primarily in Koranic schools, is now provided by government schools. Kanubans show a remarkable interest in educating their children through secondary school and even through the university level. Female education has become desirable and women have recently begun to play a role in the political life of the village. Women are now registered to vote in the election of local representatives for the National Assembly, an unprecedented phenomenon in the conservative Aswan region.

The village aspirations towards progress correspond with the Egyptian government's plans to introduce change and to promote development in the Aswan region in connection with the construction of the High Dam. Nevertheless, the village leadership did not wait for change to come; rather, it worked with both local and national authorities to secure the greatest advantages for the village. In 1963, a health clinic was built in the village and pure drinking water was made available through several faucet units. The Aswan Housing Department, with the collaboration of the village board, prepared a new design for the village and, in 1964, began constructing houses to replace those destroyed by termites.

In 1966, the village affiliated itself administratively with New Nubia in order to have access to services and advantages offered to New Nubian settlers by the national government. By 1970, the construction of 160 new houses, a village club, and a 10-class primary school was completed. In 1973, the village had electricity connected to the houses and to the streets. Many villagers have radio sets but only one, thus far, has bought a television set. There is also a television set installed in the village club. Furthermore the village persuaded the government to finance the building of a large, nicely designed mosque—currently a village landmark.

Perhaps the most important event in village history has been the success of the village leadership in working out a plan with the Ministry of Agriculture to reclaim and cultivate some 900 acres of village land on a long-term credit. Between 1968 and 1970, the land was reclaimed. Managed by the villagers as a cooperative farm, in the following years it turned green. If I had not visited the village since 1964, I would find it difficult to identify the village site. The cooperative farm has affected almost all aspects of village life as well as the people's aspirations. Reflecting the current national policy of ''economic openness'' following the 1973 war, informants talk about a 10-year plan which would include new houses for all families, a youth center equipped with a swimming pool, a consumer cooperative department, an animal husbandry project, and an agro-industrial factory.

Cultivation of the reclaimed land interestingly enough did not change the village occupational structure. Working men remained in their jobs outside the village while the farm is worked with hired labor from neighboring communities under the supervision of the elderly village men. On their return to Kanuba in the evening, the working men meet in the club to attend to the business affairs of the farm. In time of need, women and children help out on the farm. Each is assigned a task under the supervision of some village men. The village farm, in brief, cemented the existing community spirit and made life in the village socially and economically much better—to quote one informant. For the villagers of Kanuba, their cooperative farm is a symbol of dreams that can come true.

METHODOLOGICAL ISSUES

The Villagers' Attitude

The village leader once stated to me, ''We really never entirely understood what you [referring to the Kennedy research team] were doing and why. But we liked you very much.'' On another occasion he said, ''You were under the village scrutiny for a long time. As you proved to be good people, I instructed the people to cooperate with you and have you go to their homes.'' Actually, the timing of Kennedy's study in 1963–1964 came during a very critical period of the village history when hopes for change were revived, along with measures to achieve them. The village was very sensitive to our residence, highly concerned with our doings, and usually curious to know of our writings. I recall that when Kennedy went to present a paper on the village occupational structure and on job preferences before a symposium on contemporary Nubia held in Aswan in January 1964, the village sent an English-language school teacher to attend the meeting and report back to the village. The people of Kanuba seemed happy to be a subject for study which they hoped in turn would make their village known.

The village's attitude towards me personally has been constantly changing according to my status, age, and role. During my original contact with the village, I was viewed as an *Ustaz,* a respectable employee with a university background who was helping Dr. Kennedy in his study. The fact that I was married and had children impressed the villagers favorably and my coming to work in their village while leaving my wife and children in Cairo did not seem abnormal to them as they themselves often did the same. The Kanubians' attitude towards me then was relatively informal and extremely cordial.

During my first visit after my return from the United States in 1968, I was deeply moved by the warmth of their reception, though I felt a change in their attitude. Friendly and hospitable though they were, they were nonetheless relatively formal and gently reserved. Their formality was reflected in their speech. I was called ''Doctor'' rather than *Ustaz*. Their reserved attitude reflected my affiliation with an American institution at a time when the relationship between Egypt and the United States was strained. Informants also expressed their disappointment about the delay in publishing research findings on their village.

My return to Kanuba on a government assignment raised my status and their formality subsequently increased. I was not taken to the leader's house as previously but rather to the village club where people grouped to greet me while children lined up to clap whenever I passed them. This official-like reception made me feel ''out of place and as a stranger in my own home,'' as I once told the village leader. He pointed out that such a reception is a village ritual to express affection and esteem. He also added that my concern for the village, as implied by my regular visits, was admired. Because of my new role and status, my services to the village were anticipated.

The villagers of Kanuba were aware that their village was not included in the agricultural scheme that I was studying for the government; yet they felt that I could help them meet the village's needs through my official contacts. This feeling was clearly expressed in conversations with informants, especially during my most recent visit. They talked about what the village had achieved and much more about their aspirations. Their expectation of me was quite clear.

The Researcher's Attitude

My attitude toward the village people has undergone change. During the first stage of my research in Kanuba and during the years following my return from the United States, I was strictly committed to the role of an academic-oriented researcher. Recently, I have been revising both my research approach and personal stance. While I have gained professionally from my research in Kanuba and other Nubian villages, I often wonder whether the Nubians have benefited from my studies. Impressed by the progress that Kanuba achieved during the past decade and embarrassed by the Kanubans' unhappiness with my neutral role as a strict researcher, I have become consciously sympathetic to their aspirations and more willing to help them whenever possible. Recently, I tried to advocate before the relevant officials the village's request to receive International Food Aid and UNESCO vocational facilities to which New Nubian villages have had access. I do not know what will be the impact of such a new role on my future research in Kanuba.

Another important change in my attitude is connected with publication. While in the beginning I regarded publication as basically an academic activity, I have recently come to the opinion that the people under study must have access to the researcher's writings. It is true that people's desire to know what is written about them may vary but it seems only moral on the part of anthropologists to make their findings available to the studied people especially if they plan to subject them to a longitudinal research. From the Kanuba study, several articles have appeared in professional journals in English but none have been translated into Arabic. Only one article on the cooperative farm written for EOLCD was passed on to the village in Arabic.

To cope with this publication issue (which I have found to be a serious problem in regard to my ongoing Nubian research), I began presenting a series of short articles on my research findings in both Kanuba and New Nubia in "Nubia's News," a bimonthly magazine first issued in February 1975, by the Nubian club in Cairo. They aim to provide basic information on the communities studied and to introduce readers to the notion of research and its significance to the new life of the Kom Ombo Nubians and its related problems. Writing these was a difficult task, especially in terms of deciding what topics to write about and how to handle them.

In addition, I approached the publication problem on two other fronts. To my institution, I pointed out the negative implications of a research policy that mainly emphasizes academic publications in a foreign language. The policy affected both the people under study and the administrators involved in a directed change scheme. In my case, local officials and administrators often had inquiries about my institution's interests in research among Nubians; they had some concern about the lack of Arabic publications. I also explained to the officials at EOLCD that the research findings presented in my reports should be communicated (perhaps in a rather simple and brief form) to the administrators and technicians involved in the technical development schemes. In my opinion, it is useful for them to learn about the recipient groups and to know what an objective outsider feels are the problems in their administrative structure. Moreover their curiosity about the ongoing long-term research is satisfied.

Long-Term Research in the Villagers' View

In a discussion of the question of long-term research in Kanuba with a group of five informants holding leading positions in the community, some interesting views emerged. The informants tended to view a long-term study in their community as a reflection of a continuing interest on the part of the researcher in the village and its people. That was something they enjoyed and appreciated. One informant said, "You [referring to Kennedy's group] were the first people to show interest in our life style and to live with us. Many individuals and groups dropped in for a Hello–Goodbye type of research. You [referring to me] are the only person who revisits us from time to time." The village leader commented, while showing me the village's 12-year-old autograph book, "Most of the statements written here are complimentary but yours are not; we feel that your sentiments are true." He added, "We suspected your role in the beginning but over these long years, the village cannot view you other than as a true good friend."

An interesting point made by one informant was that he viewed the research as a recording of the social history of the village which, if made available in a language comprehensible to villagers, could be taught to the younger generation. This may be one positive contribution that longitudinal research can make to the community under study. Two further points were made. A long-term researcher is capable of understanding the village's needs and problems in their sociocultural and historical context. In addition, it was remarked, the village can afford to trust and have control over only one researcher in residence at a time given the absence of a large proportion of men from the village most of the day.

Kanuba, due to its orientation toward progress and the achievements it has accomplished, recently has become a place for top officials and foreign experts to visit. Several government agencies conducted uncoordinated surveys and studies in the village in the 5 years between 1970 and 1975, with villagers being subjected to many similar questionnaires in a relatively short time. When I attempted to explore further development on specific issues during my last visit, I was often told that the same questions had been asked by such-and-such a person or agency.

Like Kanuba, I suspect that other communities subjected to longitudinal study change during the course of the study in terms of their relative isolation. After a period of study, they attract attention and become open to a wider spectrum of interaction with the larger society, partly because they are known. This effect must be taken into account by those planning long-term research in such communities. The question is how to work out a flexible research strategy that allows the study to adapt to the changing conditions of the community.

Long-Term Research Strategy

An initial community study in its common anthropological sense is basic, I believe, to longitudinal research. It serves as a guide and as a base for further field research. The Kanuba community study of 1964 proved to be a very useful reference during subsequent visits. In less than a month in 1972, I was able to collect data and to draft a report on the village cooperative farm at an urgent and last minute request from EOLCD. Producing such a report in a satisfactory way would have been impossible without this reference. My continuing rapport with the village and my familiarity with its developments are also major advantages.

In my own research, I have found the problem-oriented approach to be a useful and convenient strategy to use after the original baseline study. The problems focused on can be either follow-ups of earlier interests or new concerns. In regard to research priorities, I believe that there is no need to list problems that lend themselves to long-term research. In dynamic settings, such as Kanuba, research topics significant to the development of anthropological knowledge are easily identified. The choice of research problems must depend on the resources of the project and the interests of its sponsors.

One factor affecting the strategy will be the degree to which the researchers have students or colleagues associated with them. I have not had the opportunity to have students visit or conduct research in Kanuba;

but, in March 1975, I had the chance to invite Arthur Wycoff, a social psychologist from American University in Cairo, to visit Kanuba. Wycoff came to New Nubia for a week to explore research possibilities. When the Land Reclamation Regional Office arranged his visit, I suggested that a 1-day visit to Kanuba be included. Wycoff's observations while he was in the village and his inquiries and comments proved most useful to my own study. A new input to the field situation should be viewed as a healthy approach for long-term studies. It adds new insights and so reduces the likelihood of diminishing returns. The new researcher also is less likely to ignore significant data because of a familiarity with the place and people under study.

The personal aging process is another relevant factor influencing the methodology of long-term research. In Kanuba, I noticed that my association with people has often been with the age group with whom I mixed during the 1964 study. I now am viewed and sometimes treated in a parental perspective. During my recent visit, some friends were concerned with the grey hair that has begun to show on my head. They were surprised, but admiring that my son would enter the university in 1976 and that my two daughters were no longer "little kids" as they had been a few years before. Their attitude towards me as a parent gave me the chance to talk with the women. During a recent visit (winter 1975), I was invited by my previous informants and other young men, who were children when I was first in the village, to stop by and greet their wives and children. In 1964, this was never possible.

On the other hand, when I tried to approach teenagers to explore ideas for possible future studies on the youth in Kanuba and other Nubian villages, some informants seemed unwilling to accept the idea that I conduct research among this age group. When I asked, "Why?", one informant said, "Your status, role, and age lend themselves to a more serious task."

Relationship to Informants

No informants have been paid in cash for their collaboration, either in Kennedy's study or since. Gifts to the village, such as nominal cash donations given to the construction of the village mosque, and small cash donations to individuals have been our form of remuneration. On different occasions during our stay in the village, candy was given to children and bottled fruit juice to the men, a tradition I have continued on subsequent visits. Towards the end of our stay, Kennedy's group invited all the men in the village to eat "Fatta," a favorite dish connected with ceremonial celebrations. I should also note that I have always taken a special family gift to the village leader. The reason for this special gift is that over the past years he has been related to me as a friend much more than as the village leader or as a dependable informant.

During Kennedy's study, I associated with the village leader mostly when I was involved in long interviews with him about his life history. In the summer of 1964, following the completion of fieldwork in Kanuba, Kennedy invited the leader to come to Cairo for a visit and more interviewing. During his stay, he was introduced to my family. He travelled with us to Alexandria. His sense of humor and his kindness to my children made his company pleasant to my family who had never been so close to a Nubian. While in Cairo and Alexandria, the leader and I sat together and talked for hours. We also visited several places where he was brought up and worked before returning to Kanuba. We enjoyed each other and he shared with me so much of his personal life that he once said to me, "I do not know how much is left that you do not know about me." My relationship with other informants is generally good. Yet, there are some with whom I feel more at ease and share a more intimate relationship.

Over the past years, my informants have continued to be the same except for those who have left the village or died. I have been unable to establish strong rapport with new informants, especially with newcomers to the village. This is most probably due to my residence outside the village in the city of Aswan and to the fact that my recent visits have been short. However, it is interesting that I developed a friendly relationship with the only son of the village headman. His father was a very good friend to me during the period of Kennedy's study and continued to be so until he died in 1969. During the first period, his son was completely indifferent to the research group. Since 1970, he has visited me quite often in Cairo as well as in Aswan where he now works.

I would like to suggest that an anthropologist involved in long-term research should widen the circle of his informants over the years. He should be able to draw on more varied groups. This serves to replace informants lost by relocation or death. Dealing with informants of different age groups also exposes the anthropologist to differing perspectives that provide him with a more comprehensive view of village life. Perhaps more important, long-term informants, having experienced a close relationship to the researcher and understanding his interests, may tend to answer him as they perceive that he wishes to be answered. A long-term informant may also conceal facts or twist information so as not to embarrass himself or others. He may not wish to jeopardize his relationship with the researcher.

Naming the Research Site

Anthropologists often conceal the true name of their research site under a pseudonym. In Kennedy's publications, the village studied was referred to as "Kanuba." I continued the use of this name in my own writings. It could be shocking and disappointing for the villagers, I suspect, if they read about their conflicts over ritual performances when they persistently tried to show us that these differences were minor and of no effect on the village life. It would hurt their feelings and might cause them to doubt all other writings. But, the question here is whether the researcher should maintain the pseudonym of a community subject to long-term research or use its real name. In my case, I use the pseudonym "Kanuba" in my academic papers published in English, while in my Arabic reports I use the village's true name. These reports usually present data combined with very little or no theoretical discussion. Writing these reports, however, is not an easy task.

If I were to begin a new longitudinal study in another community, I would use the actual name of the community in all my writings, because I would wish the people under study to share my perceptions and analysis of their life style. Their feedback could be an important contribution to the study. Giving pseudonyms to anthropological research sites (while a useful precaution) also may hinder communication of research findings to colleagues, students, administrators, or to others who are undertaking research or are on action-assignments in these places. I once was asked by a government agency to send publications on the Nubian village where I did field research. When I explained that I had already sent copies a long time ago, I was told that the publications I had sent concerned a different village, namely "Kanuba."

The Micro and Macro Levels

Kanuba has always been my micro research unit whereas New Nubia at large represents the macro level of my research. While field research in Kanuba has been basically anthropological in orientation and practice, my studies in other Nubian villages have mostly been of the survey-type designed to collect quantitative data. The latter method is more acceptable to government agencies.

This survey-type research in New Nubia over a long period of time gave me, as I have lately discovered, only casual contacts with the numerous new villages. I was deprived of the thorough investigation and close observations that characterized my research in Kanuba. At the intensive level, I usually felt more relaxed and almost "at home." This feeling may perhaps be attributed to the continuing solid rapport with the village people and my familiarity with the place. The value of this rapport may not be recognized and appreciated until one tries to establish it anew. In general, I feel a deficiency in my anthropological training in regard to the study of what Bernard and Pelto (1972:4) refer to as macro-technological change. Anthropologists have approached this field only recently and to a modest extent. Human problems related to large scale environmental transformation such as community relocation schemes, whether caused by dams or new towns, have not as yet been well explored. Anthropological research related to macro-technological change needs, in my view, a new perspective and training, as these projects are usually regional and national in scope while anthropological emphasis has been on the microlevel.

RESEARCH FINDINGS

During my follow-up research in Kanuba I continued my original interest in religious practices, although later I gave more emphasis to the investigation of the village farm and its impact on social and economic life. In the winter of 1975, I gathered preliminary data on the socialization of the youth and data on the transmission of the villagers' notion of what progress is and how it is to be achieved. I discovered during that recent field trip that monitoring Kanuba over the past years has raised questions relevant to the study of culture change and adaptation processes in New Nubia.

The Community Religious Life

During the 1964 study, the village religious system was characterized by a split over the doctrinal legitimacy of popular religious beliefs and practices (Fahim 1973; Kennedy and Fahim 1974). A strong Orthodox group condemned the majority's practice of ceremonial celebrations that traditionally had been community-wide events and were viewed generally by villagers as occasions for social gatherings and entertainment. This village conflict was still evident in 1969, but during my visit to Kanuba in 1975 I gathered that the village no longer is in conflict over these matters. Preoccupied with farm activities and responsibilities in the farm management, the people seem less interested in the old controversial issues. The Orthodox group leader is now in charge of the animal husbandry section of the farm business. The people favoring ceremonial gatherings have found that "the farm business is much more beneficial than arguments over Islamic legitimacy of ceremonial practices,'' the village leader told me.

The question that may arise now is whether or not better economic conditions, due to the success of the village farm, will revitalize traditional Nubian ceremonialism. During the years of economic hardship, the villagers tended to maintain traditional ceremonial activities but simplified their forms, reduced their frequency, and minimized their costs. New Nubia's settlers similarly cut short their ceremonial celebrations due to the rise in the cost of living after resettlement. I propose to follow up this question, which deals with the relationship between economy and religious life.

The Village Leadership

An interesting aspect of the village leadership is the continued role of the core leading group of 1964 through various changes in strategy. In 1964, the leader's overall strategy was based on an attempt to secure advantages for the community by impressing important government and other public personages with the needs of the village. After achieving this end and satisfying most of the village's needs, he found himself facing the many new problems created by the distribution of the new houses and the management of the cooperative farm. The leader then was required to direct his attention to internal village problems while forming a ''second line'' to take over his original leading role in ''external affairs and problems,'' to use his own words.

In dealing with internal conflicts and problems associated with social and economic developments in the village, the leader reinforced the community's spirit and succeeded in assigning participatory roles to individuals and groups. He recently told me, ''Progress is not all honey,'' while reflecting on the immense problems that progress has brought and his efforts to counter them through a smooth policy and unrushed decisions. The leader's new role has changed his character; while he is in his late forties, he acts like an elderly man. He has grown a beard, a sign of old age and piety in the villager's view. In 1964, he was addressed as *Afandi*, a title for government clerks, whereas today, he is widely known as *El-sheikh*, a title given to pious leaders.

A dynamic and achievement-oriented leadership in a community accelerates the pace of change and promotes stability. The continuation of a participatory leadership pattern in a rapidly changing community for over a decade is, I believe, a phenomenon that should be thoroughly studied to increase our knowledge of the internal factors that promote change at the local level. How long will the existing leadership pattern last? Under what circumstances will it disappear or be totally modified? What will it be like when the "second line" of young men takes over and how will this affect the village notion and practice of progress? These are some questions that are raised and can only be answered through longitudinal study.

Kanuba and New Nubia

My frequent visits to Kanuba while conducting research in New Nubia have often stimulated comparative propositions. A basic question is: Why is Kanuba a stable and progressive community whereas most Kom Ombo Nubian villages are not? Is the time factor essential for adaptation and progress as many administrators and some Nubian leaders think? Are there other factors that lend themselves to explain this situation?

My field notes over the past years show that while the villagers of Kanuba tend to be mostly future oriented, the Kom Ombo settlers, even more than 10 years after their resettlement, tend to be past-oriented. Settlers in New Nubia talk frequently about the "good old days"; they reject their present realities and hope for very little in the future. This feeling was projected and dramatized in February 1975 when the government announced plans to develop the shores of Lake Aswan and to settle new communities on the shores. The issue of returning to the original homeland was debated among Nubians and, although there were opposing views, the fact remains that many people would be willing to return to Old Nubia.

During my visit of March 1975 to some New Nubian villages, I heard many complaints because the youth are rejecting the cultural involution adopted by the Nubian community as an adaptive mechanism to relocation (see Scudder 1973). Dependency on the government, the ongoing conflict between the old and new, and the increasing gap between the elderly and the young have resulted in a status quo situation in some villages and maintained a state of dissatisfaction and stress.

In Kanuba, this sort of cultural conflict and a generation gap do exist but to a much lesser degree. One explanation lies in the success of the village leadership in building an *ésprit de corps* among the people and encouraging an outward competition—the villagers minimize the effect of their cultural differences by directing their attention to competition with other villages to secure some of the limited aid available. The Kanuba case suggests that an emphasis on participatory leadership, as a way of developing community solidarity, should be recommended policy for community developers who must cope with the stress situations often associated with community relocation schemes.

The contrasts between Kanuba and the New Nubian villages should help to pinpoint indices to be used in identifying the termination of (or the continuation of) the transitional period that follows mass population movements.

On Recent Developments in Kanuba

During my last visit to Kanuba, I was struck with both the new projects the village has undertaken during the last decade and the change in people's interests. The youth talk about traveling abroad to seek better job opportunities. A 45-year-old schoolteacher left his family in the village for a 4-year contract in Saudi Arabia; others wish to do so. Girls move more freely in and out of the village. Contacts with New Nubian villages have increased; consequently the often closed marriage circle is opening up. Even contacts with non-Nubians, whose help is needed in agriculture, have widened. I was informed of a Nubian girl who recently married a non-Nubian, an incident that would have been resented strongly by the community just a few years ago.

Women in particular are experiencing an entirely new life with the new agricultural work, new products, potable water, and electricity. As a result of these innovations, women are more involved in social and political events within the village. The village organization for community development depends basically on the participation of the women (especially the younger generation) in promoting programs relating to the nursery and to the handcrafts industry.

CONCLUSION

In concluding this article, I wish to indicate that from the beginning my research in Kanuba has been an experience that I treasure and hope to continue. In Kanuba, I have had the opportunity to practice anthropology, which previously I had only read about. In Kanuba, too, I have gone through a wonderful experience, although uneasy at times, of learning about and from other people. I recall with gratitude both the professional gains and the new personality qualities I have acquired, such as tolerance, patience, contentment, and hope. More importantly, I believe, I have acquired some wisdom of the folk people.

BIBLIOGRAPHY

Bernard, H. Russell, and Pertti J. Pelto
   1972   Introduction. In *Technology and social change,* edited by Bernard, H. Russell and Pelto, Pertti J. Pp. 1–8. New York: Macmillan.

Fahim, Hussein
   1972   *Nubian resettlement in the Sudan*. Cairo: American Univ. in Cairo, Social Research Center. Reprint series No. 13.
   1973   Change in religion in a resettled Nubian village. *International Journal of Middle Eastern Studies* 4:163–177.
Fernea, Robert, and John Kennedy
   1967   Initial adaptation to resettlement: A new life for Egyptian Nubia. *Current Anthropology* 7:349–354.
Kennedy, John, and Hussein Fahim
   1974   Nubian Dhikr rituals and culture change. *The Muslim World* 64(3):205–219.
Scudder, Thayer
   1973   The human ecology of big projects: River basin development and resettlement. In *Annual Review of Anthropology*, edited by Siegel, B. Pp. 45–55. Palo Alto: Annual Reviews Inc.

Part IV

TEAM PROJECTS

Most anthropological fieldwork, whether long-term or short-term, is done by lone ethnographers. Occasionally, a few students may join the project on a part-time basis; less often, as in the Colson–Scudder partnership, a pair of fieldworkers will jointly conduct a project while retaining a considerable measure of independence in their interests and responsibilities. Even rarer is the team project, in which a group of anthropologists (or other scientists) participate in a large-scale longitudinal research design. The experiences of two well known projects—the Harvard Chiapas Project and the Kalahari Research Project—discussed in this section will illustrate the advantages and disadvantages of team research in contemporary anthropology.

The Harvard Chiapas Project began in 1957. In the 20 years since Vogt and a single graduate student went to Mexico, this research effort has expanded to include a total of 136 participants who have cumulatively spent about 40 years in the field. The fame of the project rests on the quality of the anthropologists trained and on their remarkable scholarly productivity: 21 monographs, 100 articles, and 20 dissertations so far.

Vogt undertook the Chiapas research on the urging of Mexican anthropologists at the National Indian Institute who were familiar with his earlier work in the Ramah Project. The initial 5-year period of

275

Long-Term Field Research
in Social Anthropology

fieldwork was intended to measure the impact of governmental programs on the traditional life of the Tzotzil and Tzeltal peoples of Chiapas and, from these descriptive data, to analyze the determinants and processes of cultural change. However, this research design soon proved to be inadequate. Vogt therefore shifted the strategy toward basic linguistic and ethnographic work within a narrower area—the municipality of Zinacantan. When the research grant was renewed in 1963, a second area—the municipality of Chamula—was added to the study. At the same time, an aerial photography project was undertaken as a specialized short-term activity in conjunction with anthropologists from Chicago and Stanford. The Zinacantan and Chamula research continues to the present day, with a changing cast of fieldworkers depositing their data in a central archive at Harvard and with Vogt providing the guiding hand much as Kluckhohn did in the early Navajo research and Holmberg did at Vicos.

With such a large number of fieldworkers and such a wide area to cover, it is not surprising that the Harvard Chiapas Project has touched upon many ethnographic topics. Vogt feels that it has achieved notable results in three major areas: the study of native concepts and theories of the universe; the design and execution of specialized experiments; and a deeper understanding of cultural change and continuity. It is certain that the variety of theoretical approaches and methodologies used by the different team members has provided a much richer understanding of Tzotzil cultural domains than would have been possible for a single fieldworker. Furthermore, the wide range of ethnographic data collected through virtually continuous fieldwork, by a number of fieldworkers, has provided very accurate documentation of the impact of external forces upon traditional Tzotzil life. Indeed, Vogt finds that the continuities from pre-conquest times are quite remarkable in the face of the constant pressures toward acculturation.

These advantages of large-scale longitudinal research are partially offset by two major disadvantages. One problem is the need to continually recruit top-flight students into the project. The continuation of the research over two decades has depended in large measure on the division of labor among participants: each finds a niche within the overall research design and pursues it to completion, whether in a summer or over several years. A second problem is the administrative burden on Vogt and his primary assistants. Keeping the data files in good order, keeping the project funded, and keeping peace when the occasional conflicts among team members occur all demand time and energy that otherwise could be devoted to fieldwork and write-up.

In contrast to the Harvard Chiapas Project, the Kalahari Research Project did not begin as an explicitly longitudinal study. What began as a two-person operation involving DeVore and Lee, professor and graduate student, has become a multidisciplinary team project involving a dozen more investigators. The scope of the research has been quite broad. Beginning with the study of hunter–gatherer adaptations within an ecological, ethological, and evolutionary framework, the research has expanded to cover four major topics: ecology and social change; population and health; child development; and the cognitive world of the !Kung San (Bushmen) of northern Botswana.

The initial ethnographic work conducted by Lee and DeVore between 1963 and 1967 suggested the need for bringing in a number of specialists, including nonanthropologists, to pursue topics such as demography, archaeology, population genetics, and nutrition. By 1969, eight more fieldworkers had joined Lee and DeVore and by the early 1970s the Kalahari Research Group was a reality. The team members operate with considerable independence and only a few are likely to carry out longitudinal research within the overall design.

A major result of the Kalahari fieldwork is a reevaluation of hunting and gathering as a way of life. Continuous long-term research has demonstrated that "there is no such thing as a typical year for hunter–gatherers." As Lee's discussion of rainfall and the annual cycle of variation in group structure and his discussion of population growth and sedentarization make clear, the key to the San adaptation to marginal environments is "the flexibility to adapt to a *long run* of conditions."

After a decade of research among the San, the Research Group had become professionally and personally involved with the future of these people. All had been given names and been adopted into the San kinship system. As a result, in 1973 they created a nonprofit foundation called the Kalahari Peoples Fund (KPF) through which they could assist in projects related to San development. Already the KPF is helping the San to establish title to the lands they have traditionally occupied, is exploring the feasibility of setting up cooperatives to market traditional San crafts abroad, and is working with the Botswana government to determine what kinds of development are compatible with the survival of the San as a cultural group.

In speaking about the San's future, Lee speaks for all the anthropologists whose long-term studies are included in this volume: "No one can predict what the outcome of the coming struggle will be or what role the San will play. We will be happy to see the San enrich the future national life of Botswana as they have enriched the lives of those who worked with them."

13

The Harvard Chiapas Project: 1957–1975

Evon Z. Vogt

INTRODUCTION

The Harvard Chiapas Project was conceived in Mexico in the summer of 1955, designed during 1956–1957 at the Center for Advanced Study in the Behavioral Sciences at Stanford, and initiated in Chiapas the summer of 1957. It has been in continuous operation from 1957 to 1975 with one or more field researchers in Chiapas each year.

In the summer of 1955, I was invited by the late Dr. Alfonso Caso, then Director of the Instituto Nacional Indigenista (hereafter, INI), to attend a meeting in Mexico City of INI field center directors and other personnel to discuss and evaluate INI programs in the Indian zones in which they were operating, principally the Tzotzil–Tzeltal area of the highlands of Chiapas, the Mazatec area of the lowlands of Veracruz and Oaxaca, and the Tarahumara region of the Western Sierra Madre. Following the meeting, I was invited to visit INI centers in Chiapas and Veracruz with Manuel Gamio, then Director of the Interamerican Indian Institute, and Gonzalo Aguirre Beltrán, then Deputy Director of INI. We drove through Oaxaca to Tehuantepec and on to the highlands of Chiapas where we stayed at INI headquarters in San Cristóbal Las Casas and made daily

Long-Term Field Research
in Social Anthropology

trips out to Indian villages to visit schools, clinics, and experimental farms.

Emotionally and intellectually, it was love at first sight for me. I found the cool, high (7000–9000 feet) mountain terrain covered with pine and oak forests, the rugged barrancas carved into the limestone, and the volcanic peaks all to be breathtakingly beautiful. I was impressed by the Mayan-speaking Indians I met, with each municipio dressed uniformly in distinctive, colorful styles, and by the fact that these Tzotzil and Tzeltal communities appeared to present one of those rare opportunities for research in anthropology utilizing the method of controlled comparison (Eggan 1954; Vogt 1964c). The historical frame for the comparison has been set by the fact that the people of all 37 Tzotzil and Tzeltal communities are directly descended and differentiated from a small group of Proto-Tzeltalans who occupied the Chiapas highlands about a millennium ago. The geographical frame for the comparison is set by the natural habitat—the highlands of Central Chiapas and their immediately flanking lowlands which the 200,000 Tzotzil and Tzeltal have continued to occupy in nearly contiguous communities. The continuing uniformities observed derive from shared historical antecedents, from shared experiences with the Spanish Conquest, and subsequent political impacts. The variations derive from unique local cultural drifts as the population diversifies, from differences in adaptations to micro-niches within the ecological setting, and from detailed differences in the impacts of the Conquest and subsequent political developments. By controlled comparative analysis, I felt it should eventually be possible to state with some precision the hierarchy of decisive factors that account for the present uniformities and variations.

During 1956–1957 while a Fellow at the Center for Advanced Study in the Behavioral Sciences, I had the opportunity to think through the project design and to apply for grants. Over the Christmas holidays, the center funded a trip to Chiapas where I met with Alfonso Villa Rojas, then director of the INI Center for the Tzotzil–Tzeltal zone, and members of his staff, with whom I visited Indian communities to make additional arrangements for research.

THE FIRST PHASE

Initial funding proved difficult, but finally, for the summer of 1957, I received a grant from the "Small Grants Program" of NIMH (National Institute of Mental Health) and my graduate student assistant, Frank C. Miller, was funded by the Doherty Foundation. So, the first phase of the project began very modestly—one graduate student and a Landrover purchased in Tuxtla Gutiérrez, the capital city of Chiapas. Miller and I spent August 1957 making a reconnaissance of the Tzotzil–Tzeltal region, by Landrover, by horseback, and by foot.

With the suggestion and assistance of Villa Rojas, Miller decided to study health care delivery in the municipio of Huistán during 1957–1958, and was installed in an INI clinic in the isolated hamlet of Yalcuc. I decided to work in the municipio of Zinacantan, and began to make preliminary contacts in the ceremonial center itself, and in the hamlet of Paste?. During 1957–1958, I received the welcome news that my major application to NIMH had been successful and that I would be funded for 5 years. In the summer of 1958, I returned to Chiapas, joined by Nick and Lore Colby, who succeeded Miller as graduate student assistants and spent the 1958–1959 academic year working in Zinacantan on problems of education, Indian–Ladino relations, and the study of the Tzotzil language. They were joined by Pierre L. van den Berghe who worked on Indian–Ladino relations.

In the summer of 1959, Robert M. Laughlin served as graduate assistant, working in Zinacantan during 1959–1960 on mythology and beginning his "The Great Tzotzil Dictionary of San Lorenzo Zinacantán." At the same time, Manuel T. Zabala Cubillos came from the National School of Anthropology and History in Mexico City to do a study for us on the salt industry of Zinacantan. In 1960–1961, Frank and Francesca Cancian replaced Laughlin as student assistants and initiated their researches on the cargo system and on the study of the Tzotzil family as a small group.

My own work during the summers of 1958 and 1959 was focused on trying to get a basic grasp of some of the ethnography of Zinacantan, notably the cargo system and the organization of shamans. In the summer of 1958, my wife and I and our four children lived in quarters provided by INI at the edge of San Cristóbal, and from there I traveled to Zinacantan Center and to the hamlet of Paste? to visit Indian schools and a few families that we knew. Rapport was especially difficult to establish at first—not only all the people, but also the dogs and the sheep ran to hide in the cornfields as we drove into the hamlet in the Landrover and stopped by the trail for a picnic lunch. But after a time, curious people re-emerged from the tall corn and began to engage us in conversation—with their halting Spanish and my even more meager Tzotzil. Before long we were providing transport for people and for bags of maize and chickens to the market in San Cristóbal. Many of the Zinacantecos had never been in an automobile before; both men and women became dizzy at speeds over 5 miles per hour and the women sat, by preference, on the floor of the Landrover since they had never sat on a chair or bench in their lives.

By the summer of 1959, INI had constructed a small field house for us next to the school in Paste?, for which we paid construction costs. We spent most of the summer in the hamlet, learning a great deal about the school and its operation, but less than I would have liked about the rest of the community. I did become well acquainted with the secretary of the school committee, who later became one of my principal shaman informants, and with the Zinacanteco schoolteacher, who I learned later was the most important political boss in Zinacantan. More productive, however, in learning about the basic ethnography were long interviews with a Zinacanteco who had formerly worked in the INI puppet show and as an informant for Nick Colby. These interviews actually proved to be more fruitful when we worked in San Cristóbal—away from the noises and interruptions of hamlet life; so part of the summer was spent in an apartment we retained in town. In the spring term of 1960, I had a leave-of-absence from Harvard to engage in field research in Chiapas. Since our children were in school, I went alone. I lived in the field house in Paste? and took my meals with a neighboring Zinacanteco family. For the first time, I was observing and participating in the flow of everyday Zinacanteco life. By May, I was able to attend the all-night lineage and waterhole ceremonies performed by the shamans in this hamlet, which were crucial to our understanding of the structure and dynamics of Zinacanteco hamlet life. However, even after these 6 months in the hamlet, I was still unable to obtain permission to attend a curing ceremony. I knew they were taking place almost daily, for I would hear the chanting of the shamans and the blowing on the ritual gourds to summon the lost souls. But, it was not until the summer of 1961—4 seasons after the project began—that I was finally invited to a curing ceremony, performed in that instance by the former secretary of the school committee whom I had first met over 2 years before.

THE SECOND PHASE

Meanwhile, beginning in the summer of 1960, the second phase of the Chiapas Project was initiated—the inclusion of small numbers of carefully selected undergraduates in the summer field research. This undergraduate fieldwork began as part of an inter-university program funded by the Carnegie Corporation of New York. The Harvard Chiapas Project collaborated with Professors Charles Wagley and Marvin Harris at Columbia and Professor Alan Holmberg and his colleagues at Cornell to train and place undergraduates from the three universities at field stations in Mexico, Brazil, Peru, and Ecuador. We later added the University of

Illinois, represented by Professor Joseph B. Casagrande, to the consortium. The program was so successful that it was extended for a number of years under the sponsorship of the National Science Foundation and, in the case of Harvard, it still continues.

By the summer of 1960, there had been a shift in the field strategy of the project. My original objectives proved to be far too ambitious. Moreover, we were too closely associated with INI to get at the needed basic ethnography. I had originally proposed a 5-year project which was tightly designed to describe the changes that were occurring in the cultures of the Tzotzil and Tzeltal as a result of the action program of INI and to utilize these data for an analysis of the determinants and processes of cultural change. I argued that the field setting provided an unprecedented opportunity for controlled research on several aspects of cultural change. Within a radius of 30 miles of San Cristóbal Las Casas, a Ladino town of 25,000 inhabitants, the contemporary 200,000 Tzotzil and Tzeltal Indians live in scattered communities in the mountains. These Mayan-speaking Indians were first brought into contact with Europeans in 1528 when the town of San Cristóbal was founded by the Spanish conquerors, the ancestors of the present Ladino population.

In the 1930s, the municipio of Oxchuc was studied by Alfonso Villa Rojas (1947), and in the 1940s four additional municipios were studied by Sol Tax and a group of Mexican students. Professor Tax (1943, 1944) and his students first worked mainly in Zinacantan for a period of 6 weeks. Later, three of the students undertook further fieldwork: Fernando Cámara Barbachano (1952) in Tenejapa, Calixta Guiteras-Holmes (1961) in Chenalhó, and Ricardo Pozas (1959) in Chamula. Ruth Bunzel (1940) also worked briefly in Chamula in the 1930s before she went on to Chichicastenango in Guatemala. These data provide a useful early baseline for the investigation of more recent cultural changes.

In 1950, INI established its operating center in San Cristóbal and launched an elaborate program of change that included health education and the establishment of clinics, more formal schooling, the establishment of Indian-controlled stores in each village, the construction of roads, and the improvement of crops and agricultural practices. With this program, INI became the most important event to affect the Indian cultures since the Spanish Conquest. I proposed to take advantage of this cultural laboratory situation to describe the cultural changes that were currently occurring and could be observed first-hand. By using the baseline data from the 1930s and 1940s, by careful study of the new stimulus for change (i.e., the INI program), and by continuing observations over the years, I hoped to trace the sequences and directions of cultural change in detail.

The second aim of the project was to utilize the descriptive data for an analysis of the determinants and processes of cultural change. The crucial determinants of change fall into two major categories: (*a*) the properties of the two cultures that come into contact; (*b*) the types of interrelationships established between them (Vogt 1957). Among the properties of the culture that I proposed to study in accounting for the processes of change were the value system which appears extraordinarily persistent and exercises certain controlling effects upon the rates and directions of change (Vogt 1955); and the social structure which may (in rural Mexico) be tightly organized in a "closed" corporate community that is resistant to change, or more loosely organized in an "open" community that is more vulnerable to change (Wolf 1955). Preliminary data from Chiapas had suggested this contrast as a crucial variable in cultural change. A crucial factor in the types of relationships established between cultures appeared to be the extent to which the new program of change is "forced" or "permissive"; the thesis being that changes backed by force or power are less likely to be accepted than are new patterns presented to an American Indian group under permissive conditions that allow for freedom to make choices and for a selective process of adaptation (Dozier 1955). Preliminary data from Chiapas had also suggested that this variable was highly significant in accounting for variations in the adoption of, or resistance to, new patterns.

Inasmuch as the Indian population was relatively large and their settlements numerous, the action programs of INI reach the Indian communities in variable degrees and with variable results, a fact of importance for my research design, which was to be based upon a series of comparative studies:

1. Indian communities that have been "progressive" in accepting the modernization program compared to those that have a record of marked "resistance" to change
2. "Open" communities compared with "closed" corporate communities
3. More "permissive" programs compared with more "forced" programs of change

By 1959, it had become clear that (*a*) we had underestimated the amount and complexity of ancient Maya social organization and culture that are still viable in these communities; and (*b*) by focusing upon INI programs and the ways in which the Indians responded to these, we were obtaining only part of the data necessary for a penetrating study of the problems. We were, in a word, getting too much of an "outside" view and too little of an "inside" view. I now believe I miscalculated for two reasons: (*a*) the presence of Catholicism, including the dozens of cross shrines, the links of the communities with the Mexican government, the use of Mexican money, and the use of Spanish all led me to think that, in spite of the basic use of Tzotzil by the Indians, the people were essentially Mexican peasants, much like those described by Robert Redfield and Oscar Lewis in Tepoztlán; (b) my previous field research had been in the American southwest where all Indian cultures had been under anthropological scrutiny for a hundred years before I began my work there. Even though this early anthropological work had been spotty and some of it superficial, it nevertheless had built up an enormous corpus of basic ethnographic data—a corpus lacking in the case of the highland Chiapas cultures.

Therefore, in 1959 I decided to concentrate on basic linguistic and ethnographic work in one municipio (Zinacantan), rather than scattering our efforts over many topics and areas. This ground obviously had to be covered before much could be achieved in the study of cultural change. Lore Colby, a trained linguist, completed a study of the basic elements of Tzotzil grammar and compiled a Tzotzil–Spanish dictionary which she had started in the fall of 1958.

The change in strategy also involved detaching ourselves more and more from the government program and its technicians, and identifying ourselves more with the conservative segments of the Indian communities. Among other things, we started wearing items of Indian clothing, rather than dressing as Ladinos, and we started living in Indian houses. Both of these moves were complex procedures. We found, for example, that it was appropriate in the Indian view to dress as Indians only insofar as we learned to speak Tzotzil. We had to engage in very complicated negotiations to rent Indian houses or move in with Indian families. I mention these field procedures because while living in Navajo hogans or Zuni houses in New Mexico had long been standard operating procedure for anthropologists there, living with Indian families had rarely, if ever, been done by anthropologists in Mexico or Guatemala.

In the municipio of Zinacantan, fewer than 1000 Indians live in the ceremonial center where the churches, the town hall, and a few stores are located. The other 7000 live in outlying hamlets, ranging in population from 50 to slightly over 1000. The hamlets are subdivided into "water hole" groups of one or more patrilineages living around communal waterholes. These patrilineages consist of a series of patrilocally extended families, each occupying a *sitio* ('homestead') with two to four houses surrounded by their maize fields. Our students arrange to take up residence in one of the houses in a *sitio*. Our approach to placing students in houses is modelled on that used by the Zinacantecos themselves in asking favors of others. We visit the male head of a household, present him with a liter of sugar cane liquor, and explain that we want the student with us to live in his house, learn the Tzotzil language and customs, and help with household work. If the student is a woman, she will assist with tortilla-making and carrying wood and water; if the student is a man, he will assist with farming activities. We explain carefully that the student knows how to eat Zinacanteco food and that he or she will reimburse the family for meals, normally 5 pesos a day. We add that the student knows how to sleep on a *petate* ('reed mat') and has brought a sleeping bag for warmth at night. If the family does not wish to have a student guest, the household head will politely refuse the liquor, and we then go on to another house. If the household head accepts the liquor, this indicates that he accepts the student. He orders the liquor served to all, and by the time the ritual drinking is over, everyone is in a state of pleasant intoxication and the bargain has been sealed. The student remains from 4 days to 2 weeks at a time in the home of his Zinacanteco hosts, participating in the full flow of Tzotzil life as represented by this extended family and their neighbors. When the student tires of the diet of tortillas and beans three times a day or detects that his hosts need a rest from his presence, he will return to San Cristóbal to spend some days writing up field notes, conferring with the field director, and exchanging experiences with other members of the field party who happen to be in town at the same time. If the arrangement in the field goes well, a student may return to the same household all season. If it does not, or if the nature of his research topic demands more comparative data, the student may move to other hamlets and households during the field season.

We also shifted policy with respect to problem areas that were the focal points for study each year. We abandoned (until later) the effort to understand directly the influence of the government program on the Indian communities and moved instead to a study of a number of basic domains of the culture. By the end of 1960, the results had become exciting. We now knew we were dealing with Indian cultures that were fully as complex and intricate in religion and ceremonial organization, and to some extent in social organization, as southwestern pueblos like the Zuni and Hopi.

THE THIRD PHASE

In 1963 and 1964, I initiated the third phase of the Harvard Chiapas Project. This involved renewal of the NIMH grant and expansion of our operations to include Chamula in our intensive field research. The inclusion of Chamula made our field research even more complex and difficult. Zinacantan had proven to be complex enough, having at that time a population of some 8000 living in a ceremonial center and 15 hamlets. But Chamula had a population of about 30,000 living in a ceremonial center and nearly a hundred hamlets. More important, I added another methodological phase to our operations: the aerial photography project, funded by the National Science Foundation and sponsored jointly with Professor Norman A. McQuown of Chicago and Professor A. Kimball Romney of Stanford. From 1963 to 1969, we accomplished the following objectives: the taking of aerial photographs of three types (cartographic, High Acuity panoramic, and low-level oblique) of the highlands of Chiapas with the aid of the Itek Corporation of Palo Alto, California, and the Compañía Mexicana Aerofoto of Mexico City; the establishment of an aerial photo laboratory at Harvard with a Reader–Printer and a zoom stereoscope for viewing and working with the photographs; and the production of a basic file of photomosaics and maps for the study of settlement patterns, land use, population densities, and so on in the Chiapas highlands (Vogt 1974).

Fieldwork went well through the 1960s, and rapport with both Indians and Ladinos became better each year as we learned more fluent Tzotzil and extended our range of contacts. Each spring at Harvard we offer an informal course in Tzotzil, taught by the person who knows the most Tzotzil. Since I am not as fluent in the language as many of my gifted students, I have never taught this course. It is taught by a junior colleague or a graduate student, or at times by one or more undergraduates who prove to have superior control of the language, and I am one of the students. This course and my Seminar in Field Methods are taken by all students intending to go into the field the following summer. Some of the sessions in the methods seminar are devoted to field reports by students from the previous year; this serves to communicate experience directly and keep members of the project in intellectual and personal touch with one another through the years.

During the 1960s, we also gradually developed a series of project traditions which help to build and keep morale high among students. Most meetings between the field leader and students are on a one-to-one basis, similar to individual tutorials, held either at field headquarters or in the field situation, when the field leader visits the student in some remote hamlet or while traveling together on foot along the mountain trails. We also have an organized Mid-Summer Conference and a Final Conference at which each student gives reports and receives comments and criticisms. We also have dances at field headquarters, either with marimba bands to which our Indian and Ladino friends are invited and in which they participate, or with taped music for square dances.

Furthermore, a student whose birthday occurs in the summer field season enjoys a Mexican style celebration with mariachis playing early morning *mañanitas* with tamales, rum, and coffee for breakfast, or a gala mid-day luncheon with mariachis and always a *piñata*. These parties not only bring together all our students to honor the birthday person but also provide hospitality for our Indian and Ladino informants and friends and are often attended by 50 to 100 people. Our more athletically inclined students have also helped to provide a series of games which help to build and maintain morale at field headquarters. Volleyball, horseshoes, darts, and ping pong are played almost daily.

Research conducted in Chiapas during the 1960s includes: John D. Early's collected data on the ceremonies of the Zinacanteco cargoholders during the academic year 1962–1963; the following year, 1963–1964, Daniel B. Silver undertook a systematic study of the rituals performed by the shamans in Zinacantan. In 1965–1966, Victoria R. Bricker studied the patterns of ceremonial humor, and in 1966–1967 George and Jane Collier, who had already spent summers doing field research, returned for a full year to work on land-use and inheritance and collect law cases. They were joined by Frank and Francesca Cancian returning for a second full year in the field, and by Elena Uribe Wood who studied patterns of *compadrazgo* in Zinacantan and Chamula. During 1968–1969, Gary H. Gossen worked on Chamula oral narrative, while Victoria Bricker returned for a second field stint to study ritual humor in Chamula and Chenalhó.

THE CRISIS

Then, in December 1969, an event occurred which nearly ended the Project. Thieves, who have never been identified, broke into the Church of San Lorenzo in Zinacantan Center in the middle of the night and stole a silver cross from the wall and the golden chalice from the main altar. Zinacanteco officials saw the tracks of tennis shoes (which are often worn by anthropologists) outside the church, and within hours word spread throughout the municipio that the anthropologists must have stolen the sacred objects. Later we found that two other churches had been broken into the same night (one in San Cristóbal and the other in San Felipe at the edge of San Cristóbal) and colonial art pieces removed. Fortunately, two very experienced and gifted fieldworkers, John Haviland and Francesco Pellizzi, were in Chiapas at the time, and they managed to ride out the political storm with the aid of Mexican government authorities, the Bishop, and various priests, all of whom reassured the Zinacantecos that we were not thieves. Since the thieves have never been apprehended nor the art objects recovered, we have concluded that some kind of internationally organized "ring" dealing in stolen art was probably involved, and that the objects are now in New York, London or Paris. What made the Zinacanteco reaction especially sharp was their belief that the silver cross had been found in a cave by an ancestral figure, and that it had the power to "make money." It has taken at least 5 years for us to recover the rapport we had before this unfortunate event.

By the early 1970s, we finally had good control of the ethnographic data in Zinacantan and increasingly adequate control of the data in Chamula, especially from the work of Gary H. Gossen, Priscilla Rachun Linn, and Jeffrey C. Howry, as well as some data on the neighboring Indian municipios and the Ladino municipio of San Cristóbal Las Casas, which was particularly studied by Felisa M. Kazen in connection with her field study of a textile factory in the city. We began to engage in more controlled comparative studies and also returned to the basic questions I began with concerning the impact of Mexican government programs on the Indian cultures. These problems are being specifically investigated by the most recent graduate students on the project: Robert F. Wasserstrom, Jan Rus III, and Richard González.

Most summer seasons I have served as field leader as well as carrying on my own research. I have also had a spring term (1960) and a fall term (1971) in Chiapas, so that I have been able to witness the full calendar round. My total time in the field from 1957 to 1975 has been 50 months, and another spring term in the field (1976) has been added. The seasons when I could not be in the field throughout the summer, I appointed experienced younger colleagues to serve as field leaders: Duane Metzger in 1960, Frank Cancian in 1962, George Collier in 1964 and 1966, John Haviland in 1971, Priscilla Rachun Linn in 1972 and Jan Rus in 1975. By the summer of 1975, we have had a total of 136 fieldworkers who have engaged in research in Chiapas for a summer season or longer. Colleagues often inquire how long I plan to continue the project. My answer is that I plan to continue in Chiapas through the remainder of my professional career.

METHODOLOGY

The principal advantage of a continuous long-range project over a short-range one, or a series of revisits, is the depth, quality, and variety of understandings achieved—understandings of the basic ethnography and of the trends and processes of change. If the long-range project also involves a sizable team of students and younger colleagues who make one or more revisits and keep abreast of all the publications, then there is the added advantage of having a variety of fieldworkers with varied training and different theoretical biases who are forced to reconcile their findings and their analyses with one another.

From the start, the Chiapas Project has operated with the agreement that each fieldworker deposits a copy of his field data in the central files at Harvard and, in return, each fieldworker has access to everyone else's data; further, each fieldworker normally circulates manuscripts to other members of the project for comment and criticism in advance of publication. While I sometimes find it maddening to have to rewrite an article or chapters of a book three or four times in response to sharp comments from my colleagues, I am convinced the final products are always better for it—both ethnographically and analytically. This procedure is a far cry from the long tradition in anthropology of one fieldworker who spends 1 or 2 years with a tribe and then returns to produce *the* monograph, which not only stands as God's Truth about the tribe but also is processed into the Human Relations Area Files and thereby becomes the basis for a *case* in cross-cultural studies. It may be that the ethnographic data was excellent and basically correct, but we have only the word of one anthropologist to depend upon, and my guess is that the materials are sometimes superficial. I note with interest that whenever there has been a revisit by some other anthropologist, there has followed, I believe without exception, a celebrated controversy in the journals about who was right and who was wrong.

A second important advantage to a long-range project is the development of rapport with the communities under observation. There is something about constantly returning each season—in our case, with the rains—that seems to reassure most people and to engender feelings of mutual trust. This situation makes it possible to be doing significant fieldwork upon arrival, and the fieldworker does not have to go through the motions of coping with the local bureaucracy each season. On the Chiapas Project, this long-range rapport has led to significant results in three areas: (*a*) the study of native concepts and theories of the universe; (*b*) the design and execution of specialized experimental studies; (*c*) deeper understanding of the trends of cultural change.

(*a*) We are achieving a degree of understanding of native Tzotzil theory and belief that could not be attained in a project of shorter duration. Field studies of native cognitive structures have often suffered from either a lack of the intimate insights supplied by a thorough knowledge of the native language, or a tendency to portray belief as monolithic or unchanging across the social universe. Although the first years of our fieldwork were hampered by our lack of fluency in Tzotzil, one of our fieldworkers, Dr. Robert M. Laughlin, has over the past 13 years elicited more than 35,000 entries for a Tzotzil dictionary, and other students have developed grammatical descriptions which now allow new fieldworkers to achieve fluency in Tzotzil in 6 months of solid study.

At the same time, our varied training has importantly extended our understanding of the native conceptual system. Frank Cancian, for instance, has described the ritual cargo system of the Chiapas highlands as an economic system of social prestige ranking (1965). Others of us have incorporated Cancian's insights into an analysis of how, in native theory, the cargo system represents a complex system of prestations between men and gods.

More recently, Gary Gossen, working in Chamula on oral narrative and cosmology, discovered in the mythical order that lies behind the system of ritual cargos and curing ceremonies a correlation between mythical time and social space, social chaos and disorder being associated with times and places deep in the past and as distant and barbarous as Guatemala, Mexico City, and the United States, while social order is symbolized by current ritual behavior of the officials in the modern ceremonial centers (Gossen 1974b). Further, Gossen discovered that conservative Chamulas not only maintain the ancient Tzotzil solar calendar of 18 months of 20 days each with a 5-day unlucky period at the end, but that flower-changing ceremonies for the saints are still performed on this 20-day month basis. In addition, there are still carefully calculated cycles of time—the agricultural cycle, the weather cycle, the fiesta cycle, the phases of the moon—which permit two Chamulas conversing together to specify the exact day of the year by the ancient calendar (Gossen 1974a).

Gossen also discovered puns, riddles, and children's games that are far more subtle and complex than we previously believed to exist. The games are proving to offer models for Chamula social structure, models which are extraordinarily interesting. For example, there is one game in which five small children arrange themselves from the most senior in age to the most junior in age—reflecting the kinship system—and take the respective roles of an older, middle, and younger brother, a chicken and a weasel. The three older children join hands and place the chicken (domesticated) in the center. Then the weasel (wild) attempts to break into the protective circle to capture and kill the chicken. The game appears to represent not only one of the basic principles of Tzotzil social structure (i.e., age-grading) but also to be a metaphorical comment on the relationship between wild and domestic animals, as well as aiding socialization in teaching children to care for domestic animals.

Our understanding of these domains of Tzotzil culture has been built up, step by step, only by intimate knowledge of the Tzotzil language, of bodies of data from both Chamula and Zinacantan for controlled comparative study, and by utilizing a variety of theoretical approaches. A long-range project is imperative for these kinds of cumulative, cross-checked results.

(b) Our long-range project also has had tremendous potential for the successful execution of specialized, experimental studies. Our heavy investment in developing rapport over the years has made it possible to experiment with hundreds of subjects, rather than just a handful of them, and to draw representative, and even total, samples of the universes being studied. Richard Shweder, for example, was able to perform a variety of carefully controlled procedures matching 50 shamans with 50 nonshamans (Shweder 1972). Drs. T. Berry Brazelton, John S. Robey and George A. Collier (1969) in 2 summers of study, were able to examine and give tests of psychosocial development to nearly 100 Zinacanteco infants. Frank Cancian was able to study economic motivation in two communities of nearly 1700 people by training key informants to recruit *every* household head and administer to him a lengthy questionnaire in the Tzotzil language (Cancian 1972). George Collier, utilizing aerial photographs, completed an exhaustive study of land tenure practices in one community where, several years ago, questions of land ownership would have been too delicate to broach (Collier 1975). George Collier and John Haviland worked together on a "Who's Who in Zinacantan" in which a panel of informants from each of the major hamlets would converse freely around a tape recorder about the important people in each hamlet—political leaders, shamans, wealthy corn farmers, etc. The panel discussions not only generated penetrating data for Collier who was studying the determinants of political power, but also for Haviland who was studying gossip and utilizing it to understand the dynamics of social structure.

In each of these instances, fieldwork prior to the execution of the study allowed the researchers to formulate theoretically meaningful and, at the same time, practical, experimental designs.

(c) A third advantage of our long-term project is the opportunity it has provided to study first-hand the trends of cultural change. In order to systematize these observations on change from year to year, we attempt to take a reading each season on a number of indices of change. Our observations during the early years of the project have revealed that these indices are both crucial and measurable markers of change. Some of these mark the degree of "modernization" that is taking place in the Indian villages; other are measures of nativistic trends in traditional Indian life. Examples of these indices are:

1. *Incidence of bilingualism*. During the decades 1940 to 1960 there was a net increase in monolingualism in Tzotzil in the highlands of

Chiapas. But, by now, the scales have been tipped in the direction of increasing control of Spanish on the part of the Indians.

2. *Housing styles*. The trend is from the traditional thatched roof, with wattle-and-daub walls to tile roofs with adobe walls.

3. *Clothing styles*. The shift is from the traditional (Colonial period) Indian dress to styles of clothing worn by Mexican peasants. This change is fast for men, very slow for women. It is noteworthy, however, that traditional men's *chamarras* (jackets) and women's *rebozos* (shawls) with increasingly exuberant embroidered floral designs are retained as symbols of "Indianness."

4. *Household equipment*. This includes the addition of corn mills, tortilla presses, metal pots and pans.

5. *Roads and modes of transport*. More and better roads have led to a shift from foot travel to more bus and truck travel.

6. *Surnames*. The shift is from the traditional Tzotzil system to the Mexican system.

7. *Participation of Indians in Ladino institutions*. For example, arranging loans with governmental agencies, joining labor unions, using Ladino courts.

8. *Numbers of religious cargos and practicing shamans*. Both are increasing; index of "nativism."

9. *Shifts in drinking customs*. Not much change has occurred yet in Zinacantan, but there has been a great change in Chamula where drinking to the point of complete inebriation occurs far less for reasons we do not yet understand.

10. *Adoption of public utilities: water lines and electricity*. Acceptance is proceeding apace.

11. *Population growth*. It is explosive and a real problem.

Have we found disadvantages to our long-term research, and especially that involving teams of fieldworkers? There are two disadvantages I perceive. One is that sometimes it has been impossible to recruit top-flight students who may prefer, instead, to undertake field research in still unstudied areas of places like New Guinea or Brazil. When the Harvard Chiapas Project started, this was not a problem since it was an unstudied ethnographic area with all the usual exotic challenges. But now, as we sit in seminar rooms at Harvard and describe how tough it was in the beginning, we sometimes find we have inspired the students to look elsewhere for "wild and hairy" field sites instead of coming to work in what they perceive to be the already heavily studied highlands of Chiapas. When I point out that there are still dozens of Tzotzil and Tzeltal municipios that have scarcely been touched, I do not always succeed in convincing them.

The other disadvantage is the amount of administrative time it takes to run a long-term project. My administrative burden has not been so heavy as it might have been, for I have deliberately kept the number of graduate students small and selective—not more than one or two a year for most of the time. The undergraduates have posed more problems since there have been many applications each year, not only from Harvard and Radcliffe, but from other schools as well, and it has been difficult to keep the numbers at about six each summer, especially when former students wish to return. Since some of the best graduate students have been recruited from undergraduate field programs, I have been reluctant to limit the numbers. But perhaps the most vexing administrative problem occurs when members of the project do not get on well with one another—for various and complicated reasons—and I will not pretend that we have not had a few celebrated intra-project conflicts. In the long run, most of these have been resolved to the point where the "combatants" have participated together in symposia at anthropology meetings. Generalizing about the sources of these conflicts is difficult, but one thing seems clear. They have, surprisingly, *not* arisen over possessive feelings about field data or ideas, but rather because of differences in research style and field methods and in intellectual and political presuppositions.

If I could start over, would I do things differently? In retrospect, it would seem that I might have been able to get at more penetrating ethnographic data in the first phase of the project than I did. But, given the enormous difficulties of establishing rapport with closely and highly suspicious Indian communities, there was probably no real alternative to the different strategies we used. We were first sponsored by, and closely associated ourselves with, INI which, as a champion of Indian interests, had developed closer rapport than that enjoyed by most of the local Ladino population. Through INI, we met and employed our first informants and established our field house in Paste?. Still later, when I discovered that living next door to Indian families was much less productive than living with them, we donated the field house to the schoolteachers and established a field headquarters in rented buildings at the edge of San Cristóbal. With this headquarters as a base, we can move out to the hamlets to live with Indian families for periods of days or weeks, then return to base to write up data and, even more important, to reciprocate hospitality when our Indian friends come to see us. This pattern of alternation is crucial for our research operations, because, unlike the Mexicans, the Indians of Zinacantan and Chamula have no patterns of visiting each other unless there is some explicit purpose, such as borrowing an axe, buying a chicken, or asking for a loan of money. Furthermore, the data that can be gathered by informal interviewing and observation while living on a day and night basis in a one-room thatched house with an

Indian family so exceeds the data that can be gathered from a short stay during the day that there is no comparison. On the other hand, the periods of relative calm at field headquarters are ideal for thinking, writing up data, and for formal interviewing of informants away from the distractions of hamlet life.

RESEARCH RESULTS

Our research results are found in the 27 monographs, 100 articles, and 21 dissertations listed in the Harvard Chiapas Project Bibliography (Vogt 1978). It will be apparent that we have worked on many ethnographic fronts and have tilled different patches of theoretical turf. Over the years, I have deliberately encouraged my students and junior colleagues to develop their own ideas and work out their own methods of undertaking research. This policy was based on my experience with the previous Values Study Project in the Southwest (see Evon Z. Vogt and Ethel M. Albert 1966). I have sometimes wished that we had tried to establish a publication series with one press so that the results of the Chiapas Project would be less scattered. But presses have different interests, so we have utilized a variety of them including especially Harvard, Stanford, and Texas.

Reviewing first my own published results, I have edited an INI volume (*Los Zinacantecos: Un Pueblo Tzotzil de los Altos de Chiapas,* 1966), which is a collection of reprinted technical articles in Spanish by my students and me, done a major monograph (*Zinacantan: A Maya Community in the Highlands of Chiapas,* 1969), and a small paperback (*The Zinacantecos of Mexico: A Modern Maya Way of Life*, 1970b), which has also appeared in Spanish (*Los Zinacantecos: Un Grupo Maya en el Siglo XX,* 1973). The emphasis in these volumes is upon descriptive ethnography with some analysis.

With Alberto Ruz L., I have also edited *Desarrollo Cultural de los Mayas* (1964), based on the 1962 Burg Wartenstein Symposium, "The Cultural Development of the Maya," which contains a goodly amount of Chiapas material. A recent volume to appear, edited by me, is *Aerial Photography in Anthropological Field Research*, 1974, which contains five articles on various aspects of our aerial photo work in the highlands of Chiapas. These two volumes contain ethnographic data, but the emphasis is more methodological and theoretical. Recently published is my *Tortillas for the Gods: A Symbolic Analysis of Zinacanteco Rituals* (1976), which attempts a theoretical interpretation of ceremonial life.

In addition, I have published a number of articles, some of which were largely ethnographic in content and, for the most part, simply anticipated what later appears in my books. But I can note several which have had a theoretical and methodological impact. My early papers entitled "Some Aspects of Zinacantan Settlement Patterns and Ceremonial Organization" (1961), "Ancient Maya and Contemporary Tzotzil Cosmology: A Comment on Some Methodological Problems" (1964a), "Ancient Maya Concepts in Contemporary Zinacantan Religion" (1964b), "The Genetic Model and Maya Cultural Development" (1964c), and "Some Implications of Zinacantan Social Structure for the Study of the Ancient Maya" (1964d) triggered a controversy with certain Mayan archaeologists which has reverberated through the journals and monographs for the last 15 years. My basic argument has been that it should be fruitful to examine the social and political structure and cosmology of the contemporary Mayan peoples in areas like the highlands of Chiapas for hints about the Classic Maya, rather than utilizing what are essentially European models of kinship, priesthoods, etc. to make inferences. In particular, I hypothesize a conceptual (and perhaps historical) connection between the steep-sided mountains (that are homes of ancestral gods in Chiapas) and the pyramids in Classic sites (which it turns out are often tombs for prominent ancient Mayas). At the least, since we find a close relationship between sacred shrines devoted to ancestors and various levels of social structure in highland Chiapas, it would seem worthwhile to explore the idea that the multiple pyramids in archaeological sites may symbolize differentiated sociopolitical units in Classic Maya society.

Another paper which generated considerable interest, and which I still find pertinent in ongoing research, is "Structural and Conceptual Replication in Zinacantan Culture" (1965) in which I attempted to demonstrate how certain key structural and conceptual patterns are replicated in many domains and at various levels of the culture, ranging from child care to the supernatural world.

In recent years, I have turned more to an attempt to decode the rich ceremonial life of Zinacantan. Two preliminary papers, "Human Souls and Animal Spirits in Zinacantan" (1970a) and "Lévi-Strauss Among the Maya" (with Catherine C. Vogt, 1970), were followed shortly by the aforementioned book, *Tortillas for the Gods*. In these efforts I have developed ideas stemming from Lévi-Strauss, Leach, Turner, Geertz, Douglas, and others for what is essentially a structural analysis of the symbolism of Zinacanteco rituals. I plan another book on ritual in the near future, a general theoretical effort drawing in part on Chiapas materials.

Looking over my publications, I see that I have spent rather more time analyzing continuities than changes in Tzotzil culture. There is my paper on "Tendencias de Cambio en los Altos de Chiapas" (1967), and on "Recurrent and Directional Processes in Zinacantan" (1968), but for the most part I have left the more sustained analysis of trends and processes of change to my students and colleagues. I believe there are two reasons for this: the cultural continuities have continued to impress me and I often feel rather like A. L. Kroeber, who found that acculturation studies were "dreary." Nothing about the various trends we track and describe seems very astonishing. Tribal peoples are in effect becoming more like peasants, and peasants have a kind of dreary sameness all over the world.

Meanwhile, my former graduate students and now my junior colleagues (to say nothing of the undergraduates) have been very productive in publishing their research results. Their books are included in the bibliography.

IMPACT OF OUR RESEARCH

Our impact on the Indian cultures we study in highland Chiapas makes itself felt on two levels: (*a*) the immediate day-to-day relationships with the Indian families and communities, and (*b*) the more indirect effects stemming from our publications.

It is easy to exaggerate our day-to-day influence on the Indian cultures. For, although we have been doing fieldwork involving a large number of different researchers over the years, the Indian communities we study are relatively large. Even with a field party of as many as 15 students, we are not so conspicuous in the total Zinacanteco population of 15,000 or the Chamula population of 40,000 as a single anthropologist is in a tribe of 200 people in the interior of Brazil. Further, we never have more than two fieldworkers in a given hamlet with a population ranging between 500 and 1500. We have had an impact on selected Indian families that we have employed as informants over the years. Not only have we employed members of these families fairly steadily for months at a time, but five young men (four Zinacantecos and one Chamula) have been brought to Harvard for as long as 2 months to assist in teaching Tzotzil to new students. While at Harvard, these men have lived either with my family or with younger colleagues or graduate students. Further, two of the Zinacanteco men have spent longer periods in Santa Fe, New Mexico, and at the Smithsonian Institution in Washington, D.C., assisting Robert Laughlin with his work on the Tzotzil dictionary. The same two attended the American Anthropological Association meetings in San Francisco in 1963 and had the frightening experience of seeing Oswald shot down on the TV screen following the Kennedy assassination. Needless to say, they wanted to return immediately to the safety of the highlands of southern Mexico.

All five of these men were literate in Spanish, but we taught them to read and write in Tzotzil; three of the five even learned to touch-type quite competently. For four of the five, I believe our major impact, both in terms of the salaries we paid them and the cross-cultural experiences we provided, served mainly to speed up the processes of economic advancement and modernization in their lives that might have occurred anyway. The steady salaries we paid and the skills we taught them permitted these men to get married sooner and/or to advance in the cargo system more quickly and to acquire better jobs with government agencies than would otherwise have been the case. The major negative impact occurred in the case of the Zinacanteco we first employed and who came to be highly dependent on us. His is a very special case. His mother is a Chamula who came to Zinacantan Center to weave for a Zinacanteco family and later married a Zinacanteco man. The father abandoned the mother, hence our informant was brought up without the father's guidance and did not learn the proper techniques and usual corn-farming skills. He probably would have drifted away from the traditional way of life, even had we not appeared—in fact, he was working as a puppeteer for INI when we first hired him. He is the only one who is still really dependent on members of the project for economic support to get through his cargos and support his wife and five children, because his corn-farming efforts are always failures and he does not have steady employment elsewhere. He also suffers from cirrhosis of the liver from excessive drinking that usually begins in connection with his ceremonial duties and is then prolonged by his psychological problems. Fortunately, his wife and children seem to maintain a warm family relationship with him, despite all, and his elder sons will shortly be able to handle the corn-farming.

On another level, our publications have had some effects on the communities, although they are difficult to specify. We have made it a practice to give copies of our publications (especially those that appear in Spanish and/or have many photographs) to our Indian friends. They spend hours pouring over the photographs and read selectively in the texts. Some of the books are proudly kept in boxes on household altars and brought out to show visitors. I suppose there is some small Hawthorn effect in this, insofar as it makes the Indians aware that they and their culture are important enough to be studied and written about. Perhaps somewhat more important are effects that stem from the reading of our books by government officials. We know that the governor of Chiapas and the president of the Republic have copies of my monograph on Zinacantan.

When I gave a copy to the governor, he promptly gave it to the president and wrote me for another copy. The president has probably looked at the photographs, but I do not know whether he has read the monograph. The governor, a well-educated neuro-surgeon, we know does read our books and tries to learn from them. Whether any particular item of government policy toward the Indians has been altered by what he has read, except the governor's insistence that government publications using Tzotzil follow the orthography we use, is not clear to me, except for one major development. This was the establishment of a government radio station in San Cristóbal which broadcasts in Tzotzil. This station might eventually have been established, but I am certain that it was put into operation years earlier than it might have been as a consequence of the governor's reading and acting upon one of the predictions in the final chapter of my monograph.

ACKNOWLEDGMENTS

This paper has benefited from comments and suggestions by Suzanne Abel, John B. Haviland, Robert M. Laughlin, and the members of the 67th Burg Wartenstein Symposium.

BIBLIOGRAPHY[1]

Blaffer, Sarah C.
　*1972　*The black-man of Zinacantan: A Central American legend.* Austin: Univ. of Texas Press.
Brazelton, T. Berry, John S. Robey, and George A. Collier
　*1969　Infant development in the Zinacanteco Indians of Southern Mexico. *Pediatrics 44*(2):274–293.
Bricker, Victoria R.
　*1973　*Ritual humor in Highland Chiapas.* Austin: Univ. of Texas Press.
Bunzel, Ruth
　1940　The role of alcoholism in two Central American cultures. *Psychiatry 3*:361–387.
Cámara Barbachano, Fernando
　1952　Organización religiosa y política de Tenejapa. *Anales del instituto nacional de antropología e história 4*:263–277.
Cancian, Francesca M.
　*1975　*What are norms? A study of belief and action in a Maya Community.* Cambridge: Cambridge Univ. Press.
Cancian, Frank
　*1965　*Economics and prestige in a Maya community: A study of the religious cargo system in Zinacantan, Chiapas, Mexico.* Stanford: Stanford Univ. Press.
　*1972　*Change and uncertainty in a peasant economy: The Maya corn farmers of Zinacantan.* Stanford: Stanford Univ. Press.

---

[1] Publications of the Harvard Chiapas Project are marked with an asterisk.

*1974   *Another place: Photographs of a Maya community.* San Francisco: Scrimshaw Press.

Colby, B. N.
*1966   *Ethnic relations in the Chiapas highlands.* Santa Fe: Museum of New Mexico Press.

Collier, George A.
*1975   *Fields of the Tzotzil: The ecological bases of tradition in Highland Chiapas.* Austin: Univ. of Texas Press.

Collier, Jane F.
*1973   *Law and social change in Zinacantan.* Stanford: Stanford Univ. Press.

Dozier, Edward P.
1955   Forced and permissive acculturation. *American Indian* 7:38–44.

Eggan, Fred
1954   Social anthropology and the method of controlled comparison. *American Anthropologist* 56:743–763.

Gossen, Gary H.
*1974a A Chamula calendar board from Chiapas, Mexico. In *Meso–American archaeology: New approaches,* edited by Hammond, Norman. Pp. 217–254. Austin: Univ. of Texas Press.
*1974b *Chamulas in the world of the sun: Time and space in a Maya oral tradition.* Cambridge, Massachusetts: Harvard Univ. Press.

Guiteras-Holmes, Calixta
1961   *Perils of the soul: The world view of a Tzotzil Indian.* Glencoe, Illinois: Free Press.

Haviland, John B.
*1977   *Gossip, Reputation, and Knowledge in Zinacantan.* Chicago: Univ. of Chicago Press.

Krebs, Stephanie L.
*1967   *Shunka's story: A woman's life in Zinacantan.* (20 min., 16-mm color film).

Laughlin, Robert M.
*1975   *The great Tzotzil dictionary of San Lorenzo Zinacantán.* Smithsonian contributions to anthropology, No. 19. Washington, D.C.: Smithsonian Institution Press.

Pozas, Ricardo
1959   Chamula, un pueblo indio de los altos de Chiapas. *Memorias del instituto nacional indigenista,* Mexico, No. 8.

Shweder, Richard A.
*1972   Aspects of cognition in Zinacanteco shamans: Experimental results. In *Reader in comparative religion: An anthropological approach,* edited by Lessa, W. A. and Vogt, E. Z. Pp. 407–412. New York: Harper and Row.

Tax, Sol
1943   *Notas sobre Zinacantan, Chiapas.* University of Chicago Library, Microfilm Collection of Manuscripts on Middle American Cultural Anthropology, No. 20.
1944   Information about the municipio of Zinacantan, Chiapas. *Revista Mexicana de estudios antropológicos* 6:181–195.

Villa Rojas, Alfonso
1947   Kinship and nagualism in a Tzeltal community, Southeastern Mexico. *American Anthropologist* 49:578–588.

Vogt, Evon Z.
1955   *Modern homesteaders: The life of a twentieth-century frontier community.* Cambridge, Massachusetts: Belknap Press of Harvard Univ. Press.
1957   The acculturation of the American Indians. *Annals of American Academy of Political and Social Science,* May. Pp. 137–146.

*1961   Some aspects of Zinacantan settlement patterns and ceremonial organization. *Estudios de cultura Maya, Universidad Nacional Autónoma de México 1*:131–146.

*1964a   Ancient Maya and contemporary Tzotzil cosmology: A comment on some methodological problems. *American Antiquity 30*:192–195.

*1964b   Ancient Maya concepts in contemporary Zinacantan religion. *VIᵉ Congrès International des Sciences Anthropologiques et Ethnologiques*, Paris, Vol. 2. Pp. 497–502.

*1964c   The genetic model and Maya cultural development. In *Desarrollo Cultural de los Mayas*, edited by Vogt, E. Z. and Ruz L., Alberto. Pp. 9–48. Mexico City: Universidad Nacional Autómona de México.

*1964d   Some implications of Zinacantan social structure for the study of the ancient Maya. *Actas y Memorias del XXXV Congreso Internacional de Americanistas*, México, Vol. 1. Pp. 307–319.

*1965   Structural and conceptual replication in Zinacantan culture. *American Anthropologist 67*:342–353.

*1966   (ed.) Los Zinacantecos: Un pueblo Tzotzil de los altos de Chiapas. *Instituto Nacional Indigenista, Colección de Antropología Social*, Vol. 7. Mexico City.

*1967   Tendencias de cambio en las tierras altas de Chiapas. *América Indígena 27*:199–222.

*1968   Recurrent and directional processes in Zinacantan. *Actas y Memorias del XXXVII Congreso Internacional de Americanistas*, Buenos Aires, Vol. 1. Pp. 441–447.

*1969   *Zinacantan: A Maya community in the highlands of Chiapas*. Cambridge, Massachusetts: Belknap Press of Harvard Univ. Press.

*1970a   Human souls and animal spirits in Zinacantan. In *Echanges et Communications: Mélanges offerts à Claude Lévi-Strauss à l'occasion de son 60ème anniversaire*. Compositors Jean Pouillon and Pierre Maranda. Pp. 1148–1167. The Hague: Mouton.

*1970b   *The Zinacantecos of Mexico: A modern Maya way of life*. New York: Holt, Rinehart and Winston.

*1973   *Los Zinacantecos: Un grupo Maya en el siglo XX*. Mexico City: SepSetentas 69.

*1974   (ed.) *Aerial photography in anthropological field research*. Cambridge, Massachusetts: Harvard Univ. Press.

*1976   *Tortillas for the gods: A symbolic analysis of Zinacanteco rituals*. Cambridge, Massachusetts: Harvard Univ. Press.

*1978   *Bibliography of the Harvard Chiapas Project*. Peabody Museum, Harvard Univ.

Vogt, Evon Z., and Ethel M. Albert, eds.

1966   *People of Rimrock: A study of values in five cultures*. Cambridge, Massachusetts: Harvard Univ. Press.

Vogt, Evon Z., and Alberto Ruz L., eds.

1964   *Desarrollo cultural de los Mayas*. Mexico City: Seminario de Cultura Maya, Universidad Nacional Autónoma de México. 2nd edition, 1971.

Vogt, Evon Z., and Catherine C. Vogt

*1970   Lévi-Strauss among the Maya. *Man 5*:379–392.

Wilson, Carter

*1966   *Crazy February*. Philadelphia: J. B. Lippincott.

*1972   *A green tree and a dry tree*. New York: Macmillan.

Wolf, Eric

1955   Types of Latin American peasantry. *American Anthropologist 57*:452–471.

14

Hunter–Gatherers in Process:
The Kalahari Research Project,
1963–1976[1]

Richard B. Lee

INTRODUCTION

Since 1963 a group of investigators has been studying the !Kung San (Bushmen), a hunting and gathering people in northwestern Botswana. The overall goal of the study, directed by Irven DeVore and me, has been to develop as complete a picture as possible of the hunting and gathering way of life, an adaptation that was, until 10,000 years ago, a human universal.

Our interest in the San was sparked in 1962 at the University of California (Berkeley) by Sherwood Washburn and J. Desmond Clark. Washburn argued that the study of living hunting and gathering peoples might throw light on the evolution of human behavior and ecology; Clark believed that the study of campsite behavior would be an aid in the interpretation of prehistoric living sites. In the early 1960s, the anthropological world was excited by the new data pouring in from field

[1] The financial support of the following is gratefully acknowledged: the National Science Foundation (U.S.), the National Institute of Mental Health (U.S.), the Wenner–Gren Foundation for Anthropological Research, and the Canada Council.

303

Long-Term Field Research
in Social Anthropology

studies on nonhuman primates and from the Leakeys' discoveries of ancient living floors associated with fossil man. The ethnographic study of a contemporary hunter–gatherer group seemed to be the next logical step.

Irven DeVore and I chose to work in Africa rather than in Australia because we wanted to be close to the actual faunal and floral environment occupied by early man. After 2 months of survey in Botswana in mid-1963, we decided to concentrate on an isolated region in northwestern Ngamiland that we named the Dobe Area after the water hole where I first camped in October 1963.

When DeVore and I began planning fieldwork with the San, a 13-year commitment of time and energy was not anticipated. DeVore was seeking to expand his interest from the ecology and behavior of nonhuman primates to the ecology and behavior of a human group. A graduate student, I was looking for a dissertation project in which to pursue my interests in human ecology, economic systems, and social evolution.

At first our project was a two-person operation. Later it expanded not only in time, but also in personnel. While continuing to do our own work, DeVore and I supported the work of students and specialists in a range of related fields: medicine, demography, psychology, ethology, archaeology, and folklore.

In all, some 14 investigators associated with the project have carried out major studies of the San (see Appendix at the end of the chapter). Although the scope of our studies has been considerable, four major groups of research problems can be distinguished: ecology and social change, population and health, child development, and the cognitive world.

Each of these studies has contributed in its way to a dozen or more specialties in anthropology and related fields. What these diverse projects have in common is a shared theoretical orientation that can be broadly defined as ecological, ethological, and evolutionary. All of the project workers have sought to relate their data to the basic adaptive strategies of the hunting and gathering way of life. The full range of studies has been brought together in Lee and DeVore, 1976.

A HISTORY OF SAN STUDIES

The San, called Basarwa locally and formerly known widely as the Bushmen, represent the oldest cultural stratum surviving among the peoples of Botswana and Southern Africa. For a people of such importance to science, surprisingly little has been known about the San. Although some medical research was carried out among the Kalahari San in the 1930s (e.g., Dart 1937), serious ethnographic fieldwork did not get underway until 1951! In that year, Laurence and Lorna Marshall began their work among the Nyae Nyae !Kung of South West Africa. Since then, the Marshall family expeditions have produced a distinguished series of publications, films and books (Marshall 1960, 1976).

Later long-term research was initiated among the /Gwi and //Gana peoples of the Central Kalahari Desert by George Silberbauer (Silberbauer 1965; Silberbauer and Kuper 1966), and by H. J. Heinz among the !Xo peoples of southern Botswana (Heinz 1966). Medical, ecological and physiological research has been carried out by Phillip Tobias, C. H. Wyndham, and the other members of the Kalahari Research Committee of the University of the Witwatersrand in Johannesburg (Tobias 1964). Important linguistic work has been carried out by Westphal (1963) and Traill (1973).

In 1967, a Japanese expedition came out to do San fieldwork in Botswana. Jiro Tanaka studied the /Gwi and //Gana on two field trips, the second one under the auspices of the Harvard Kalahari Research Group (Tanaka 1969, 1976). Mathias Guenther from the University of Toronto studied a mission station on the Ghanzi Farms in 1968–1970, and was among the first to work with San in highly acculturated situations (1976).

The Kalahari Research Project, Stage One: Lee and Devore, 1963–1967

Our own work has centered on the Dobe area, a line of water holes in the northwest corner of Botswana straddling the Namibian border. Within its area of about 10,000 km² live some 450 !Kung residents augmented by an equal number of seasonal and occasional visitors. There are eight water holes in the !Kangwa Valley, and south of the Aha Hills one large water hole at /Xai /Xai. The !Kung share these water holes with several hundred Herero and Tswana cattle people and their livestock.

After our initial contact with the Dobe !Kung in October 1963, I spent 15 months and DeVore 2 months living in the area in 1963–1964. In line with our original research interests, we focused heavily on ecology— mainly hunting and gathering techniques, land use, and group structure. The results were summarized in my doctoral dissertation (1965) and in several papers (Lee 1968a, b, 1969).

This first field study yielded new data on hunters and gatherers that seemed to cast doubt on some of the then current views of the hunting and gathering way of life. At the suggestion of Sol Tax, we organized the symposium on "Man the Hunter," held in Chicago in April 1966. The conference brought together students of hunter–gatherers from all over the world and helped to stimulate new research directions (Lee and DeVore 1968).

Two practical consequences emerged from the first field study and from the Symposium on "Man the Hunter." First, it became clear that before studies of hunter–gatherers could be of real usefulness to students of human evolution, a great deal more had to be known about the ethnography, adaptations, and acculturation status of contemporary peoples. Second, it became clear that the range of specialized information required was too broad for any single investigator to collect.

These considerations led to the planning of the second field study. The central ethnographic and ecological interests of DeVore and myself were continued, but the research design was expanded to include specialists in demography, child development, archaeology, population genetics, medicine, and nutrition.

Stage Two: Lee, DeVore, Howell, Draper, Harpending, Yellen, the Doctors, and Katz, 1967–1969

In 1967, DeVore and I returned to the Dobe area to continue the work. In late 1967, Nancy Howell began research on San demography; her study later grew to include reproductive histories of virtually all the adult women of the Dobe area (Howell 1976a). Howell also studied the networks of kinship and acquaintance that held together the widely dispersed San population of Dobe and adjacent areas.

In early 1968, Patricia Draper, Henry Harpending, and John Yellen arrived at Dobe. Draper did an 18-month study of child rearing and subsistence of both nomadic and settled !Kung (1975). Harpending's work in genetic demography took him to camps all over northwestern Botswana where he interviewed and collected blood samples from nearly 2000 San. Yellen, in collaboration with DeVore, did a two-part study of hunting behavior and settlement patterns. They followed hunters on actual hunts and carefully traced the butchering and distribution of the meat and the final scattering of the bone remains. They also plotted the floor plans of recently occupied campsites (Yellen 1976). Yellen also conducted excavations of Stone Age sites in the area.

In 1967–1968, a medical team composed of Doctors Stewart Truswell and John Hansen made two trips to Dobe to examine !Kung adults and children. Truswell and Dr. B. M. Kennelly made a third trip in 1969 to work on heart disease. Medical research was also carried out by Doctors Trefor Jenkins and Jack Metz (Truswell and Hansen 1976). In September 1968, Richard Katz, a psychologist, came out for several months to study the !Kung healing dance in collaboration with me (Katz 1976).

Stage Three: Konner, Shostak, Tanaka, and Biesele, 1969–1972

In mid-1969, Mel Konner and Marjorie Shostak joined Harpending, Draper, and Yellen at Dobe, Konner to work on the ethology of early infant development (Konner 1976). Later, he was joined by Nicholas Blurton Jones from the Institute of Child Study, University of London. Together they worked on several projects including the !Kungs' knowledge of animal behavior (Blurton Jones and Konner 1976). Shostak made studies of beadwork and musical instruments and collected in-depth life history materials from eight San women (1976).

Jiro Tanaka of Kyoto University, who had worked with the /Gwi in 1967–1968, returned in 1971 to the Central Kalahari Reserve to continue his ecological studies in parallel with my own ecological work in the Dobe area, 400 km to the north (1976).

In late 1970, Megan Biesele, a folklorist and anthropologist, arrived in the Dobe area to study oral literature, myth, and ritual of the !Kung. Most of her work was done at Kauri, about 150 km southeast of Dobe (1976). In addition to her ethnographic work, Biesele focused on the problems of social and economic change among the San. Her findings showed that drastic changes were in the offing for the remaining San groups.

Stage Four: The AAA Symposium on Bushmen Studies and the Founding of the Kalahari Peoples' Fund, 1971 to the Present

With the return of most of the fieldworkers by 1971, the time seemed ripe for a major presentation of our results. DeVore and I organized the "Symposium on Bushmen Studies" that was held at the annual meetings of the American Anthropological Association in New York in November, 1971. An audience of over 400 people heard papers by Howell, Harpending, Yellen, and DeVore in the morning, and Katz, Konner, Draper, Guenther, and me in the afternoon. An important contribution was made by the discussants who offered constructive criticism of the papers and helped to put our data into perspective. These included Milton Freeman, Jean MacCluer, and Charles Nelson on the demographic and ecological papers; June Helm and Michael Harner on the sociological papers; and Margaret Bacon and Nicholas Blurton Jones on the papers on child development. Sherwood Washburn made some general remarks and also wrote the foreword for the book that came out of the symposium (Lee and DeVore 1976).

A sense of the accelerating pace of change emerged clearly at this symposium. As concerned anthropologists, we began to explore how our work could be of maximum benefit to the San. These discussions resulted

in the formation of the Kalahari Peoples' Fund in January 1973. The goals
and activities of the Fund are discussed in the concluding section.

THE LOGISTICS OF TEAM RESEARCH IN THE FIELD

Coordinating the work of a dozen investigators over more than a decade
has proved to be a formidable task. During most of the period, there were
from one to three researchers in the Dobe area at any one time, although
in peak periods there were as many as eight. The abundance of investigators created logistical problems, although we would like to think that
the returns in valuable data across a wide range of fields more than offset
the drawbacks of too many researchers. Also, the continuing infusion of
new research people helped develop an *ésprit de corps,* kept the "senior"
researchers on their toes, and yielded practical benefits for language
learning, orientation in the field for newcomers, and continuity of observation.

What follows is a critical discussion of our practice as fieldworkers
pointing out some of the mistakes we made, and some of the things we did
right as well. After 1967, the camp at Dobe water hole became a base
camp for the entire research project, from which researchers could branch
out on lightly equipped extended visits to remote water holes and rainy
season camps. Dispersing the investigators at widely separated points was
a necessary strategy; however, it was marred by the fact that the Dobe
San people themselves were continuously part of the study population.
The Dobe residents enjoyed unprecedented popularity (and later resentment) among other San because of our presence at their water hole. It
seems clear in hindsight that our research group exerted a major accul-
turative impact on the Dobe camps, though one that can be identified and
remedied in the analysis. In hindsight, it would have been better to
situate the base camp on neutral ground or at the district headquarters to
minimize such effects.

Team research also brought with it problems of relations between
researchers themselves. The recruitment of new fieldworkers was in part
based on gaps in our data that DeVore and I felt had to be filled. Certain
areas were given high priority, such as demography, archaeology, and
child-rearing practices. In part recruitment was a process of self-selection
by the researchers themselves; students who demonstrated a keen interest in the San and a strong motivation to brave the rigors of desert life
found a place in the project. Physical fitness was a characteristic common
to all the fieldworkers. When the project reached its present size in 1972,
we consciously scaled it down by not actively continuing to recruit new

researchers. This was partly to give the !Kung a rest, but mainly to allow us time to assimilate and publish what we had found out.

Each researcher defined for himself a topical niche that had a core of subject matter that became that person's responsibility. In addition, each research worker identified several topics which touched on the interests of others involved in the project. In this way the interconnections between studies were complementary rather than duplicative or competitive. The advantage (and challenge) of collaborative research of this kind is the necessity to submit one's findings to the critical evaluation of one's colleagues within the project. The result has been that a number of individual findings have failed to be confirmed by other workers, while those results that have been corroborated by five or six observers have gained correspondingly in strength.

Another problem area concerned language learning and use. The !Kung language is unwritten and not extensively described. In 1963, no !Kung spoke English. In order to communicate with the !Kung, I had to learn in the field Setswana, the language of the dominant Botswana people. Speaking in Setswana with the aid of an interpreter, I was able to elicit vocabulary in !Kung until late 1964, when I struck out on my own. Back in Cambridge, Massachusetts, I taught the rudiments of !Kung to the next wave of fieldworkers. Since then, returning fieldworkers have taught the language to those embarking for the Kalahari. Most of the later researchers started work directly in !Kung and bypassed interpreters entirely.

When it became clear that many fieldworkers would be researching and writing about the Dobe area !Kung, standardization of format became a high priority. A standard orthography and coded lists of place names and personal names have been used by all members of the research group since 1973. Perhaps of greater significance to long-term field research is the problem of identification of individuals. Nearly 1000 !Kung live in or visit the Dobe area. Because of the peculiar system of inheritance of personal names, dozens of people may share the same given name; since there are no surnames, this creates real dangers of misidentification. If one meets a man named "≠toma," for example, how can it be determined which of the 25 "≠toma's" he is or whether he is the same "≠toma" studied by Lee 10 years before?

We solved the problem by assigning each person a master number from 1 to 1000. In 1964, some 460 residents were enumerated. Thereafter new !Kung entering the population through birth or migration were assigned a number. A master file containing a short biography, a genealogy, and a photo of every individual became the core data base of the Dobe area research. It was kept up to date from 1963 to 1973 and has been periodically updated since then; it is the standard work referred to by all the researchers. This core data base is especially useful for demographic and other quantitative analyses and allows for computer cross-tabulations among a wide range of variables. It helps to maintain the clarity of the boundaries of the study population and gives the research group a handle on accounting for discrepancies if one set of observations is at odds with another. This factor was of crucial importance in the study of social process, since the Dobe area population was undergoing microevolutionary changes throughout the period 1963–1973. Identifying these processes and weighing their differential impact on the various geographic divisions of the population became crucial to the understanding of the !Kung hunting and gathering way of life and its transformations.

HOW THE DOBE AREA CHANGED

In 1963, the San of the Dobe area were the most isolated and traditional hunter–gatherers we could find in northern Botswana. Our choice of Dobe as a study site did not spring from archaism or romanticism; rather to achieve our goal of preserving a record of the hunting and gathering way of life, it was necessary to find the most unacculturated group.

The Dobe area is cut off from the rest of what was then the Bechuanaland Protectorate by a 100 km stretch of waterless country that takes two or three days to cross on foot or by donkey. When I first arrived at Dobe in October 1963, the area had no stores or schools and only intermittent contact with the outside world. A government truck would come out about once a month, but the main concern of its crew was the Bantu-speaking cattle people and not the San themselves. At that time, the San planted no crops and kept no domesticated animals except for the dog. The majority of the people lived mainly by hunting and gathering. The pastoralists lived at eight of the nine water holes, but beyond these areas stretched a vast uncharted, unfenced hinterland 10,000 km² used almost exclusively by hunting and gathering groups of San.

For the foraging peoples, group structure was intact, traditional kinship patterns were very strong and the people moved freely back and forth across the unfenced boundary between Bechuanaland and South West Africa. In 1960–1961, a government settlement station had been set up by the South Africans at Chum!kwe, 50 km west of the Dobe area, but this had barely begun to affect the lives of the Bechuanaland !Kung. Dobe appeared to be an ideal area to study the hunting and gathering way of life.

As our fieldwork continued, a more realistic picture of the "pristine" nature of the Dobe area began to emerge. Most of the men of the Dobe area at some point in their lives had had some experience herding the Bantu cattle and, at any one time, about 20% of the young men were working with cattle. Some men had even owned cattle or goats in the past. Similarly, the !Kung were not total strangers to agriculture. Many had learned the techniques by assisting their Bantu neighbors in planting and, in years of good rainfall, some had planted and harvested small plots themselves. However, because of the extreme unreliability of the rainfall, none of the San had succeeded in establishing himself on an agricultural basis. Hunting and gathering continued to be by far the most reliable and therefore dominant means of subsistence.

We sensed that the !Kung were on the threshold of great changes, but we could not have anticipated how rapidly these changes would come or what their consequences would be. In 1964, after the first census of the area, the !Kung were canvassed in a voter registration drive, this being one of their first direct contacts with the central government of the country. In 1965, the Dobe area San voted in the first election and became, along with their fellow countrymen, citizens of the independent Republic of Botswana in 1966. In 1965, the previously unguarded international border that runs through the Dobe area was fenced and began to be patrolled regularly by the South African occupation forces in Namibia (South West Africa). This fencing limited access to the western hunting areas of the Dobe area and in the mid-1960s, a number of Dobe area families decided to emigrate permanently to Chum!kwe where the South Africans were providing jobs and rations.

In 1967, a trading store was built at !Kangwa in the heart of the Dobe area and, for the first time, store-bought food and dry goods were available for cash. The San women of !Kangwa immediately set up a thriving business in home-brew beer using brown sugar from the store as the main ingredient. The arrival of the store and the increase in government services after 1966 reduced the isolation of the Dobe area. In 1967–1968, an average of one truck a week arrived at !Kangwa from the outside world. This improvement in transportation made it much easier for Dobe area San to travel out; in the years 1964–1968, about 20 young men went to work in the gold mines of the Witwatersrand in South Africa.

A period of high rainfall was 1967–1970 and the San took this opportunity to plant and harvest extensive crops of maize, sorghum and melons. However, when the rainfall failed in 1972–1973, they again fell back on hunting and gathering. The 1960s also saw a sharp increase in livestock holdings. Whether purchased with cash from mine wages or obtained in payment for herding services, these goats, cattle, donkeys, and horses came into the San economy by the dozens. By 1973, at least 20 families (particularly at !Goshe water hole) were deriving more of their subsistence from pastoralism than from hunting and gathering.

Two further developments occurred in the early 1970s. In 1973, a primary school opened at !Kangwa offering Standards I–IV. This was an incentive to the cash economy-oriented !Kung to stay in Botswana rather than emigrate to Chum!kwe to put their children into school. Counteracting this incentive was the campaign on the South African side of the border to organize some !Kung into paramilitary units of trackers in South Africa's counter-insurgency warfare against the African liberation forces. The implications of these developments are discussed in the concluding section.

THE IMPLICATIONS OF LONG-TERM FIELDWORK

The changes we observed in the Dobe area provide the background to what we have learned by doing long-term fieldwork. Observing the San over a 13-year period forcibly impressed upon us that a sense of history is essential to an understanding of social structure. Hunter–gatherer societies are strongly influenced by seasonal and annual variation in climate and resources. Thirteen years of work brought home to us the annual range of variation in ecological conditions. There is no such thing as a typical year for hunter–gatherers. In the case of the !Kung the annual cycle in group structure looks very different in a wet year from a dry year, and the key to their adaptation is the flexibility to adapt to a *long run* of conditions (Lee 1972a).

In addition to these cyclical ecological changes are the long-term acculturation trends in the direction of the way of life of their pastoral and farming neighbors. Although the Dobe area !Kung have been in intermittent contact with the Tswana since the 1880s, administrative control was only established in 1948. Since then the !Kung have been moving in fits and starts towards the adoption of herding and farming. The pace of this change, however, is strongly affected by the climatic cycles mentioned above. Two examples will serve to illustrate the articulation of these two kinds of trends—cyclical and secular. Secular here is used in the sense of unidirectional and irreversible.

Rainfall and the Annual Cycle in Group Structure

During the first period of my fieldwork (October 1963–December 1964), all the San of the Dobe area were full-time hunter–gatherers. When the rains came (November–March), they dispersed in small groups to the seasonal water holes. When these dried out (April–May), they converged into larger groups to winter at the nine permanent water holes of the area (June–September). When the rains came the following year, the pattern of dispersion was repeated. This was the pattern I described in my 1965 dissertation.

Returning to the Dobe water hole in August 1967 with this pattern fixed in my mind, I expected to find a large concentration of San wintering there. I was surprised to find Dobe almost deserted! Most of the Dobe people were to be found wintering at !Gausha, a "summer" water hole 16 km to the north of Dobe. To make matters even more confusing, when the rains came, the people moved *back* to the permanent water holes, exactly the reverse of the pattern I had observed in 1963–1964.

How were we to account for this apparent reversal in the annual cycle of group movement? A clue to the answer appeared when, taking advantage of the good rains of 1967–1968, a number of people began planting small gardens near the permanent water holes. Those who did not plant dispersed out to the summer water sources. As the season progressed, those whose crops failed also moved out to these summer water sources, while the successful farmers confined themselves to short 2–5-day visits to the summer areas returning frequently to tend their fields. In autumn 1968 (April–May), several families harvested crops. These were rapidly consumed by kinfolk and neighbors, and, by mid-June, the farming families, along with a number of others, had moved out to the numerous water points that held water well into the winter months.

Comparing 1967–1968 to 1963–1964, two kinds of changes were in evidence. First was the *cycle* of rainfall. The dry years (1960–1964) had been marked by full-time hunting and gathering and a fairly strict adherence to the pattern of winter concentration and summer dispersion. With a run of good rainfall years beginning in 1965, the seasonal water points persisted into the winter months. This extra water gave the San the *choice* of wintering at permanent *or* temporary water holes, the conditions I observed in 1967–1968. During 1963–1964 fieldwork, this choice was not available.

The second kind of change is that of the long-term *trend* towards farming and herding. This also influenced the various choices that people made during the 1967–1968 rainy season. The nonplanters adhered more or less closely to the winter concentration–summer dispersion pattern, while the planters were mainly responsible for the apparent reversal of this pattern. This new insight, plus a very detailed reconstruction of the patterns of group movement during the 1920s (before the arrival of the Bantu-speaking colonists), enabled me to confirm that the pattern observed in 1963–1964 possessed a substantial historical validity. This revised model of !Kung group movement under traditional hunting and gathering conditions was presented in my paper "!Kung Spatial Organization: An Ecological and Historical Perspective" (1972a).

Population Growth and Sedentarization

A second example of the importance of long-term fieldwork concerns the demographic changes that have taken place in the Dobe area since 1963. Starting with July 1963, our research project has maintained a registry of all Dobe area births and deaths. When workers are in the field, birth dates are recorded by direct observation: these dates are usually accurate to ± 5 days. For periods when there has been no observer in the field, birth dates have been reconstructed through interviews. These dates are usually accurate to ± 30 days. In all, we have followed the reproductive lives of 256 adult women over the 10-year period.

During the 1960s, a process of sedentarization was going on in the Dobe area, but this had a markedly differential effect on groups at different water holes. At one eastern water hole (!Goshe), the San had built a village of mud huts in the early 1960s, which they occupied throughout the study period. They continued to hunt and gather on short trips but an increasing proportion of their subsistence came from cows' milk and cultivated grains. At the other extreme of mobility were the /Du/da subpopulation 60 km south of the Dobe area who continued to move camp five or six times a year in a classic foraging pattern. The remainder of the population exhibited patterns intermediate between these two poles.

These varied adaptations offered a natural laboratory for testing hypotheses about the social, economic, and demographic effects of sedentarization. My main hunch concerned the role of sedentarization in triggering population growth. Could the mere fact of settling down increase the birth rate even in the absence of an expansion of the food supply? If so, what form would it take and what would be the possible mechanisms involved?

In a paper written in 1970, based on 1963–1969 data (Lee 1972b), I pointed out that long birth spacing of 3 or 4 years was essential to the subsistence economy of the !Kung San. Since women were highly mobile (1500 km of travel per year) and since it was necessary to carry the infants and toddlers for much of the first 4 years of life, long birth spacing was necessary to maintain a mobile mother's burden at a tolerable level. A woman with 4-year birth spacing would have only one child to carry at a time, while a woman with 2-year birth spacing would have twice the burden to carry, placing her and her offspring at a distinct disadvantage in terms of survival. The model also predicted that even partial reduction of mobility would lessen the deleterious effects of short birth spacing and might lead to an increase in the birth rate. There seemed to be some indication that at !Goshe, the easternmost water hole, such a process was already under way.

I returned to the Dobe area in 1973 to complete the full 10-year record of births and deaths and to provide data for testing the model of birth spacing and sedentarization. Data on 256 adult women, including virtually all of the resident women of reproductive age in the population, were recorded. Of these, 119 had had no pregnancies during the period 1 July 1963–30 June 1973, 43 had had only one birth, and for 2 other women data were incomplete. This left 92 women with two or more births and hence with one or more measurable birth intervals.

The average interval between successive live births for all 92 women (165 intervals) was 37.23 months. That means that over 3 years elapsed between births whether or not the first baby died. This figure varied from a low of 11 months in the case of a woman whose infant died in the first month of life and who conceived soon after, to a high of over 8 years. A 3-year interval is very high for a population in which no forms of contraception are practiced.

In order to eliminate the effects of infant mortality, I abstracted from the data those birth intervals in which the first child survived to the birth of the second. I further divided the population into two groups: more nomadic women and more sedentary women. Finally I divided the 10-year run of data into two 5-year periods. This last division yielded three temporally related sets of data:

1. Intervals falling within the period 1 July 1963–30 June 1968
2. Intervals falling within the period 1 July 1968–30 June 1973
3. Intervals straddling the mid-1968 boundary

By comparing Period 1 with Period 2, I could discern possible secular trends through the 10-year period.

The results are set out in Table 14.1. The mean birth interval for nomadic women was 44.11 months and for sedentary women 36.17 months, indicating that throughout the period sedentary women tended to reconceive about 8 months earlier than nomadic women. This 8-month difference would significantly increase both the birth rate and completed family size for the sedentary women.

The difference between the more nomadic and the more sedentary women is even more striking when we consider the time dimension. The entire population was undergoing sedentarization during the period 1963–1973; this is reflected in the fact that the birth interval dropped from

TABLE 14.1

Intervals in Months between Successive Live Births to !Kung Women during the Period 1963–1973

	Mean length of birth interval in months (*n*)			
	1963–1968	1968–1973	1963–1973	Mean of all three periods
More nomadic women	42.27 (11)	36.42 (12)	47.63 (32)	44.11 (55)
More sedentary women	38.35 (17)	29.82 (22)	40.12 (26)	36.17 (65)
All women	39.89 (28)	32.15 (34)	44.26 (58)	39.81 (120)

39.89 months in Period 1 to 32.15 months in Period 2. This shortening of the birth interval was particularly marked for the more sedentary women, with a drop of 8.53 months, but the process is apparent in the more nomadic women as well, who exhibited a decrease of 5.85 months.

The increase in fertility was most marked at the most settled village— !Goshe—where each of four young women had had two successive live births spaced 22, 23, 21, and 20 months apart respectively in the period 1968–1973. Several women at !Goshe and other water holes asked me for birth control assistance (a pill to make them stop having babies)! This request indicated that even for sedentary women the rapid succession of births was not an unmixed blessing.

The probable mechanism for this decreased birth spacing is not hard to find. The nomadic !Kung diet, though rich in nutrients, is deficient in suitable weaning foods, such as milk and porridge which are easily digested by infants and toddlers. As a result, though infants are introduced to solid foods by 6 months of age, mother's milk continues to be an important part of the child's diet into the third year of life. At !Goshe and other more settled !Kung villages there is a more plentiful supply of milk and cultivated grains. This availability of alternative food lessens the child's need for breast milk. The lowered level of lactation in turn may trigger the resumption of a woman's ovulation as early as 11 to 14 months after giving birth. The shortening of the birth interval may also be connected with the earlier restoring of critical fat levels in nursing mothers (Frisch and McArthur 1974; Howell 1976b).

I have discussed these results in some detail in order to make two points. First, the evidence strongly supports the hypothesis that sedentarization is associated with an increase in the birth rate and that this increase is expressed through a shortening of the interval between birth and reconception. Second, this important finding could only have been determined by *the continuing observation of a population over a period of years*. Periodic recensuses 5 or 10 years apart or restrospective reproductive histories can only imperfectly reflect the actual changes that take place.

LONG-TERM FIELDWORK AND THE FUTURE OF TRADITIONAL SOCIETIES

Up to 1973, the Dobe area !Kung had shown extraordinary resilience, having survived as an independent hunting and gathering people long after most of the world's hunter–gatherers have been subjugated by and incorporated into more powerful societies. Yet we had no illusions about their future. Their lands were becoming increasingly fenced in, missions and schools were opening in their midst, and, most sinister of all, the South African military were recruiting the San as trackers in their border patrols against African liberation movements. There was also the danger that the Dobe !Kung and other San groups would be swallowed up and dispersed in rural and peri-urban slums in the cities and towns of Botswana and Namibia (Biesele and Lee 1974).

Throughout our years of fieldwork, the San have shown us great hospitality. In 1963, I was given the personal name /Tontah; I was adopted by a family and incorporated into the kinship system. Since then, every other research worker has also been named and adopted by someone, so that all of us feel a personal, as well as a professional, involvement with the San.

In January 1973, the Kalahari Research group met in Hancock, New Hampshire, to discuss the future of the San, including our own relationship to them. After much debate we agreed that our responsibility went beyond merely publishing the results of our studies in the appropriate journals. It also included working with the people in their struggle to determine their own futures. As a focus for our efforts in this direction we created a nonprofit foundation called the Kalahari Peoples' Fund (KPF) and assigned the royalties from a forthcoming book of ours to the Fund. To give the KPF more working capital, most of us turn over a portion of our royalties and fees from writing or film-making projects on the San. The Kalahari Peoples' Fund (P.O. Box 4973, Austin, Texas 78751) has initiated several projects relating to San development. In 1973, we presented a complete set of the published output of the Research Group (65 items at the time) to the Botswana cabinet minister responsible for Bushman affairs. Scholarships were provided for 22 !Kung children to enter the !Kangwa Primary School in January 1974. The Government of Botswana through the local District put up a matching grant. At the invitation of the Government in 1975, the KPF sent a full-time representative to work with the Office of Basarwa Development. This was Megan Biesele whose participation was made possible by grants from the Marshall family. During her year of liaison work, Biesele visited all the northern San communities to find out what kinds of development are socially and ecologically feasible. Biesele also assisted the San in applying to the government's land board to establish legal rights to parts of the lands they have traditionally occupied.

The KPF is also exploring the kinds of economic possibilities which are compatible with San survival as a cultural group. First is their transition to a settled village life based on horticulture and livestock. This is the dominant mode of subsistence for Botswana peasants. Ecologically, farming is unreliable except in the Okavango Swamps. Cattle raising, as practiced locally, has high initial returns but these will fall off after a generation due to a lowering of the water table and a decline in the quality of forage because of overgrazing.

The disadvantages of farming and herding have directed attention to a second alternative: the harvesting of mongongo nuts and other wild staples for subsistence and as a wild cash crop. The mongongo fruit and nut are excellent food sources, so abundant that part of each year's crop rots on the ground for want of being eaten (Lee 1973). The San are well set up to harvest large quantities of these nuts, eat what they need, and export the rest to the towns where they would provide a much needed source of protein. Mongongo forests are plentiful in northwestern and northeastern Botswana; in the center and south, the Tsin bean is an equally abundant food source. The regular marketing of these high quality wild foods might also be tied in with the marketing of traditional San crafts. Their bead and leather work is well known and brings high prices. The Canadian Eskimo artists' and craftsmen's Coops may provide a model for the San.

Because of the variety of settings in which the Botswana San are found, no single economic alternative will work in all cases. Probably a mix of foraging, farming, stock-raising, cash cropping (of wild foods) and craft work will be worked out that will suit the needs of each local community. As a result, in part, of KPF's initial groundwork, the Botswana Government has earmarked funds in each year's budget for Basarwa development projects, while the Basarwa Office now has five full- and part-time Basarwa Development Officers working throughout the country.

Although the Kalahari Peoples' Fund is only a few years old, there are already signs that the intervention of concerned outsiders has started to arrest the processes of proletarianization, dispersal, and militarization that we saw at work through the 1960s and early 1970s. Ultimately the future of the San is tied in with the future of all the peoples of Southern Africa. No one can predict what the outcome of the coming struggle there will be or what role the San will play. We will be happy to see the San enrich the future national life of Botswana as they have enriched the lives of those who worked with them.

Name/department/university	Topic	Dates
1. Megan Biesele Kalahari Peoples Fund, Austin, Texas	Folklore, music, applied social change	1970–1972 1975–1976
2. Nicholas Blurton Jones Child Study, London	Ethology, animal behavior	1971
3. Irven DeVore Anthropology, Harvard	Hunting behavior	1963, 1964 1967–1968
4. Patricia Draper Anthropology, New Mexico	Child rearing, sex roles	1968–1969 1975
5. John Hansen Child Health, Witwatersrand	Pediatrics	1967, 1968
6. Henry Harpending Anthropology, New Mexico	Genetic demography	1968–1969 1975
7. Nancy Howell Sociology, Toronto	Demography, networks	1967–1969
8. Richard Katz Psychology, Harvard	Ritual healing dance	1968
9. Melvin Konner Anthropology, Harvard	Ethology, infant behavior	1969–1971 1975
10. Richard Lee Anthropology. Toronto	Ecology, social organization, ritual	1963–1964 1967–1969 1973
11. Marjorie Shostak Radcliffe Institute	Life history, music, crafts	1969–1971 1975
12. Jiro Tanaka Primate Ecology, Kyoto	Ecology and social organization (/Gwi and //Gana)	1967–1968 1971–1972 1975
13. Stewart Truswell Nutrition, London	Medicine, nutrition, cardiology	1967, 1968 1969
14. John Yellen Anthropology, Smithsonian Institution	Archaeology, hunting settlement patterns	1968–1970 1975–1976

[2] In addition, observations have been carried out by the following: Sue Bucklin (1964–rock art), Mathias Guenther (1968–70–sociocultural change), Trefor Jenkins (1963, 1968, 1969–genetics), Brian Kennelly (1969–cardiology), Francis Van Noten (1964–settlement archaeology), Polly Weissner (1973–1975–exchange systems), Marjorie Whiting (1967–nutrition), Edwin Wilmsen (1973–1974, 1975–1976–ecology and archaeology), James Woodburn (1967–social anthropology).

BIBLIOGRAPHY

Biesele, M.
1976 Aspects of !Kung folklore. In *Kalahari hunter–gatherers: Studies of the !Kung and their neighbors,* edited by Lee, R. and DeVore, I. Pp. 302–324. Cambridge, Massachusetts: Harvard Univ. Press.

Biesele, M., and R. Lee
1974 Hunters, clients, and squatters: The Kalahari San today. Paper presented at the Symposium on the Future of Traditional Societies. Cambridge University, December.

Blurton Jones, N., and M. Konner
1976 !Kung knowledge of animal behavior. In *Kalahari hunter–gatherers: Studies of the !Kung and their neighbors,* edited by Lee, R. and DeVore, I., Pp. 325–348. Cambridge, Massachusetts: Harvard Univ. Press.

Dart, R.
1937 Some physical characteristics of the /auni-≠Khomani Bushmen. *Bantu Studies 11:*175–246.

Draper, P.
1975 !Kung Women: Contrasts in sexual egalitarianism in foraging and sedentary contexts. In *Toward an Anthropology of Women,* edited by Reiter, R. Pp. 77–109. New York: Monthly Review Press.

Frisch, R., and J. McArthur
1974 Menstrual cycles: Fatness as a determinant of minimum weight for height necessary for their maintenance or onset. *Science 185:*949–951.

Guenther, Mathias
1976 From hunters to squatters: Social and cultural change among the farm San of Ghanzi, Botswana. In *Kalahari hunter–gatherers: Studies of the !Kung and their neighbors,* edited by Lee, R. and Devore, I. Pp. 137–151. Cambridge, Massachusetts: Harvard Univ. Press.

Heinz, H. J.
1966 Social organization of the !Ko bushmen. Unpublished master's thesis. Univ. of South Africa, Pretoria.

Howell, N.
1976a The Population of the Dobe Area !Kung. In *Kalahari hunter–gatherers: Studies of the !Kung and their neighbors,* edited by Lee, R. and DeVore, I. Pp. 137–151. Cambridge, Massachusetts: Harvard Univ. Press.

1976b Toward a uniformitarian theory of human paleodemography. *Journal of Human Evolution* 5:25–40.

Katz, R.
1976 Education for transcendance: !Kia healing with the Kalahari !Kung. In *Kalahari hunter–gatherers: Studies of the !King and their neighbors,* edited by Lee, R. and DeVore, I. Pp. 281–301. Cambridge, Massachusetts: Harvard Univ. Press.

Konner, M.
1976 Maternal care, infant behavior, and development among the !Kung. In *Kalahari hunter–gatherers: Studies of the !Kung and their neighbors,* edited by Lee, R. and DeVore, I. Pp. 218–245. Cambridge, Massachusetts: Harvard Univ. Press.

Lee, R.
1965 Subsistence ecology of !Kung Bushmen. Ph.D. dissertation, Department of Anthropology, Univ. of California, Berkeley.

1968a The Sociology of !Kung Bushman trance performances. In *Trance and Possession States,* edited by Prince, R. Pp. 35–54. Montreal: R. M. Bucke Memorial Society.

1968b What hunters do for a living, or how to make out on scarce resources. In *Man the hunter,* edited by Lee, R. and DeVore, I. Pp. 30–48. Chicago: Aldine.

1969   !Kung Bushman subsistence: An input-output analysis. In *Environment and cultural behavior*, edited by Vayda, A. P. Pp. 47–79. New York: Natural History Press.

1972a   !Kung spatial organization: An ecological and historical perspective. *Human Ecology 1*:125–147. (Reprinted in Lee and DeVore 1976.)

1972b   Population growth and the beginnings of sedentary life among the !Kung Bushmen. In *Population growth: Anthropological implications*, edited by Spooner, B. Pp. 329–342. Cambridge, Massachusetts: MIT Press.

1973   Mongongo: The ethnography of a major wild food resource. *Ecology of food and nutrition 2*:307–321.

Lee, R., and I. DeVore, eds.

1968   *Man the hunter.* Chicago: Aldine.

1976   *Kalahari hunter–gatherers: Studies of the !Kung and their neighbors.* Cambridge, Massachusetts: Harvard Univ. Press.

Marshall, L.

1960   !Kung Bushman bands. *Africa 30*:325–355.

1976   *The !Kung of Nyae Nyae.* Cambridge, Massachusetts: Harvard Univ. Press.

Schapera, I.

1930   *The Khoisan peoples of South Africa: Bushmen and Hottentots.* London: Routledge and Kegan Paul.

Shostak, M.

1976   A !Kung woman's memories of childhood. In *Kalahari hunter–gatherers: Studies of the !Kung and their neighbors*, edited by Lee, R. and DeVore, I. Pp. 246–277. Cambridge, Massachusetts: Harvard Univ. Press.

Silberbauer, G.

1965   Bushman survey report. Bechuanaland Government, Gaborone.

Silberbauer, G., and A. Kuper

1966   Kalahari masters and bushman serfs: Some observations. *African Studies 25*:171–179.

Tanaka, J.

1969   The ecology and social structure of Central Kalahari bushmen. In *Kyoto African studies III*, edited by Umesao, T. Kyoto: Kyoto Univ. Press.

1976   Subsistence ecology of the central Kalahari San. In *Kalahari hunter–gatherers: Studies of the !Kung and their neighbors*, edited by Lee, R. and DeVore, I. Pp. 98–119. Cambridge, Massachusetts: Harvard Univ. Press.

Tobias, P.

1964   Bushman hunter–gatherers: A study in human ecology. In *Ecological studies in Southern Africa*, edited by Davis, D. H. S. The Hague: W. Junk.

Traill, A.

1973   The complete guide to the Koon. Mimeographed manuscript, Department of Linguistics, Univ. of the Witwatersrand, Johannesburg.

Truswell, A. S., and J. D. L. Hansen

1976   Medical research among the !Kung. In *Kalahari hunter–gatherers: Studies of the !Kung and their neighbors*, edited by Lee, R. and DeVore, I. Pp. 166–194. Cambridge, Massachusetts: Harvard Univ. Press.

Westphal, E. O. J.

1963   The linguistic prehistory of Southern Africa: Bush, Kwadi, Hottentot, and Bantu linguistic relationships. *Africa 33*:237–265.

Yellen, J.

1976   Settlement patterns of the !Kung: An archaeological perspective. In *Kalahari hunter–gatherers: Studies of the !Kung and their neighbors*, edited by Lee, R. and DeVore, I. Pp. 47–72. Cambridge, Massachusetts: Harvard Univ. Press.

Conclusion:
The Long-Term Study
in Perspective

*George M. Foster, Thayer Scudder, Elizabeth
Colson, Robert V. Kemper*

INTRODUCTION

In this concluding chapter, we return to the questions posed in the
Introduction and attempt a synthesis of the experience of those who
attended the Burg Wartenstein conference.

A long-term study is a rich, personal experience. Without exception,
the authors are enthusiastic about their research, at least most of the time;
without exception, they anticipate return visits and, in fact, at least half
returned to the field during the 12 months following the 1975 conference.
The principal question that must be asked about long-term research,
however, is not, "Is it personally gratifying?" Rather, one must ask,
"Does it produce results not so readily obtained, if at all, from more
traditional research? And are these results of such significance and importance as to justify the expenditure of money and professional time?"

The answer appears to be, not that long-term research can be justified,
but another question: How much and what kinds of long-term research
should appear in the total mix of anthropological investigation? Should
young anthropologists routinely be encouraged to think in terms of repeat
visits to their first research site? Should they take special pains to gather

*Long-Term Field Research
in Social Anthropology*

core data not necessarily central to their immediate research goals, in case return visits materialize? Or, should such planning be restricted to special situations that promise exceptional dividends in learning about change processes or other topics? Is it preferable for the anthropologist to range the world widely, or is it more productive to confine one's interest to one or two groups, to be intensively studied? There are no simple answers to such questions, but conference participants felt it possible to delineate many of the criteria that should be considered in making decisions. These criteria are discussed in the following pages under the headings of Theoretical Justifications; Research Design, Methodology, and Operations; and Ethical and Policy Considerations.

THEORETICAL JUSTIFICATIONS

Sociocultural Change

In beginning our deliberations, most of us assumed that the primary justification for long-range study is the greater insight that should come with respect to change processes and possible predictive ability. Process and prediction continued to be dominant justifications for long-term research, but increasingly participants felt that opportunity to learn about a society in detail and depth impossible in a single visit was also highly important. As Pospisil puts it, "a longer research period will allow for achievement of greater depth and for coverage of a wider field of inquiry and accumulation of more data." The best long-term research seems marked by shifting emphases as the researcher or team exhausts (at least temporarily) one theme, and turns to others for more intensive investigation. Some topics, such as Vogt's study of native concepts and theories of the universe and of symbolic meaning, seem simply to require time and repeated visits for the researcher to develop the necessary ideas and insights and for the accumulation of the data needed. Nevertheless, change processes are the focus of many of the studies.

Long-term study is congenial to the analysis of change processes for a number of reasons. First, in a diachronic study the observation of what actually happens over, say, a generation provides more valid data than historical reconstruction or projections into the future. The data are there, and they cannot be disputed. Second, although the "annual cycle plus two months" often is viewed as a desirable length of time for a field study, especially for doctoral candidates, many phenomena, even in simple societies, need much longer cycles. The hypothetical case of the New Guinea ethnologist studying American presidential politics was cited: He would need 8 years to observe the "natural" cycle and he would have to be present during the two major election periods themselves. Similarly, as Pospisil notes, the American ethnologist in New Guinea cannot fully comprehend the pig festival from a single visit. Less formal cyclical events—the domestic household cycle, for example—are best understood when the actual movements of actual people are observed over time. Hofer gives a particularly good example of informal cyclical process: "We could observe how neighbors came to be on bad terms or held a grudge against each other, and how, after attempts for several years at smoothing things over, a solemn peace-making occurred." A static recording of enmities and friendships tells little about the dynamic processes of ongoing relationships.

Third, quite apart from ritual, social, and informal cycles, there are other fluctuations that are best observed over time. These may be called "out-of-the-ordinary events" which are, in fact, the rule rather than the exception. Years of drought are followed by years of excess rain; behavior under starvation conditions will be quite different from that in times of plenty. War, the decision of a distant government to build a dam, or to cut a major highway through a jungle—events such as these, and their impact, must be observed if the ethnologist hopes to understand the long-range coping mechanisms of the society concerned. In short, normative behavior cannot really be described for a group unless its behavior is observed under most of the situations in which it may find itself.

Prediction and Predictive Models within the Context of Dynamic and Open-Ended Societies

One way to improve one's understanding of social dynamics is to develop a set of predictions, and then see where and why one went wrong. Conference participants agreed that we have been negligent in not routinely making predictions to be tested on follow-up visits. We have had "impressions," we have "guessed" as to what might happen but we have been—as a group—unsystematic in publishing or otherwise formulating predictions. While we have shared this failing with anthropologists as a whole, we have a major responsibility to formulate predictive statements simply because we anticipate return visits.

Part of the problem lies in our increasing awareness that social systems are more complicated, or at least more dynamic and open-ended, than previously realized—an awareness that long-term research in particular has fostered among its practitioners. Conventional short-term studies have predisposed anthropologists for too long to think about societies as if they were relatively closed systems in which the nature of the interrelationships between activities and ideologies precluded rapid change as a "normal" feature.

The Static Bias of Anthropological Models

The reports of conference participants suggest that the speed and extent of change in the traditional world is even greater than is usually assumed. Pospisil records the change, in scarcely a decade, of a "religious Central European peasant community, with its traditional culture and economy based on mountain farming and cattle breeding, into a secular settlement with a diversified commercialized economy based largely on tourism." Colson and Scudder describe Gwembe Valley Tonga as moving from isolated village subsistence farmers to the possibility of becoming bank tellers. Mangin tells of the emergence of Vicos peons from a feudal existence to partners in a cooperative farm. Everywhere the story is the same: A transformation that would have looked impossible a generation ago happens.

Anthropologists, of course, have been concerned with processes of culture change for nearly half a century. In the United States, the "acculturation" studies of Herskovits, Redfield, Linton, E. C. Parsons and many others come to mind. In England, "culture change" was a topic of major interest to such anthropologists as Hunter, Mair, Schapera, Malinowski, and Godfrey Wilson in the 1930s. Yet in spite of this recognition of change, an underlying "static bias" has characterized a great deal of theory during this same half century. As Meggitt expressed it at the conference, "stability is taken to be the norm and change the problem to be explained." This "bias" is apparent in Kaberry's comments on the work of Radcliffe–Brown, his students, and "other adherents of his theory":

> In the utilization of ethnographic data, the underlying assumption in most of these structural analyses is that societies are in more or less stable equilibrium and that "morals, law, etiquette, religion, government, and education are all parts of the complex mechanism by which a social structure exists and persists" [Kaberry 1957:87]. [The quote-within-a-quote is from Radcliffe–Brown, "On Social Structure."]

Also illustrative of the static bias is Reo Fortune's *Sorcerers of Dobu*: the book has not a word on history or change, past or present. The author's first words are "The ideal village of Dobu is a circle of huts facing inward to a central, often elevated mound, which is the village graveyard [Fortune 1932:1]." Evans-Pritchard spent about a year among the Nuer between 1930 and 1936. But this 6-year time span plays no role whatsoever in his analysis, which is unconcerned with change (Evans-Pritchard 1940). In contrast, it is inconceivable that in the 1970s an anthropologist could spend a similar amount of time, over a like number of years, without being profoundly impressed with change.

Among the chapters in this volume, the implications of static or equilibrium models are perhaps best illustrated by Foster's concept of Limited Good, formulated initially (Foster 1965) on the basis of data from Tzintzuntzan and generalized for peasant society as a whole to explain how peasants perceive their world. Abstracted from detailed observation of peasant behavior and peasant explanations prior to the 1960s, this model has considerable utility in explaining the nature of peasant societies in the past. But it has less and less explanatory value today, simply because villages like Tzintzuntzan are increasingly dynamic and open to the world about them. Not only is this clear from Foster's subsequent research in the village, but it is especially emphasized by Kemper's work among Tzintzuntzeños living and working in Mexico City.

The Gwembe research has revealed a similar pattern of rapid change which outdates early models of society and culture. In 1949 when Colson first visited the Gwembe Tonga, the people lived in discrete neighborhoods of 1000 to 2000 people. Neighborhoods most of the time were self-sufficient—as economic, social, political, and religious entities. Furthermore when 55,000 Gwembe Tonga were forced to move in the late 1950s because of the construction of the Kariba Dam, the relocatees behaved during the transition period that accompanied forced removal as if a social system was indeed a closed system—an observation that Scudder has extended to all rural communities undergoing compulsory relocation. The relocation period, however, was only a phase in Tonga history, and Colson's visit in 1949 also must not be viewed in any way as a baseline situation, granted the long and complicated history of the Middle Zambezi Valley. Today the combination of education and opportunity are facilitating the rapid emergence of a middle class among the formerly egalitarian Tonga which, in moving onto the national scene, has rapidly broadened its horizons while maintaining historical roots. For this elite, the world is a very different one from that of their parents and grandparents.

The incorporation of once isolated, relatively "closed" communities into national and international political and economic structures has drastically altered the world studied by anthropologists. As a result, conference participants were particularly aware of the limitations of classical equilibrium models and of the need for developing new methodologies, new concepts, and new theories. The task is not an easy one. In the past, the significance of "outside" influence affecting change has not been adequately appreciated by most anthropologists. With these influences growing rapidly in number and strength, no longer are we able to act "as if" the community were an isolate, not significantly affected by extra-community forces. This recognition presents methodological problems. We will need to study national economic policies and trends, local and national political systems, government welfare institutions, educational systems, and the formal and informal mechanisms that tie these and many other strands together. Yet while doing all this, we must not overemphasize the extent to which local populations are passive players in a drama over which they have little control. Not only do they retain the capacity to make choices between options, but they can and do increase this capacity through an active involvement in a wider social field in which there are new opportunities for both educational and socioeconomic advancement. Methodologically, all this will not be easy for anthropologists. There are problems of establishing rapport with the appropriate sources for the wider range of information needed and in identifying and running down these sources. More interdisciplinary research seems to be at least a partial answer, as does a greater emphasis on the processes whereby individuals as members of domestic and other social units choose between a variety of options.

As for new concepts and new theories, although increasingly we are learning what kinds of systems societies are not, we have still to conceptualize the nature of a society which has moved into a dynamic open-ended period of activity and belief formulation. While long-term studies are very much in their infancy and, hence, have still to prove their worth, we believe their future contribution to this domain of social theory will be considerable. This is especially so with those studies, most of which so far are only partially reported in the literature, which are based on extensive and intensive time-series data maintained over a 10–20-year period.

Against this background, it is not surprising that conference participants found it difficult to pinpoint major theoretical or even methodological advances in anthropology which could be directly attributed to longterm research. More specifically, it is not surprising that we have hesitated to publish predictive statements, often preferring to keep our hunches to ourselves for further research during subsequent visits. Among ourselves, we were unable to agree as to how successful we have been in sharpening anthropology's predictive capacity. It was suggested that we must distinguish between (*a*) ability to predict in a specific situation and (*b*) predictive models. A predictive model is a statement about principles of change, or regularities that have been observed in a variety of settings, and has predictive value cross-culturally. An example of a predictive model noted by several participants is that nascent class distinctions begin to appear in simple, essentially homogeneous communities when opportunities for educational advancement and/or economic accumulation arise. However, the model does not automatically apply to all situations.

In reviewing our individual track records as prophets, Epstein was perhaps most content with the extent to which major predictions made at the time of her first study had been borne out 14 years later—although Colson and Scudder could also claim some success, including a predictive model relating to how a wide variety of communities respond to compulsory relocation that grew directly out of their long-term study of the Gwembe Tonga.

Other participants were more impressed with what poor prophets they had been. Villa Rojas had assumed initially that the sacred aspects of life in Chan Kom would give way to the secular, basing this on current theory that held that such change is a process that occurs with the passage of time. Yet, 45 years later, just the opposite has happened, and sacred rites have taken on added meaning to the villagers. Vogt has noted a comparable phenomenon in Chiapas. Whereas in central Mexico the religious *mayordomía* system and the numbers of practicing shamans and curers have declined dramatically since World War II, numbers of religious "cargos" and practicing shamans have increased among the peoples he has studied. Foster reports another unfulfilled prophecy: With the end of the Mexican *bracero* program of short-term indentured farm laborers in the United States in 1964, he anticipated serious social unrest in Tzintzuntzan and rural Mexico in general because of unemployment. He vastly underestimated the capacity of Mexican cities to absorb millions of rural migrants and to provide reasonably adequate work for them; this is a specific example of our past failure to pay sufficient attention to the wider national context.

Study in Depth

As we recounted and compared our research experiences, increasingly we realized that a greater depth and understanding of the whole spectrum of culture achieved through observations over time is a highly important theoretical justification for long-term research. Vogt argued this point particularly effectively: "The principal advantage of a continuous long-range project over a short-range one, or a series of revisits, is the depth, quality, and variety of understandings achieved—understanding of the basic ethnography and of the trends and processes of change." He noted that he has become more concerned with cultural continuities than with change and that, in his studies of symbolic behavior, only long and intimate contact with the Zinacantecos has made possible his rich understanding of meaning. The intricacies of a cultural fabric, the delicacy of the weaving, the blending of colors and their changing hues in different lights—time, and time alone, brings these nuances to the full awareness of the investigator.

When, in long-term studies, anthropologists live with community families, there are added opportunities for serendipitous observations that open new and previously unthought of lines of investigation. Villa Rojas has found, "The factor of serendipity . . . is one of the best allies of any good researcher. . . ." Serendipity, of course, is not limited to long-term situations, but since it so often builds on accumulated observations, it perhaps plays a more important role in these settings. Foster describes serendipity as involving "trigger mechanisms"—chance observations of seemingly inconsequential behavior in the family with whom he lives, which spark a near-instantaneous recall of episodes of relevant prior behavior that, until that moment, had fitted into no apparent coherent patterns. Those conference participants who routinely returned to the peoples they studied felt that their awareness of the depth of the cultures was aided by time at home to review notes, to reflect, to try out ideas on students, and to work out lines of questioning on specific topics prior to departure on the next trip.

RESEARCH DESIGN, METHODOLOGY, AND OPERATIONS

The Personal Equation

When the anthropologist thinks of change, the reference is usually the community under observation. Yet, there are in fact three interlocking change domains. Research interests, like societies, Epstein points out, rarely remain static so that the researcher is apt to introduce new variables and deemphasize others within the context of a continuing study. The investigator also changes through time. The anthropologist at 60 years of age is a very different person than the one just emerged from graduate school. The seasoned fieldworker is technically more skilled and theoretically more sophisticated. He or she has engaged in a number of lines of investigation, abandoning some when interest dropped to turn to new themes that serendipitously appear, that become fashionable in the field at large, or that are carefully selected on the basis of past research experience. Psychologically, the seasoned worker probably also has an advantage. Return to the field is associated with a sense of anticipation that is hard to equal. Not only is it a pleasure to renew acquaintances, to see the genuine pleasure of those who welcome the anthropologist back, and to catch up on local gossip and developments, but psychologically reentry is easier than shifting to a totally different society. Not only is "culture shock" minimized, but often the anthropologist is fully engaged in research within a few hours of arrival. Under such circumstances, it was a common observation among conference participants that entry becomes easier with each successive visit unless the habitat, livelihood, and standing of the host community has deteriorated markedly over the duration of the study period.

The technical advantages of repeated visits derive much from the fact that in doing field research we are involved as social persons. During any long stay, we build sets of relationships that can be limiting as well as helpful. We become categorized and are expected to behave in a particular fashion. By leaving and returning, we have a chance to break molds imposed upon us. We may return as old friends, but our friends have replaced us in our absence with other interests and arranged their lives in new patterns. Enemies have sometimes forgotten some of the reasons why they disliked us, or they have redefined their alliances so that they can now include us among their friends, although as Meggitt warns us, this is not inevitable. When we left, we were assumed to know certain things and therefore found it difficult to learn about them; on the other hand, it was assumed that some things should be hidden from us. During each absence, much of this may be forgotten so that we come back on a new footing.

The return is also a reaffirmation of concern and interest in the people with whom we work and gives new validation to our right to learn. As visits continue, we also find that information becomes available to us because we are moving into age brackets, along with our contemporaries, to which that knowledge is appropriate. As they learn, so do we. Most anthropologists begin fieldwork as young men and women—indeed, one of the problems with assessing the value of anthropological data is that so much of it reflects the interests and perspectives of young people in their twenties and early thirties. As the years of long-term research pass, the former graduate student is accepted as a mature adult coping with easily recognized common problems and with whom it is now appropriate to compare experience. Still later, the fieldworker is recognized as a contemporary of the elders. In fact, the anthropologist follows a trajectory from whippersnapper to elder and reaps the benefit. No doubt, an aging anthropologist reevaluates field records collected at a younger age, but equally there is no doubt that what seems to be significant or what can be learned is different at different periods.

Field teams composed of anthropologists of different ages who can diversify their social relationships and link into different local networks may have some of the same advantages as the long-term study involving the same fieldworker or the same small team of fieldworkers. The Chiapas Project has an impressive record in utilizing the varying interests and social characteristics of the many people who have joined the project for short periods. Even so, it is Vogt's own experience of over 20 years with the project that gives the continuity, while the major integration of the knowledge gained by the various workers comes through his own deepening involvement with Tzetal thought.

Core Data

The research planning and design and the field techniques described in the preceding chapters have been very much a function of the personalities of the individuals concerned. They have been influenced by the shifting interests of the same researcher, partnership, or team, as well as by the extent to which theoretical interests reflect a primary interest in belief systems or in behavior varying through time.

Such differences and shifts create serious methodological problems, since baseline data from initial studies may not provide a basis for subsequent comparison. Referring to her own fieldwork among the Navajo, Lamphere was disappointed to learn that "most of the Ramah personality data do not fit into contemporary frameworks nor are they relevant to recent interests in social structure, economy, and political organization" in spite of Kluckhohn's pioneering role in initiating long-term research. Examining our own studies, we realized that in most cases the long-term pattern, like Topsy, "just growed" so that a new generation of researchers might be equally disappointed with our own baseline data.

Looking to the future, we believe that the problem appears more serious than is, in fact, the case. The Navajo example is a complicated and exceptional one because a comparatively large number of investigators have been involved over an extended time period with very little direct communication among the different teams or researchers in regard to data collection, definition of such basic terms as "household," and theoretical interests. As for our own research, few of us initially realized that we would eventually find ourselves caught up in a long-term study involving a major professional commitment in time, resources and emotional ties. Exceptions included Colson, Meggitt, Pospisil, and Scudder. Along with Epstein and Foster, neither of whom saw themselves as embarking upon long-term research initially, they made a conscious attempt from the very beginning of their research to collect at least certain types of "minimum core data" (Table 15.1). Such data, conference participants agreed,

TABLE 15.1

Standardization of Minimum Core Data

Accelerating rates of change and increases in complexity require reliable reference points for successive and cross-societal comparison.

From the start, each investigator should define his sample(s) and parent populations in space and time.

Definition of terms (e.g., household) must be consistent and unambiguous.

Minimum core data should be recorded for each individual in the sample according to the following categories:
Name
Sex
Date and place of birth and of death
Marital and Parental status (including number of all children with their dates of birth and death)
Unit(s) of affiliation, past and present
  (a) Social
  (b) Residential
Occupation(s) and their locations, past and present
Education
Religion
Resource Base (minimum descriptive data)
  (a) Ecological categories
  (b) Economic categories
Sociopolitical differentiation (e.g., rank, title, caste, office, political roles, etc.)

should include maps, vital statistics, census material (including marital and parental status, social and residential units of affiliation, occupations, education, and religion); resource base (minimal descriptive data on ecological and economic categories); and sociopolitical differentiation. Core data are by no means exclusively quantitative in nature. Given the importance of change in long-term research, we felt it essential to record the dates of appearance of new traits and the disappearance of old ones: radio, television, motor vehicles, tools, and household equipment among the new, and the loss of traditional dress, agricultural tools, and rituals among the old. Inventory checklists would be useful for this purpose. Other kinds of data are what Meggitt called "standard," and hardly need quantification. Generally, we felt that solid, factual data of earlier years, whether gathered by the current researcher or a predecessor, have proven to be more valuable than the theoretical interests of the person who gathered them. Ideally, minimum core data should be standardized to the greatest extent possible so as to facilitate cross-societal comparison of both changes and continuities.

We wish to emphasize, however, that the minimum core data approach includes major risks to the balance of future work. Simply because the collection of such data is immensely time-consuming and, in its own way, rewarding as an end in itself, the researcher may not have the time or inclination to examine developments that cannot be measured by the indices in question. Obviously, ongoing and future long-term studies must involve both rigor and openness. Wherever there is the possibility of a given study developing into a long-term research program, core data should be systematically gathered from the start on the basis of a carefully thought-out rationale. At the same time, a high degree of openness in orientation must be retained; otherwise, the investigator may not see, let alone investigate, the types of shifts in emphasis in human affairs and beliefs that can be expected to occur within the contemporary world. Important as core data are, their collection should not dominate research, nor interfere with the exploration of new topics. Here it is important to emphasize that long-term longitudinal field research is not necessarily written up in a single publication covering the full flow of events. Where openness is maintained, researchers can incorporate new interests and write a number of discreet papers on such topics as the emergence of an elite class or of a new economic system, which unfold themselves during relatively short time periods.

Data Banks

Core data and all other field records require an orderly filing system that facilitates information retrieval for the researcher(s) and others who may have interest in the project. Most files in the team research that has been described here have been kept in such a haphazard fashion as to be of little use to other people; the Chiapas project, with its Harvard-based data bank, is the exception to the rule. Lamphere found that the extensive Navajo Ramah and Values Project files were of little use to her and other recent researchers for mechanical and theoretical reasons. Basic demographic, census, and land use data are missing and economic data can be found only "in bits and pieces." The Human Relations Area Files coding system was used, but individual slips had the numbers only, without topical headings. To make matters worse, the HRAF coding system has been significantly revised since the time of the processing of the original field notes. Lamphere found that the published data of Father Bernard were of more value to her than the raw field data of other workers. Nevertheless, Blanchard (1977) seems to have been able to make extensive use of the data in the Ramah file in his own study of religious conversion.

The Vicos data bank, too, was not systematically handled, and much tension has stemmed from conflicting claims to the materials. Henry Dobyns has gathered much of the material together, and it is to be under the care of a librarian at Cornell University. But other information is in such places as the Harry Stack Sullivan Institute in New York City, where it was brought by nonanthropologists who did research in Vicos. Other researchers, while sharing their notes with interested people, have kept their materials as personal files. Even in the Colson–Scudder partnership, each researcher has an individual file although all typewritten notes were prepared in duplicate and exchanged. The evidence indicates that in major team research a good data bank requires the personal attention of the team leader or a major participant. To date, there appears to be no case of a well-maintained data bank being passed on in such fashion that significant use has been made of it by researchers not associated with the early stages of the project or not associated with the principal investigator or team leader. Perhaps a dominant principal investigator is essential to a useful data bank. In the case of the Navajo, Lamphere found that "It was as if the 'key' to the Ramah Files had died with Kluckhohn, and only hours of digging through 'cut up' field notes revealed facts that might have come to light in a conversation with him."

Initially, we discussed data banks from the standpoint of recording, coding, filing, and easy retrieval. But as we considered the changing realities of ethnographic research, we began to think that the problem is not basically filing and retrieval, but that of security and protection of subjects—and perhaps ethnographers as well. Traditionally, ethnographic data have been gathered on the assumption that their circulation would be strictly limited. Personal names have been used and dates and places have been recorded. Such notes sometimes contain items that could be harmful to individuals or their communities. It has been the responsibility of the ethnographers, in preparing materials for publication, to take such steps as seem indicated to preserve anonymity. Raw field data rarely were seen by more than one or two people.

Today conditions are changed. Some countries ask, not unreasonably, that copies of all research materials be left in national museums or research institutes. Growing numbers of anthropologists believe that human subjects should also have the right to see what is being attributed to them. In addition to the possibility of injury to people because of such "legitimate" access to field data, there are dangers from illicit use of such materials. If the "open file" comes to be the norm, with access available to anyone who expresses interest, individuals with ulterior motives might well use data to injure informants, their communities, or the anthropologists who have gathered the data. Some of us began to think that a centralized, well-maintained, open data bank may very well be a time bomb, whose explosive potentialities cannot be predicted. More thought must be given to these complex problems.

Long-Term Planning

Long-term planning involves personal, political, and financial factors. Individual studies are particularly vulnerable to a wide range of personal factors including illness (and death), conflicting professional demands, and family obligations—all of which can interfere with the timing and length of return visits. While these vulnerabilities can be offset by team research, or some sort of arrangement to pass on the mantle to another colleague or student, the same cannot be said for disruptions of a political nature.

A generation ago, we assumed that the anthropologist who had a vision (as in the case of Alan Holmberg in Vicos) for an ongoing project, and who could raise money and interest other personnel, was free to carry out work almost any place in the noncommunist world. But, just as the principal forces affecting today's communities come from the outside, so many of the limitations on long-term planning are beyond the control of anthropologists. Political factors increasingly place restrictions on freedom of access to peoples that anthropologists may want to study. And when access is granted, governments, especially in the Third World, as Fahim points out, are more apt to insist that research include an applied emphasis. That is, unless a research topic shows some relevance to national planning, governments may be reluctant to authorize it. If it is authorized, they may insist on periodic practical, readily utilizable reports as a condition to continued work, whether done by national or foreign anthropologists.

While problems with visas and foreign research permits, the increased emphasis placed on applied research by national governments, and sudden civil disturbances may affect any first-time anthropologist, opinions differed among conference participants as to whether or not long-term research was especially vulnerable. Some thought it was and even wondered if the planning of new major long-term projects was defensible in today's troubled world—a world in which some ongoing studies probably could not be initiated in the same locales if they were to start today rather than 10 to 20 years ago (an argument, incidentally, which points up the importance of continuing those studies currently underway).

Other participants disagreed strongly with this view. Although they agreed that anthropologists who wish to initiate new research today face a greater degree of uncertainty than in the past, they also felt it was easier to continue research once initiated than to start new projects elsewhere.

Over the years, those involved in long-term research build up a rapport, or at least a presence, which makes it easier to obtain the necessary permits and clearances. Known quantities, with ties and support among both local and national officials and among host country scholars, they are "part of the scene," so to speak, and, as such, have built up a series of contacts that stretch from the village to the capital. At the same time, those involved in long-term studies usually can point to concrete results in the form of publications that often find their way into local school and university libraries. Initial studies often have been carefully scrutinized by educated members of the host community, and the investigators "taken over the coals" for publishing statements and photographs which are considered biased or otherwise inappropriate. Such experiences, plus a deepening understanding that comes from years spent in the same area or among the same people, help the anthropologist identify those local and national sensitivities which can be easily aroused through simplistic and invidious statements.

The Gwembe project is an example of how long-term research can continue in spite of difficult conditions. Working close to the Zambian–Rhodesian border, the investigators never know when factors beyond their control will restrict their access to the frontier. Partly for this reason, they have expanded their research to include Gwembe Tonga wherever they live and work within Zambia. Hesitant to return in 1976 to the community that he has been following over a 20-year period, Scudder nonetheless was able to continue the collection of core data through the assistance of seven secondary school students—all of whom are from the community in question and some of whom have been working with him since 1970. Planning his return to coincide with their holidays, he was able to employ them for a month each, briefing them before they returned home and then meeting them again at the end of the holidays to discuss the results of their work. In the meanwhile, he continued his research among the new Gwembe elite living in urban centers on the Zambian Plateau.

Financially, long-term research may be less expensive than fieldwork carried out during a similar time period in two or more countries since equipment is accumulated over the years. The researcher is also more familiar with the area in which he lives, which tends to reduce costs for both daily provisioning and shelter. At least for the present, long-term research seems also to be easier to fund. With some justification, donor agencies are more apt to query the funding of one more community study just because the community is there and the ethnic population involved has never been studied. Though the situation may change, none of the editors have had difficulty in funding ongoing research nor are we aware of funding being an insurmountable problem for other conference participants. We do not wish to imply, however, that certain types of funding should be restricted to long-term research. Rather we are stating that competitively speaking, such research may well have a comparative advantage in terms of its ability to produce an expected set of results, both in regard to the study of specified topics and in regard to the training of future anthropologists who do benefit from the opportunity to observe at firsthand a society on which information has been gathered over an extended time period.

Time Allocations in Long-Term Research

In long-term research, only a part of the anthropologist's life can be allocated to the project. What are the criteria on which decisions about length and frequency of visits can be made? In team research, especially when graduate students are involved, the problem is less pressing, for they can be scheduled for succeeding years and perhaps be asked to help keep up the core data file. The initial question most frequently asked by conference participants was, "What is the appropriate time interval between visits?" We quickly realized, however, that this is not the right question. In general, we concluded, as Meggitt put it, that the optimum time is a function of the problems being investigated. But even this rule is difficult to apply. In the Gwembe Valley Tonga study, for example, Scudder thinks that his and Colson's failure to be present at the time of the physical relocation of the Tonga was a major flaw in the research design. Colson is less sure, believing that at a time of such turmoil and misery it would have been difficult to make systematic records. When a population includes literate members, when vital statistics and other demographic data are recorded by the people themselves, when land sales and purchases are written down, and when tax records are kept, longer gaps between visits are more defensible than when a population is totally illiterate. Yet, it is Pospisil and Foster, who work under these conditions, whose work has had the greatest degree of continuity.

Participants who work in communities relatively accessible from their homes and who return on an annual basis find it hard to see how intimate contacts can be maintained with friends and community on any other basis. Those whose field sites are farther from their homes and where annual visits are not practicable thought that 3–5-year intervals are not unreasonable. Everyone, Epstein included, regarded the 14 years between her first and second visits as longer than desirable. Fortunately, any return to an ongoing society is likely to coincide with an important series of events, since no social group lives completely by routine.

Repeated visits to the same group limits, or even precludes, research among other peoples in other places. Do such possible restrictions adversely affect the intellectual development of an anthropologist? The large majority of conference participants, it turned out, had had research experience in two or more cultures, and all felt they were better anthropologists for this exposure. They found that contrasting research settings caused them to ask new questions about their major projects, or brought into perspective past observations that had seemed to have little significance. Foster, for example, pointed out that his model of Limited Good and the concept of implicit premises on which it is built, which began to take shape in Tzintzuntzan, owed much to a stint in (then) Northern Rhodesia. "Crystallization of the implicit premises way of looking at behavior required a field experience totally outside the realm of Tzintzuntzan," is the way he put it in conference discussions. All participants felt that anthropologists contemplating long-term research should have additional field experience before or during their intensive studies to keep their sense of problem and their awareness of how cultures differ, and to be exposed to stimuli in one area that may be immediately relevant to interpretation in another.

Team Research

Long-term research involving two or more people presents administrative and coordination problems. The former are obvious: the more people and money, the greater the administrative chores which must be done by someone, usually the project director. The latter present problems of a different nature, particularly having to do with dividing research tasks and allocating primary rights to certain materials. Anthropologists have a long tradition of selecting a community and making it their own. They have been more reluctant to share research tasks and field data and to engage in joint authorship than other behavioral scientists. But in team research, the traditional pattern must be modified. In searching for a model to coordinate the research of a number of people, we borrowed from ecology the concept of *niche*. In the Kalahari Project, for example, Lee points out how students were given a "piece" of the project with fairly clear-cut "boundaries," logical units that lend themselves to individual pursuit. In other words, each student found his or her investigative niche. The niche model, participants noted, places special demands on every investigator to keep up part of the core data for the benefit of the project as a whole.

In general, division of research responsibilities and data rights have been less of a problem in team research than might have been expected. Vogt noted, for example, that while there have been "a few celebrated intra-project conflicts," these have arisen because of differences in re-search styles and field methods rather than from over possessive feelings about field data or ideas.

Team research seems most fruitful when formal mechanisms bring participants and their ideas together. In the Kalahari Project, a major symposium in 1966 led to planning the second phase of the research, which in turn led to a 1971 symposium. Both meetings produced major volumes. Lee believes that joint authorship of papers is an important way to avoid possible fractioning of project unity, an ever-present possibility with the niche model of research. The Chiapas Project has also made use of symposia, but Vogt stresses particularly the pattern whereby field-workers circulate manuscript drafts among other participants for criticism and comment prior to putting them in final form. In spite of the extra time involved because of the need to rewrite articles and chapters, Vogt thinks the results are ethnographically and analytically superior to what they would be without mutual criticism. In projects involving fewer personnel than these two, informal discussions and exchanges of ideas and occasional joint authorship play a comparable role. All conference participants agreed that opportunity to discuss specific hypotheses, hunches, and data with other partners or team mates leads to a better final product.

The Point of Diminishing Returns

Granted the increasingly open-ended and dynamic nature of many societies, it is unlikely that a point of diminishing returns will be reached in terms of the opportunity presented by a given long-term study to contribute to our knowledge of the nature of social systems. On the other hand, conference participants were concerned with the problem of di-minishing returns from the standpoint of individual researchers. The methodological advantages of long-term research for the anthropologist are many. There are also disadvantages, the greatest of which may well be the danger of boredom, growing stale, finding that long familiarity with a way of life dull's one's sense of the new, the novel, the significant. Foster reports fewer "fresh ideas" in Tzintzuntzan than in earlier years, and wonders whether it is due to age or familiarity with a way of life that no longer seems exotic. Helm, on the other hand, notes that since her first research in 1951, "there have always been emergent or unfinished ethnological questions, so that my research has been continually creating itself."

The introduction of new colleagues or students into ongoing studies, who bring fresh points of view and undulled curiosity, is perhaps the best way to counter this danger. The bringing in of short-term consultants or participants from other disciplines, Fahim suggested, is a useful way to keep one's theoretical outlook sharpened. Several participants also found that short visits to anthropologists working in very different settings and consultancies that took them to different countries play an important revitalizing role. Meggitt, though recognizing the possibility of diminishing returns, nonetheless thinks "the anthropologist who makes but one sojourn in an alien society and then spends the rest of his academic career sorting and resorting the one collection of data" is in much greater danger of dulled perception than is the long-term researcher. "Such an anthropologist is much more likely to make the mistake of believing that he has seen all there is to see of significance in that society and in the data, and that in some osmotic way he really understands all about them."

Student Training in Long-Term Research

Many of the problems of long-term research appear to be common to social anthropology. Perhaps the key technical problems unique to the long-term study lie in discovering how to build viable research teams that can recruit and retain younger colleagues with a commitment to the continuation of the research after the retirement or demise of its originators. So far, admittedly, anthropologists have had little incentive to join ongoing studies. Few of the long-term studies, which rely upon the close monitoring of events, have been in progress long enough for their advantages to be clearly demonstrated. Anthropologists will only want to join in such enterprises when there is a clear demonstration of a payoff through more comprehensive and more effective understanding of how people organize themselves and order their experience. In the meanwhile, those executing long-term research will find the recruitment of students as the best means to draw in "new blood."

Students have been involved in a number of the studies described in this volume. In most cases, initial participation took the form of supervised field training, seen as a part of doctoral programs (only in the Chiapas Project were undergraduate students also included). Not surprisingly, a good many of these students returned to the same or adjacent areas to pursue subsequent research, thus becoming full members of team enterprises. Although a professor can take students to an area known to none of them, an ongoing project, particularly one with some kind of field headquarters, offers better opportunities to initiate students into the intricacies of fieldwork. They can observe an older anthropologist in action in a familiar milieu and they can test the water themselves under a watchful eye. When several students are together, formal seminars give them an opportunity to see how data are analyzed and utilized in the formulation of additional research topics.

It was with students in mind that the conference organizers asked participants to consider the problem of "passing the mantle," of making provision for continuing research after they no longer wished, or were no longer able, to return to the field. The "mantle" does not necessarily have to be passed to students or former students, of course, but they are the most likely candidates. Although some long-term projects may not justify indefinite continuation, others do: We thought how exciting it would be, for example, if anthropology now had one hundred years of systematic recording of life in Tepoztlán. Mantle passing, however, is not an exact science. Fortuitous circumstances will play the major role in determining whether individual projects are or are not continued. To date we have no models to go by, for the term applies neither to the Navajo nor to Vicos. Currently, the Chiapas Project, with its army of youthful and enthusiastic participants, is the most viable candidate for indefinite long-term research. Tzintzuntzan is a second possibility. In both cases, former students, though influenced by the initiator's style and interests, have branched out on their own to become true collaborators.

Data Management, Analysis, and Write-up

The vast amount of data accumulated during long-term studies is both a strength and a weakness of this kind of research. Those of us who have accumulated time-series data in particular suffer from the sensation of being buried beneath our data. Just to face these at times brings on a feeling of extreme ennui alternating with a desire for deliverance. Certainly we must continually ask, as Vogt did at the conference, if we overestimate data accumulation as an end in itself—"Do we really use our vast data or do our insights emerge otherwise?" Serendipity does play an important role, with unexpected events and statements acting as illuminating trigger mechanisms. On the other hand, there is no substitute for slogging through the data for purposes of reconstruction, generalization, and validation.

As we compared notes at the conference, it became increasingly obvious that we could greatly simplify our data management problems by better prefield planning and by better data processing in the field. Time spent in carefully predesigning forms for the coding of minimum core data in the field, for example, would not only allow the fieldworker to consider the adequacy of data shortly after its accumulation, but it would also reduce the seemingly endless periods of coding that confront us back in the office. Too frequently, we turn this over to inexperienced research assistants and hence risk losing that sense of familiarity with data which should remain one of the hallmarks of the field anthropologist. The time has come for departments of anthropology to deal with data management problems as an integral part of the curriculum for the next generation of fieldworkers. Students should be familiarized with different approaches to data management, including, of course, the costs and benefits of computer versus hand processing of data. Though some participants already rely to a considerable extent on computers for storage, retrieval, and analytical purposes, the positive and negative implications of the new generation of relatively format-free software systems that are being designed for interactive use by social and behavioral science users were clear to none of us.

Those involved in long-term research must also subject themselves to an active schedule for publishing results as soon as possible after each return from the field. From personal experience, we know that this is not easy. Knowing that a return to the field is imminent and that *that* will be the time to tie up those final loose ends, it is all too easy to substitute further fieldwork for analysis and write-up. If we have learned anything at all from long-term studies, we have learned not to expect closure in human affairs; conversely, we have also learned that it is seldom too early to put on paper the results of completed work, including especially predictions about the implications for the future of current trends.

ETHICAL AND POLICY CONSIDERATIONS

The Policy Implications of Long-Term Research

The results of long-term research almost inevitably have important implications for the national planning, execution, and evaluation of development policies. Fahim in particular stressed the benefits that long-term studies can provide to the host communities and/or to the nations of which they are part. While host country anthropologists with close ties to planners and policymakers are probably in a better position to push for such benefits, the same sort of ethical questions arise regardless of the nationality of the anthropologist.

Conference participants considered three ethical stances that characterize the ways in which anthropologists have related themselves to the people studied. These we labeled the "professional," the "action-oriented," and the "advocacy" stances.

The "Professional" Stance

This stance resembles the code of personal professional ethics that has been widely adopted in American anthropology in recent years. Our primary responsibility is not to bring harm by our research to the people studied. A second aspect is the safeguarding of data banks with sensitive information and the preservation where necessary of an informant's anonymity. However, there is no positive injunction to benefit the people studied through one's research.

The "Action-Oriented" Stance

In this stance, the investigator takes on the additional responsibility to help constructively the studied population by participating in programs introducing health, housing, schools, or other attempts to raise the standard of living. The action-oriented anthropologist both facilitates the introduction of change and helps people to adapt to change within the framework of national goals.

The "Advocacy" Stance

This stance has become increasingly common during the last 10 years. It involves working with people who are struggling with change agencies even if this position brings the anthropologist into opposition to the agency. Examples include resisting external attempts to relocate local communities forcibly, supporting native political struggles, studying the power structure imposed upon native peoples ("studying up"), and disseminating information about cases of ethnocide and genocide.

Research "on" versus "for" People

No one at the conference defended the stance of maintaining complete research objectivity, in the sense of not intervening in community life if intervention seemed feasible and might further community-defined interests. Possibly because of their personal involvement over time with the people of the communities they study, conference participants felt they are more "action" or "advocacy" oriented than anthropologists who do not contemplate enduring ties with the people they study. On the other hand, conference participants disagreed as to how far anthropologists should go in active support of the communities they know, and appreciate. Helm describes her roles in support of the Indian Brotherhood of the Northwest Territories as, first, expert witness on traditional land usages and land holdings, and, second, as advisor to the Land Claims Research Project of the Brotherhood. In the latter role, she provided a research design for field research to be carried out by local Indians. Conference participants agreed these are laudable and desirable roles.

Other participants took a much stronger "action-oriented" or "advocacy" stance as a general position, arguing that research cannot be justified unless obvious good is likely to accrue to the people studied as a consequence. This position includes the obligation of the anthropologist to engage in activities designed to further the well-being of the people in question, activities that are little if at all concerned with research. The Kalahari Peoples Fund, described by Lee, is the most far-reaching attempt at "working with the people in their struggle to determine their own future" that we considered.

Lamphere also forcefully argued the importance of advocacy ethics, that research should be *for* rather than *on* people. Looking back on the Ramah project, she found "the cultural, value, and personality data collected during the years of research at Ramah of little relevance to present-day Navajo." A majority of conference participants agreed that while it is desirable, when possible, to use research findings to help the peoples studied, a full advocacy stance is not necessary to justify research. Villa Rojas, who has devoted a lifetime to furthering the well-being of Mexican Indians, believes that when a project does not have scientific goals, whatever its potential for helping people, it fails. Fortunately, when science is the aim, the value of applied results may be greater than in narrowly conceived applied work. As Scudder pointed out, the beneficial implications of research results may extend well beyond the studied population. While he and Colson have pushed neither an "action-oriented" nor an "advocacy" position during their long-term research among the Gwembe Tonga, as an advocacy-oriented consultant to the Navajo Tribal Council, Scudder has drawn heavily upon that research to oppose the forced removal of Navajo from the Joint Use Area in Arizona.

Uncritical acceptance of an advocacy stance leads to difficult questions. What happens, it was asked, when a dissident group is considering action inimical to a national government, however unjust that government may seem? Does the anthropologist wholeheartedly join in with his subjects? Political activism, especially by foreign anthropologists, is tricky business at best. Anthropologists have obligations to their colleagues as well as to the people they study. In their defense of the latter, how far can they risk unilateral action that may exclude other foreign researchers? The answers are complex and unclear.

Conference participants also wondered what form "positive good" takes for a community and how much is necessary to justify research, if this must be a predictable outcome of a project. The Kalahari Peoples Fund is designed to work with people "in their struggle to determine their own futures." It emphasizes economic, political, and educational goals.

But are there not other less tangible manifestations of "positive good"? Hofer points out that Hungarian ethnographic research contributes to an important self-image of the study communities. Here and elsewhere, the anthropologist has played an important role as social historian or chronicler. Foster believes his major positive impact in Tzintzuntzan "has been to give villagers a sense of ésprit that would otherwise be lacking." They take pride in the fact that he finds them sufficiently interesting and enjoyable to return year after year, to write about them, and to spread the word that Tzintzuntzan is worth visiting. Kemper's work among Tzintzuntzeños in Mexico City led to the establishment of a migrants' association, designed to foster closer ties in the city, and to remind people of their common origin. None of this is research "for" people, but it can be argued that it has beneficial effects.

Although generally we felt that our research had not affected adversely the peoples with whom we have worked, we noted an occasional ethical problem not encountered in more traditional work: the professional informant who becomes dependent on a research project for a livelihood. Five Zinacanteco Indians have been employed for long periods by the Chiapas Project. They have been brought to Harvard to serve as linguistic informants in classes, and they have visited Washington, Santa Fe, San Francisco, and other American cities. Four of the five, Vogt believes, have benefited from these experiences and have advanced more rapidly in their personal lives than would have been possible without project work. The fifth has remained essentially dependent on the project: basic and preexisting psychological problems may well have been accentuated by associations with the Chiapas Project. This example should teach caution to anthropologists in establishing long-term monetary ties with local people; they seem sufficiently rare, however, as not to constitute a major ethical problem.

Responsibilities to Colleagues

Anthropologists have obligations to the people they study; they also have obligations to their colleagues, both those in the country where they are guests and in their country of origin. Many of these obligations are the same. Above all, research results should be made available in publications, in preliminary reports, in symposia, and in lectures at the earliest time consistent with professional standards of excellence. It seems particularly important for foreign anthropologists to communicate their findings to local anthropologists, who have a primary interest in what has been found in their countries. In Fahim's opinion, it is important to make the results available to the people studied in a form that they can understand, an obligation that may require translation into a local vernacular.

Conference participants from less wealthy countries pointed out a problem that well-financed American anthropologists sometimes unwittingly cause them. Their living and spending habits and the financial aid they give informants often raise community expectations of what can be expected of anthropologists above what local anthropologists can afford. Clearly, in planning research American anthropologists must consider their potential impact on local science as well as on the peoples they study.

Vested Interests in Research Sites

Finally, conference participants considered the question of whether anthropologists acquire exclusive rights or vested interests through long-term research in a particular community. Put simply, the question is whether any anthropologist has the ethical right to initiate research in a community currently under investigation by a prior arrival, except upon invitation by that person. Is such an act "poaching," or is it a legitimate right in free science? Many communities are difficult of access: People are suspicious, months are needed to establish rapport, and the intrusion of uninvited outsiders may threaten the delicate balance that has been achieved. Vogt has described the problems in building rapport in Zinacantan, the loss of this rapport when unknown persons suspected by the local population of being anthropologists stole sacred objects from the church, and the five years necessary to rebuild this rapport.

While all participants agreed that, as a minimum, professional courtesy requires consultation with the personnel of established research projects by other anthropologists hoping to work in the same area, opinions varied as to "rights." Some—Foster among them—argued that communities which continue to be active research laboratories should be off-bounds to other anthropologists, unless invited to join in, until the project is terminated. Foster qualified his position, however, by saying that foreign anthropologists cannot reasonably expect exclusive rights that would prevent nationals of the country concerned from entering the community. Others—Colson and Meggitt among them—argued that no anthropologist has a right to "stake a claim in perpetuity" to a people, society, or community, and try for no other compelling reason to discourage other anthropologists from going there. The size and nature of a community obviously will have a bearing on the ethical question. Tzintzuntzan has less than 2500 inhabitants, all living within a closely circumscribed area. The introduction of an additional researcher here is apt to have very different consequences from the introduction of an additional researcher among the 100,000 Gwembe Tonga, scattered in many communities over a wide area. Whereas in the urban situation described by Kemper, the issue can hardly arise, one or two researchers without previous involvement in the village might be highly disruptive to Villa Rojas' planned continuing observations in Chan Kom aimed at rounding out a 50-year time span.

CONCLUSIONS

The conference confirmed the participants' beliefs that long-term research, whatever form it takes, offers many theoretical and methodological advantages over short-term research, even though few convincing examples of major theoretical formulations have yet to emerge largely or entirely from this type of research. This poses a dilemma: If most contemporary social anthropological theory continues to be based on traditional, or more time limited research, does this mean (*a*) that long-term research is of less theoretical value than the participants believe, or (*b*) that long-term research is so recent, with most studies still ongoing, that it accounts for but a small fraction of all past and current research, and that much of the data accumulated and insights gained have yet to be thought through and/or published? While it is too soon to say, the next decade should begin to provide the answers.

BIBLIOGRAPHY

Blanchard, Kendall A.
  1977 *The economics of sainthood: Religious change among the Rimrock Navajos*. Rutherford, New Jersey: Fairleigh Dickinson Univ. Press.
Evans–Pritchard, E. E.
  1940 *The Nuer*. Oxford: Clarendon Press.
Fortune, R. F.
  1932 *Sorcerers of Dobu*. New York: E. P. Dutton.
Foster, George M.
  1965 Peasant society and the image of limited good. *American Anthropologist* 67:293–315.
Kaberry, Phyllis
  1957 Malinowski's contribution to fieldwork methods and the writing of ethnography. In *Man and culture*, edited by Firth, Raymond. Pp. 71–92. London: Routledge and Kegan Paul.

Subject Index